AIRLINERS
from 1919 to the Present Day

AIRLINERS
from 1919 to the Present Day

by
Kenneth Munson

Illustrated by
JOHN W. WOOD

Michael Baber
Bob Corrall
Frank Friend
Brian Hiley
William Hobson
Alan Holliday
Tony Mitchell
Jack Pelling
Allen Randall

Exeter Books

NEW YORK

CONTENTS

BOOK I

AIRLINERS BETWEEN
THE WARS 1919-1939

In the period between World Wars 1 and 2, two great competitive flying events stand out above all others – the contests for the Schneider Trophy, which ended with a British victory in 1931, and the 'MacRobertson' race from England to Australia in 1934. The latter event was held as part of the centenary celebrations of the state of Victoria and of Melbourne, its capital, with prizes donated by Sir William MacPherson Robertson. The race was open to all nationalities, and was divided into a speed section (based on elapsed time for the journey) and a handicap section (based on flying time only). It started from Mildenhall, Suffolk, and ended at Flemington racecourse, Melbourne, with main control points at Baghdad, Allahabad, Singapore, Darwin and Charleville; the total distance was 11,300 miles (18,185 km).

So far as the record books are concerned, the 'MacRobertson' also ended in a British victory: the de Havilland D.H.88 Comet was designed to win the race, and it did so. But of infinitely greater significance was the identity of the second aircraft to arrive in Melbourne, which had flown a standard commercial route of 12,530 miles (19,875 km) – 1,230 miles (1,690 km) longer than the prescribed route – and had done so in only $5\frac{3}{4}$ hours' flying time more than the D.H.88. Its average speed for the whole journey was about 160 mph (257 km/hr).

This aircraft was a twin-engined Douglas DC-2 of KLM Royal Dutch Airlines, carrying a 4-man crew, 3 fare-paying passengers and a 420 lb (191 kg) cargo of mail. Before the race, many people had been sceptical of the chances of a normally-loaded commercial transport aircraft flown by an airline crew. It would be competing against several faster aeroplanes, some of them flown by such eminent competitive pilots as Charles Scott and Tom Campbell Black, Roscoe

7

Turner and Clyde Pangborn, James and Amy Mollison, and Jacqueline Cochrane. Indeed, one London newspaper was moved to dismiss the KLM entry as 'an audacious assumption that such a ship could expect to compete with the fastest planes on the Continent'. KLM, however, knew a thing or two about its latest American acquisition, and proved – as it had set out to do – that a standard, modern commercial transport aircraft, carrying a useful payload, could cover the world's longest air route in less than 4 days, without any sacrifice of its passengers' comfort. The successes of both the D.H.88 and the DC-2 proved, more convincingly than ever before, that the retractable undercarriage and variable-pitch propeller were henceforth essential ingredients for commercial aircraft of the future.

Until that time, the air transport scene the world over had been dominated first by biplanes and then by lumbering, fixed-gear tri-motors. Prior to World War 1 there had been no scheduled airline services in existence, apart from those operated in Germany with Zeppelin airships, and hence the early 1920s saw not only the beginnings of air transport as a business, but the use of many improvised 'airliners', many of them embodying only the minimum of conversion from the wartime roles for which they were designed. In some of these primitive conversions, the passengers were as exposed to the elements as the pilots, and had likewise to be provided with leather coats, flying helmets, gloves, goggles, and – in extreme cases – a hot water bottle as well.

Thus, perhaps, the most pressing initial need of the embryo airlines was to offer their passengers a reasonable standard of comfort, and evidence of the importance attached to this need was soon to be seen in such post-war designs as the Westland Limousine and the Blériot-Spad 'berlines', and in the restaurant facilities introduced on several European routes. Operating economics were not at first of widespread concern, at least on the continent of Europe, where most of the early pioneering airlines received substantial government assistance. The lack of such assistance was felt keenly in Britain, where the four major airlines of the early 1920s had to struggle hard for survival until the government decided to amalgamate them in 1924 to form Imperial Airways, the 'chosen instrument' of a new British air transport policy. The world 'imperial' did not then provoke the inflammatory reaction that it does today. Indeed, one may well ponder how different the world air transport scene might have been if there had been no empires forty years ago to provide the incentive to pioneer the global and transcontinental air routes which we now take for granted. The air transport adventure of the 1920s and 1930s might have followed a very different path without the initiative of Great Britain in opening up air routes to the Middle East, South Africa, India and Australia; of France to North Africa and the Orient; of Belgium to the Congo; of the Netherlands to the East and West Indies; and of Germany to South America.

Comfort, safety and speed : these were the attractions with which the airlines set out to win their prospective public. Designing comfort into an aeroplane was no great problem, but the number of airline accidents in the early years of operation was too high to become an accepted norm. Operating conditions, including the need to maintain schedules in often unfavourable weather, were partly to blame, but all too often aircraft succumbed to circumstances which more powerful or more reliable engines would have overcome. Improvements in aero-engine design and output, and in particular the progress made with air-cooled radial engines after the war, played a large part in the improvement in the general safety record of air transport as the years went by. Nor is it mere coincidence that many of the most successful airliners of the inter-war period were those which flew with many different types of engine. Anthony Fokker, one of the shrewdest salesmen in the aviation business, very soon realised that the powerplant of an aeroplane was, as often as not, the factor which decided a customer for or against the purchase of a particular type of aircraft. His policy therefore was to produce basic airframe designs that could be adapted readily to the powerplant of a customer's choice, and it paid off handsomely, especially in the case of the F.VIIb-3m tri-motor. The same degree of adaptability undoubtedly influenced the popularity of many other types, including the Junkers F 13 and the Ford Tri-motor.

Speed, the one selling factor paramount today over surface transport, was slow to come to air transport. Paradoxically, it came at last from the United States, where passenger transport, playing second fiddle to the transportation of mail by air, had been relatively slow to develop. The turning-point came in 1927, the year in which the US government threw open all air mail operations to private enterprise and the year in which Charles Lindbergh flew alone across the Atlantic. Within months of Lindbergh's epic flight orders were rolling in for the little Ryan Brougham, sister-ship of his *Spirit of St Louis*, but the aeroplane which truly ushered in the speed era of air transport in the US was the Vega – the first of Lockheed's famous 'plywood bullets'.

By the beginning of the 1930s, the world's airlines had to a great extent succeeded in making air transport attractive to a large section of the public. They had yet to solve the problem of making it attractive to themselves, in terms of operating costs. The aircraft which could carry a worthwhile payload over a reasonable range were obsolescent and slow, while the faster types could carry only a small load over shorter distances. Throughout the 1920s dozens of small airlines had been absorbed in mergers to form larger and financially healthier organisations, while others had disappeared altogether through failure to make their operations pay their way. The time was ripe for a breakthrough, in the form of an aircraft that could combine the requirements of comfort, safety and speed with the best payload/range capabilities of existing types.

The first sign of such a breakthrough came with the Boeing 247, which first flew on 8 February 1933 and entered service with United Air Lines in the same year. United's unprecedentedly large order for the 247 was a family affair, for both it and Boeing were members of the huge United Aircraft and Transport Corporation, but this cannot obscure the advance in state-of-the-art airliner design which the Boeing 247 represented. Apart from its cantilever monoplane layout, retractable landing gear and use of all-metal construction, it introduced many other, lesser innovations. Among these were the first use, in a production airliner, of supercharged engines and control surface trim tabs. Here was an aircraft that, in its definitive Model 247D form, could cruise at 189 mph (304 km/hr) with a 2,582 lb (1,171 kg) payload of 10 passengers and baggage over a 750 mile (1,207 km) range, and could climb under full load on one engine.

At last the cost-effective modern airliner was in sight; but the Boeing 247 was to maintain its lead for only a comparatively brief period. Little more than a year after it began airline operation it, too, was entered in the 1934 'MacRobertson' race. It was the third of the competing aircraft to reach Melbourne, but in doing so it took 12¼ hours longer than the DC-2. 'The results of the England-Australia air race', said the London *Morning Post*, 'have fallen like a bomb in the midst of British every-day commercial and military aviation'; and what was true for Britain was almost equally true for the rest of Europe. The paper went on : 'Preconceived ideas of the maximum speed limitations of standard commercial aeroplanes have been blown sky-high. It has suddenly and vividly been brought home that, while the race has been a triumph for the British de Havilland Comet, British *standard* aeroplane development, both commercial and military, has been standing still while America has been going ahead. It has been realised with astonishment that America now has, in hundreds, standard commercial aeroplanes with a higher top speed than the fastest aeroplane in regular service in any squadron in the whole of the Royal Air Force'.

Reaction reached its peak, however, when Douglas produced the DC-3 in late 1935. Prompted by American Airlines, whose lumbering Curtiss Condors and Fokker trimotors were no match for the Boeing 247s and DC-2s of its rivals, Douglas evolved the Douglas Sleeper Transport, which required a wider fuselage than the DC-2 to accommodate 14 sleeping berths. Almost immediately, Douglas realised that, within this wider cabin, the daytime seating capacity of the DC-2 could be increased by 50 per cent – and the DC-3 was born. Already, in 1934, the presence of the DC-2 had caused United Air Lines to transfer its Boeing 247s to less competitive routes, and when the DC-3 entered service they were eclipsed completely. From then until the outbreak of war, airlines ordered DC-3s as fast as Douglas could build them, and their impact upon air transport both inside and outside the United States reached an unparallelled level. Even the appearance of the Lockheed 'twins' – which were faster, but carried a smaller payload – had little effect on the DC-3's progress.

In 1936 the Collier Trophy was awarded to the DC-3 as the outstanding twin-engined commercial transport aeroplane of the year. In words which, in retrospect, seem a masterpiece of understatement, the citation declared that 'this airplane, by reason of its high speed, economy, and quiet passenger comfort, has been generally adopted by transport lines throughout the United States. Its merit has been further recognised by its adoption abroad, and its influence on foreign design is already apparent'. At that time, even the DC-3's most ardent supporters would have found it hard to believe that, thirty-five years later, more than eight hundred examples of this remarkable aeroplane would still be in operation with over two hundred of the world's airlines, having survived innumerable attempts, all abortive, to find a 'DC-3 replacement'. There could have been no more fitting title than that chosen for a full-length book which has been written of the career of the DC-3 : *The Plane That Changed The World.*

INTERNATIONAL CIVIL AIRCRAFT REGISTRATION PREFIX LETTERS

Country	Early 1920s	1939
Afghanistan		YA-
Albania		ZA-
Argentina		*R-
Australia	G-AU	VH-
Austria		*A-

Country	Early 1920s	1939
Bahamas		VP-B
Barbados		VQ-B
Belgium and Colonies	O-B	OO-
Bermuda		VR-B
Bolivia	C-V	CP-
Brazil	P-B	PP-
British Guiana		VP-G
British Honduras		VP-H
Brunei		VR-U
Bulgaria	LZ-	LZ-
Canada	G-C	CF-
Ceylon		VP-C
Chile		CC-
China	X-C	XT-
Colombia		HJ-, HK-
Costa Rica		TI-
Cuba	C-C	CL-, CM-
Curaçao		PJ-
Cyprus		VQ-C
Czechoslovakia	L-B	OK-
Danzig		YM-
Denmark	T-D	OY-
Ecuador	E-E	HC-
Egypt		SU-
Eire	EI-	EI-
Estonia		ES-
Ethiopia		ET-
Falkland Islands		VP-F
Federated Malay States		VR-R
Fiji		VQ-F
Finland	K-S	OH-
France and Colonies	F-	F-

Country	Early 1920s	1939
Gambia		VP-X
Germany		D-
Gibraltar		VR-G
Great Britain	G-E	G-
Greece	S-G	SX-
Grenada		VQ-G
Gold Coast		VP-A
Guatemala	L-G	TG-
Haiti	H-H	HH-
Hejaz (Saudi Arabia)	A-H	UH-
Honduras	X-H	HR-
Hong Kong		VR-H
Hungary		HA-
Iceland		TF-
India	G-I	VT-
Iran		RV-
Iraq		YI-
Italy and Colonies	I-	I-
Jamaica		VP-J
Japan	J-	J-
Johore		VR-J
Kenya		
Latvia	B-L	YL-
Leeward Islands		VP-L
Liberia	L-L	EL-
Lithuania		RY-
Luxembourg	L-U	UL-
Malta		VP-M
Mauritius		VQ-M
Mexico		XA-, XB-
Monaco		CZ-
Morocco		CN-

Country	Early 1920s	1939
Netherlands	H-N	PH-
Netherlands East Indies		PK-
Newfoundland		VO-
New Hebrides		YJ-
New Zealand	G-NZ	ZK-
Nicaragua	A-N	YN-
Nigeria		VR-N
Northern Rhodesia		VP-R
Norway	*N-	LN-
Nyasaland		VP-N
Palestine		VQ-P
Panama	S-P	RX-
Paraguay		ZP-
Peru	O-P	OB-
Poland	P-P	SP-
Portugal	C-P	CS-
Portuguese Colonies		CR-
Romania	C-R	YR-
St Helena		VQ-H
St Lucia		VQ-L
St Vincent		VP-V
Saar Territories	TS-	EZ-
Salvador		YS-
Santo Domingo		HI-
Seychelles		VQ-S
Siam	H-S	HS-
Sierra Leone		VR-L
Southern Rhodesia		VP-Y
Spain	M-A to M-N	EC-
Straits Settlements		VR-S
Surinam		PZ-
Sweden	S-A	SE-
Switzerland	*CH	HB-

15

Country	Early 1920s	1939
Tanganyika Territory		`VR-T
Trinidad and Tobago		VP-T
Turkey		TC-
Uganda		VP-U
Union of South Africa	G-U	ZS-
Uruguay	C-U	CX-
USA	N-	†*N
USSR		*URSS
Venezuela	††X-S	YV-
Wei-hai-wei (China)		VP-W
Western Pacific Islands		VP-P
Yugoslavia		YU-
Zanzibar		VP-Z

*prefix followed by numerals instead of letters
†followed by second prefix letter indicating certification category :
    X (Experimental), C (Commercial) or R (Restricted)
††Serbia, Croatia and Slavonia

THE COLOUR PLATES

As an aid to identification, the colour plates which follow have been arranged in an essentially visual order, with biplanes followed by monoplanes, grouped broadly according to wing position and in ascending order of the number of engines. The reference number of each type corresponds to the appropriate text matter, and an index to all types appears on pp. 349–350.

The 'split' plan view, adopted to give both upper and lower surface markings within a single plan outline, depicts the colour scheme appearing above and below either the port or starboard half of the aircraft, according to whichever aspect is shown in the side elevation.

BREGUET 14 (France)

1

Breguet 14T2 Salon of Compagnie des Messageries Aériennes (CMA), 1920. *Engine:* One 300 h.p. Renault 12Fe twelve-cylinder Vee type. *Span:* 47 ft. 1¼ in. (14.36 m.). *Length:* 29 ft. 6¼ in. (9.00 m.). *Wing area:* 538.2 sq.ft. (50.00 sq.m.). *Take-off weight:* 4,374 lb. (1,984 kg.). *Cruising speed:* 78 m.p.h. (125 km/hr.) at 6,560 ft. (2,000 m.). *Service ceiling:* 14,765 ft. (4,500 m.). *Range:* 286 miles (460 km.)

D.H.4A (U.K.)

2

De Havilland D.H.4A *City of York* of Instone Air Line Ltd, *ca* late 1922/early 1923. *Engine:* One 350 h.p. Rolls-Royce Eagle VIII twelve-cylinder Vee type. *Span:* 42 ft. 4⅝ in. (12.92 m.). *Length:* 30 ft. 6 in. (9.30 m.). *Wing area:* 434.0 sq.ft. (40.32 sq.m.). *Take-off weight:* 3,720 lb. (1,687 kg.). *Maximum speed:* 121· m.p.h. (195 km/hr.). *Service ceiling:* approx 20,000 ft. (6,100 m.). *Range:* 250 miles (402 km.).

LIMOUSINE (U.K.)

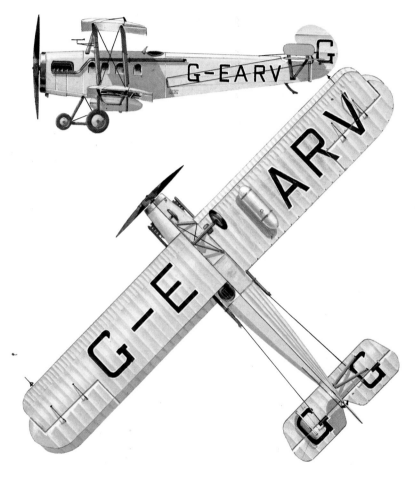

3
Westland Limousine III, winner in the 1920 Air Ministry Commercial Aeroplane Competition. *Engine:* One 450 h.p. Napier Lion IB twelve-cylinder 'broad arrow' type. *Span:* 54 ft. 0 in. (16.46 m.). *Length:* 33 ft. 6 in. (10.21 m.). *Wing area:* 726.0 sq.ft. (67.45 sq.m.). *Take-off weight:* 5,850 lb. (2,653 kg.). *Cruising speed:* 90 m.p.h. (145 km/hr.). *Service ceiling:* 12,300 ft. (3,750 m.). *Range:* 520 miles (837 km.).

D.H.34 (U.K.)

4

De Havilland D.H.34 of Daimler Hire Ltd, 1922. *Engine:* One 450 h.p. Napier Lion twelve-cylinder 'broad arrow' type. *Span:* 51 ft. 0 in. (15.54 m.). *Length:* 39 ft. 0 in. (11.89 m.). *Wing area:* 590.0 sq.ft. (54.81 sq.m.). *Take-off weight:* 7,200 lb. (3,266 kg.). *Cruising speed:* 105 m.p.h. (169 km/hr.). *Service ceiling:* 14,500 tt. (4,420 m.). *Range:* 365 miles (587 km.).

D.H.50 (U.K.)

5

De Havilland D.H.50 prototype, in the markings of de Havilland Hire Service, *ca* 1924. *Engine:* One 240 h.p. Siddeley Puma six-cylinder in-line. *Span:* 42 ft. 9 in. (13.03 m.). *Length:* 29 ft. 9 in. (9.07 m.). *Wing area:* 434.0 sq.ft. (40.32 sq.m.). *Take-off weight:* 4,200 lb. (1,905 kg.). *Cruising speed:* 95 m.p.h. (153 km/hr.). *Service ceiling:* 14,600 ft. (4,450 m.). *Range:* 380 miles (611 km.).

BLÉRIOT-SPAD (France)

6

Blériot-Spad Type 56-4 of Compagnie Internationale de Navigation Aérienne (CIDNA), *ca* 1927-28. *Engine:* One 420 h.p. Gnome-Rhône (Bristol) Jupiter 9Ac nine-cylinder radial. *Span:* 43 ft. 1 in. (13.13 m.). *Length:* 29 ft. 6¼ in. (9.00 m.). *Wing area:* 523.1 sq.ft. (48.60 sq.m.). *Take-off weight:* 5,979 lb. (2,712 kg).. *Cruising speed:* 99 m.p.h. (160 km/hr.). *Service ceiling:* 13,125 ft. (4,000 m.). *Range:* 301 miles (485 km.).

AVIA BH-25 (Czechoslovakia)

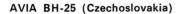

7

Avia BH-25 of Ceskoslovenská Letecka Spolecnost (CLS), *ca* 1929. *Engine:* One 450 h.p. Walter (Bristol) Jupiter IV nine-cylinder radial. *Span:* 50 ft. 2¼ in. (15.30 m.). *Length:* 41 ft. 4½ in. (12.61 m.). *Wing area:* 672.7 sq.ft. (62.50 sq.m.). *Take-off weight:* 6,393 lb. (2,900 kg.). *Cruising speed:* 99 m.p.h. (160 km/hr.). *Service ceiling:* 13,450 ft. (4,100 m.). *Range:* 373 miles (600 km.).

VIMY COMMERCIAL (U.K.)

8

Vickers Vimy Commercial *City of London* of S. Instone &
Co. Ltd. Aerial Transport Department, 1920. *Engines:* Two
360 h.p. Rolls-Royce Eagle VIII twelve-cylinder Vee type.
Span: 67 ft. 2 in. (20. 47 m.). *Length:* 42 ft. 8 in. (13.00 m.).
Wing area: 1,330.0 sq.ft. (123.56 sq.m.). *Take-off weight:*
12,500 lb. (5,670 kg.). *Cruising speed:* 84 m.p.h. (135 km/
hr.). *Service ceiling:* 10,500 ft. (3,200 m.). *Range:* 450
miles (724 km.).

GOLIATH (France)

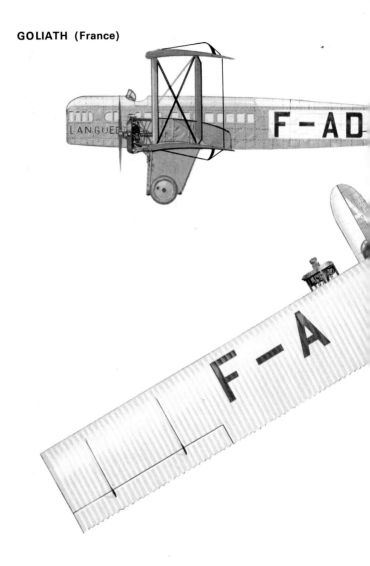

9

Farman F.60 Goliath *Languedoc* of Air Union, 1923. *Engines:* Two 260 h.p. Salmson 9Cm nine-cylinder radials. *Span:* 86 ft. 11¼ in. (26.50 m.). *Length:* 47 ft. 0¼ in. (14.33 m.). *Wing area:* 1,733.0 sq.ft. (161.00 sq.m.) *Take-off weight:* 10,516 lb. (4,770 kg.). *Cruising speed:* 75 m.p.h. (120 km/hr.). at 6,560 ft. (2,000 m.). *Service ceiling:* 13,125 ft. (4,000 m.). *Range:* 248 miles (400 km.).

LIORÉ et OLIVIER 21 (France)

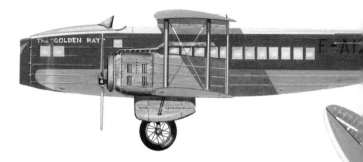

10

Lioré et Olivier 213 of Air Union, 1931-32. *Engines:* Two
450 h.p. Renault 12Ja twelve-cylinder Vee type. *Span:* 76
ft. 10½ in. (23.43 m.). *Length:* 52 ft. 4 in. (15.95 m.). *Wing
area:* 1,167.9 sq.ft. (108.50 sq.m.). *Take-off weight:* 12,566
lb. (5,700 kg.). *Cruising speed:* 109 m.p.h. (175 km/hr.) at
3,280 ft. (1,000 m.). *Service ceiling:* 14,765 ft. (4,500 m.).
Range: 348 miles (560 km.).

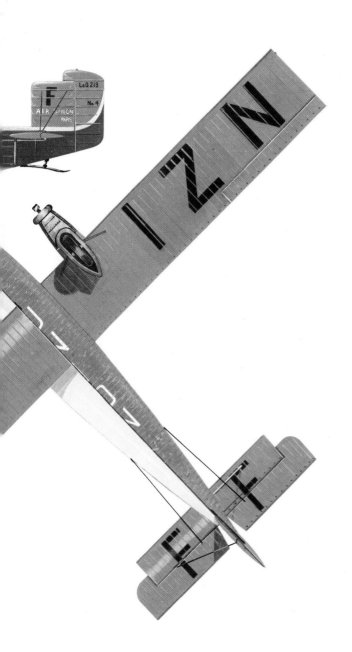

HANDLEY PAGE W.8b (U.K.)

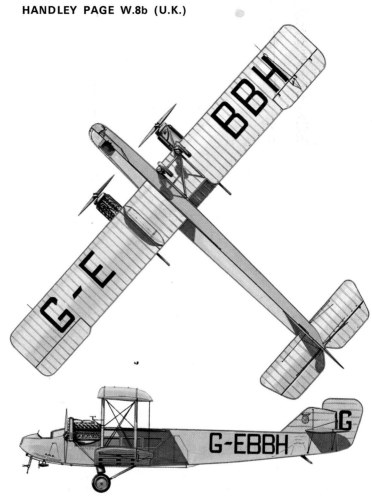

11

Handley Page W.8b *RMA Prince George* of Handley Page Transport Ltd., 1922. *Engines:* Two 360 h.p. Rolls-Royce Eagle VIII twelve-cylinder Vee type. *Span:* 75 ft. 0 in. (22.86 m.). *Length:* 60 ft. 1 in. (18.31 m.). *Wing area:* 1,456.0 sq.ft. (135.26 sq.m.). *Take-off weight:* 12,000 lb. (5,443 kg.). *Maximum cruising speed:* 101 m.p.h. (163 km/hr.). *Service ceiling:* 10,000 ft. (3,050 m.). *Range:* 400 miles (644 km.).

ARGOSY (U.K.)

12

Armstrong Whitworth A.W. 155 Argosy I *City of Birmingham* of Imperial Airways Ltd., autumn 1926. *Engines:* Three 385 h.p. Armstrong Siddeley Jaguar III fourteen-cylinder radials. *Span:* 90 ft. 0 in. (27.43 m.). *Length:* 64 ft. 6 in. (19.66 m.). *Wing area:* 1,890.0 sq.ft. (175.59 sq.m.) *Take-off weight:* 18,000 lb. (8,165 kg.). *Cruising speed:* 90 m.p.h. (145 km/hr.). *Range:* 405 miles (652 km.).

HERCULES (U.K.)

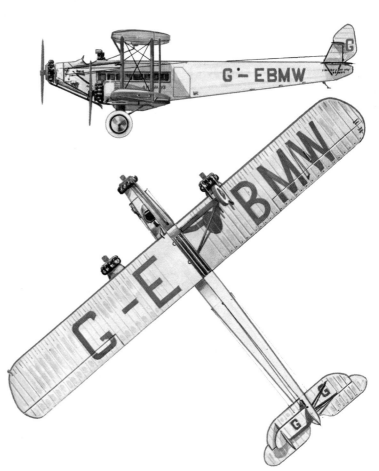

13

De Havilland D.H.66 Hercules *City of Cairo* of Imperial Airways Ltd., *ca* 1927. *Engines:* Three 420 h.p. Bristol Jupiter VI nine-cylinder radials. *Span:* 79 ft. 6 in. (24.23 m.). *Length:* 55 ft. 6 in. (16.92 m.). *Wing area:* 1,547.0 sq.ft. (143.72 sq.m.). *Take-off weight:* 15,600 lb. (7,076 kg.). *Cruising speed:* 110 m.p.h. (177 km/hr.). *Service ceiling:* 13,000 ft. (3,960 m.).

BOEING 80A (U.S.A.)

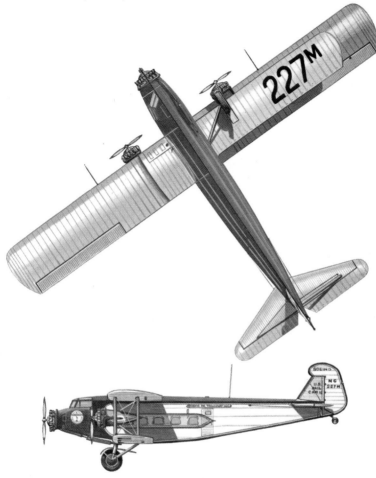

14

Boeing Model 80A of Boeing Air Transport Inc, *ca* 1930-31. *Engines:* Three 525 h.p. Pratt & Whitney Hornet B nine-cylinder radials. *Span:* 80 ft. 0 in. (24.38 m.). *Length:* 56 ft. 6 in. (17.22 m.). *Wing area:* 1,220.0 sq.ft. (113.34 sq.m.). *Take-off weight:* 17,500 lb. (7,938 kg.). *Cruising speed:* 125 m.p.h. (201 km/hr.). *Service ceiling:* 14,000 ft. (4,267 m.). *Range:* 460 miles (740 km.).

HANDLEY PAGE H.P.42 (U.K.)

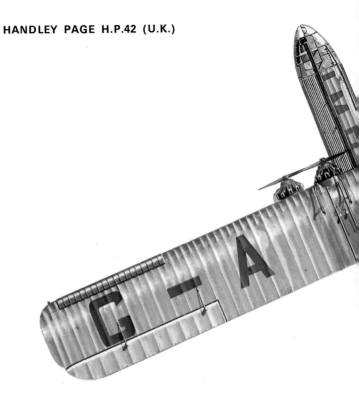

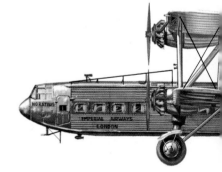

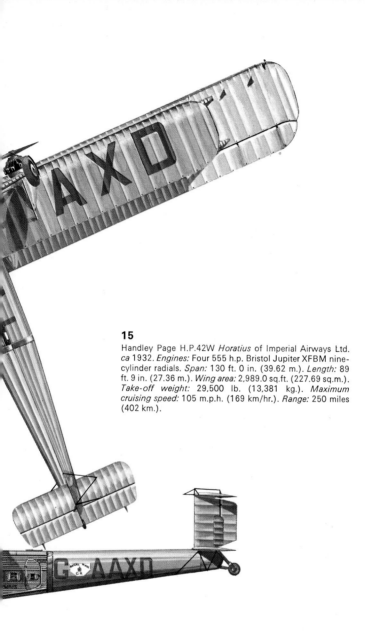

15

Handley Page H.P.42W *Horatius* of Imperial Airways Ltd. *ca* 1932. *Engines:* Four 555 h.p. Bristol Jupiter XFBM nine-cylinder radials. *Span:* 130 ft. 0 in. (39.62 m.). *Length:* 89 ft. 9 in. (27.36 m.). *Wing area:* 2,989.0 sq.ft. (227.69 sq.m.). *Take-off weight:* 29,500 lb. (13,381 kg.). *Maximum cruising speed:* 105 m.p.h. (169 km/hr.). *Range:* 250 miles (402 km.).

CONDOR (U.S.A.)

16

Curtiss Model AT-32-A Condor of American Airways, 1934. *Engines:* Two 710 h.p. Wright Cyclone SGR-1820-F3 nine-cylinder radials. *Span:* 82 ft. 0 in. (24.99 m.). *Length:* 48 ft. 7 in. (14.81 m.). *Wing area:* 1,208.0 sq.ft. (112.22 sq.m.). *Take-off weight:* 17,500 lb. (7,938 kg.). *Speed:* 167 m.p.h. (269 km/hr.) at 8,000 ft. (2,438 m.).*Service ceiling:* 23,000 ft. (7,010 m.). *Maximum range:* 716 miles (1,152 km.).

DRAGON (U.K.)

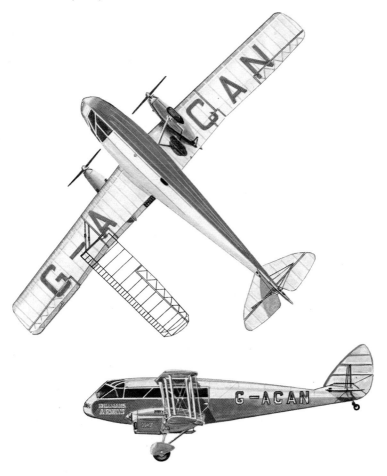

17

Prototype de Havilland D.H.84 Dragon 1, as *Maylands* of Hillman's Airways Ltd,
early 1933. *Engines:* Two 130 h.p. de Havilland Gipsy Major I four-cylinder in-lines.
Span: 47 ft. 4 in. (14.43 m.). *Length:* 34 ft. 6 in. (10.52 m.). *Wing area:* 376.0 sq.ft.
(34.93 m.). *Take-off weight:* 4,200 lb. (1,905 kg.). *Cruising speed:* 109 m.p.h. (175
km/hr.) at 1,000 ft. (305 m.). *Service ceiling:* 12,500 ft. (3,810 m.). *Range:* 460
miles (740 km.).

DRAGON RAPIDE (U.K.)

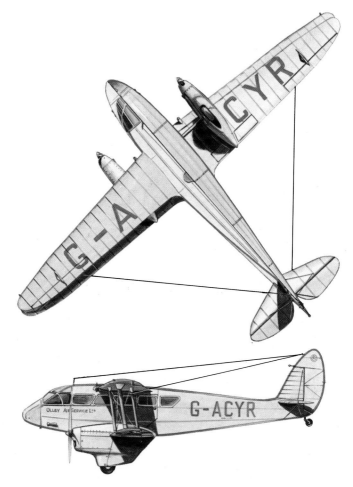

18

De Havilland D.H.89A Dragon Rapide of Olley Air Service Ltd., 1935. *Engines:* Two 200 h.p. de Havilland Gipsy Six I six-cylinder in-lines. *Span:* 48 ft 0 in. (14.63 m.). *Length:* 34 ft. 6 in. (10.52 m.). *Wing area:* 336.0 sq.ft. (31.22 sq.m.). *Take-off weight:* 5,500 lb. (2,495 kg.). *Cruising speed:* 133 m.p.h. (214 km/hr.). *Service ceiling:* 16,700 ft. (5,090 m.). *Range:* 578 miles (930 km.).

D.H.86 (U.K.)

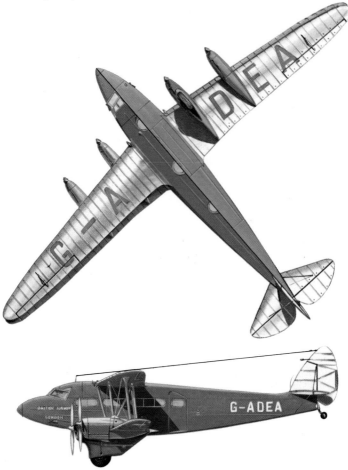

19

De Havilland D.H.86A of British Airways, 1936. *Engines:* Four 200 h.p. de Havilland Gipsy Six I six-cylinder in-lines. *Span:* 64 ft. 6 in. (19.66 m.). *Length:* 46 ft. 1¼ in. (14.05 m.). *Wing area:* 641.0 sq.ft. (59.55 sq.m.). *Take-off weight:* 10,250 lb. (4,650 kg.). *Cruising speed:* 145 m.p.h. (233 km/hr.). *Service ceiling:* 17,400 ft. (5,300 m.). *Range:* 764 miles (1,230 km.).

MERKUR (Germany)

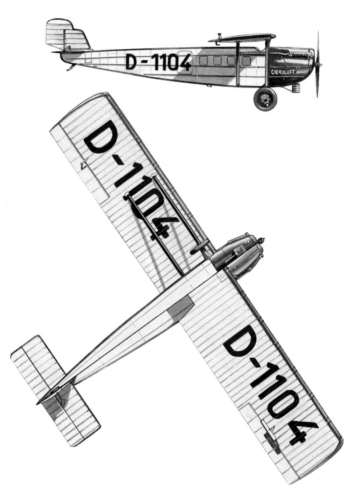

20

Dornier Merkur of Deruluft, *ca* 1927-28. *Engine:* One 600 h.p. BMW VI twelve-cylinder Vee type. *Span:* 64 ft. 3¾ in. (19.60 m.). *Length:* 41 ft. 0 in. (12.50 m.). *Wing area:* 667.4 sq.ft. (62.00 sq.m.). *Take-off-weight:* 7,936 lb. (3,600 kg.). *Cruising speed:* 112 m.p.h. (180 km/hr.) *Service ceiling:* 17,060 ft. (5,200 m.).

FOCKE-WULF A 17 (Germany)

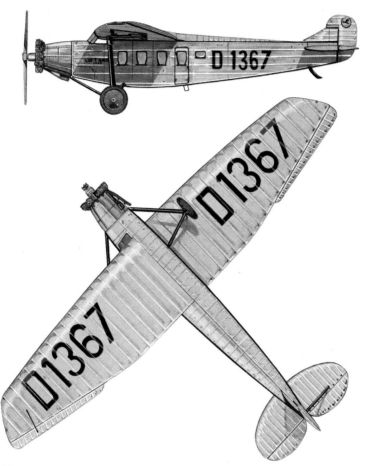

21

Focke-Wulf A 17a Möwe *Leer* of Deutsche Luft Hansa, *ca* 1932. *Engine:* One 480 h.p. Siemens-built Bristol Jupiter VI nine-cylinder radial. *Span:* 65 ft. 7½ in. (20.00 m.) *Length:* 48 ft. 0 in. (14.63 m.). *Wing area:* 672.7 sq.ft. (62.50 sq.m.). *Take-off weight:* 8,818 lb. (4,000 kg.). *Maximum cruising speed:* 109 m.p.h. (175 km/hr.). *Service ceiling:* 16,400 ft. (5,000 m.). *Range:* 497 miles (800 km.).

FOKKER F.III (Netherlands)

22

Fokker F.III of Koninklijke Luchtvaart Maatschappij (KLM), 1921-22. *Engine:* One 245 h.p. Siddeley Puma six-cylinder in-line. *Span:* 57 ft. 9¾ in. (17.62 m.). *Length:* 36 ft. 3¾ in. (11.07 m.). *Wing area:* 420.9 sq.ft. (39.10 sq.m.). *Take-off weight:* 4,850 lb. (2,200 kg.). *Cruising speed:* 81 m.p.h. (130 km/hr.). *Endurance:* 5 hours.

SUPER UNIVERSAL (U.S.A.)

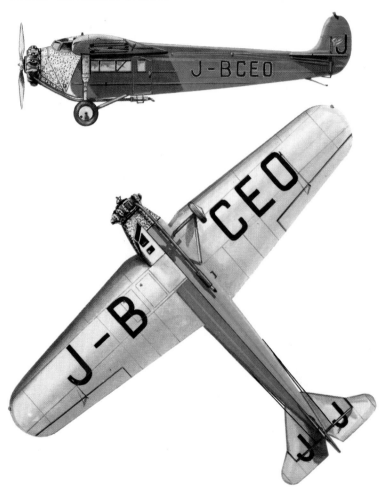

23

Nakajima-built Fokker Super Universal of the Manchurian Air Transport Company, late 1932. *Engine:* One 450 h.p. Nakajima-built Bristol Jupiter nine-cylinder radial. *Span:* 50 ft. 7¾ in. (15.44 m.). *Length:* 36 ft. 7 in. (11.15 m.). *Wing area:* 370 sq.ft. (34.37 sq. m.). *Take-off weight:* 5,271 lb. (2,391 kg.). *Cruising speed:* 118 m.p.h. (190 km/hr.). *Service ceiling:* 18,000 ft. (5.486 m.). *Range:* 675 miles (1,086 km.).

DETROITER (U.S.A.)

24

Stinson Model SM-1 Detroiter of Braniff Airways, 1928. *Engine:* One 220 h.p. Wright Whirlwind J5C nine-cylinder radial. *Span:* 45 ft. 10 in. (13.97 m.). *Length:* 32 ft. 10 in. (10.01 m.). *Wing area:* 292.0 sq.ft. (27.13 sq.m.). *Take-off weight:* 3,485 lb. (1,580 kg.). *Cruising speed:* 105 m.p.h. (169 km/hr.). *Service ceiling:* 14,000 ft. (4,267 m.). *Range:* 700 miles (1,125 km.).

BROUGHAM (U.S.A.)

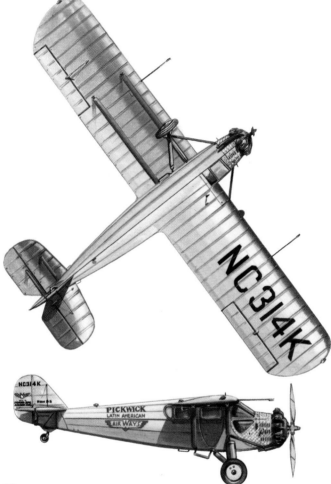

25

Ryan Model B-5 Brougham of Pickwick Latin American Airways, *ca* 1929-30. *Engine:* One 300 h.p. Wright Whirlwind J6 nine-cylinder radial. *Span:* 42 ft. 4 in. (12.90 m.). *Length:* 28 ft. 4 in. (8.64 m.). *Wing area:* 280.0 sq. ft. (26.01 sq. m.). *Take-off weight:* 4,000 lb. (1,814 kg.). *Cruising speed:* 120 m.p.h. (193 km/hr.). *Service ceiling:* 18,000 ft. (5,486 m.). *Range:* 720 miles (1,158 km).

P.W.S.24 (Poland)

26

Podlaska Wytwornia Samolotow P.W.S.24 *Filip* of Polskie Linie Lotnicze (Lot), 1933. *Engine:* One 220 h.p. Skoda-built Wright J5 Whirlwind seven-cylinder radial. *Span:* 49 ft. 2½ in. (15.00 m.). *Length:* 31 ft. 8 in. (9.65 m.). *Wing area:* 341.7 sq.ft. (31.75 sq.m.). *Normal take-off weight:* 4,078 lb. (1,850 kg.). *Best cruising speed:* 99 m.p.h. (160 km/hr.). *Service ceiling:* 11,480 ft. (3,500 m.). *Range:* 577 miles (930 km.).

KALININ K-5 (U.S.S.R.)

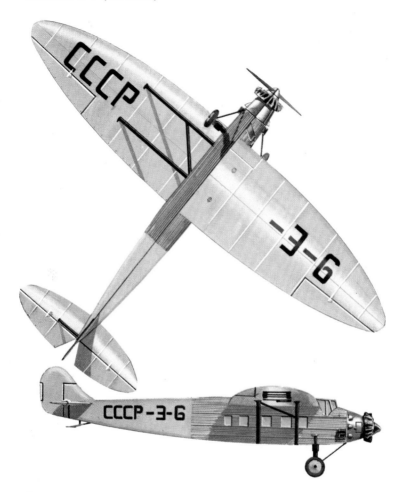

27

Kalinin K-5 of Dobrolet, *ca* 1930. *Engine:* One 450 h.p. M-15 (Bristol Jupiter) nine-cylinder radial. *Span:* 67 ft. 3 in. (20.50 m.). *Length:* 52 ft. 0¾ in. (15.87 m.). *Wing area:* 710.4 sq.ft. (66.00 sq.m.). *Maximum take-off weight:* 8,267 lb. (3,750 kg.). *Cruising speed:* 97.5 m.p.h. (157 km/hr.). *Service ceiling:* 15,680 ft. (4,780 m.). *Range:* 590 miles (950 km.).

FLEETSTER (U.S.A.)

28

Consolidated Model 17 Fleetster floatplane of New York, Rio and Buenos Aires Line Inc, 1930. *Engine:* One 575 h.p. Pratt & Whitney R-1860 Hornet B nine-cylinder radial. *Span:* 45 ft. 0 in. (13.72 m.). *Length* (landplane): 31 ft. 9 in. (9.68 m.). *Wing area:* 313.5 sq.ft. (29.125 sq.m.). *Take-off weight:* 5,570 lb. (2,527 kg.). *Cruising speed:* 145 m.p.h. (233 km/hr.). *Service ceiling:* 17,000 ft. (5,182 m.). *Range:* 600 miles (966 km.).

LATÉCOÈRE 28 (France)

29

Latécoère 283 *Comte de la Vaulx* of Compagnie Générale Aéropostale, flown by Jean Mermoz, 1930. *Engine:* One 750 h.p. Hispano Suiza 12 Lbr twelve-cylinder Vee type. *Span:* 63 ft. 1¾ in. (19.25 m.). *Length:* 47 ft. 0 in. (14.325 m.) (floatplane); 44 ft. 9¼ in. (13.645 m.) (landplane). *Wing area:* 626.5 sq.ft. (58.20 sq.m.). *Take-off weight:* 11,060 lb. (5,017 kg.). *Cruising speed:* approx 124 m.p.h. (200 km/hr.) at 9,845 ft. (3,000 m.). *Range:* 1,988 miles (3,200 km).

VEGA (U.S.A.)

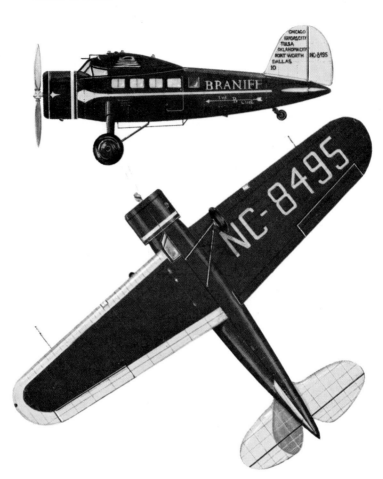

30
Lockheed Vega Model DL-1 of Braniff Airways, *ca* 1934-35. *Engine:* One 450 h.p.
Pratt & Whitney Wasp C1 nine-cylinder radial. *Span:* 41 ft. 0 in. (12.50 m.). *Length:*
27 ft. 6 in. (8.38 m.). *Wing area:* 275.0 sq. ft. (25.55 sq. m.). *Take-off weight:* 4,270
lb. (1,937 kg.). *Cruising speed:* 150 m.p.h. (241 km/hr.). *Service ceiling:* approx
22,000 ft. (6,705 m.). *Range:* approx 700 miles (1,126 km.)

AIRCRUISER (U.S.A.)

31

Bellanca Model 66-70 Cargo Aircruiser of Mackenzie Air Service Ltd, 1935. *Engine:* One 658 h.p. Canadian-built Wright Cyclone nine-cylinder radial. *Span:* 65 ft. 0 in. (19.81 m.). *Length:* 42 ft. 9 in. (13.03 m.). *Wing area:* 664.0 sq.ft. (61.69 sq.m.). *Take-off weight:* 11,400 lb. (5,171 kg.). *Speed:* 154 m.p.h. (248 km/hr.) at 12,000 ft. (3,658 m.). *Service ceiling:* 20,000 ft. (6,100 m.). *Range with maximum payload of 4,000 lb. (1,814 kg):* 550 miles (885 km.).

TUPOLEV ANT-9 (U.S.S.R.)

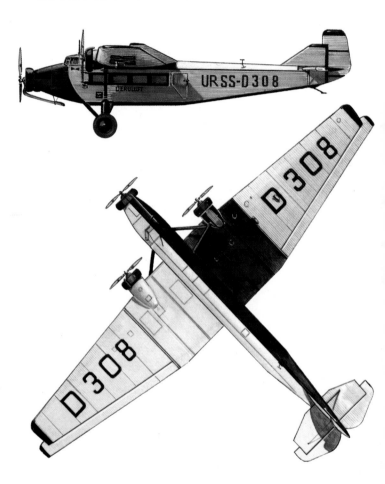

32

Tupolev ANT-9 *Chaika* (Seagull) of Deruluft, *ca* 1932-33. *Engines:* Three 300 h.p. M-26 (Wright J6 Whirlwind) seven-cylinder radials *Span:* 77 ft. 10¼ in. (23.73 m.). *Length:* 55 ft. 9¼ in. (17.00 m.). *Wing area:* 904.2 sq.ft. (84.00 sq.m.). *Take-off weight:* 13,228 lb. (6,000 kg.). *Cruising speed:* 115 m.p.h. (185 km/hr.) *Service ceiling:* 11,155 ft. (3,400 m.). *Range:* 620 miles (1,000 km.).

ROHRBACH Ro VIII ROLAND (Germany)

33

Rohrbach Ro VIII Roland I of Compania Aérea de Transportes (Iberia), *ca* 1928. *Engines:* Three 230 h.p. BMW IV six-cylinder in-lines. *Span:* 86 ft. 3½ in. (26.30 m.). *Length:* 52 ft. 9¾ in. (16.10 m.). *Wing area:* 958.0 sq.ft. (89.00 sq.m.). *Take-off weight:* 15,763 lb. (7,150 kg.). *Cruising speed:* 109 m.p.h. (175 km/hr.). *Service ceiling:* 13,125 ft. (4,000 m.). *Maximum range:* 932 miles (1,500 km.).

FORD TRI-MOTOR (U.S.A.)

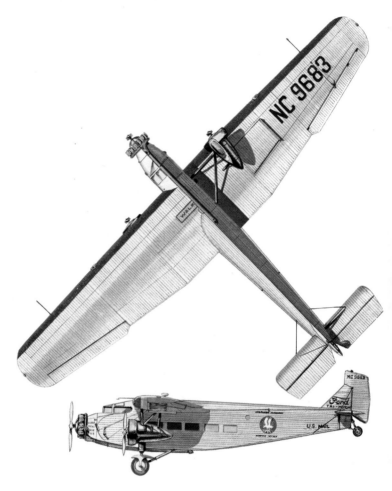

34

Ford Model 5-AT-B of American Airways, 1931. *Engines:* Three 420 h.p. Pratt & Whitney Wasp C-1 or SC-1 nine-cylinder radials. *Span:* 77 ft. 10 in. (23.72 m.). *Length:* 49 ft. 10 in. (15.19 m.). *Wing area:* 835.0 sq.ft. (77.57 sq.m.). *Typical take-off weight:* 13,000 lb. (5,897 kg.). *Typical cruising speed:* 122 m.p.h. (196 km/hr.) *Service ceiling:* 18,500 ft. (5,639 m.). *Typical range:* 550 miles (885 km.).

SAVOIA-MARCHETTI S.71 (Italy)

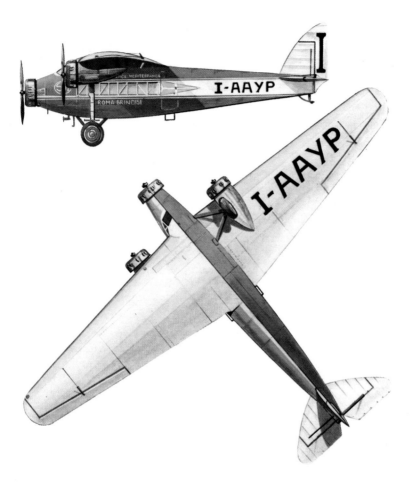

35

Savoia-Marchetti S.71 of Società Aerea Mediterranea, *ca* 1932. *Engines:* Three 240 h.p. Walter Castor seven-cylinder radials. *Span:* 69 ft. 6¾ in. (21.20 m.). *Length:* 45 ft. 11¼ in. (14.00 m.). *Wing area:* 645.8 sq.ft. (60.00 sq.m.). *Take-off weight:* 10,140 lb. (4,600 kg.). *Cruising speed:* 112 m.p.h. (180 km/hr.). *Service ceiling:* 19,685 ft. (6,000 m.). *Maximum range:* 777 miles (1,250 km.).

FOKKER F.VII and F.VIIa/3m (Netherlands)

36

Bottom: Fokker F.VII prototype of Koninklijke Luchtvaart Maatschappij (KLM), 1924. *Engine:* One 360 h.p. Rolls-Royce Eagle IX twelve-cylinder Vee type. *Span:* 72 ft. $2\frac{1}{4}$ in. (22.00 m.). *Length:* 44 ft. $3\frac{1}{2}$ in. (13.50 m.). *Wing area:* 772.5 sq.ft. (71.77 sq.m.). *Take-off weight:* 8,080 lb. (3,665 kg.). *Cruising speed:* 81 m.p.h. (130 km/hr.). *Service ceiling:* 14,765 ft. (4,500 m.).

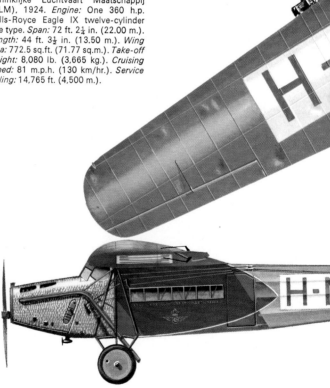

Fokker F.VIIa/3m of Koninklijke Luchtvaart Maatschappij (KLM), 1926.
Engines: Three 220 h.p. Armstrong
Siddeley Lynx IVC seven-cylinder radials.
Span: 63 ft. 4¼ in. (19.31 m.). *Length:* 47
ft. 1 in. (14.35 m.). *Wing area:* 627.6 sq.
ft. (58.50 sq.m.). *Take-off weight:* 7,937
lb. (3,600 kg.). *Speed:* 106 m.p.h. (170
km/hr.). *Service ceiling:* 15,420 ft.
(4,700 m.). *Range:* approx 550 miles
(885 km.).

AVRO TEN (U.K.)

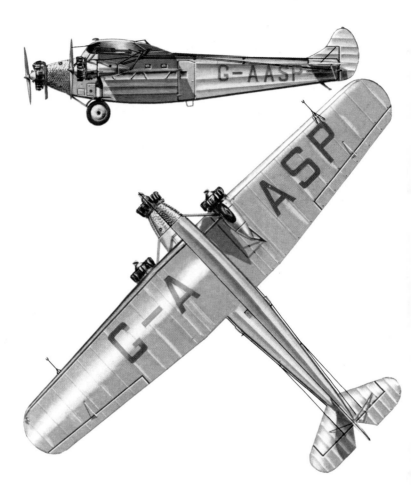

37

Avro Type 618 Ten *Achilles* of Imperial Airways Ltd., 1930-31. *Engines:* Three 215 h.p. Armstrong Siddeley Lynx IVC seven-cylinder radials. *Span:* 71 ft. 3 in. (21.72 m.). *Length:* 47 ft. 6 in. (14.48 m.). *Wing area:* 772.0 sq.ft. (71.72 sq.m.). *Take-off weight:* 10,600 lb. (4,808 kg.). *Cruising speed:* 100 m.p.h. (161 km/hr.). *Service ceiling:* 16,000 ft. (4,880 m.). *Range:* 400 miles (644 km.).

FOKKER F.XII (Netherlands)

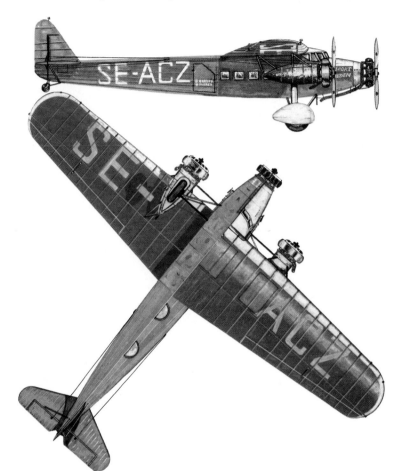

38

Fokker F.XII *Värmland* of AB Aerotransport, 1932-33. *Engines:* Three 500 h.p. Pratt & Whitney Wasp T1D1 nine-cylinder radials. *Span:* 75 ft. 6¼ in. (23.02 m.). *Length:* 58 ft. 4¾ in. (17.80 m.). *Wing area:* 893.4 sq.ft. (83.00 sq.m.). *Take-off weight:* 15,983 lb. (7,250 kg.). *Cruising speed:* 130 m.p.h. (210 km/hr.). *Service ceiling:* 11,155 ft. (3,400 m.). *Range with maximum fuel:* 808 miles (1,300 km.).

JUNKERS G 38 (Germany)

39

Junkers G 38ce *Generalfeldmarschall von Hindenburg* of
Deutsche Luft Hansa, 1933. *Engines:* Four 775 h.p. Junkers
L 88a twelve-cylinder Vee type. *Span:* 144 ft. 4¼ in. (44.00
m.). *Length:* 76 ft. 1½ in. (23.20 m.). *Wing area:* 3,229.2
sq.ft. (300.00 sq.m.). *Maximum take-off weight:* 52,910 lb.
(24,000 kg.). *Cruising speed:* 112 m.p.h. (180 km/hr.).
Service ceiling: 8,200 ft. (2,500 m.). *Range:* 2,175 miles
(3,500 km.)

POTEZ 62 (France)

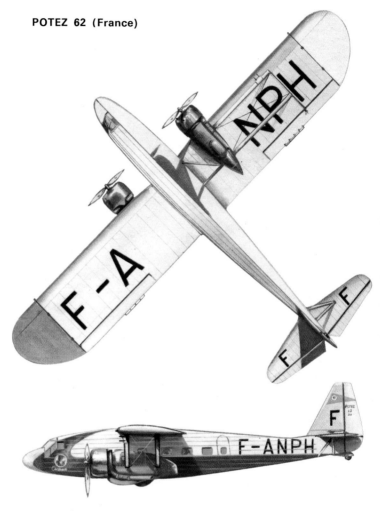

40

Potez 62-0 *Cormoran* of Air France, 1935. *Engines:* Two 870 h.p. Gnome-Rhône 14Kdrs Mistral Major fourteen-cylinder radials. *Span:* 73 ft. 7¾ in. (22.45 m.). *Length:* 56 ft. 10 in. (17.32 m.). *Wing area:* 818.1 sq.ft. (76.00 sq.m.). *Normal take-off weight:* 15,785 lb. (7,160 kg.). *Cruising speed:* 174 m.p.h. (280 km/hr.) at 6,560 ft. (2,000 m.). *Absolute ceiling:* 24,605 ft. (7,500 m.). *Normal range:* 620 miles (1,000 km.).

ATALANTA (U.K.)

41
Armstrong Whitworth A.W.15 Atalanta *Arethusa* of Indian Trans-Continental Airways, late 1933. *Engines:* Four 340 h.p. Armstrong Siddeley Serval III ten-cylinder radials. *Span:* 90 ft. 0 in. (27.43 m.). *Length:* 71 ft. 6 in. (21.79 m.). *Wing area:* 1,285.0 sq.ft. (119.38 sq.m.). *Take-off weight:* 21,000 lb. (9.525 kg.). *Cruising speed:* 130 m.p.h. (209 km/hr.). *Service ceiling:* 13,000 ft. (3,962 m.). *Range:* 400 miles (644 km.).

ENSIGN (U.K.)

42

Armstrong Whitworth A.W.27 Ensign *Ensign* of Imperial Airways Ltd, 1938-39. *Engines:* Four 880 h.p. Armstrong Siddeley Tiger IX fourteen-cylinder radials. *Span:* 123 ft. 0 in. (37.49 m.). *Length:* 114 ft. 0 in. (34.75 m.). *Wing area:* 2,450.0 sq.ft. (227.61 sq.m.). *Take-off weight:* 49,000 lb. (22,226 kg.). *Cruising speed:* 170 m.p.h. (274 km/hr.). *Service ceiling:* 18,000 ft. (5,490 m.). *Range:* 800 miles (1,287 km.).

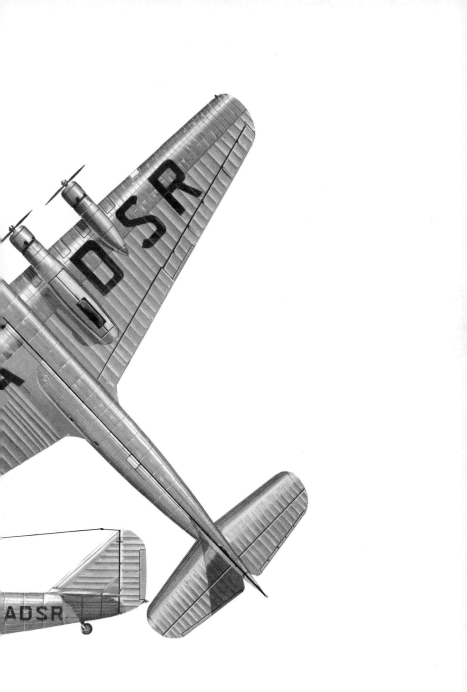

JUNKERS F 13 (Germany)

43

Junkers F 13 of AB Aerotransport, 1928. *Engine:* One 310 h.p. Junkers L5 six-cylinder in-line. *Span:* 56 ft. 3¼ in. (17.15 m.). *Length:* 31 ft. 6 in. (9.60 m.). *Wing area:* 430.6 sq. ft. (40.00 sq. m.). *Take-off weight:* 4,244 lb. (1,925 kg.). *Cruising speed:* 99 m.p.h. (160 km/hr.) at 6,560 ft. (2,000 m.). *Service ceiling:* 8,200 ft. (2,500 m.). *Range:* 528 miles (850 km.).

JUNKERS G 24 (Germany)

44

Junkers G 24W *Suomi* of Aero O/Y (Finnair), *ca* 1928. *Engines:* Three 310 h.p.
Junkers L5 six-cylinder in-lines. *Span:* 96 ft. 4¼ in. (29.37 m.). *Length:* 54 ft. 9½ in.
(16.70 m.). *Wing area:* 1,087.2 sq.ft. (101.00 sq.m.) *Take-off weight:* 14,330 lb.
(6,500 kg.). *Cruising speed:* 102.5 m.p.h. (165 km/hr.) at 6,560 ft. (2,000 m.).
Service ceiling: 14,100 ft. (4,300 m.).

JUNKERS W 34 (Germany)

45

Swedish-built Junkers W 34 *Ternen* of Det Norske Luftruter, *ca* 1931. *Engine:* One 600 h.p. BMW Hornet C nine-cylinder radial. *Span:* 60 ft. 7½ in. (18.48 m.). *Length:* 36 ft. 6¼ in. (11.13 m.). *Wing area:* 473.6 sq.ft. (44.00 sq.m.). *Maximum take-off weight:* 7,055 lb. (3,200 kg.). *Maximum cruising speed:* 134 m.p.h. (215 km/hr.) at 3,280 ft. (1,000 m.). *Service ceiling:* 20,340 ft. (6,200 m.).

DELTA (U.S.A.)

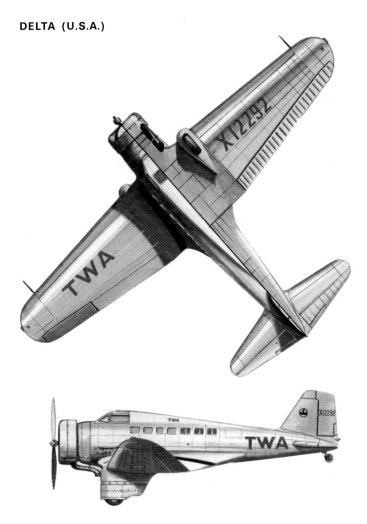

46

Northrop Delta of Transcontinental and Western Air (TWA), 1933. *Engine:* One 575 h.p. Wright Cyclone nine-cylinder radial. *Span:* 47 ft. $9\frac{1}{2}$ in. (14.57 m.). *Length:* 33 ft. 1 in. (10.08 m.). *Wing area:* 363.0 sq. ft. (33.72 sq. m.). *Take-off weight:* 7,350 lb. (3,334 kg.). *Cruising speed:* 208 m.p.h. (335 km/hr.) at 12,700 ft. (3,870 m.). *Service ceiling:* 23,500 ft. (7,163 m.). *Range:* 1,650 miles (2,655 km.).

MONOMAIL (U.S.A.)

47

Boeing Model 221A (originally Model 200) Monomail of United Air Lines (Boeing Air Transport Division), *ca* 1932. *Engine:* One 575 h.p. Pratt & Whitney Hornet B nine-cylinder radial. *Span:* 59 ft. 1½ in. (18.02 m.). *Length:* 44 ft. 1½ in. (13.45 m.). *Wing area:* 535.0 sq.ft. (49.70 sq.m.). *Take-off weight:* 8,000 lb. (3.629 kg.). *Cruising speed:* 137 m.p.h. (220 km/hr.). *Service ceiling:* 14,700 ft. (4,480 m.). *Range:* 540 miles (869 km.).

COURIER (U.K.)

48
Airspeed A.S.5 Courier prototype, built for non-stop flight to India in 1934 by Sir Alan Cobham. *Engine:* One 240 h.p. Armstrong Siddeley Lynx IVC seven-cylinder radial. *Span:* 47 ft. 0 in. (14.33 m.). *Length:* 28 ft. 6 in. (8.69 m.). *Wing area:* 250.0 sq.ft. (23.23 sq.m.). *Take-off weight:* 3,900 lb. (1.769 kg.). *Cruising speed:* 132 m.p.h. (212 km/hr.) at 1,000 ft. (305 m.). *Service ceiling:* 13,500 ft. (4,115 m.). *Range:* 638 miles (1,027 km.).

ORION (U.S.A.)

49

Lockheed Model 9 Orion *South Wind* of Varney Speed Lanes, 1930. *Engine:* One 450 h.p. Pratt & Whitney Wasp S1D1 nine-cylinder radial. *Span:* 42 ft. 9¼ in. (13.04 m.). *Length:* 27 ft. 6 in. (8.38 m.). *Wing area:* 294.1 sq.ft. (27.32 sq.m.). *Take-off weight (mail version):* 5,400 lb. (2,449 kg.). *Cruising speed:* 175 m.p.h. (282 km/hr.) at 11,000 ft. (3,353 m.). *Service ceiling:* 22,000 ft. (6,706 m.). *Range:* 750 miles (1,207 km.).

CLARK G.A.43 (U.S.A.)

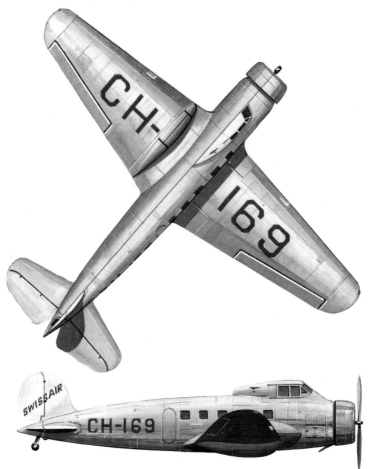

50

General Aviation (Clark) G.A.43 of Swiss Air Lines (Swissair), *ca* 1934-35. *Engine:* One 700 h.p. Wright GR-1820-F1 Cyclone nine-cylinder radial. *Span:* 53 ft. 0 in. (16.15 m.). *Length:* 43 ft. 1 in (13.13 m.). *Wing area:* 464.0 sq. ft. (43.11 sq. m.). *Take-off weight:* 8,750 lb. (3,969 kg.). *Cruising speed:* 162 m.p.h. (261 km/hr.) at 10,000 ft. (3,050 m.). *Service ceiling:* 18,000 ft. (5,486 m.). *Range:* 850 miles (1,368 km.).

MONOSPAR (U.K.)

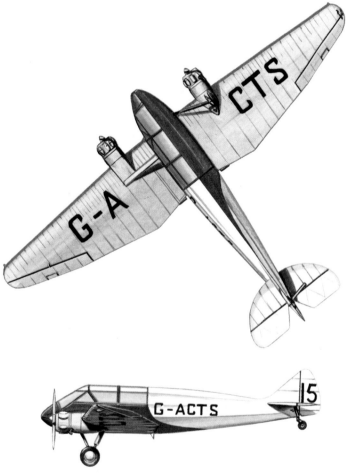

51

General Aircraft Monospar ST-10, winner of 1934 King's Cup air race. *Engines:* Two 90 h.p. Pobjoy Niagara I seven-cylinder radials. *Span:* 40 ft. 2 in. (12.24 m.). *Length:* 26 ft. 4 in. (8.03 m.). *Wing area:* 217.0 sq.ft. (20.16 sq.m.). *Take-off weight:* 2,750 lb. (1,451 kg.). *Cruising speed:* 130 m.p.h. (209 km/hr.). *Service ceiling:* 18,000 ft. (2,900 m.). *Range:* 585 miles (941 km.).

BOEING 247 (U.S.A.)

Legend on fuselage reads:
'THIS PLANE CARRIED THE STARS AND
STRIPES ACROSS THE FINISHING
LINE IN THE WORLD'S
GREATEST AIR RACE'

52

United Air Lines' Boeing 247D, flown to third place in the 1934 'MacRobertson'
race by Roscoe Turner and Clyde Pangborn, after its return to airline service. *Engines:*
Two 550 h.p. Pratt & Whitney Wasp S1H1-G nine-cylinder radials. *Span:* 74 ft. 0 in.
(22.56 m.). *Length:* 51 ft. 7 in. (15.72 m.). *Wing area:* 836.13 sq.ft. (77.68 sq.m.).
Take-off weight: 13,650 lb. (6,192 kg.). *Speed:* 189 m.p.h. (304 km/hr.) at 12,000
ft. (3,658 m.). *Service ceiling:* 25,400 ft. (7,742 m.). *Maximum range:* 840 miles
(1,352 km.).

DOUGLAS DC-2 (U.S.A.)

53

Douglas DC-2 of Swiss Air Lines (Swissair), *ca* 1935. *Engines:* Two 720 h.p. Wright
Cyclone SGR-1820-F2 nine-cylinder radials. *Span:* 85 ft. 0 in. (25.91 m.). *Length:*
61 ft. 11$\frac{1}{4}$ in. (18.88 m.). *Wing area:* 939.0 sq.ft. (87.24 sq.m.). *Take-off weight:*
18,000 lb. (8,615 kg.). *Cruising speed:* 196 m.p.h. (315 km/hr.). *Service ceiling:*
23,600 ft. (7,193 m.). *Range:* 1,060 miles (1,706 km.).

DOUGLAS DC-3 (U.S.A.)

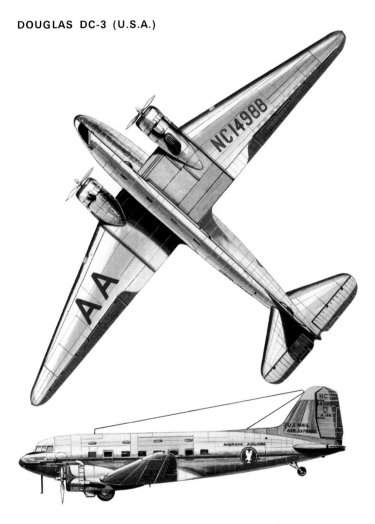

54

Douglas DC-3 (DST) prototype, as *Flagship Texas* of American Airlines Inc, 1936. *Engines:* Two 900 h.p. Wright GR-1820-G102A Cyclone nine-cylinder radials. *Span:* 95 ft. 0 in. (28.96 m.). *Length:* 64 ft. 6 in. (19.66 m.). *Wing area:* 987.0 sq.ft. (91.70 sq.m.). *Take-off weight:* 24,000 lb. (10,886 kg.). *Cruising speed:* 185 m.p.h. (298 km/hr.). *Service ceiling:* 23,200 ft. (7,070 m.). *Range:* 1,500 miles (2,414 km.).

MITSUBISHI G3M (Japan)

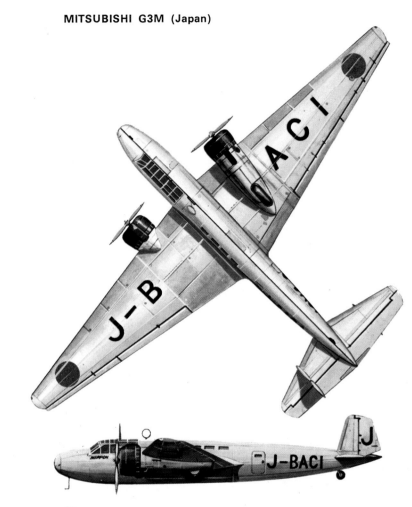

55

Converted Mitsubishi G3M2 Model 21/22 *Nippon* which made a round-the-world demonstration flight, August-October 1939. *Engines:* Two 900 h.p. Mitsubishi Kinsei 41 fourteen-cylinder radials. *Span:* 82 ft. 0¼ in. (25.00 m.). *Length:* 53 ft. 11¾ in. (16.45 m.). *Wing area:* 807.3 sq.ft. (75.00 sq.m.). *Take-off weight:* 20,282 lb. (9,200 kg.). *Cruising speed:* 174 m.p.h. (280 km/hr.) *Service ceiling:* 26,250 ft, (8,000 m.). *Range:* 2,175 miles (3,500 km.).

JUNKERS Ju 86 (Germany)

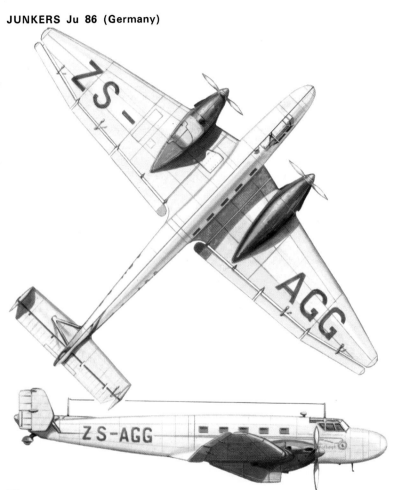

56

Junkers Ju 86 *Ryk Tulbagh* in 1936, with 745 h.p. Rolls-Royce Kestrel XVI twelve-cylinder Vee-type engines, prior to delivery to South African Airways. Later converted to Ju 86Z-7 standard, to which the following data apply. *Engines:* Two 800 h.p. Pratt & Whitney Hornet S1E-G nine-cylinder radials. *Span:* 73 ft. 9¾ in. (22.50 m.). *Length:* 57 ft. 5 in. (17.50 m.). *Wing area:* 882.6 sq. ft. (82.00 sq. m.). *Take-off weight:* 17,637 lb. (8,000 kg.). *Maximum cruising speed:* 224 m.p.h. (360 km/hr.) at 11,480 ft. (3,500 m.). *Service ceiling:* 25,590 ft. (7,800 m.). *Range:* 932 miles (1,500 km.).

ELECTRA (U.S.A.)

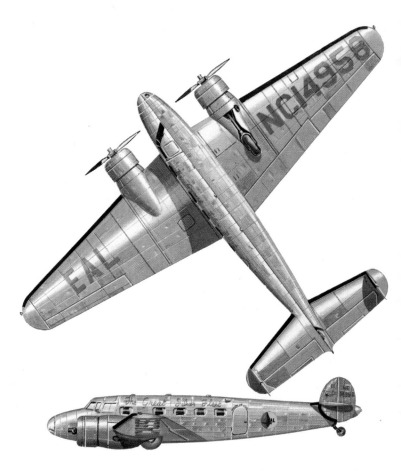

57

Lockheed Model 10 Electra of Eastern Air Lines, *ca* 1934-35. *Engines:* Two 440 h.p. Wright R-975-E3 Whirlwind nine-cylinder radials. *Span:* 55 ft. 0 in. (16.76 m.). *Length:* 38 ft. 7 in. (11.76 m.). *Wing area:* 458.5 sq.ft. (42.60 sq.m.). *Take-off weight:* 9,750 lb. (4,423 kg.). *Cruising speed:* 182 m.p.h. (293 km/hr.) at 5,000 ft. (1,524 m.). *Service ceiling:* 21,650 ft. (6,600 m.). *Range:* 810 miles (1,304 km.).

LOCKHEED MODEL 14 (U.S.A.)

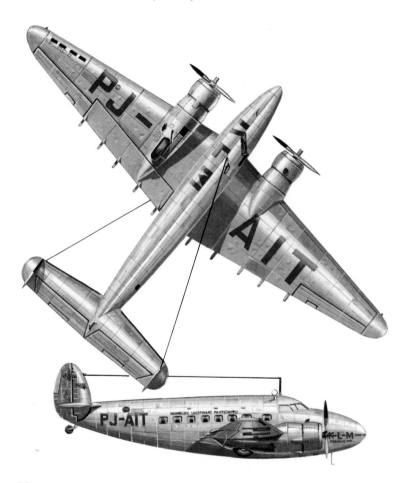

58

Lockheed Model 14 of Koninklijke Luchtvaart Maatschappij (KLM), 1938. *Engines.* Two 860 h.p. Wright Cyclone GR-1820-F62 nine-cylinder radials. *Span:* 65 ft. 6 in: (19.96 m.). *Length:* 44 ft. 4 in. (13.51 m.). *Wing area:* 551.0 sq.ft. (51.19 sq.m.). *Take-off weight:* 17,500 lb. (7,938 kg.). *Cruising speed:* 225 m.p.h. (362 km/hr.) at 13,000 ft. (3,962 m.). *Service ceiling:* 21,500 ft. (6,553 m.). *Range:* 1,590 miles (2,560 km.).

BLOCH 220 (France)

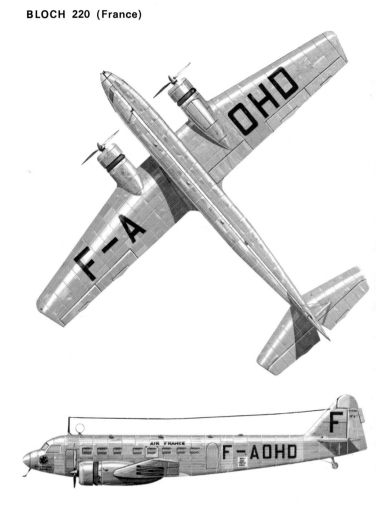

59

Bloch 220 *Auvergne* of Air France, *ca* 1937-38. *Engines:* Two 985 h.p. Gnome-Rhône 14N 16/17 fourteen-cylinder radials. *Span:* 74 ft. 10½ in. (22.82 m.). *Length:* 63 ft. 1¾ in. (19.25 m.). *Wing area:* 807.3 sq.ft. (75.00 sq.m.). *Take-off weight:* 20,944 lb. (9,500 kg.). *Cruising speed:* 174 m.p.h. (280 km/hr.). *Service ceiling:* 22,965 ft. (7,000 m.). *Range:* 870 miles (1,400 km.).

TUPOLEV ANT-35 (U.S.S.R.)

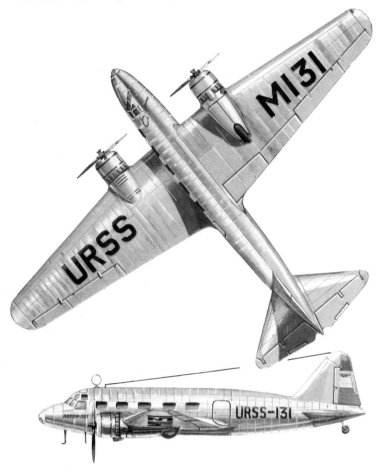

60

Tupolev ANT-35 (PS-35) of Aeroflot, early 1938. *Engines:* Two 850 h.p. M-85
(Gnome-Rhône 14N) fourteen-cylinder radials. *Span:* 68 ft. 3 in. (20.80 m.).
Length: 49 ft. 0½ in. (14.95 m.). *Wing area:* 624.3 sq.ft. (58.00 sq.m.). *Take-off
weight:* 14,594 lb. (6,620 kg.). *Cruising speed:* approx 217 m.p.h. (350 km/hr.).
Service ceiling: 27,890 ft. (8,500 m.). *Range:* 1,243 miles (2,000 km.).

JUNKERS Ju 52/3m (Germany)

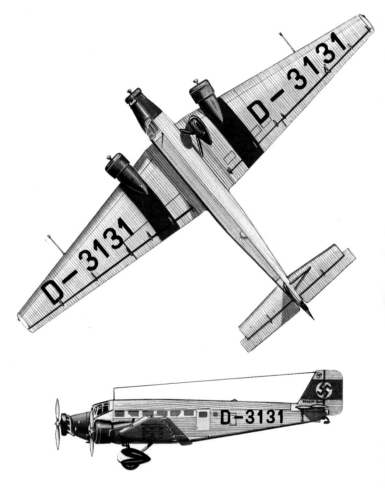

61

Junkers Ju 52/3m ge *Werner Voss* of Deutsche Luft Hansa, *ca* 1933. *Engines:* Three 660 h.p. BMW 132A-1 nine-cylinder radials. *Span:* 95 ft. 11½ in. (29.25 m.). *Length:* 62 ft. 0 in. (18.90 m.). *Wing area:* 1,189.4 sq.ft. (110.50 sq.m.). *Normal take-off weight:* 20,282 lb. (9,200 kg.). *Cruising speed:* 152 m.p.h. (245 km/hr.). *Service ceiling:* 17,060 ft. (5,200 m.). *Range:* 568 miles (915 km.).

CRUISER (U.K.)

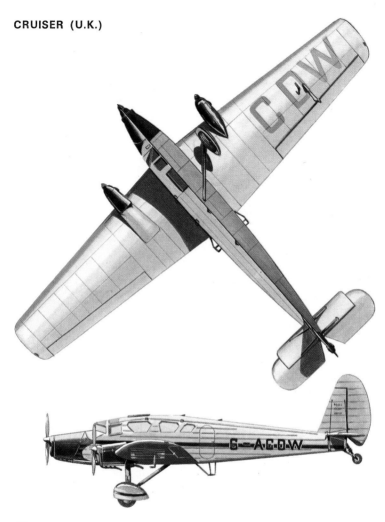

62

Spartan Cruiser II *Faithful City* of Spartan Air Lines Ltd, 1933. *Engines:* Three 130 h.p. de Havilland Gipsy Major six-cylinder in-lines. *Span:* 54 ft. 0 in. (16.46 m.). *Length:* 39 ft. 2 in. (11.94 m.). *Wing area:* 436.0 sq.ft. (40.50 sq.m.). *Take-off weight:* 6,200 lb. (2,812 kg.). *Cruising speed:* 115 m.p.h. (185 km/hr.). *Service ceiling:* 15,000 ft. (4,570 m.). *Range:* 310 miles (499 km.).

STINSON MODEL A (U.S.A.)

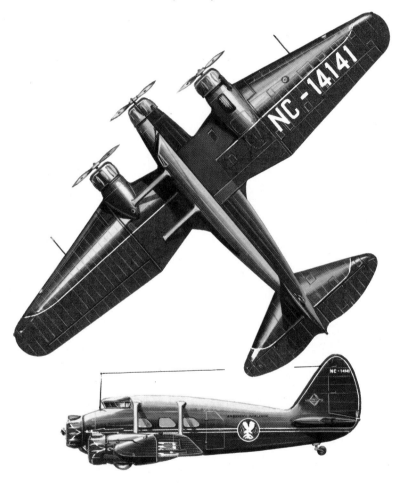

63

Stinson Model A of American Airlines Inc., *ca* 1936. *Engines:* Three 260 h.p. Lycoming R-680-5 nine-cylinder radials. *Span:* 60 ft. 0 in. (18.29 m.). *Length:* 36 ft. 10 in. (11.23 m.). *Wing area:* 500.0 sq.ft. (46.45 sq.m.). *Take-off weight:* 9,875 lb. (4,479 kg.). *Cruising speed:* 162 m.p.h. (261 km/hr.) at 5,000 ft. (1,524 m.). *Service ceiling:* 15,000 ft. (4,572 m.). *Range:* 400 miles (644 km.).

WIBAULT-PENHOËT 28 (France)

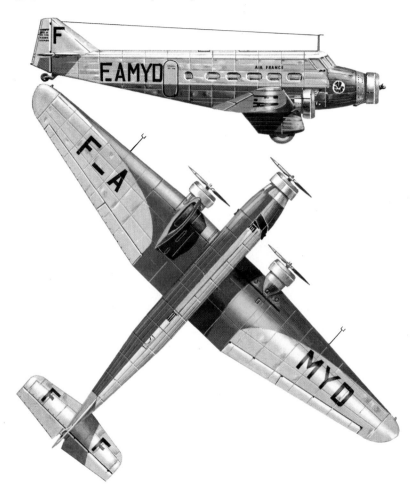

64

Wibault-Penhoët 283.T12 *Le Glorieux* of Air France, *ca* 1934. *Engines:* Three 350 h.p. Gnome-Rhône Titan Major 7Kd seven-cylinder radials. *Span:* 74 ft. 2¼ in. (22.61 m.). *Length:* 55 ft. 9¼ in. (17.00 m.). *Wing area:* 693.2 sq.ft. (64.40 sq.m.). *Take-off weight:* 14,000 lb. (6,350 kg.). *Cruising speed:* 143 m.p.h. (230 km/hr.). *Service ceiling:* 17,060 ft. (5,200 m.). *Range:* 620 miles (1,000 km.).

SAVOIA-MARCHETTI S.M.75 (Italy)

65

Savoia-Marchetti S.M.75 of Ala Littoria SA, 1938. *Engines:* Three 750 h.p. Alfa Romeo 126 RC 34 nine-cylinder radials. *Span:* 97 ft. 5¼ in. (29.70 m.). *Length:* 70 ft. 10½ in. (21.60 m.). *Wing area:* 1,276.6 sq.ft. (118.60 sq.m.). *Take-off weight:* 31,967 lb. (14,500 kg.). *Cruising speed:* 202 m.p.h. (325 km/hr.) at 13,125 ft. (4,000 m.). *Service ceiling:* 22,965 ft. (7,000 m.). *Maximum range:* 1,417 miles (2,280 km.).

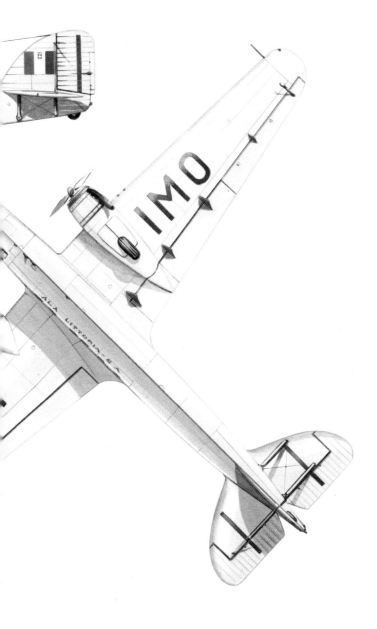

DEWOITINE 338 (France)

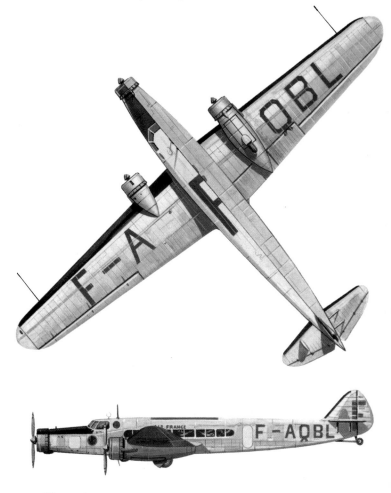

66

Dewoitine 338 *Ville d'Orléans* of Air France, *ca* 1938. *Engines:* Three 650 h.p. Hispano Suiza 9V 16/17 nine-cylinder radials. *Span:* 96 ft. 4¾ in. (29.38 m.). *Length:* 72 ft. 7¼ in. (22.13 m.). *Wing area:* 1,065.6 sq.ft. (99.00 sq.m.). *Take-off weight:* 24,582 lb. (11,150 kg.). *Cruising speed:* 162 m.p.h. (260 km/hr.). *Service ceiling:* 16,075 ft. (4,900 m.). *Range:* 1,212 miles (1,950 km.).

CONDOR (Germany)

67

Focke-Wulf Fw 200 V2 Condor *Westfalen* of Deutsche Lufthansa, 1938. *Engines:* Four 720 h.p. BMW 132G-1 nine-cylinder radials. *Span(V2):* 107 ft. 9 in. (32.84 m.); *span (production version):* 108 ft. 3¼ in. (33.00 m.). *Length:* 78 ft. 3 in. (23.85 m.). *Wing area (V2):* 1,270.1 sq.ft. (118.00 sq.m.); *wing area (production version):* 1,291.7 sq.ft. (120.00 sq.m.). *Take-off weight:* 32,188 lb. (14,600 kg.). *Cruising speed:* 202 m.p.h. (325 km/hr.) at 9,845 ft. (3,000 m.). *Service ceiling:* 21,980 ft. (6,700 m.). *Normal range:* 777 miles (1,250 km.).

JUNKERS Ju 90 (Germany)

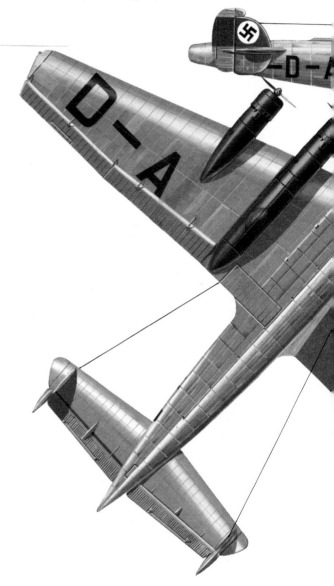

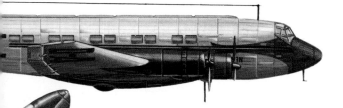

68

Junkers Ju 90 V3 *Bayern* of Deutsche
Lufthansa, 1938. *Engines:* Four 830 h.p.
BMW 132H nine-cylinder radials. *Span:*
114 ft. 10¾ in. (35.02 m.). *Length:* 86 ft.
3½ in. (26.30 m.). *Wing area:* 1,980.6
sq.ft. (184.00 sq.m.). *Take-off weight:*
50,705 lb. (23,000 kg.). *Cruising speed:*
199 m.p.h. (320 km/hr.) at 9,845 ft.
(3,000 m.). *Service ceiling:* 18,045 ft.
(5,500 m.). *Maximum range:* 1,305
miles (2,100 km.).

STRATOLINER (U.S.A.)

69

Boeing Model SA-307B Stratoliner of Transcontinental and Western Air (TWA), 1940. *Engines:* Four 1,100 h.p. Wright GR-1820-G105A Cyclone nine-cylinder radials. *Span:* 107 ft. 3 in. (32.69 m.). *Length:* 74 ft. 4 in. (22.66 m.). *Wing area:* 1,485.8 sq.ft. (138.03 sq.m.). *Take-off weight:* 45,000 lb. (20,412 kg.). *Cruising speed:* 222 m.p.h. (357 km/hr.) at 19,000 ft. (5,790 m.). *Service ceiling:* 23,800 ft. (7,255 m.). *Range with maximum payload:* 1,675 miles (2,695 km.).

ALBATROSS (U.K.)

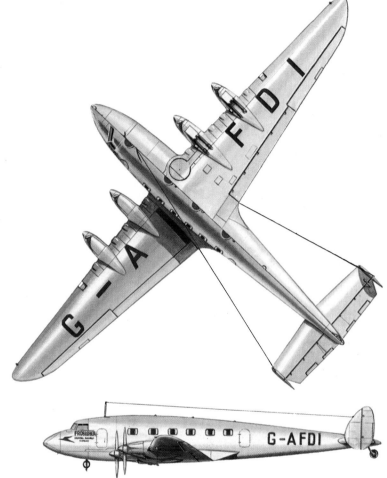

70

De Havilland D.H.91 Albatross *Frobisher* of Imperial Airways Ltd, 1939. *Engines:* Four 525 h.p. de Havilland Gipsy Twelve Series I twelve-cylinder inverted-Vee type. *Span:* 105 ft. 0 in. (32.00 m.). *Length:* 71 ft. 6 in. (21.79 m.). *Wing area:* 1,078.0 sq.ft. (100.15 sq.m.). *Normal take-off weight:* 29,500 lb. (13,381 kg.). *Maximum cruising speed:* 210 m.p.h. (338 km/hr.) at 11,000 ft. (3,355 m.). *Service ceiling:* 17,900 ft. (5,455 m.). *Normal range:* 1,040 miles (1,674 km.).

1 Breguet 14

The Breguet 14, one of France's finest bomber and reconnaissance aircraft of World War 1, remained in production until 1926, by which time about eight thousand had been built. These were mostly for military use, and the Breguet 14's wartime use is described in the *Bombers 1914–19* volume. After the war somewhere in the region of a hundred and fifty served in a civilian role, including many converted specially for the carriage of mails, passengers or cargo. The first, and by far the largest, commercial operator of the Breguet 14 was Lignes Aériennes Latécoère, which opened its first service, from Toulouse to Barcelona, on 25 December 1918. This was but the first stage in a prolonged and courageous movement to establish a regular scheduled service between France and South America. In September 1919 the network was extended to Rabat, in April 1920 to Casablanca, in October 1922 to Oran, and in June 1925 to Dakar. In all, 'The Line' acquired no fewer than one hundred and six Breguet 14's, most of them of the standard Br.14A2 (military 2-seat reconnaissance) type with minimal modification. The Latécoère fleet also included a few ex-bomber Br.14B2's, and some civil Breguet 14T and 14T*bis*.

The second-largest operator, with twenty-five Breguet 14T/14T2/ 14T*bis*, was Compagnie des Messageries Aériennes (CMA). This was formed in early 1919 by a consortium which included some of the most famous names in French aviation history – Louis Blériot, Louis Breguet, René Caudron, Henry Farman, Robert Morane, Louis Renault and L. Saulnier – and it began operations on 18 April 1919 with a cargo service between Paris and Lille. With subsequent expansion it, too, carried passengers and mail, and extended its services from Paris to Brussels (August 1919), London (September 1919), Amsterdam (June 1921) and Marseilles (May 1922). The first passenger service was flown on 19 September 1919. Subsequent CMA disposals included two or more to Latécoère, but at least ten were absorbed into the fleet of Air Union, formed in January 1923 from a merger of CMA and CGEA. Breguet 14's were also operated in small numbers by the Belgian airline SNETA, which had three Fiat-engined Br.14A2's; by Compagnie des Transports Aériens Guyanais in French Guiana, which used five or more on a short-lived service from St Laurent to Cayenne and Inihi in 1919–20; by the Thailand Royal Aeronautical Service, which operated a non-scheduled mail service between Korat and Ubol, starting in 1922, and possibly passenger services thereafter; by Compania Rio-platense de Aviacion in Argentina, which (also in 1922) flew a service between Buenos Aires and Montevideo for a short period; and in 1928 by Aeroposta Argentinas, a subsidiary of the Latécoère successor, Aéropostale. One Breguet 14, possibly Italian-built, was operated by SA Navigazione Aerea in 1925, and two Breguet 14T*bis* were flown by the Swedish Red Cross.

The precise designation of the civil Breguet 14 versions is not entirely clear. The standard A2 and B2 military versions seated 2 persons, in separate open cockpits in tandem aft of the wings. The Latécoère fleet included at least eighty-one A2's and four B2's; there were at least five examples of a version known as the Torpédo, a name signifying 'open tourer' which is believed to apply also to the A2 in its civilian form. There were two aircraft, possibly more, known as Limousines, a designation which may relate to a known Latécoère conversion which provided a crude cabin enclosure over the rear cockpit. Latécoère carried out considerable overhaul and modification of his Breguet fleet, most of which were purchased as war-surplus military machines. The principal conversion was made for the mail-carrying operations which constituted the bulk of the airline's business. For these operations the aircraft were at first flown as single-seaters, and the mail carried in two streamlined containers, one attached beneath each lower wing. Later, as the network extended across French North Africa, the mail was often stowed in the rear fuselage. This provided a somewhat lumpy seat in the rear cockpit for a Moorish interpreter, whose presence was deemed necessary after a number of Aéropostale's Breguets had been destroyed in the desert by marauding tribesmen.

The true cabin versions of the Breguet 14 seem to have originated with the 14T2 Salon, a 2-passenger version which first appeared (F-CMAA) in 1919. This housed the passenger within the forward fuselage, with small rectangular windows provided in the upper decking. Breguet also produced in 1919 the Br.18T Berline, a larger aircraft based on the Br.16 bomber, powered by a 450 hp Renault 12Ja engine and seating 4 passengers. So far as is known only one (F-CMAX) was built, though a 3-seat version of the T2 appeared later. The final model, the 14T*bis*, combined features of both the Br.18T and the 14T2. The prototype, F-CMAL, was flown for the first time on 13 September 1921, and a military ambulance version was also developed. Many Breguet 14's were operated, at some period during their lives, on a float landing gear, and in the case of the Swedish ambulance aircraft a ski gear was also in use at times.

2 de Havilland D.H.4A, D.H.9, D.H.16 and D.H.18

The British government authorised the post-war resumption of civil flying to and from the UK with effect from 15 July 1919, and on that day Britain's first airline carried its first fare-paying passenger. It was a charter flight, from London to Paris, and was made in a de Havilland D.H.9B. Just over a month later, on 25 August, Captain Bill Lawford of Air Transport and Travel Ltd flew with another passenger to Paris, this time in a D.H.4A, in what was probably a positioning flight for the departure flight later that day from Paris to London. The true inaugural flight by AT & T, of the first regular daily international service, was made in yet another de Havilland type: a D.H.16, piloted by Major Cyril Patteson, who left London at 12.30 pm on 25 August carrying 4 passengers for Le Bourget.

AT & T, before it went out of business at the end of 1920, had on charge two D.H.4's, four D.H.4A's, sixteen D.H.9's or D.H.9B's, eight D.H.16's and three D.H.18's. The D.H.4's were simply ex-RAF machines with their armament removed and a 2-seat open rear cockpit, but the D.H.4A was a genuine civil conversion with an enclosed 2-seat passenger cabin aft of the front cockpit. In addition to those converted for AT & T, two were completed for Handley Page Transport Ltd, for services to Paris and Schiphol, and one other was operated by The Instone Air Line Ltd. This last-named aircraft, G-EAMU, was originally an ex-RAF D.H.4 and bore the Instone fleet name *City of Cardiff* when it began operation on 12 October 1919. Sixteen months later it was converted to D.H.4A standard and placed in service between Croydon and Paris as *City of York*; it survived to be taken over – though not operated – by Imperial Airways in 1924.

In addition to the AT & T D.H.9's, ten others formed part of the Handley Page Transport fleet from 1920, and AT & T sold four of its D.H.9's to KLM, on whose behalf it had previously flown them on services to Amsterdam. Another 2-seat cabin conversion, recognisable by its sweptback wings, was the D.H.9C, five of which were operated on charter and taxi flights by the de Havilland Aeroplane Hire Service. The cabin conversion approach was taken a stage further with the D.H.16, which was based on the airframe and powerplant of the wartime D.H.9A but had the rear fuselage enlarged to seat 4 passengers in the cabin. Nine were built, five of the AT & T aircraft having 320 hp Rolls-Royce Eagle VIII engines and the other three having 450 hp Napier Lions. The remaining aircraft was sold to Compania Rioplatense de Aviacion in Argentina.

The first de Havilland type designed from the outset for airline work was the D.H.18, whose prototype (G-EARI) flew for the first time in early 1920. This was also Lion-powered, had a gross weight of 7,116 lb (3,228 kg) and a cabin seating up to 8 passengers. The pilot occupied an open cockpit aft of the cabin. Wing span and area were, respectively, 51 ft 3 in (15.62 m) and 621.0 sq ft (57.69 sq m), overall length was 39 ft 0 in (11.89 m), and the D.H.18 had a cruising range of 400 miles (644 km). The three AT & T D.H.18's passed in 1921 to Instone, which also acquired a fourth. One of these, G-EAWO, was loaned to The Daimler Airway in 1922 and promptly became the victim of a head-on collision with a Farman Goliath while on its first flight for its new operator. The three surviving Instone D.H.18's were retired from airline service in 1923.

3 Westland Limousine

As its name suggests, the Limousine was an attempt, by the Westland design staff led by Arthur Davenport, to introduce saloon-car comfort as an improvement upon the often crudely-furnished converted World War 1 aeroplanes that were the first post-war entrants into the field of air transport. The prototype Limousine I (K-126) made its first flight in July 1919, powered by a 275 hp Rolls-Royce Falcon III fitted with a circular radiator – an installation closely resembling that in the Bristol Fighter. Access was gained via a door on the starboard side. The interior was arranged with separate, well-upholstered armchair seats in two side-by-side pairs. The front starboard seat faced rearward, the other three forward, and there was a small table in front of the forward seat on the port side. The pilot occupied the rear port-side seat, elevated 2 ft 6 in (0.76 m) above the others to enable his head and shoulders to protrude through a hole in the roof. With the passenger seats removed, the aircraft could carry 540 lb (245 kg) of cargo. The Limousine I, later re-registered G-EAFO, was Westland's first civil product, and made many demonstration appearances during its first year. While doing so it featured in one of the earliest recorded uses of an aeroplane as a business executive transport when Robert J. Norton, Westland's commercial manager, dictated letters to his secretary during a flight and had them typed, signed and ready to post when the Limousine landed. In October 1919 Westland completed a prototype (G-EAJL) of the Limousine II – still a 4-seater, but with the Falcon III engine fitted with a rectangular radiator and other structural changes which included a slightly shorter wing span and an increase in the fin and rudder area. During the summer and autumn of 1920 these two Limousines were loaned to Air Post of Banks Ltd for an experimental mail service between Croydon and Paris. Afterwards, G-EAFO went back to Westland as company communications aircraft until September 1925, when it was destroyed at RAF Netheravon.

Four other Limousine II's (G-EAMV, G-EARE, G-EARF and G-EARG) were built in 1920; the registration G-EARH was also allotted, but this sixth Limousine II is not thought to have been completed. Of the others, G-EAMV, first flown in April 1920, was initially completed as a testbed for the Cosmos Jupiter III radial engine (later to become the famous Bristol Jupiter), but subsequently became a standard Falcon-engined machine, as was G-EARG. The other two Limousine II's were leased to The

Instone Air Line in late 1920. They were powered by 300 hp Hispano-Suiza engines and carried their fuel in tanks beneath the lower wings, a safety factor to permit passengers to smoke in the cabin during a flight. Instone bought the two aircraft outright in June 1922, and kept them in operation until about a year later.

Meanwhile, Westland had also produced in 1920 an enlarged, 6-seat Limousine III, powered by a 450 hp Napier Lion engine. The prototype, G-EARV, was entered in 1920 in an Air Ministry competition to find safe, comfortable commercial aircraft to operate European services. The Limousine III had mainwheel braking and a pair of small anti-noseover wheels ahead of the main gear; the underwing fuel system, as on the Instone Limousine II's, was retained. The Limousine III won the £7,500 first prize in the small aeroplane class, but the expected commercial demand did not materialise and only one other (G-EAWF) was built. This was sold in April 1921 to the Air Council, which loaned it to Instone until 1923 as a reserve aircraft; it was scrapped at the end of 1925. The original Limousine III had, in the meantime, been sold to F. S. (Sidney) Cotton, of 'Sidcot' flying suit fame, in January 1921. Cotton's Aerial Survey Company operated it in Newfoundland as a seal- and fish-spotting aircraft, fitting it with a ski landing gear during the winter months. Later, it took part in a 'gold rush', when a strike was reported at Stag Bay, Labrador. Cotton, at least, was evidently impressed with the Limousine's capabilities, for in 1922 he also purchased the three Falcon-engined Limousine II's for similar duties.

4 de Havilland D.H.34

Succeeding the D.H.18 as de Havilland's next production airliner, the D.H.34 also utilised the reliable Napier Lion as powerplant, and had cabin seating for up to 9 passengers in individual chairs. The cockpit, however, was moved to a new position ahead of the wings, and seated 2 pilots side by side. Provision was made to carry a spare engine, stowed athwart the fuselage behind the rear seats; the cabin door was shaped so as to permit straight-in loading of the engine, and the propeller shaft protruded through a hole in the starboard cabin wall which was covered by a plate when no spare engine was carried.

First airline customer was Daimler Hire Ltd, owner and operator of The Daimler Airway, which placed an initial order for two. The first D.H.34 to fly, G-EBBQ, on 26 March 1922, was one of this pair, the other being G-EBBS; it was delivered to the airline five days later, and flew its first operational service, to Paris, on 2 April 1922. Under the purchasing policy prevalent at the time the Air Council also ordered seven D.H.34's (later increased to nine), and four of the first batch (G-EBBR *City of Glasgow*, G-EBBT *City of New York*, G-EBBV *City of Washington* and G-EBBW *City of Chicago*) were loaned to Instone Air Line, which flew its inaugural D.H.34 service to Paris on the same day as Daimler. Four of the others (G-EBBU, G-EBBX, G-EBBY and G-EBCX), were loaned to Daimler, the final Air Council machine (G-EBCY) being allocated to the Royal Aircraft Establishment at Farnborough. One other D.H.34, bringing the total built to twelve, was completed and delivered to the Soviet airline Dobrolet.

In the early post-war years there was much wasteful competition between the small, struggling British airlines in the form of unnecessary route duplication. In 1922 this was regularised by the allocation of specific routes to particular airlines, and thereafter Instone was allotted the Brussels and Cologne service while Daimler operated a new service to Berlin via Amsterdam and either Hanover or Hamburg, opened by G-EBBS on 30 April 1923. By the time the two fleets became part of Imperial Airways in 1924, Instone had lost one D.H.34 and Daimler three in crashes; in 1926 the four Imperial Airways survivors (two more having been lost in crashes in the meantime) were scrapped.

5 de Havilland D.H.50

The satisfactory service given by civil D.H.9's on short-range scheduled services and aerial taxi work led to the development of the D.H.50 as a peacetime successor. The D.H.50 bore many similarities to the D.H.9, had the same 230 hp Siddeley Puma engine, and could accommodate 4 passengers in an enclosed cabin. The pilot occupied an open cockpit aft of this cabin. It proved extremely economical and reliable and was built under licence in three countries. It was also the aircraft flown by Alan Cobham on several long-distance flights which not only earned their pilot a well-deserved knighthood but pioneered some of the Empire routes later to be flown by Imperial Airways.

The prototype D.H.50 (G-EBFN *Galatea*) was flown for the first time in early August 1923, and served for some $2\frac{1}{2}$ years with the de Havilland Hire Service before being sold in February 1926 to West Australian Airways as G-AUEY. The second D.H.50, G-EBFO, was used by Cobham for the Empire flights, which began with a 17,000 mile (27,360 km) journey from England to Rangoon between 20 November 1924 and 18 March 1925. The aircraft was refitted with an uncowled 385 hp Armstrong Siddeley Jaguar III radial engine, giving it the new designation D.H.50J, before undertaking a 16,000 mile (25,750 km) survey flight from Croydon to Cape Town between 16 November 1925 and 17 February 1926. It underwent a third major change, to a twin-float landing gear, before leaving Rochester on 30 June 1926 for Melbourne. The final landing back in London, on 1 October 1926, was made on the Thames at Westminster, opposite the Houses of Parliament. These flights covered, in all, a distance of some 62,000 miles (99,780 km).

Fourteen of the remaining fifteen aircraft built by de Havilland were D.H.50A's, these having a slightly longer cabin, greater radiator area for the Puma engine and minor changes to the centre-section strutting and landing gear position. They were built for Imperial Airways for charter operations (G-EBFP and G-EBKZ); for Air Taxis (G-EBQI); for West Australian Airways' Wyndham-Perth-Adelaide service (G-AUEL and G-AUEM); QANTAS (G-AUER); Australian Aerial Services for the Adelaide-Sydney air mail run (G-AUEI, G-AUEJ and G-AUEK); the Royal Australian Air Force (G-AUAB and A8-1); Australia's Controller of Civil Aviation (G-AUAY); the New Zealand Air Force (serial number 135); and the Czechoslovak govern-

ment (L-BAHG). The British total was made up by G-EBOP *Pelican,* built for the North Sea Aerial and General Transport Co as a D.H.50J floatplane, the J suffix in this case denoting installation of a 420 hp Bristol Jupiter IV engine. West Australian Airways added a fourth British-built D.H.50 to its fleet in January 1929 by acquiring Cobham's famous G-EBFO, refitted with a 300 hp ADC Nimbus engine; it also built three D.H.50A's (G-AUFD, 'FE, and 'FN) under licence at Perth in 1927. In all, twenty-one D.H.50's were built under foreign licence, to bring total production of the type to thirty-eight. QANTAS (Queensland And Northern Territory Aerial Services), having passed on G-AUER to become *Hermes* (later *Victory*), the first aircraft of the Australian Flying Doctor Service, built at Longreach between 1926 and 1929 four Puma-engined D.H.50A's (G-AUFA/FW/GD/HE) and three D.H.50J's (G-AUHI and 'JS and VH-ULG) with 450 hp Bristol Jupiter VI engines. One other D.H.50A was built in Australia, this being VH-UMN, completed by the Larkin Aircraft Supply Co for Australian Aerial Services. A number of the D.H.50A's operating in Australia were subsequently fitted with Jupiter powerplants. The delivery of L-BAHG to Czechoslovakia in early 1925 was followed in 1926 by the licence manufacture of seven more D.H.50A's (L-BALA to 'LG) by Aero, which were powered by 240 hp Walter W-4 in-line engines and operated by CLS (Ceskoslovenská Letecka Spolecnost). Three others (O-BAHV, 'HW and 'HX) were built in Belgium by SABCA in 1925 and operated on Sabena's Congo route between Kinshasa and

Stanleyville.

Many D.H.50's continued in service until the mid-1930s, and a few were still extant at and after the outbreak of World War 2.

6 Spad 27/33/46/50/56 series

If the celebrated Spad fighters of World War 1 are indissolubly associated with the name of their chief designer, Louis Béchereau, then the family of Spad biplanes and monoplanes which appeared in the 1920s and 1930s are no less of a tribute to André Herbemont, who inherited from Béchereau the continued development of Spad aeroplanes. Herbemont's first association was with the Spad XX 2-seat fighter, from which stemmed a line of military types typified by the Spad 510 described in the volume on *Fighters 1919–39*; and there is a detectable family resemblance between these and the series of commercial passenger-carrying 'berlines' which emanated from the same design source during the 1920s.

Built by the Société Anonyme Blériot-Aéronautique, these began with the appearance of the Spad 27, flown for the first time in November 1919. Built for Compagnie des Messageries Aériennes (CMA), the Spad 27 was in essence a 'limousine' version of the Spad XX, having an open single cockpit for the pilot and an enclosed cabin for 2 passengers in the rear fuselage. Powered by a 270 hp Hispano-Suiza 8Fa engine, it was capable of a maximum speed of 155 mph (250 km/hr), and on 24 December 1919 a Spad 27 with a pilot and one passenger on board was flown to a world altitude record of 24,770 ft (7,550 m). The Spad 27 was operated by CMA between Paris and London, and it is believed that ten examples were built, although comparatively few can be confirmed by known registrations. One of these, F-CMAW, was a version with 3 passenger seats in open cockpits, known as the Spad 37.

The first major production 'berline' was the Spad 33, whose prototype (F-CMAZ) made its first flight on 12 December 1920. Forty production aircraft were built, to fulfil orders from CMA (fifteen), Compagnie Franco-Roumaine de Navigation Aérienne (twenty) and the Belgian airline SNETA (five). The aircraft operated by CMA, which included the prototype, had 250 hp Salmson 9Z water-cooled radial engines, the remainder being fitted with the Salmson 9Cm of 260 hp. Four passengers were accommodated in the cabin in the front of the fuselage, and aft of this were two side-by-side open cockpits for the pilot and a fifth passenger. A small number of Spad 33's were used for experimental purposes. One CIDNA aircraft (F-AICC) was fitted with enlarged wings and dual controls as an airline trainer for blind-flying instruction, and in 1922 another CIDNA machine became a Spad 33*bis* (later redesignated Spad 47) when fitted with a 300 hp Salmson engine. One of CFRNA's aircraft (F-FRAU) became, in 1921, the sole Spad 48 when fitted with a 275 hp Lorraine engine. Studies were undertaken, on behalf of SNETA, for a Spad 49 version powered by a 350 hp Rolls-Royce Eagle VIII engine, but no such aircraft was built. The production career of the Spad commercials continued with the Spad 46, manufacture of which also amounted to forty examples, excluding the prototype. Of the same seating capacity as the Spad 33, it had a wing span increased from 38 ft 3 in (11.66 m) to 41 ft 5½ in (12.64 m) and was powered by a 370 hp Lorraine-Dietrich 12Da Vee-type engine, increasing the maximum speed from 112 mph (180 km/hr) to 133 mph (214 km/hr). This speed increase was at some cost in range, which dropped from 670 miles (1,080 km) in the Spad 33 to 497 miles (800 km) in the Spad 46. The prototype Spad 46 (F-AGFD) was flown on 16 June 1921; this machine and thirty-eight of the production aircraft were delivered to CFRNA, which became CIDNA (Compagnie Internationale de Navigation Aérienne) on 1 January 1925. More than forty of CIDNA's Spad 33's and 46's later underwent detail improvements, after which they were redesignated Spad 66. Another, F-AEHH, was refitted with a 450 hp Renault 12Ja to become the sole Spad 116. One aircraft (F-AHDI) became the Spad 86 when fitted with an early example of 450 hp Lorraine-Dietrich W-type engine in 1922, and Spad 126 in 1929 after refitting with a 450 hp Hispano-Suiza 12Ha. Neither version attained production status, and proposals for a strut-braced monoplane version of the former, as the Spad 86bis, were not pursued.

Two prototypes were built of the Spad 50, the first of which (F-ESAX, later F-ADAR) was flown on 23 December 1921. This was, essentially, the Spad 33 airframe fitted with a 275 hp Hispano-Suiza 8Fg or 8Fd engine. No production was undertaken, although three Spad 33's were re-engined to the same standard. All five became part of the Air Union fleet. The final production model was the Spad 56, which appeared in six versions, all powered by Gnome-Rhône-built Bristol Jupiter engines. Representing the sole Spad 56-1, the prototype which flew first (3 February 1923) was F-AGEO, powered by a 380 hp Jupiter 9Aa. This version had metal-structure wings, with the span increased to 42 ft 11 in (13.08 m); maximum speed was 122 mph (196 km/hr). Total passenger capacity remained as before, but the twin open cockpits were merged into one and there was an additional door to the cabin. The Spad 56-2 (F-AIDC, first flight 28 September 1925) was a single example, with a 400 hp Jupiter 9Ab, equipped for the personal use of Louis Blériot. The next airframe change came with the Spad 56-3, in which the wing span was further increased to 43 ft 1 in (13.13 m). Six with 380 hp Jupiter 9Aa engines were built for CIDNA (first flight 14 June 1926, by F-AIEE), and two with 420 hp Jupiter 9Ac engines for Air Union. The Spad 56-4, first flown on 25 October 1926 (possibly F-AIMN), was, although retaining the same overall dimensions, a version with more power (420 hp Jupiter 9Ac), cabin accommodation for 6 persons, and a single cockpit located forward of a raised upper wing. Five were built for Air Union and three for CIDNA, the latter airline also converting two of its Spad 56-3's to this standard. The Spad 56-5 was a convertible passenger/cargo version, in which the cabin was partitioned aft of the 4 front seats, the rear compartment being usable either for 2 more passengers or for freight. It flew for the first time in 1928, the prototype being converted from the Spad 56-3 F-AIEM. The only operator was CIDNA, which had seven, produced by converting six of its 56-3's and one 56-4. The final version of the Spad 56 was the 56-6, which had a 380 hp Jupiter and a 4-passenger cabin. Two were built, the first example (F-AJVA) being flown on 6 September 1929, but neither of these was for airline use.

The Blériot-Spad 'berlines' operated through many of the countries of Europe throughout the 1920s, and some were still in service as late as 1930. With CMA, and later with Air Union, they were used on services from Paris to London, Amsterdam, Brussels, Marseilles and elsewhere; CFRNA/CIDNA routes included Paris to Bucharest (via Strasbourg, Zurich, Innsbruck, Vienna, Budapest and Belgrade) and branches from Vienna to Warsaw (via Prague) and Bucharest to Constantinople; SNETA shared some early routes with CMA.

7 Avia BH-25

The output of nationally-designed transport aircraft by the Czechoslovak aircraft industry between 1919 and 1939 was extremely small, both in terms of individual types and of overall production. Of eight native designs known to have operated in regular airline service – most of them with CSA, the national carrier – none, so far as can be ascertained, achieved a production run that went into double figures. Only two types – the Aero A-35 and Letov S-32 – were monoplanes, and only these two and the Aero A-38 had enclosed cockpits for the crew. All were single-engined except the S-32, which was a tri-motor, and passenger seating capacity ranged from 3 in the Aero A-10 (Czechoslovakia's first commercial transport type) and A-22 to 8 in the A-38.

Typical of the industry's products of the period was the BH-25, de-signed by Paul Benes and Miroslav Hajn and manufactured by Avia at Prague-Cakovice. It was unusual in that the lower wings were of slightly greater span than the upper one. Forward of the wings was an open cockpit, with side-by-side seating for the crew. The enclosed passenger cabin had seats for 6 persons and space for up to 220 lb (100 kg) of baggage, equivalent to a total useful load of 1,278 lb (580 kg). All 6 circular cabin windows could be opened in flight, and an escape hatch was provided in the top of the fuselage.

The BH-25 prototype (L-BABA) was powered by a 450 hp Skoda-built Lorraine-Dietrich water-cooled 'W' engine, and first flew in July 1926. After flight testing, a number of major airframe modifications were made before production began. These included a change of powerplant, to the 420 hp Walter-built Bristol Jupiter IV radial; an increase in the length of the nose section of the fuselage; the addition of a vertical fin with a non-balanced rudder (the aircraft having originally had a balanced rudder and no fin); and the transfer of the twin fuel tanks from beneath to above the centre-section of the upper wing. Production BH-25's were similar except that the fuel was housed in a wider but shallower single tank.

Two airline operators of the BH-25 are known. The Czechoslovak airline CLS (Ceskoslovenská Letecka Spolecnost) operated the prototype and four other aircraft (L-BABA/B/C/E/F, later re-registered OK-ABA/B/C/E/F) on services from Prague to Berlin and Rotterdam; and SNNA (Serviciul National de Navigatie Aeriana) of Romania operated four aircraft

(YR-AAA/B/C/D) on internal services in about 1928.

8 Vickers Vimy (civil) and Vimy Commercial

As described in the *Bombers 1914–19* volume in this series, the Vickers F.B.27 Vimy twin-engined bomber was developed too late to perform operational service during World War 1, although it was to remain a standard RAF post-war type until the early 1930s (see *Bombers 1919–39*). Within a matter of months after the Armistice, however, the name Vimy was to achieve a prominence that by the end of 1919 was literally world-wide. First came the non-stop trans-Atlantic flight by Capt John Alcock and Lt Arthur Whitten-Brown, made in a specially-modified standard Eagle-engined Vimy that had been flown for the first time (by Alcock) on 18 April 1919. With modified seating, and carrying extra fuel tanks in the fuselage, this aircraft was flown on 14–15 June 1919 from St Johns, Newfoundland, to Clifden, on the west coast of Ireland, to win the £10,000 prize offered by the *Daily Mail* for the first non-stop aeroplane crossing of the Atlantic Ocean. Earlier that year, in March, the Australian government had offered a prize of £A10,000 for the first flight from England to Australia by an Australian crew in a British aeroplane. After Alcock and Brown's success, the Vimy was a natural choice for the attempt, which was made by two brothers, Capt Ross and Lt Keith Smith of the Australian Flying Corps, with two fellow-Australians, Sgts J. M. Bennett and W. H. Shiers, as mechanics. The Vimy used for the flight was an ex-RAF machine, F8630; it received the civil registration G-EAOU, which a would-be wit was prompted to suggest stood for 'God 'Elp All Of Us'. His pessimism was unjustified, however, for G-EAOU achieved its goal in the remarkable space of 135 hours 55 minutes flying time. It left Hounslow on 12 November 1919, and arrived at Fanny Bay, Darwin, on 10 December. Both of these historic aircraft may still be seen, the trans-Atlantic Vimy in the Science Museum in London and the England-Australia aircraft in Adelaide. The other historic Vimys of 1919–20 did not, unfortunately, survive for posterity. The first of these was G-UABA *Silver Queen*, built for an attempt to win another £10,000 *Daily Mail* prize, for a flight from Cairo to Cape Town. Flown by Lt Col Pierre van Ryneveld and Major C. J. Quintin Brand, with two mechanics, it left Cairo on 10 February 1920 but crashed at Korosko in Upper Egypt. The crew borrowed another Vimy from the RAF in Egypt, named it *Silver Queen II* and tried again on 22 February. This time they reached Bulawayo, but their aircraft then crashed during take-off. They were, however, finally awarded the prize after completing the journey in a borrowed D.H.9. Another attempt for the same prize was made in G-EAAV, the prototype Vimy Commercial, sponsored by *The Times* and piloted by two Vickers test pilots, Capts S. Cockerell and F. C. G. Broome; but this ended when the aircraft crashed on take-off at Tabora, Tanganyika, on 27 February 1920. Two other standard Vimys were allocated British civil registrations. That of G-EAAR, for an early Vickers demonstrator, was never worn; the aircraft carried instead its constructor's number C-105, during its brief career in 1919–20. The other aircraft was G-EAOL (formerly F8625 of the RAF), which flew to Madrid for evaluation by the Spanish government and apparently remained in that country.

First flown on 13 April 1919, the Vimy Commercial prototype was originally registered K-107, changed to G-EAAV prior to its attempt for the Cairo-Cape Town prize. It retained the wings, powerplant, landing gear and tail assembly of the standard Vimy bomber, but the fuselage was an entirely new structure, of ample proportions, accommodating a crew of 2 in open cockpits and 10 passengers inside the cabin. The loss of the prototype did not affect a substantial order, for forty aircraft, placed by the Chinese government. These were built at Weybridge, beginning in April 1920. There is reason to doubt whether many were actually assembled and flown after their arrival in China, but at least two were used, and an air mail service between Peking and Tsinan was inaugurated on 1 July 1921 with aircraft of this type. Those delivered to China may have included two Vimy Commercials which appeared on the British Civil Register as G-EAUL and G-EAUY. Of these, the former was runner-up in the Air Ministry competition at Martlesham in August 1921 for heavy commercial aircraft. The most famous Vimy Commercial, without doubt, was 'old go-easy' – G-EASI *City of London*, built for the Air Transport Department of S. Instone & Co and used to inaugurate Instone's Croydon-Brussels service on 9 May 1920. It has been said of G-EASI that it flew 'continuously, almost relentlessly' on Instone's Paris, Brussels and Cologne services, and when absorbed into the Imperial Airways fleet on 1 April 1924 it had flown a total of 107,950 miles (173,728 km). It continued in service with Imperial Airways until scrapped in 1926. Two other Vimy Commercials are known, both powered by 450 hp Napier Lion engines. One was operated in France by Grands Express Aériens as F-ADER, and the other was delivered in September 1922 to the USSR. The latter, which may have been operated for a time by Dobrolet from 1924, was a hybrid aircraft, having some features of the Vimy Ambulance (five of which were built for the RAF) and being, in effect, prototype for the Vernon bomber-transport built for the RAF – whose career included operation of the Cairo-Baghdad air mail in 1926.

9 Farman F.50P and F.60 Goliath series

One of the stalwarts of early French airline operation, the Farman Goliath originated as a design for a 2-seat, twin-engined night bomber, but was not developed in time to serve operationally in World War 1. It was preceded in the bomber role by the F.50, a somewhat smaller aircraft of similar general appearance, which saw limited service with the French and American forces in France during 1918, and after the war three were converted for use as F.50P public transport aircraft. They were powered by a pair of 275 hp Lorraine-Dietrich 8Bd eight-cylinder Vee-type engines, had a wing span of 74 ft 11½ in (22.85 m), and could cruise at about 62 mph (100 km/hr) at a gross weight of

6,856 lb (3,110 kg). The Farman brothers had the appropriately registered F-HMFO, which apparently was not placed in airline service; it may perhaps have been a transport trials aircraft. Compagnie des Grands Express Aériens operated F-GEAV on its services from Paris to Brussels and Amsterdam in 1920; this aircraft evidently did not remain long in regular operation with CGEA, but it was acquired in 1923 by Air Union, which was also the owner of the third F.50P, F-AECK.

The larger Goliath first appeared in 1918 as the FF.60, a bomber prototype powered by two 230 hp Salmson 9Z water-cooled radial engines. Soon after the Armistice the fuselage was converted by having a well-lit passenger cabin and an extended nose. At this stage it still bore its original overhanging balanced ailerons, but production Goliaths had square-tipped wings with inset ailerons and were re-engined with 260 hp Salmson 9Cm radials. The 2-man crew were seated side by side in an elevated open cockpit between the front (4-seat) and rear (8-seat) passenger compartments. The passenger accommodation, at first primitive in the extreme, improved considerably later as competing airlines strove to improve their 'image' to the travelling public.

The major early operators of the Goliath were the Farmans' own airline, Lignes Aériennes Farman (approx eighteen), CMA (sixteen or more) and CGEA (twelve); others were delivered to SNETA of Belgium (six) and CSA of Czechoslovakia (six, licence-built by Avia and Letov), and Goliaths are known to have operated also in Romania and Latin America. Air Union, upon its creation in 1923, inherited at least fifteen from CMA and CGEA; it still numbered four Farmans in its fleet as late as 1931, and the Goliath appears to have remained in service with this operator and some others for at least two years after that. The fuselage of Air Union's F-HMFU *Ile de France* can still be seen in the Musée de l'Air in Paris.

It appears that somewhere in the region of sixty Goliaths were operated in airline service. During their career versions with several different powerplants appeared, some of which may have been conversions, and production was integrated with military bomber or ambulance versions, which makes a detailed list of variants difficult. Known designations for civil Goliaths include the F.60*bis* (300 hp Salmson 9Az), F.61 (300 hp Renault 12Fe), F.62, F.63, F.63*bis* (380 hp Gnome-Rhône Jupiter 9A), F.63*ter* (also Jupiter-powered), and there were versions with Lorraine-Dietrich or Maybach engines. The Czech-built Goliaths had Lorraine or Jupiter engines built by Skoda and Walter respectively. One Goliath set up three world load-to-height records in 1919, the best of which was for reaching 16,732 ft (5,100 m) carrying 25 passengers; later that year a non-stop distance record of 1,274 miles (2,050 km) was set up on a flight from Paris to Casablanca. Farman produced a four-engined 'Super Goliath', the F.140, in 1923, which in November 1925 captured 12 world records for height and endurance with payloads of 8,818 lb (4,000 kg) and 13,228 lb (6,000 kg). Six were ordered for experimental flights, but the F.140 was not built for commercial service.

10 Lioré et Olivier LeO 21

From the LeO 12 twin-engined bomber biplane, which first flew in June 1924, Lioré et Olivier evolved in 1925–26 two modified versions, with Gnome-Rhône (Bristol) Jupiter engines in place of the original Lorraine-Dietrich powerplant. These were the LeO 121 12-passenger commercial transport and the LeO 122 bomber. From the latter was developed the LeO 20 4/5-seat night bomber, described in the *Bombers 1919–39* volume; in similar fashion, the LeO 121 design was developed into the larger LeO 21 passenger transport.

Two prototype LeO 21's were built (F-AIFD and F-AIFE), each originally powered by two 420 hp Gnome-Rhône Jupiter 9Ab uncowled radial engines. Certification was received in August 1926, and in the following month the LeO 21 was awarded the highest marks in a competition for transport aircraft staged by the Service Technique Aéronautique. It took first place in the transport class at two meetings during 1927, and the two prototypes, named *Capitaine Ferber* and *L. P. Mouillard* respectively, were introduced on Air Union's Paris-London route on 30 July 1927. The second machine was refitted with two 450 hp Renault 12Ja twelve-cylinder Vee-type engines (with which it was redesignated LeO 212), and this became the standard powerplant for the LeO 213 production version, of which the first example (F-AIVG) was built in 1928. The LeO 21 was flown by a 2-man crew, seated side by side in a communal open cockpit just forward of the wings. Internal accommodation was for 6 passengers in a forward cabin in the nose, which was connected by a corridor to the 12-passenger main cabin at the rear. The first LeO 21 was converted in 1929, to become the LeO 211, equipped with a bar and barman; the LeO 212's main cabin was converted, in collaboration with the Compagnie des Wagons-Lits, into a 12-seat restaurant complete with bar and barman.

Ten further LeO 213's were built in 1929–31, registered F-AIZN and 'ZO, F-AJBE and 'NS and F-ALCS/CY/GF/GG/GH/GI; all were delivered to Air Union. Unlike the original pair, the production aircraft were not allocated individual fleet names, but all thirteen aircraft operated by Air Union bore the fleet title 'le Rayon d'Or' on the starboard side of the nose, with its English equivalent, 'The Golden Ray', on the port side. (The name was corrupted by the LeO 213's ground crews into 'Les Gueules de Raies' – 'the red stripes'.) The LeO 213 had a greater span and wing area than the original LeO 21's and a longer fuselage with a corresponding increase in the size of the main cabin. The front cabin was then taken over as an additional baggage compartment, and the windows in the extreme nose were omitted. The 2-man crew sat in separate open cockpits, which were equipped with dual controls. Air Union operated these aircraft on Paris-London, Paris-Lyons-Marseilles and Paris-Geneva services. All eleven LeO 213's were passed on to Air France in August 1933, and at the end of their commercial career they had amassed some 20,000 flying hours. F-AIVG, destroyed when it flew into a pylon during a flight to Croydon on 31 May 1934, had completed 1,461 hours of flying. The two LeO 21 prototypes were converted again, in

1931 and 1932, for an all-cargo role; F-AIVG was also on a mail cargo flight when it was lost, and F-AIZO (and perhaps other LeO 213's) were similarly converted. Some were converted for night flying (designation LeO 213N), these having an enlarged cabin door, strengthened cabin floor, non-openable cabin windows and a modified fuel system. In 1932 F-AJNS was fitted with 500 hp Renault 12Jb engines, with reduction gearing, and another attempt to 'improve the breed' was the proposed LeO 214, with 500 hp Renault 12Jc engines and accommodation for 16 passengers. Neither this nor the projected LeO 21S (Sanitaire) ambulance version was built.

In 1934 Air France began to replace its LeO 213's with the Potez 62, and during the year passed on nine of its LeO's to the Armée de l'Air.

11 **Handley Page W8, W9 and W10**
Handley Page was involved in the very beginnings of transport aircraft development in Britain, for two of its O/400 bombers were engaged in 1918 in bringing back ferry pilots from France, and eight converted O/400's of the RAF's No 1 (Communications) Squadron flew a regular service between London and Paris during the peace talks of 1919. It formed its own separate operating company, Handley Page Transport Ltd – later to become one of the major constituents of Imperial Airways Ltd – on 14 June 1919. The first-ever British Certificates of Airworthiness for civil operation were awarded to four Handley Page O/400's on 1 May 1919, and HPT's early services –

mostly to Le Bourget, Brussels or Amsterdam – were flown with aircraft of this type, either with minimal conversion from their original bomber configuration or as fully-converted all-passenger O/7's and O/10's or mixed passenger/cargo O/11's. These converted aircraft were, however, far from competitive, and by 1923 those which had not been lost in crashes (of which there were several) were sold, scrapped or otherwise disposed of.

Well before this, however, Handley Page had foreseen the need for a tailor-made commercial transport aircraft, and soon after the end of World War 1 had initiated such a design. This was the W8, which was flown for the first time (G-EAPJ) on 4 December 1919, powered by two 450 hp Napier Lion engines. On 4 May 1920 it set up a British height-with-payload record by lifting 3,690 lb (1,674 kg) to an altitude of 14,000 ft (4,267 m), and in the following August was declared by the Air Ministry to be the best heavy commercial aircraft then developed in terms of comfort, speed and reliability. It operated a London-Paris service from 21 October 1921, but was destroyed in a bad-weather landing just over two years later. A W8a version was proposed, but was not built although the registration G-EAVJ was reserved for the prototype. The next version to appear was thus the W8b, of which three were ordered to Air Ministry Specification 16/21. They were powered by 360 hp Rolls-Royce Eagle VIII engines, and conformed to Air Ministry requirements in having the passenger capacity limited to 12 (the original W8 had been designed to seat 15) and in having the fuel tanks located above the top wing instead of in the rear of extended engine nacelles. The first W8b was G-EBBG *Bombay*; this aircraft was renamed *Princess Mary* in May 1922, when Handley Page Transport also took delivery of G-EBBH *Prince George* and G-EBBI *Prince Henry*. This trio operated on HPT's Paris and Brussels services until the absorption into Imperial Airways on 1 April 1924; G-EBBG eventually crashed in February 1928, and 'BH and 'BI were scrapped in February 1931 and October 1932 respectively. The remaining W8 civil variants were tri-motors, the first to appear being the W8e, with a single 360 hp Eagle IX in the nose and two 240 hp Siddeley Pumas. The first and only British-built example was delivered to Sabena as O-BAHG in May 1924, and four similar aircraft were built in Belgium by SABCA for the same airline later that year. The W8f Hamilton (G-EBIX), first flown on 20 June 1924, was built for Imperial Airways as *City of Washington* and was generally similar to the W8e except in having a cabin heating system. Ten aircraft of the same type were built by SABCA for Sabena, which employed them on its Belgian Congo network for many years from April 1925. In later years G-EBIX was given vertical tail surfaces similar to the W10 (see below), and in November 1929 was redesignated W8g when the nose engine was deleted and the two outboard engines were replaced by Rolls-Royce F.IX's.

This trial-and-error experimentation with various twin- and triple-engined layouts was symptomatic of the W types' chief failing, and the next version to appear was the only member of the whole W8/9/10 family capable of maintaining height with one engine cut. This was the tri-motor W9a Hampstead, a 14-seater powered initially by three 385 hp Armstrong Siddeley Jaguar IV radials and flown for the first time on 1 October 1925. Only one example, G-EBLE *City of New York*, was built; this entered service with Imperial Airways on 3 November 1925. In the following April it was refitted with 450 hp Bristol Jupiter VI radials, and was sold in New Guinea in 1929 as VH-ULK.

Last of the W types was the W10, which seated 14 passengers and reverted to twin-engined configuration with a pair of 450 hp Napier Lions. During development of the W8 series, a bomber version had emerged as the W8d Hyderabad, of which a distinguishing feature was a more angular-shaped vertical tail. (This is illustrated on pages 56–57 of the *Bombers 1919–39* volume.) This and other design aspects of the Hyderabad were incorporated in the W10, four of which were built for Imperial Airways. The first flight was made by G-EBMM *City of Melbourne* on 10 February 1926; the others were G-EBMR *City of Pretoria*, G-EBMS *City of London* and G-EBMT *City of Ottawa*. All four had been delivered by the end of March 1926, but 'MS was lost through engine failure in October of that year and 'MT suffered a similar fate in June 1929. Like G-EBBI, the remaining pair survived until replacement by the H.P.42 in 1931. In September 1934 they were used by Sir Alan Cobham to refuel his Airspeed Courier G-ABXN on its attempted flight to India; 'MM was lost in a crash later the same month.

12 Armstrong Whitworth Argosy
Upon its formation on 1 April 1924, Imperial Airways inherited a fleet which included quite a number of single-engined aircraft. One of its first actions was to stipulate that its future acquisitions should all be multi-engined types, as an earnest of its intent to place passenger safety high on its list of priorities. This policy was first put into practice in the designs of the de Havilland Hercules (which see) and the Argosy. The Argosy was Armstrong Whitworth's first venture into the commercial transport aircraft market, and was built exclusively for Imperial Airways, which eventually acquired seven. The first of these to fly, in the spring of 1926, was G-EBLF, first of an initial order for three Argosies. It was later named *City of Glasgow*, and was delivered to the airline in the following September. Prior to this, on 5 August 1926, the first London-Paris Argosy service had been opened by the second aircraft, G-EBLO *City of Birmingham*, a service eventually extended to include Brussels, Cologne and Basle. The third Argosy, G-EBOZ, was named *City of Wellington*, and later *City of Arundel*, in airline service. These first three aircraft were designated Argosy I, and were powered by 385 hp Jaguar III radial engines. Accommodation included side-by-side seats in an open cockpit for the crew of 2, and cabin seating for up to 20 passengers, with toilet and baggage space at the rear. On 1 May 1927 the Argosy inaugurated Imperial Airways', and the world's, first named air service – Silver Wing – in which a steward was carried and the 2 rear passenger seats were removed to make room for a bar.

During the first half of 1929 the airline took delivery of a second batch of three Argosies, these being designated Argosy II. They were powered by 420 hp geared Jaguar IVA engines, installed in conical nacelles and fitted with Townend cowling rings; Handley Page wing slats were fitted, and the passenger accommodation was increased to 28. The three Argosy II's were G-AACH *City of Edinburgh*, G-AACI *City of Liverpool* and G-AACJ *City of Manchester*; a fourth, G-AAEJ *City of Coventry*, joined the fleet later. In 1930 the Argosy I's were re-engined to the same standard, two being sent overseas to operate the Cairo-Khartoum sector of the route to South Africa; G-EBLO was lost, in June 1931, when it crashed at Aswan. This was the second Argosy casualty, G-AACH having crashed at Croydon in the previous April. G-EBLF was flown out to replace 'LO, but both it and 'OZ had been reallocated to Europe-only operation by the end of 1931. There was one other casualty in Imperial Airways service – G-AACI, which crashed near Dixmude in March 1933 – but by this time the H.P.42 had begun to appear on the European routes and the four surviving Argosies were withdrawn at the end of 1934. Three were scrapped in 1935, and the fourth (after brief ownership by United Airways and used for joy-riding at Blackpool) at the end of summer 1936.

13 de Havilland D.H.66 Hercules
The formation of Imperial Airways in 1924 was a major step towards a unified British national air transport policy. One of the major tasks of the new airline was the carriage

of all Empire mails by air, and although this ambition was not achieved to the full until the mid-1930s the first steps were taken not long after the end of World War 1. In the Middle East, the RAF built up a highly successful desert air mail service between Cairo and Baghdad. This was inaugurated in 1920, and the RAF continued to operate it until 1926, but in 1925 it was decided that responsibility should eventually pass to Imperial Airways, which was to develop and extend it into a regular fortnightly service as far eastward as Karachi.

None of the aircraft then in the Imperial Airways fleet had either the structural ruggedness or the reserve of power necessary for arduous operation over such difficult terrain in tropical weather; a new type was clearly needed. This need was met by the D.H.66 Hercules. Imperial Airways ordered an initial fleet of five, and the first of these (G-EBMW) was flown for the first time on 30 September 1926, powered by three 420 hp Bristol Jupiter VI radial engines. The 2 pilots sat side by side in a communal cockpit ahead of the wings; inside the cabin were seats for the wireless operator and 7 passengers, plus a 465 cu ft (13.2 cu m) compartment for mail or cargo, and there was an additional 155 cu ft (4.4 cu m) of mail/cargo space in the rear of the fuselage. In mid-December 1926, G-EBMW flew to Cairo, from where, after being named City of Cairo, it made the first eastbound scheduled flight of the new service on 12 January 1927. Shortly before this, on 8 January, the second Hercules (G-EBMX) had arrived in Delhi to mark the official hand-over of the air mail service from the RAF to Imperial Airways. Carrying the Secretary of State for Air (Sir Samuel Hoare) and his wife, G-EBMX left Croydon on 27 December 1926, and was christened City of Delhi upon its arrival in India. The three other Imperial Airways Hercules (G-EBMY City of Baghdad, G-EBMZ City of Jerusalem and G-EBNA City of Teheran) had all been delivered by the spring of 1927, but for the first two years the desert service flew eastward only as far as Basra. It was extended to Karachi in April 1929, and to Jodhpur and Delhi later the same year.

Meanwhile, in 1928, a second Hercules customer had materialised. West Australian Airways had been chosen to operate a new passenger/mail service between Perth and Adelaide, a route with conditions comparable to those flown by Imperial Airways in the Middle East. The D.H.66 was therefore an obvious choice, and WAA ordered four, which were delivered in the spring of 1929 as G-AUJO City of Perth, G-AUJP City of Adelaide, G-AUJQ and G-AUJR. The Australian Hercules had a number of modifications compared with the original five aircraft, the principal ones being a cockpit enclosure for the 2 pilots and seating for up to 14 passengers in addition to the mail load. The first Perth-Adelaide service of WAA was flown on 2 June 1929 by G-AUJO, with a payload which included 856 lb (388 kg) of mail.

Imperial Airways ordered a sixth D.H.66, G-AAJH City of Basra, which joined the fleet in Cairo in June 1929. It was fitted with the enclosed flight deck of the Australian machines, and this feature was added retrospectively to the earlier examples. The difficult flying conditions of the Cairo-Delhi route, however, soon began to take their toll of the original fleet, from which three were lost in crashes : G-EBMZ in September 1929, G-EBNA in February 1930 and G-EBMW in April 1931. To replace 'MZ the airline ordered a seventh aircraft, G-AARY *City of Karachi*, from de Havilland, so bringing the number built to eleven. By the time of the losses of G-EBNA and G-EBMW, however, the production line had closed, but the airline made up the deficiency by purchasing the third and fourth WAA Hercules, which became G-ABMT *City of Cape Town* and G-ABCP *Cty of Jodhpur* respectively. The loss of G-EBMW on 13 April 1931 was doubly unfortunate, for it came when the aircraft was en route from Karachi to Darwin with the first experimental through air mail service between Croydon and Melbourne. The crew were lost, but the mail was salvaged and was flown to Darwin by the Australian pilot Charles Kingsford Smith in his celebrated Fokker tri-motor *Southern Cross*. The naming of G-ABMT acknowledged the extension of Imperial Airways' African services southwards to Cape Town. These services were not flown by Hercules, but the preliminary survey flight for the route was made in the Hercules G-AARY in late 1931. Imperial Airways lost G-ABCP in a crash in November 1935, but by then its Hercules fleet had reached virtually the end of its useful life. In the following month G-EBMY and G-AARY were withdrawn and scrapped; and G-AAJH, G-ABMT and G-EBMX were sold to the South African Air Force.

14 **Boeing Model 40 and Model 80**
Most of the scheduled air services in the United States during the first half of the 1920s were devoted to the carriage of the mails under government contract, an area which Boeing first entered as early as March 1919. The standard type on most US Post Office Department routes was for many years the British-designed, American-built DH-4, and in 1925 the Department held a design competition to find its successor. Boeing entered an elegant biplane, the Model 40, powered (as specified) by a neatly-installed 400 hp Liberty engine. The Post Office purchased the unregistered Model 40 prototype, which made its first flight on 7 July 1925, but placed no production contract. Since there was, at that time, no other possible US customer for the aircraft, Boeing temporarily shelved the project, but later in 1925 it was announced that from July 1927 all domestic trans-continental air mail contracts would be placed with private operators. Accordingly, under the design leadership of Phil G. Johnson, Boeing updated the original proposal into the Model 40A, replacing the smooth wood-veneer fuselage covering with fabric and substituting for the Liberty a 420 hp uncowled Pratt & Whitney Wasp radial engine. As a result, the aeroplane lost much of its outward elegance, but it was a more viable product economically. There were two mail compartments in the fuselage, and between them was a small cabin to seat 2 passengers; the pilot occupied an open cockpit well behind the wings, aft of the rear mail compartment. With the 40A Boeing won from the Post Office a contract to operate the San Francisco-

Chicago mail route, which enabled it to initiate production of twenty-five Model 40A's and to form a new company, Boeing Air Transport Inc, to operate the service. The first production aircraft was flown on 20 May 1927, and the BAT service opened on 1 July 1927, with a fleet of twenty-four aircraft. Data for the Model 40A were as follows: wing span 44 ft 2 in (13.46 m); wing area 547.0 sq ft (50.82 sq m); length 33 ft 0 in (10.06 m); gross weight 6,000 lb (2,722 kg); cruising speed 105 mph (169 km/hr); range 650 miles (1,046 km). The twenty-fifth Model 40A went to Pratt & Whitney as an engine testbed, and when the new 525 hp Hornet radial became available in early 1928 nineteen surviving airline 40A's were fitted with these engines and redesignated Model 40B. Gross weight was then 6,079 lb (2,758 kg) and cruising speed 110 mph (177 km/hr). Two aircraft were also modified to have a second cockpit, in tandem, and dual controls. In mid-1928, Boeing produced the Model 40C, a version with a 450 hp Wasp engine and enlarged cabin to seat 4 passengers. Nine were built for Pacific Air Transport and a tenth was delivered to National Park Airways. Two other specially-modified 40C's, designated 40X and 40Y, were built for Associated Oil and Standard Oil. In July 1929 type certification was awarded to the final production model, an improved version of the 40B seating 4 passengers. Powered by the 525 hp Hornet engine, it was designated 40B-4, the original 2-seat version then being redesignated 40B-2. The first 40B-4 was flown on 5 October 1929. Thirty-eight Model 40B-4's were built, twenty having Townend cowling rings, radio and steerable

tailwheels. One other was completed as an engine testbed for Pratt & Whitney, and four 40H-4's were built by Boeing's Canadian factory. Customers included BAT, Varney Air Lines, Western Airlines and Western Canada Airways.

As evidenced by the modest increase in the passenger-carrying capacity of the Model 40 series, the potential of this side of the transport business was beginning to expand by the late 1920s. The extent of this expansion encouraged Boeing to design a new and much larger biplane primarily for passenger-carrying, and this emerged as the Model 80. It was powered by three 410 hp Wasp engines, and the first of four examples was flown in early August 1928. The 2-man crew occupied an enclosed cockpit just behind the nose engine, and the main cabin accommodated 12 passengers in a 3-abreast seating layout. In 1929 the Model 80 was followed by ten examples of the Model 80A, an improved version with Hornet B engines, increased fuel capacity, modified fin and rudder contours, and a cabin large enough to accommodate 18 passengers. There was a 39 cu ft (1.10 cu m) baggage compartment beneath the pilot's cabin floor. The Models 80 and 80A were employed by Boeing Air Transport, and by mid-1930 were flying a daily round-trip service between Chicago and San Francisco. In passenger service, travellers' comforts were at first attended to by male 'couriers', but, beginning on the Golden Gate-Lake Michigan route (which it later extended to New York), BAT introduced eight trained nurses as the world's first airline stewardesses. The Model 80A's were in due course converted to Model 80A-1 standard, this being a mixed-traffic layout for 12 passengers and up to 1,145 lb (519 kg) of mail or cargo. A reduced fuel load was carried, and in a further tail modification small auxiliary fins and rudders were mounted on the tailplane. With these aircraft, BAT inaugurated scheduled night mail services between Salt Lake City and Oakland, California, with the passenger seats removed and the cabin equipped as an airborne post office and sorting office. One other aircraft, designated 80B-1, was built for BAT, whose crews did not at first take kindly to an enclosed cockpit. This aircraft, powered by Hornet engines, had an open cockpit, elevated over a built-up nose so that the crew could see rearward over the upper wing. Later, after pilots grew accustomed to the advantages of an enclosed flight deck, it was converted to an 80A-1. Boeing also built one 6-seat Model 226 executive aircraft for the Standard Oil Company of California, based on the Model 80A. The 80C was a proposed all-freight version, but was not built. The Model 80 series was withdrawn from United (BAT) regular services in 1933, following the appearance of the twin-engined Boeing 247 monoplane (which see).

15   Handley Page H.P.42

The first four-engined airliner in the world to go into regular passenger service, the H.P.42 was one of the small band of aeroplanes which became a legend in its own lifetime. It was not without its critics, and one need only consider the huge wings with their heavy Warren-type bracing, the two-up, two-down arrangement of the uncowled engines, and the triple-finned biplane tail unit, to understand those who made fun of its 'built-in headwinds'. Yet, somehow, these and other features, which individually may have justified the criticism that they invoked, blended to give the H.P.42 a gentle, lumbering grace that was all its own. In time, the image of the H.P.42 came to be equated with that of Imperial Airways itself: 'safe, reliable – and slow'; and even this, in the prevailing climate of British civil aviation in the early 1930s, was construed virtually as a compliment. Nearly a decade after it was designed, when in most respects it had been far outclassed by the rising generation of smooth-skinned all-metal monoplane airliners, the H.P.42 still had something to offer, as *The Aeroplane Spotter* recorded in its issue of 16 December 1943:

'As late as 1938, one could stand on the tarmac at Croydon in the morning and watch Wibault, Douglas, Lockheed, Bloch, Focke-Wulf and other modern monoplanes taking half the aerodrome to become airborne while *Heracles* left the ground on occasions without running over the Customs apron'.

The H.P.42 was designed for service on the European and the eastern sectors of the Empire routes of Imperial Airways. A cabin mock-up was exhibited at the Olympia Aero Show in July 1929, and on 17 November 1930 the prototype, G-AAGX *Hannibal*, made its maiden flight from Handley Page's airfield at Radlett, Hertfordshire. From the outset, attention was paid to a high standard of comfort for the passengers. The location of the Jupiter engines – two on the upper wing and one in each angle of the inverted-gull lower wings – was intended to minimise noise and vibration in the passenger cabins, which were situated forward and aft of the wings. They were separated by a large area accommodating the mail and baggage holds, kitchen and toilets. The crew comprised captain, first officer, radio officer and 2 cabin stewards.

There were two basic models, the H.P.42E (for Eastern services) and H.P.42W (for Western, i.e. European, services), differing only in powerplant and cabin arrangement, and four aircraft were completed initially to each configuration. The H.P.42E's (G-AAGX, G-AAUC *Horsa*, G-AAUD *Hanno* and G-AAUE *Hadrian*) were powered by Bristol Jupiter XI.F engines, and seated 6 (later 12) passengers in the forward cabin and 12 in the rear cabin, with 500 cu ft (14.2 cu m) of mail/baggage space between. Power unit for the H.P.42W's (G-AAXC *Heracles*, G-AAXD *Horatius*, G-AAXE *Hengist* and G-AAXF *Helena*) was the Jupiter X.FBM with a reduced fuel load; the forward and rear cabins seated 18 and 20 respectively, and were separated by a smaller mail/baggage space of 250 cu ft (7.1 cu m).

The first proving flight, from London to Paris, was made by *Hannibal* on 9 June 1931, and two days later this aircraft inaugurated a scheduled service on this route. In August it left for Cairo, to take up its proper duty as one of the Eastern quartet, and was joined by the other three H.P.42E's by the end of the year. By January 1932 the last of the H.P.42W's had also been delivered, and on 20 January *Helena* flew to Paris on the first leg of the first through air mail

service to Cape Town. The Western models eventually flew on services from Croydon to Brussels, Cologne, Le Touquet, Basle and Zurich, while the Cairo-based Eastern models (later, but erroneously, described as H.P.45's) flew southwards to Kisumu and eastwards to Karachi and Delhi. Utilisation was high – during their lifetime, none of the eight flew less than 12,000 hours, and their aggregate mileage exceeded 10 million (16,093,400 km). The individual record was set by *Heracles*, which in 8½ years of operation flew 1,318,990 miles (2,122,660 km) and carried more than 160,000 passengers. On 8 December 1934 *Hengist*, emulating *Helena* nearly three years earlier, flew to Paris on the first leg of the first through air mail service to Australia. Early in 1935 it was converted to Eastern standard, but its career ended on 31 May 1937, when it was burned out in a hangar fire at Karachi. To replace *Hengist* on the European routes, *Hanno* was converted to an H.P.42W, and *Helena* was converted from Western to Eastern standard.

Up to the outbreak of World War 2, *Hengist* was the only casualty from the fleet of eight aircraft, but on 7 November 1939 *Horatius* was wrecked. Ironically, after their thousands of hours of safe, reliable peacetime flying, all but one of the six remaining aircraft were lost during 1940. The last survivor, *Helena*, was dismantled in August 1941 at RNAS Donibristle.

16 Curtiss Condor

Two separate types of Condor airliner were built by Curtiss, the first being the Model 18, a derivative ot the XB-2 Condor bomber of 1927. First flown in the summer of 1929 (probably July), the Model 18 Condor was powered by two 600 hp Curtiss GV-1570 Conqueror twelve-cylinder Vee-type engines, carried a crew of 3 and had accommodation for 18 passengers in three 6-seat cabins. Chief designer was George R. Page Jr, assisted by T. P. Wright and Alexander Noble, and six examples were built at Garden City, Long Island. They entered service in 1930 with Eastern Air Transport and Transcontinental Air Transport. The Model 18 had a wing span of 91 ft 8 in (27.94 m), length of 57 ft 1 in (17.40 m), wing area of 1,512 sq ft (140.46 sq m), gross weight of 17,378 lb (7,882 kg) and cruising speed of 116 mph (187 km/hr).

By 1932 Curtiss, in common with the rest of the US aviation industry, urgently needed a new, saleable, short-term product to spur its recovery from the effects of the recent economic depression. George Page and his colleagues were therefore given the task of designing a new transport aircraft. Design work began in April 1932, using as a basis an earlier project, the XT-32. From this there emerged the T-32, for which the name Condor was retained. The T-32 was for a time referred to as the Condor II, but despite a superficial outward resemblance it bore little or no design connection with the Model 18. The first T-32, registered 12353, was flown for the first time on 30 January 1933. Immediately-detectable differences between the new Condor and the Model 18 were the more portly fuselage, the elegant single-fin-and-rudder tail assembly (the Model 18

had a biplane tail with twin fins and rudders), and the neat nacelles of its two 750 hp Wright SGR-1820-3 Cyclone radial engines, into which the main landing gear could be almost fully retracted. Eastern Air Transport and American Airways each placed initial orders for five T-32's, each subsequently increasing its order to nine. Delivery began in the spring of 1933, and they entered service shortly after the award of a type certificate in March 1933. Twenty-one T-32 Condors were built, the remaining three consisting of two YC-30 transports for the US Army Air Corps and one specially-equipped Condor for the 1933–35 Byrd Antarctic Expedition.

The performance of the T-32 had been somewhat hampered by the necessity to use propellers whose pitch could only be adjusted on the ground. With the availability in 1934 of variable-pitch propellers, Curtiss took the opportunity to introduce a new model, the AT-32, which had such additional improvements as supercharged Cyclone engines, in more streamlined nacelles, and increased fuel tankage. Thirteen AT-32's were built, ten going to American Airways (renamed American Airlines in 1934) in the form of three AT-32-A's, three AT-32-B's and four AT-32-D's. These sub-types were, respectively, 12-passenger daytime/sleeper transports with 710 hp SGR-1820-F3 or 720 hp SGR-1820-F2 engines, and a 15-seat day passenger model with -F2 engines. American subsequently had eight of its original T-32's brought up to AT-32 standard; these were then redesignated T-32C. One AT-32-C, for Swissair, was generally similar to the -D model; it was delivered in spring

1934 and used on the Zurich-Berlin service, but was lost in a crash in July of the same year. The other two AT-32's were 12-seat daytime transport AT-32-E's, delivered to the US Navy as R4C-1's. The forty-five Condors built – production ended in September 1934 – were completed by five BT-32 bombers, three CT-32 naval transports and three T-32 military transports; a description of these appears in the *Bombers 1919–39* volume.

Although ousted from the fleets of Eastern and American by the new Douglas and Lockheed monoplane airliners by the mid-1930s, the Condor enjoyed a long and far-reaching career in subsequent years, with operators as far afield as Alaska, Burma, Canada, Central and South America, China and Mexico. In addition to the Swissair Condor, four others also served briefly in Europe. These were ex-Eastern T-32's, acquired in 1937 by the UK operator International Air Freight Ltd as G-AEWD/WE/WF/ZE. Until the autumn of 1938 they were used on freight services from Croydon to Brussels, Amsterdam and other points in Europe. They were then purchased by the Air Ministry, were stored until November 1939 and then scrapped. A number of Condors survived the war, some by several years; the last known operational Condor, belonging to the Peruvian Air Force, was not withdrawn and scrapped until the autumn of 1956.

17 de Havilland D.H.84 Dragon

At first sight it might seem unlikely that a desert light bomber and an economical feeder-line transport would have very much in common, yet such was the dual requirement which produced the D.H.84 Dragon in 1932. On the one hand the Iraqi government had asked de Havilland for a twin-engined military aircraft, armed with three machine-guns and able to carry up to sixteen 20 lb (9 kg) bombs; on the other, Edward Hillman of Hillman's Airways, impressed by the operating economics of de Havilland's single-engined 4-passenger Fox Moth, wanted a 6-passenger twin-engined transport with which to open a service to Paris in the spring of 1933. To meet the two requirements a de Havilland team led by A. E. Hagg designed the D.H.84, the prototype of which flew on 24 November 1932. A little less than a month later, as G-ACAN, it was delivered to Hillman's and given the fleet name *Maylands*. The Hillman's Romford-Paris service was opened on 1 April 1933; the fleet by then including three more Dragons, G-ACAO, 'AP and 'BW. Such was their popularity, and the amount of traffic engendered, that Hillman ordered two more (G-ACEU and 'EV), and had all six aircraft converted to 8-seaters. The eight military Dragons, characterised by their gun mountings and a curved dorsal fin, were delivered to Iraq in May 1933.

Commercially, the Dragon proved an instant success, its operating economics being even better than those of the Fox Moth and its cruising speed some 10 mph (16 km/hr) higher. It rapidly attracted orders from small airline, air taxi and charter operators at home and abroad, which kept it in steady production until 1936. Altogether, de Havilland built one hundred and fifteen Dragons, comprising sixty-two Mk 1's and fifty-three Mk 2's

Differences were comparatively slight, the Mk 2 being distinguishable by individually-framed cabin windows, larger main-wheel spats and fully-faired undercarriage legs and struts. The first aircraft of Mk 2 standard to fly was G-ACKU in the autumn of 1933.

Sixty-eight appeared on the British civil register, most of them with airline or charter/taxi operators. They were particularly prominent in Scotland and the north of England, and original customers for the Mk 1 included Highland Airways (one); Hillman's Airways (six); Jersey Airways (one); The King's Flight (one); Midland and Scottish Air Ferries (three); Northern and Scottish Airways (two); Railway Air Services (one); and the Scottish Motor Traction Company (three). The Mk 2 was purchased by Aberdeen Airways (two); Blackpool and West Coast Air Services (two); Highland Airways (one); Jersey Airways (six); Portsmouth, Southsea and Isle of Wight Aviation (one); and Railway Air Services (seven). A number of these operators subsequently increased their D.H.84 fleets by the purchase of second-hand aircraft. Exports of the Dragon Mk 1 were made to African Air Transport, South Africa (three); Automobiles Fernandez, Spain (one); Canadian Airways (one); Indian National Airways (two); Misr Airwork, Egypt (three); West Australian Airways (one); and Wilson Airways, Kenya (two). Foreign sales of the Mk 2 were made to Aer Lingus (one); Canadian Airways (one); East Coast Airways, New Zealand (two); Indian National Airways (one); MacRobertson - Miller Aviation, Australia (three); VASP, Brazil (one); and West Australian Airways (one). Additional military sales were two Mk 1's to the Royal Danish Army Aviation and three Mk 2's to the Portuguese Air Force. In 1942 the Dragon went back into production, this time by de Havilland Australia, which built eighty-seven for the RAAF for use as radio/navigation trainers and communications aircraft.

18 de Havilland D.H.89 Dragon Rapide

The D.H.89 was, in essence, an updating of the D.H.84 with increases in speed and passenger comfort, making use of the six-cylinder Gipsy Six engine produced for the four-engined D.H.86. The new design, like that of its predecessor, was the responsibility of A. E. Hagg, and to denote the change of powerplant it was known originally as the Dragon Six. In early 1935 this was changed to Dragon Rapide, and before long the 'Dragon' part of the name was dropped in everyday usage and the aircraft became known simply as the Rapide. It was powered initially by two 200 hp de Havilland Gipsy Six and flew for the first time on 17 April 1934. Like the Dragon, it was flown by one pilot only, but had a larger cabin which could seat up to 8 passengers, although 6 was a more usual number.

The first commercial order came from Hillman's Airways, which, with seven Rapides, was one of the two largest pre-war operators of these aircraft. More than a dozen scheduled operators in the UK, and many air charter and taxi concerns, were customers for the Rapide before 1939. The principal British airlines were

Aberdeen Airways (two); Blackpool and West Coast Air Services (three); British Continental Airways (three); Jersey Airways (two); North Eastern Airways (four); Personal Airways (three); Railway Air Services (eight); Scottish Airways (two); United Airways (two); and Wrightways (two). Overseas operators included Canadian Airways (three); Quebec Airways (four); Misr Airwork, Egypt (five); Société de Transports du Proche-Orient (two); Tata Airlines, India (three); Ala Littoria, Italy (one); Wilson Airways, Kenya (five); Rhodesia and Nyasaland Airways (four); LARES, Romania (four); Wearne's Air Services, Singapore (two); LAPE, Spain (one); Alpar, Switzerland (two); and Devlet Hava Yollari, Turkey (four).

Production continued up to the outbreak of World War 2, during which time two hundred and five were built at Hatfield. Many were impressed for military service with the RAF, RAAF and Air Transport Auxiliary, and production continued in wartime of the military Dominie Mk I and Mk II, of which one hundred and eighty-six were built by de Havilland and three hundred and thirty-five by Brush Coachworks Ltd. Two additional Rapides were assembled from spares in 1947, to bring overall D.H.89 production to seven hundred and twenty-eight.

A number of detail and styling improvements were introduced in the pre-war Rapides. After about sixty had been built, a range of modifications introduced in early 1936 included lengthened cabin rear windows, provision of a landing light in the nose, thicker wingtips, a rearranged cabin interior with 5-passenger seating and a toilet, and a cabin heating system. The first aircraft with these improvements was G-ADWZ. In November 1936 a D.H.89 was flown with small split flaps on each side of the engine nacelles, to improve the landing characteristics. This feature was adopted for subsequent production Rapides, the designation of this version being D.H.89A, and most earlier Rapides were brought up to a similar standard. The designation D.H.89B was allotted to the wartime Dominies, many of which were released on to the civil market at the end of World War 2. These, and the post-war career of the Rapide, are described further in the volume *Private, Business and General Purpose Aircraft since 1946.*

19 **de Havilland D.H.86**

Although, from its general appearance and from the name 'Dragon Express' often applied to it, the D.H.86 appeared to belong to the same family as the D.H.84 and D.H.89, it was produced to meet a very different and more stringent requirement. It was agreed between the governments of Great Britain, India and Australia that a through passenger service between England and Australia should be inaugurated in 1934, and a new aircraft was required to operate the route sector between Singapore and Brisbane. With large stretches of water to be covered, and tropical weather conditions to be endured, the requirement was as demanding as that which had resulted in the D.H.66 for the desert air routes some 8 years earlier, and the same priorities were afforded – plenty of cabin space and comfort, multiengine configuration for maximum safety, and ample reserve power. To meet the last of these conditions Major Frank Halford of the de Havilland Engine Co evolved the 200 hp Gipsy Six engine, which, as its name implied, was an enlarged version of the four-cylinder Gipsy Major in-line with two extra cylinders. Four of these engines were fitted in the D.H.86, which otherwise was in appearance and construction a scaled-up D.H.84. It had the same narrow nose, with a seat for one pilot only; the wireless operator sat in front of the 10 passengers in the main cabin, and there was a mail compartment at the rear.

The first D.H.86 was flown on 14 January 1934, only some four months from the start of design work. It gained its C of A on 30 January, after which, with a few detail improvements, it was delivered to Railway Air Services as G-ACPL. Two other D.H.86's were acquired by RAS, and in August 1934 they inaugurated the airline's Croydon-Belfast-Renfrew service. As a result of Australian government requirements, all subsequent aircraft had a 2-pilot layout, with a captain and first officer seated side by side in an elongated nose, and increased fuel capacity. Another improvement introduced at this stage was the provision of split trailing-edge flaps. Twenty-nine 2-pilot D.H.86's were built, these being delivered to Imperial Airways (four, for operation in Europe and Africa); Jersey Airways (six); Hillman's Airways (three); and Wrightways (one), all in the UK. The remainder were delivered to Misr Airwork in Egypt (two); to Holyman's Airways (four) and Qantas Empire Airways (six), both in Australia; and the last three to Union Airways in New Zealand.

The early loss of two Qantas D.H.86's led to further exploratory flight trials during the 1934-35 winter. These disclosed no basic faults in design or construction, but some modification and strengthening of the tail surfaces was carried out as a precautionary measure. Towards the end of 1935 further improvements were introduced, with which the aircraft became designated D.H.86A. A metal-framed rudder, larger tailwheel, pneumatic shock-absorption and improved brakes on the main landing gear, and a less steeply-sloped cockpit windscreen were the principal modifications. Twenty D.H.86A's were built, including one tested briefly with 205 hp Gipsy Six II engines. They were delivered to British Airways (eight); Imperial Airways (seven); Blackpool and West Coast Air Services (two); and one each to Railway Air Services, Wrightways and Misr Airwork. All were brought up to D.H.86B standard in 1937 by the addition of a small elliptical fin at each extremity of the tailplane. Production of D.H.86 variants, which totalled sixty-two aircraft, came to an end in 1937 after the completion of ten new D.H.86B's which, in addition to the auxiliary fins, had tailplanes with increased tip chord and an improved system of aileron control. Allied Airways, Blackpool and West Coast Air Services, and Railway Air Services, each received one new D.H.86B; the others were exported to DHY, the Turkish national airline (four), and W. R. Carpenter and Co in Australia (three).

About half of the D.H.86's saw

wartime service with the RAF or RAAF; comparatively few survived the war, but one ex-Jersey Airways machine, after much renovation, did so until September 1958.

20 Dornier Komet and Merkur

The Dornier Do C III Komet I, first flown in 1921, was a single-engined transport which clearly shared some design ancestry with the Do Cs II Delphin flying-boat. A noteworthy feature was its very large wing, which spanned 55 ft 9¼ in (17.00 m) and whose constant chord of 9 ft 10 in (3.00 m) represented almost one-third of the aeroplane's overall length of 29 ft 10¼ in (9.10 m). Dornier's pride in the rigidity and strength of this structure was expressed in a publicity photograph showing no fewer than 69 persons standing or sitting on the wing! The actual accommodation of the aircraft, however, was much more modest, the Komet I having a single open cockpit for the pilot and an enclosed cabin for 4 passengers, in fore-and-aft facing pairs. Production Komet I's powered either by a 180 hp BMW III or 185 hp BMW IIIa engine, were supplied in small numbers to Deutsche Luft-Reederei, later serving with Deutscher Aero Lloyd in 1924 and eventually with Deutsche Luft Hansa upon its formation two years later. Meanwhile Dornier had produced a modified version, utilising the same wings but having a 250 hp BMW IV and an overall length of 33 ft 9½ in (10.30 m); this made its first flight on 9 October 1922. Seating capacity remained the same, despite the increase in overall length. The Ukrainian airline Ukrvozdukhput ordered six Komet II's, which were delivered in 1923, and others were sold to airline operators in Colombia, Spain (Union Aérea Espanola), Switzerland (Ad Astra Aero) and the USSR. The DLH fleet also numbered some Komet II's, though some were probably converted from existing Komet I's. The German airline ceased to operate the Komet II in the autumn of 1928.

Well before this, there had appeared the Komet III, first flown on 7 December 1924, which was an enlarged version capable of seating 6 passengers and having a crew of 1 or 2 men, still in an open cockpit. It was powered originally by a 360 hp Rolls-Royce Eagle IX engine, although offered later with either the 400 hp Liberty or the 450 hp Napier Lion. Surviving records make it impossible to judge the number of Komet III's built, particularly as many later underwent conversion to become Merkurs. However, seven were ordered by Ukrvozdukhput in 1925 for its Moscow-Kharkov-Odessa-Kiev-Rostov services, one was sold to DDL of Denmark, at least two others went to a Swiss customer, and operators of eleven known German-registered Komet III's included Deutscher Aero Lloyd, DVL and DVS. A small batch was built under licence by Kawasaki in Japan, including three used by Tozai Teiki Kokukai on services between Tokyo and Osaka.

The Merkur, or Dornier Do B, first flown on 10 February 1925, was outwardly little different from the Komet III, and the subsequent conversion of several Komet III's into Merkurs took place. The main airframe changes were to be seen in the enlarged vertical tail surfaces, unbraced tailplane, and a cut-out in the centre-section trailing-edge of the wings, whose span was slightly increased by 1 ft 11½ in (0.60 m). The powerplant was a 600 hp BMW VI engine. Later production aircraft, with increased take-off weight and BMW VIu engines, were designated Merkur II. The largest Merkur operator was undoubtedly Deutsche Luft Hansa, which employed twenty-two of these aircraft on its night service between Berlin and Königsberg, and may have had some three dozen in all, including at least seven converted from Komet III's. Deruluft, the Russo-German airline, inaugurated a Berlin - Königsberg - Riga - Moscow service with Merkurs on 15 July 1927, and a Tashkent-Kabul service later the same year; it had at least nine Merkurs, possibly more. Exported examples included two to Ad Astra Aero, which later served with Swissair; one each to the Chilean Air Force and Tozai Teiki Kokukai in Japan; and two floatplane versions – one each to Sindicato Condor in Brazil and SCADTA in Colombia. Notable demonstration or proving flights by Merkurs included one in September 1926 of some 4,350 miles (7,000 km) over the route Friedrichshafen-Berlin - Königsberg - Moscow - Kharkov - Tiflis - Baku - Kharkov, and shortly afterwards, with 6 passengers and baggage representing a payload of 3,527 lb (1,600 kg), the first aeroplane crossing of the Caucasus mountains, made between Elbruz and Kasbek at an altitude of 17,720 ft (5,400 m). One of the Swissair Merkurs, flown by Walter Mittelholzer, flew from Zurich to Cape Town between 7 December 1926 and 21 February 1927, in 100 hr flying time, on an aerial survey flight.

21 Focke-Wulf A 17, A 29 and A38 Möwe (Seagull)

The Focke-Wulf Möwe series of short-range transports were produced in limited numbers in Germany during the late 1920s and early 1930s.

The first to appear was the A 17, powered by a 420 hp Gnome-Rhône (Bristol) Jupiter 9Ab uncowled radial engine. The prototype (D-1149) flew for the first time in 1927. The 2-man crew sat side by side in an enclosed cockpit, with one double and 6 single passenger seats to the rear. Maximum payload was 8 passengers and up to 440 lb (200 kg) of baggage and/or mail. The prototype was followed by eleven production A 17's, of which ten (D-1342 *Emden,* D-1358 *Aurich,* D-1367 *Leer,* D-1380 *Oldenburg,* D-1388 *Stade,* D-1403 *Lüneburg,* D-1416 *Osnabrück,* D-1430 *Hannover,* D-1444 *Münster* and D-1484 *Bielefeld*) were delivered to Deutsche Luft Hansa for internal and foreign services. These had slightly larger rudders and modified landing gear; several were later redesignated A 17a after being refitted with 480 hp Siemens-built Jupiter VI engines. The prototype, after service with Nord Deutscher Luftverkehr and Nordbayerische Verkehrsflugzeug, eventually joined the DLH fleet and was given the name *Bremen.* The eleventh A 17 was used for a time by DVL (Deutsche Versuchsanstalt für Luftfahrt); D-1444 was redesignated A 17c after being modified with an enlarged fin and a 520 hp Junkers Jumo 5 engine.

The A 29 Möwe, which appeared in 1929, had basically the same airframe and accommodation as the A 17, though the overall length was increased to 48 ft 6¾ in

(14.80 m) and it was powered by a 750 hp BMW Vee-type engine. Five were built, four of them (D-1757 *Friesland*, D-1775 *Jeverland*, D-1867 *Westfalen* and D-1922 *Saarland*) being delivered to Deutsche Luft Hansa in 1929–30. The fifth was used for airline training at the Deutsche Verkehrsfliegerschüle (DVS).

The A 38 Möwe had a somewhat more extensively redesigned fuselage and tail assembly. Overall length was increased to 50 ft 6¼ in (15.40 m), permitting the carriage of a wireless operator and 2 additional passengers. Rudder area was substantially increased, and a tailwheel was fitted instead of the former tailskid. The A 38 also reverted to a radial engine installation, originally the 400 hp Siemens-built Jupiter. Later, the 500 hp Siemens Sh 20u was substituted, the aircraft then being known as the A 38b. Only four were produced, and delivered to DLH as D-2073 *Bückeburg*, D-2082 *Hessen*, D-2107 *Lipper* and D-2114 *Thüringen*.

Most DLH routes on which the Möwe series was flown were those radiating from Berlin to Berne, Cologne, Königsberg, Marienbad, Munich, Paris, Saarbrucken and Vienna. The A 17a was also used for cargo services between Cologne and Nuremberg, and the A 38 over part of DLH's Berlin-Oslo route. Most A 29's and A 38's had been retired by 1933 or 1934; two A 17a's survived until 1936 before being scrapped.

22   Fokker F.II and F.III

The F.II was produced before the Fokker company became established in Holland. At the end of World War 1 Fokker's chief designer, Reinhold Platz, produced two single-engined transport designs, V44 and V45. The former, a 6-seater with open cockpits, was not built, but a prototype of the V45, or Fokker F.II, flew for the first time in October 1919, powered by a 185 hp BMW IIIa in-line engine. Two more F.II's were built at Schwerin, the prototype and one of these going to KLM as H-NABC and 'BD and the other to Deutsche Luft-Reederei. Ultimately, about two dozen F.II's were completed, most of them assembled at Staaken under the supervision of Dr Ing Karl Grulich, Technical Manager of DLR, and known as Fokker-Grulich F.II's. This operator was the customer for nineteen or more of the F.II's that were built; they passed to Deutscher Aero Lloyd upon its formation in 1924, and into Deutsche Luft Hansa ownership in 1926; except for one (sold to Balair in Switzerland), they remained in full service until 1934-35. The two KLM F.II's, which entered service in September 1920, were sold to Sabena in 1927; one later returned to Holland and was still in existence at the outbreak of World War 2. The original Fokker-designed F.II had an enclosed cabin for 4 passengers and an open cockpit at the front for a pilot and one passenger seated side by side. Wing span and area were 52 ft 9¾ in (16.10 m) and 452.1 sq ft (42.00 sq m), and overall length 38 ft 2¾ in (11.65 m). At a gross weight of 4,188 lb (1,900 kg), it had a cruising speed of 75 mph (120 km/hr) at sea level and a maximum range of 745 miles (1,200 km). The Fokker-Grulich F.II's were powered by 250 hp BMW IV engines and had modifications to the cockpits, cabin windows and landing gear.

The F.III was essentially a slightly enlarged version of the F.II, with all 5 passengers accommodated in a bigger cabin, a single-seat cockpit and an increased-span wing which, unlike the F.II, was fully cantilevered. Other improvements were made to the rear fuselage and the rudder. The prototype, also utilising the BMW IIIa as powerplant, flew in April 1921. During 1921–22 twelve F.III's, powered by 240 hp Siddeley Puma in-line engines, were built for KLM. One or two others were built, from spares, by the airline itself; five of the KLM aircraft were later sold to Balair, which resold two to Italy. Six were delivered to Malert, four with BMW IIIa's and two with 230 hp Hiero IVH engines. At least ten were built for Deruluft, all powered by 360 hp Rolls-Royce Eagle VIII engines; some of these were modified as parasol monoplanes. Two Eagle-engined parasol F.III's were delivered to KLM in 1922. These were the last of about thirty-one F.III's built by Fokker, but the DLR/DAL organisation at Staaken also built the type as the Fokker-Grulich F.III, primarily for German operation. Standard powerplant for these was the 250 hp BMW IV, although the Siddeley Puma was fitted to some aircraft, and others were later refitted with 320 hp BMW Va's. The major operator of the Fokker-Grulich F.III was Deutscher Aero Lloyd, which had about twenty, of which sixteen passed into DLH ownership in 1926.

Total F.III production was probably about fifty to sixty aircraft. They were widely used throughout Europe, though two went to the United States, two to the UK, and others found their way in later years to Canada and New Guinea.

23 Fokker Universal and Super Universal

The Universal and Super Universal, produced by Fokker Aircraft Corporation and Atlantic Aircraft Corporation, were the first types bearing the Fokker name to be designed entirely in the United States. The Model 4 Universal, designed by Robert Noorduyn, first appeared in late 1925, and was powered initially by a 200 hp Wright J4 uncowled radial engine. Structure was generally similar to contemporary Dutch-built Fokker transports, but the wings had strut bracing. The first production Universal (N-AABA) was delivered to Colonial Air Transport in May 1926, and forty-five were built before production ended in the spring of 1931. About half of these were J4-powered, but an improved version appeared from 1928, having a 220 hp Wright J5 engine, and some late-production Universals were fitted with a 330 hp J6. There was accommodation for a crew of 1 or 2 in open cockpits, and 4 passengers on individual staggered seats in the cabin. Dimensions included a wing span and area of 47 ft 9 in (14.55 m) and 330.0 sq ft (30.66 sq m), and an overall length of 35 ft 6 in (10.82 m). Performance of the J5-engined version included a maximum speed of 118 mph (190 km/hr) at a gross weight of 3,810 lb (1,728 kg). Principal airline customers were Western Canada Airways (seven or more) and Standard Air Lines (four). Other North American operators included California Airways, Continental Air Express, Dominion Airways, Northwest Air Service, Northwest Airways, Reynolds Airways, and St Tammany Gulf Coast Airways.

In late 1927 the first example (3318) appeared of the Model 8 Super Universal, known originally as the Universal Special. This was a much-improved model, the prototype having an enclosed cockpit for the crew, increased overall dimensions, a more powerful engine (420 hp Wasp) and higher operating weights and performance. The cabin was lengthened to accommodate 6 passengers. Further improvements in the production version, of which eighty were built in the US, included the elimination of the wing bracing struts, straight-tapered wings with inset instead of overhung ailerons, modified main landing gear similar to that of the Fokker F.VIIa, and an improved crew enclosure. The first production Super Universal became the Byrd Antarctic Expedition's *Virginia*, and fourteen others were exported. Major North American operators were National Parks Airways (six); St Tammany (five); Standard Air Lines (three); Universal Air Lines (two); Western Air Express (five); and Western Canada Airways (nine). Other Universals and Super Universals served with operators in Argentina, Australia, Canada, Colombia, Mexico, South Africa and the UK. In addition to US production, fourteen Super Universals were licence-built in Canada by Canadian Vickers; Nakajima in Japan built nine civil examples (with 450 hp Jupiter engines) and about twenty others for military use. Fokker in Holland built three examples of the basically similar F.XI Universal in 1929, these going to Alpar (one, with 240 hp Lorraine 7Aa engine) and Malert (two, with 480 hp Gnome-Rhône Jupiters).

24 Stinson Detroiter

One of the best-known and best-liked American cabin transports of the inter-war years, the Detroiter did not attract a great number of airline customers, and the bulk of those built were employed by business corporations, aerial taxi operators and wealthy private owners.

The first Detroiter, the SB-1, was a biplane. Designed by Edward A. Stinson and Frederick Verville, it flew for the first time on 25 January 1926. Interest shown by local businessmen prompted the formation of the Stinson Airplane Corporation some four months later, and the first production SB-1 was completed in the following August. Powered by either a J4 or J5 Wright Whirlwind seven-cylinder radial engine, the 4-seat SB-1 had a wing span and area of 35 ft 10 in (10.92 m) and 350.0 sq ft (32.52 sq m) and an overall length of 28 ft 10 in (8.79 m). At a gross weight of 2,900 lb (1,315 kg) it had a range of 600 miles (965 km), and the J4-powered version could cruise at 100 mph (161 km/hr). Operable for passenger and/or mail services, it entered service in September 1926 with Florida Airways. Other airline customers included Northwest Airways (three), Wien Airlines and Patricia Airways. Total SB-1 production, which ended in June 1927, amounted to about twenty-two.

The Detroiter achieved its principal fame as a high-wing monoplane, the first and major version of which was the SM-1, certificated in November 1927. This was a 6-seater (pilot and 5 passengers), and was powered by a 225 hp J5 Whirlwind engine. Seventy-four were built, including the SM-1B, which had a wider-track landing gear. Airline customers included Paul R. Braniff Inc, which flew its first-ever scheduled service on 20 June 1928 wth a single SM-1 (NC1929) and was soon flying three round trips a day between Oklahoma City and Tulsa. Later in 1928 Braniff acquired a second Detroiter monoplane, and in early 1929 the line was extended to Wichita Falls. During 1929–30 Stinson produced, mostly in small quantities, various modified versions which included the SM-1D, SM-1DA and SM-1DB (minor improvements to landing gear, brakes, engine cowling and interior); SM-1DC and SM-1DD (2-seaters for record flights and cargo-carrying); SM-1F (6-seater with 300 hp J6 Whirlwind); and SM-1FS (twin-float version of the SM-1F). Of these, only the SM-1F achieved substantial production status. About twenty-six are believed to have been built, including four which, in 1928, operated the first regular air mail service in China. The largest Detroiter monoplane was the SM-6B, which appeared in mid-1929. Powered by a 450 hp Wasp C1 engine, it could accommodate 7 or 8 passengers or a 954 lb (432 kg) load of mail or cargo. About a dozen were built.

By this time, however, Stinson had begun to concentrate on production and marketing of the smaller Detroiter Junior, which first appeared as the SM-2 in early 1928. Scaled down to a 3/4-seater, the SM-2 was powered by a 110 hp seven-cylinder Warner Scarab engine and was aimed primarily at the business and general aviation market.

52 Ryan Brougham

The career of the Ryan Brougham appears to have been – by comparison with other and less noteworthy types – a singularly unobtrusive one. This is the more remarkable in a type of which more than two hundred examples were built and which was, moreover, a sister-ship of Charles Lindbergh's world-famous trans-Atlantic monoplane *Spirit of St Louis*.

In early 1926 T. Claude Ryan began the manufacture of the first aeroplane of his own design, the M-1, an open-cockpit 3-seat high-wing monoplane intended for the expanding air mail business in the United States. Customers included Pacific Air Transport, which operated a service from Seattle to Los Angeles via San Francisco, one of the longest and most difficult of the early routes. The Brougham was foreshadowed later in 1926 by the Ryan M-2 Bluebird, an improved M-1 seating a pilot and 4 passengers in fully-enclosed accommodation.

About twenty-eight M-1/M-2's were built. The M-2, normally powered by a Hispano-Suiza engine, was used from 1927-29 by Yukon Airways in north-western Canada to fly a service between Whitehorse and Dawson. The first Brougham was, essentially, an M-2 airframe powered by a 220 hp Wright J5 Whirlwind seven-cylinder radial engine, and was under construction at the time the company undertook to build the special NYP (New York-Paris) monoplane for Lindbergh.

Lessons learned with the NYP were incorporated into the initial production model, the B-1, and the Brougham quickly became a success. Frank Hawks flew a B-1 to eighth place in the 1927 Ford Air Tour, and later won the speed prize in the National Air Races, and with such achievements as these, coupled with the attention attracted by the Lindbergh flight, the Brougham was soon in demand. By the latter part of 1928 one hundred and fifty B-1 Broughams had been built. In October of that year Mahoney sold his interest in the company to the Detroit Aircraft Corporation, which transferred the production centre to Lambert Field, St Louis. The next airline version was the B-3, with the same seating capacity as the B-1 (pilot and 4 passengers) but increased baggage capacity, improved main landing gear struts, enlarged tail surfaces, modified engine cowling and wider cabin. Standard powerplant was the 220 hp Wright J5, though the 300 hp J6 was fitted in some aircraft. Only eight more B-3's were built, in 1929, including one converted to B-3A with additional fuel capacity.

The first version built from the outset at Lambert Field was the B-5, which adopted the 300 hp J6 Whirlwind as standard and had cabin accommodation for 5 passengers and 73 lb (33 kg) of baggage. All-round performance included a take-off run of less than 300 ft (91 m). Forty-eight B-5's were completed, nine of them for China. The next model to appear, the B-7, was the last true Brougham type to be built. This also seated 5 passengers, with a baggage allowance increased to 100 lb (45 kg), and was basically a slightly bigger B-5 with a longer fuselage, enlarged tail surfaces, and a 420 hp Wasp C1 engine. However, the fortunes of the Detroit Aircraft Corporation were by this time showing a marked downward trend, and only six B-7's

were built. The Brougham line ended in 1931 with three Brougham-type aircraft bearing the Model number C-1. Known variously as the Foursome or Baby Brougham, the C-1 was a smaller edition of the Brougham having a 225 hp J6 Whirlwind engine. Seating 3 passengers only, it was intended for the business executive or rich private owner rather than for airline use, as reflected by the more luxurious furnishing and larger cabin door.

Overall production of the Brougham, excluding the C-1, thus amounted to two hundred and twelve aircraft. By no means all of those built were for airline customers, and it is virtually impossible to state just how many were used in airline service, or even how many air transport companies included Broughams in their fleets. Ryan Airlines itself was naturally a regular operator, and Pickwick Latin American Airways was among the major users. Its services extended from Los Angeles to Mexico City, Guatemala City and San Salvador, and it may have had as many as a dozen Broughams altogether. Other known operators (not all of scheduled passenger services) included Aeronautica del Sur of Tabasco, Mexico (about ten); Bowman Airways of Alaska; Corporacion Aeronautica de Transportes of Coahuilla, Mexico; Embry-Riddle (Chicago-Cincinnati on air mail route 24); National Airlines Air Taxi Service (St Petersburg-Tampa-Lakeland-Orlando-Daytona Beach); Pike's Peak Air Lines; Robertson Airplane Service (Kansas City-Minneapolis); Thompson Flying Service (Chicago-Bay City-Pontiac); and Tri-State Airlines of Sioux City, Iowa.

26 P.W.S.24

Upon its formation on 1 January 1929 the Polish national airline, Polskie Linie Lotnicze (Lot) formulated a requirement for an aircraft to replace the Junkers F 13 on its internal network. Two competing designs were approved for comparative evaluation: the Lublin R-XI, and the P.W.S.21 designed under the leadership of Stanislaw Cywinski of the Podlaska Wytwornia Samolotow Sp Akc. Neither was accepted, but three new prototypes, the Lublin R-XVI, P.Z.L.16 and P.W.S.24T, were developed in late 1930 to a less rigid specification. Of these, the choice was made in favour of the P.W.S. design, the prototype of which (SP-AGR) made its first flight in August 1931, powered by a 220 hp Skoda-built Wright Whirlwind J5 radial engine. With detail modifications, SP-AGR was handed over to the airline in April 1932 for route-proving, by which time an initial batch of five P.W.S.24's had been ordered. Accommodation was for a pilot and 4 passengers, and the aircraft had a cruising speed of 100 mph (160 km/hr). Further modifications were introduced to the production aircraft (SP-AJF/G/H/J/K), delivery of which began in early 1933. On 1 May 1933 these five aircraft, together with the prototype, began scheduled operations, initially on the service between Warsaw and Poznan.

Lot, however, had already suggested that performance could be improved by the use of a more powerful engine, and P.W.S. first refitted the prototype with a 387 hp Lorraine 9Na engine. In this form it was test-flown extensively during the early weeks of 1933, after which it underwent further trials with a 420 hp Pratt & Whitney Wasp Junior radial. This latter engine was ultimately chosen to power a second production batch of five aircraft (SP-AMN/O/P/R/S), which received the designation P.W.S.24*bis*. The P.W.S.24*bis* went into service in the spring of 1935, being joined a few months later by a seventh aircraft (SP-AJH) brought up to similar standard and re-registered SP-ASY. However, despite the improvement in speed, the aircraft's range and payload were modest in the extreme, and all were withdrawn from passenger service in the spring of 1936.

27 Kalinin K types

Konstantin Alexievich Kalinin was among the more talented Soviet designers of the inter-war period and, prior to his arrest and the disbandment of his design bureau in 1938, had designed no fewer than 16 individual aircraft types in almost as many years. Kalinin was among the first to appreciate the aerodynamic attractions of an elliptical wing planform, for which he took out a patent in 1923, and most of his subsequent aircraft designs were based upon wings of this shape. The first to appear, in 1925, was the K-1 (also known as the RBZ-6), a small high-wing monoplane with seating for 3 passengers. Powered by a 170 hp Salmson engine, it had a speed of 100 mph (161 km/hr) and was used for a time on feeder services between Moscow and Nishnii Novgorod. A year later this was succeeded by the K-2, essentially similar to the K-1 but with a 240 hp BMW IV engine giving sufficient power to enable 4 passengers to be carried. A variant, with the same powerplant and a cabin modified to accommodate 3 stretchers, was designated K-3. The first flight was made in 1928 of the prototype K-4, which was registered RRUAX. This 4-passenger aircraft was reportedly powered by a 300 hp BMW VI engine, but the 240 hp BMW IV remained standard for the first production examples, which appeared on the internal services of Dobrolet and the Ukrainian airline Ukrvozdukhput. An ambulance version, carrying 2 stretchers and having a starboard-side rear loading door, was powered by a 300 hp M-6 engine, and the 310 hp Junkers L 5 engine was available as a third choice. Twenty-two K-4's are believed to have been built at Kharkov, including a small number for aerial photography duties.

The most successful type was the K-5, which was essentially a scaled-up K-4. It first appeared in 1929, and some two hundred and sixty were built during 1930–34. The first examples had M-15 (Bristol Jupiter) or Pratt & Whitney Hornet radial engines, but later series were powered by 480 hp M-22 or 500 hp M-17F engines. Improvements included an enclosed cockpit for the 2-man crew, cabin accommodation for up to 8 passengers, and vertical tail surfaces closely resembling those of contemporary Fokker airliners. The K-5 was used by Dobrolet on services within the USSR. A slightly smaller development was the K-6, a parasol-wing mailplane powered by a 420 hp Gnome-Rhône Jupiter VI engine, but this is not thought to have been produced in quantity.

28 **Consolidated Models 17 and 20 Fleetster**

A contemporary of the Lockheed Air Express and Vega, which it closely resembled, the Fleetster did not achieve the same eminence, although the score or so examples built were popular with pilots and passengers alike. The Fleetster owed its inception, and its name, to Rueben H. Fleet, president and general manager of Consolidated Aircraft Corporation, who was also one of the prime movers in forming the New York, Rio and Buenos Aires Line to operate air services between North and South America. The main sectors of NYRBA's network were flown initially by Consolidated Commodore flying-boats, but Fleet wanted a small, fast aeroplane to fly supporting feeder services between the principal South American stopovers and the hinterland areas, and to meet this requirement the Fleetster was produced.

Designed by I. M. Laddon, the prototype Model 17 Fleetster (X657M) flew for the first time in October 1929, and test flying was conducted with both Wasp and Hornet engines. The 575 hp Hornet B was selected, and after certification in January 1930 three Fleetsters were delivered to NYRBA: the prototype (re-registered NC657M), NC671M and NC672M. Typical routes were Rio de Janeiro-Puerto Allegre (Brazil), and from Buenos Aires into Bolivia, Paraguay, Uruguay and Chile. The original machine was operated for part of its career as a twin-float seaplane, and the other pair may have been similarly equipped. One passenger sat beside the pilot, and 5 more were accommodated in the cabin, which could be stripped for cargo-carrying. When NYRBA became part of the Pan American Airways System in September 1930, NC657M was sold; the other two were scrapped by Pan American in October 1934. One other Model 17 was built as the personal transport of the US Assistant Secretary for War.

There were two variants of the original Fleetster, the first being the Model 17-2C, one example of which (NC750V) was built in 1930 for a private owner but passed in 1933 to Pacific International Airways for operation in Alaska. Possibly the only Model 17-2C built, it had a 575 hp Wright Cyclone engine and forward-facing passenger seats. The last Model 17 variant, the 17-AF, was powered by a 575 hp R-1820-E Cyclone, with the 650 hp R-1820-F available as an alternative. It had an enclosed cockpit forward of the wing, accommodation for 9 passengers, a new low-drag main landing gear and enlarged wings of 50 ft 0 in (15.24 m) span. Three Model 17-AF's (NC703Y to NC705Y) were built for Ludington Airlines; the first was delivered in June 1932, and they were used for a fast shuttle service between New York and Washington, DC, making four round trips per day. All three were acquired by Pan American in June 1933, one being resold to Pacific-Alaska Airways in 1934.

Meanwhile, Consolidated had evolved in 1930 another version of the Fleetster, known as the Model 20 and also produced initially for NYRBA. To make better use of the available fuselage space, the Model 20 adopted a parasol-wing layout. The cockpit, which was open, was repositioned aft of the wings, enabling a 60 cu ft (1.7 cu m) cargo hold to be accommodated in the deep forward fuselage between the passenger cabin and the engine bay. The Model 20, like the Model 17, was operable either in mixed passenger/cargo configuration or as an all-cargo aircraft. Two Model 20's (NC673M) and NC674M) were

built for NYRBA, passing in late 1930 to Pan American, which purchased a third as NC675M. A fourth was supplied to a Canadian operator as CF-AIP.

The final Fleetster, the Model 20-A, was essentially an alliance of the parasol-wing Model 20 with the longer wings, modified undercarriage and other improvements of the Model 17-AF. It had seating for up to 7 passengers, or fewer passengers with enhanced cargo load. In 1932 seven were built (NC13208 to NC13214) for Transcontinental and Western Air (TWA) to operate a Detroit-Toledo-Fort Wayne-Indianapolis service to connect with westbound trunk routes. They entered service in October 1932 and, except for one lost in a crash, operated until February 1935 before being withdrawn. Three were later sold privately; the other three (NC13208, '211 and '213) found their way to Spain, where they were used on transport duties by the Republican forces in the Civil War.

29 Latécoère 28
Pierre G. Latécoère, founder of Lignes Aériennes Latécoère, one of France's first airlines, also set up in 1919 his own aircraft manufacturing company, Forges et Ateliers de Construction Latécoère, to manufacture aircraft of its own design for the airline's air mail service. At the Paris Salon in December 1919 it exhibited the first such aeroplane to appear, the Latécoère 3, powered by a 260 hp Salmson 9Z radial engine. Two years later there appeared the 5-seat Latécoère 8, an ugly, square-cut biplane with a 300 hp Renault engine. Whether either of these achieved production status is uncertain, but in 1925 about ten or a dozen examples were built of

the Latécoère 15, a parasol monoplane powered by two 275 hp Lorraine-Dietrich engines and as ugly as its predecessor. These were operated by 'The Line', probably between Toulouse and Casablanca; some were equipped as twin-float seaplanes.

Aesthetically, at least, the company's aircraft designs began to take a turn for the better with the appearance in the mid-1920s of the Latécoère 17, 25 and 26 series of single-engined parasol monoplanes. Somewhere in the region of a hundred and twenty were built, the Laté 26 predominating. When Aéropostale gave way to Air France in 1933 the latter inherited thirty-eight Laté 25's (some of which were conversions from Laté 17's) and forty-one Laté 26's.

The single-engine formula was continued in 1929 with the considerably more attractive Latécoère 28. Two initial versions appeared, the Laté 28-0 (500 hp Renault 12Jb) and Laté 28-1 (500 hp Hispano-Suiza 12Hbr). Apart from their powerplants they were apparently alike, each having accommodation for up to 8 passengers and an enclosed cockpit for a 2-man crew.

There was a certain amount of conversion from one model to another, making it impossible to establish exactly how many of each individual version were manufactured. At least thirty-eight were built for Aéropostale, three were delivered to Aviacion Nacional Venezolana, two to Linea Aeropostal Venezolana and four to Aeroposta Argentina. In addition to the two passenger-carrying models already mentioned, other designations included twin-float mailplane versions with greater wing area and either

a 600 hp Hispano-Suiza 12Lbr engine (Laté 28-3) or a 650 hp Hispano-Suiza 12Nb (Laté 28-5); the ANV trio were designated Laté 28-6. The Latécoère 28-5 was a special aircraft, flown under French Navy auspices and named *La Frégate*. Piloted by Lt de Vaisseau Paris, it set up in 1930 nine world speed, endurance and distance records with payloads ranging from 500 kg (1,102 lb) to 2,000 kg (4,409 lb). Undoubtedly the most historic flight by a Laté 28, however, was that by the 28-3 F-AJNQ *Comte de la Vaulx*, which crossed the South Atlantic from St Louis, Senegal, to Natal, Brazil, as part of the first experimental through air mail route from Toulouse to Rio de Janeiro. The crossing, made on 12/13 May 1930, took 21 hours, and was made by one of France's most celebrated pilots, Jean Mermoz, with crew members J. Dabry and L. Gimié.

30 Lockheed Vega and Air Express

Allan and Malcolm Loughead designed their first aeroplane, the Model G, in 1913, but were unable to compete with the glut of war-surplus military aircraft that flooded the civilian market, and their company was disbanded in 1921. The aeroplane which brought it together again, in 1926 in a Hollywood garage, was a highly attractive little high-wing monoplane designed by a former associate, John K. Northrop – the Lockheed Vega. When production ended 8 years later Lockheed had not only built and sold one hundred and twenty-eight Vegas but had evolved from the original design a whole family of fast transport and racing aircraft – 'Lockheed's plywood bullets', they have been called – which firmly established the new Lockheed Aircraft Company on the road to future success.

The original Vega, which made its first flight on 4 July 1927, was sold to the US newspaper magnate George Hearst Jr, who named it *Golden Eagle* and entered it in the Dole race from Oakland, California, to Hawaii. Flown by John W. Frost, with Gordon Scott as navigator, it took off from Oakland on 16 August 1927, but disappeared en route and was never heard of again. Despite this inauspicious start to its career, the Vega was an almost instant success. Lockheed retained the second Vega as a demonstrator, and the third was purchased by Captain G. H. (later Sir Hubert) Wilkins for his 1928 Arctic Expedition. The secret of the Vega's attraction, and of its excellent performance, lay in the beautifully streamlined fuselage, which was an extremely smooth semi-monocoque, built in two halves inside a concrete mould. Many early Vegas achieved renown as race-winners and record-setters. The initial version, the Vega Model 1, was powered by a 220 hp Wright J5 Whirlwind radial engine. It seated a pilot and up to 4 passengers, and at a gross weight of 3,470 lb (1,574 kg) was capable of 135 mph (217 km/hr). Twenty-eight of this version were built. The next to appear was the Vega Model 5, with the same dimensions and seating capacity but a 450 hp Pratt & Whitney Wasp B engine, gross weight of 4,033 lb (1,829 kg) in landplane form, and top speed of 185 mph (298 km/hr). Forty-two were completed, including seven converted from other models. Five of these seven were twin-float sea-planes, with 4,698 lb (2,131 kg) gross weight and a top speed of 172 mph (277 km/hr). Two Vega 5's were converted to 6-seaters for operation by Pan American-Grace Airways, and nine others were built as executive Vega 5A's.

The next version to appear was the Vega 2, a 5-seater with a 300 hp Whirlwind J6 engine, of which six were built including one converted from a Vega 1. One other was built as a 6-passenger Vega 2A. The most celebrated version was the Vega 5B, with a 450 hp Wasp C engine and passenger seating for 6. Thirty-four were completed, including three land-plane and two floatplane conversions from other models. The Vega 5B served widely with many US domestic, Mexican and foreign air-lines, and one became the famous *Winnie Mae* in which Wiley Post and Harold Gatty made their round-the-world flight in June/July 1931, the first such flight by a commercial aeroplane. Two years later, after its conversion to a Vega 5C (Wasp C1 engine and enlarged tail surfaces), Post flew *Winnie Mae* on the first solo flight round the world. Twenty-seven Vegas were in due course converted to 5C standard, and six others were built from the outset as 5C's. Apart from eight custom-built Vega 'Specials' (of various models), the only remaining Vega was the DL-1, with duralumin instead of plywood for the fuselage skin. With 6-passenger seating and a Wasp C1 engine, the DL-1 was built by Detroit Aircraft Corporation, which obtained financial control of Lockheed in early 1929, only to go into receivership in October 1931. Northrop, who left Lockheed in June 1928, was succeeded by Gerard F. Vultee, who was responsible for development of the later Vega models until his own departure in early 1930. Ten DL-1's were built, including three DL-1B's and three 'Specials'.

Very early in the life of the Vega, Lockheed had also developed a similar aircraft, using Northrop's basic fuselage design with a parasol wing of slightly greater span than the Vega. This was the Model 3 Air Express, designed to meet the requirements of Western Air Express. Seven Air Expresses were built for airline customers, the first being delivered to WAE in March 1928. Other operators were NYRBA and Pan American (two each), and American Airways and Texas Air Transport (one each). An eighth aircraft was completed as a 'Special'.

Airline use of the Vega during the late 1920s and early 1930s was widespread. About three dozen US domestic scheduled operators, or their heirs or successors, operated Vegas with outstanding success. Most had small fleets of four or less, but among the larger fleets were those of Braniff (ten); Alaska-Washington Airways (seven); Hanford Tri-State Airlines (six); Varney Speed Lines (five); and Wedell-Williams Air Service (five). Thirty-one Vegas at some time bore Mexican registrations, the major fleets being those of Lineas Aéreas Mineras (eleven) and Corporación Aéronautica de Transportes (ten). Other airline Vegas served with operators in Argentina, Australia, Canada, Costa Rica, Nicaragua, Norway, Panama and the UK.

31 **Bellanca Airbus and Aircruiser**
Giuseppe Mario Bellanca was rightly held in high esteem in the US aircraft industry of the 1920s

and 1930s. Born in Italy, where he built his first aeroplane in 1908, Bellanca emigrated to the United States in 1911 and later opened a flying school at Mineola. During World War 1 he was an aircraft designer, and after the war was engaged to design an aircraft to be powered by the new 200 hp Wright J4 Whirlwind engine. The result, the 1925 Wright-Bellanca WB-1, was followed by the WB-2, which became the *Columbia* in which Chamberlin and Levine flew across the North Atlantic to Germany a month after Lindbergh's epic flight to Paris in the *Spirit of St Louis* in 1927. Bellanca parted company with Wright in 1927, but by that time he was already known as a designer of light cabin monoplanes, his first having been the Air Sedan of 1923, which carried 5 people and had a 100 hp Anzani engine. Bellanca had a passionate belief in making his designs aerodynamically efficient: he appreciated, better than most, that an aeroplane is a vehicle for transporting a useful load from A to B, and every ingredient of his designs was aimed at doing this in the most efficient way. He was, also, not generally in favour of multi-engined aircraft, taking the view that one powerful, well-maintained engine was to be preferred wherever possible.

This philosophy was in evidence from the very start of Bellanca's career, for the prominent aerofoil struts and 'bow-legged' main landing gear were to be seen in the WB-1. Bellanca's first big commercial success was the Pacemaker series of general-purpose aircraft, in which the high-mounted wings were braced on each side by two struts with wide, aerofoil-section fairings contributing to the total lift.

Bellanca's concept of the single-engined, high-efficiency load-carrier reached its peak in the Airbus and Aircruiser, which could carry a payload comparable with that of many three-engined transports of their day. These were, in effect, sesquiplanes, with a pattern of faired-in undercarriage and wing bracing struts that gave additional lifting area to supplement that of the main high-mounted wing. They consisted of a parallel-section stub-wing inboard of each main under-carriage unit and an inverted 'V' section outboard. The inboard sections were of sufficient depth to be utilised as storage compartments for baggage, mail or freight. The first Airbus to appear was the Model P-100, which flew in May 1930, although its ancestry was traceable to the long-range Model K built some two years earlier. Unfortunately for the P-100, its airframe qualities were not matched by those of its 600 hp Curtiss Conqueror liquid-cooled engine, and only one (NC684W) was built. Nevertheless, even in this form the Airbus could lift a 3,000 lb (1,360 kg) payload, and had an outstanding short-field performance. Once fitted with a satisfactory powerplant – usually the Wright Cyclone or Pratt & Whitney Hornet – it became much more viable economically. Unfortunately, the Airbus/Aircruiser was offered when the US market was still suffering from the effects of the economic depression, and did not achieve the sales which it deserved. The Airbus existed in two major production models, the 12-passenger P-200 (to which standard the P-100 was converted) and the 15-passenger P-300. Only a small number of civil Air-buses were built, including one, with a twin-float landing gear, used on a commuter service in the summer of 1934 by New York and Suburban Airlines. Fourteen were, however, built for the US Army Air Corps as four Y1C-27's and ten C-27A's. The Model 66 Aircruiser was a cargo-carrying equivalent of the Airbus, with the same basic dimensions but slightly increased wing area. In one of its later forms the Aircruiser had an 850 hp GR-1820-G3 Cyclone engine and a gross weight of 11,400 lb (5,171 kg), of which 4,021 lb (1,825 kg) was payload. Aircruiser operators included Central Northern Airways and Mackenzie Air Service in Canada.

32   Tupolev ANT-9

As head of the design department of the TsAGI (Central Aero and Hydrodynamic Institute) from 1920, and chairman of the Soviet aviation committee formed to develop all-metal aircraft, Andrei N. Tupolev was ideally placed to be among the first Soviet designers to incorporate the latest techniques in this field into aircraft of his own design. Russian domestic production of aluminium (Kolchug-alumin) and duralumin began in 1922 and, as might be expected, was at first adopted for military purposes. However, in 1929 there appeared the prototype (URSS - 309) of the ANT - 9 tri - motor passenger transport. (Available records describe this as being 'completed' on 28 April 1929; whether this was the date on which it first flew has not been established.) Eventually to become one of the most successful Soviet transports of the inter-war period, the prototype ANT-9 was powered by three 230 hp Gnome-Rhône Titan uncowled radial engines. It had a wing span of 77 ft 9 in (23.70 m), an overall length of 55 ft 9¼ in (17.00 m), a maximum speed of 130 mph (209 km/hr) and a range of 620 miles (1,000 km). On 6–12 June 1929 it made a demonstration tour within the Soviet Union (Moscow-Odessa-Sevastopol - Odessa - Kiev - Moscow); subsequently, with the name *Krilya Sovetov* (Wings of the Soviets), it set out on 10 July 1929 on a tour of European cities, flying from Moscow to Travemünde, Berlin, Paris, Rome, Marseilles, London, Paris, Berlin and Warsaw before returning to Moscow on 8 August, a total distance of 5,615 miles (9,037 km), covered at an average flying speed of 110 mph (117 km/hr).

There were two production versions of the ANT-9, the first of similar overall dimensions to the prototype and powered by three 300 hp M-26 radial engines. An alternative version was available with 300 hp Wright J6 Whirlwind engines, offering a maximum speed of 127.4 mph (205 km/hr) – 12.4 mph (20 km/hr) better than the M-26 version – but with range reduced from 620 miles (1,000 km) to 435 miles (700 km). The Whirlwind-engined ANT-9 had a slightly-increased wing span of 78 ft 3 in (23.85 m), though wing area remained the same, and the overall length was reduced to 54 ft 7½ in (16.65 m). Accommodation in both versions was for a crew of 2, in an enclosed cockpit, and 9 passengers in the main cabin, which also incorporated a rear baggage compartment and toilet. The wheeled landing gear could be exchanged for skis for winter operation. As many as sixty ANT-9's

may have been built, including nine Whirlwind-engined aircraft operated by Deruluft on Berlin-Moscow and other services.

The designation PS-9, indicating *Passazhirskii* (Passenger) or *Pochtovii Samolet* (Postal Aircraft), has been applied generally to the ANT-9, but there is reason to believe that this should be applied only to the twin-engined version which appeared in 1933. Due to the much-increased power available from two 680 hp M-17 (licence BMW VI) Vee-type engines, the nose-mounted third engine could be dispensed with, despite an increase in gross weight to 13,668 lb (6,200 kg), and still give a maximum speed of 134 mph (215 km/hr). Overall dimensions remained similar to those of the Whirlwind-engined ANT-9. Dobrolet and Aeroflot had a total of about seventy ANT-9's, among which the twin-engined version was predominant. One PS-9, named *Krokodil*, was painted to resemble its saurian namesake and used by the Maxim Gorki propaganda squadron.

33 Rohrbach Ro VIII Roland

The Roland was a product of the Rohrbach-Metall-Flugzeugbau GmbH, established in Berlin in 1922 by Dr Ing Adolf Rohrbach, formerly of the wartime Zeppelin-Werke GmbH. Like Prof Hugo Junkers, Dr Rohrbach was an early protagonist of metal construction and cantilever wings, and both features were reflected in the Roland prototype (D-991) which flew in 1926. It was powered by three 230 hp BMW IV six--cylinder in-line engines and accommodated a crew of 2 and up to 10 passengers. Construction was entirely of metal, with a covering of duralumin sheet. The crew cockpit, with side-by-side seats, was enclosed on the prototype but open on the Roland I initial production version. Passengers occupied individual seats on each side of a central aisle; aft of the final pair of seats were a toilet and a mail/baggage hold.

In 1926–27 Deutsche Luft Hansa took delivery of the prototype, which it named *Zugspitze,* and five production Ro VIII Roland I's (D-999 *Watzmann,* D-1124 *Schneekoppe,* D-1280 *Feldberg,* D-1292 *Brocken* and D-1297 *Wasserkuppe*), which entered service in 1927 from Berlin to London via Hanover and Amsterdam. During July 1927 a Roland set up an international endurance record by flying for 14 hours 23 minutes 40 seconds over a closed circuit with a 2,205 lb (1,000 kg) payload, covering a total distance of 1,438 miles (2,315 km). In 1927–28 three of the Roland I's (D-999, D-1280 and D-1292) were acquired by Iberia and, as M-CBBB, M-CAEE and M-CCCC respectively, inaugurated a service between Madrid and Barcelona.

Their place in the DLH fleet was taken in 1928 by three Rolands of an improved type: D-1314 *Jnselberg,* D-1327 *Hohentwiel* and D-1338 *Zugspitze;* the naming of the third aircraft (which later became Iberia's M-CADD) suggests that the prototype may have been disposed of or lost. The Ro VIIIa had an 11¾ in (0.30 m) longer fuselage than the Ro VIII and a slightly higher gross weight, but the major difference from its predecessor lay in the improved powerplant of three 320 hp BMW Va engines. The remaining DLH Ro VIII's had themselves been refitted

by this time with 250 hp BMW IVa engines; later still, they were brought up to BMW V standard. The airline crews had come to accept the virtues of an enclosed cockpit, too; this feature was built into the Ro VIIIa and fitted retrospectively to the earlier machines.

The final production version was the Roland II, which had a much-redesigned crew cabin with generous window area. Another major structural change concerned the wing, now positioned on top of the fuselage with less dihedral than that of the earlier Rolands. Powerplant was the same as for the Ro VIIIa. Nine Roland II's were delivered to DLH in 1929: D-1692 *Stolzenfels,* D-1710 *Rheinstein,* D-1712 *Schönburg,* D-1720 *Niederwald,* D-1727 *Freienfels,* D-1729 *Drachenfels,* D-1735 *Marksburg,* D-1745 *Siegburg* and D-1756 *Rolandseck.* At the peak of their service, in 1931, the DLH Rolands were operating, wholly or partially, seven routes of the airline's large central European network, and Hamburg - Malmö and Berlin - Munich were still being flown by Rolands in 1936. By this time the DLH fleet had been reduced by the transfer of at least three Roland II's (D-1712, D-1729 and D-1735) to Deruluft, and most of the remaining aircraft, including one Ro VIIIa (probably D-1314), had been refitted with 280 hp Junkers L 5 engines.

34 Ford 4-AT and 5-AT Tri-motor
One of the immortals of air transport history, the Ford Tri-motor, 'Tin Lizzie' or 'Tin Goose' has more than 40 years of hard work to justify the esteem and affection in which it is rightly held by pilots

and passengers the world over. Seldom can an aeroplane of its type have been subjected to such onerous demands during its lifetime, ranging from snap rolls, low-level loops and other barnstorming aerobatics to heavy-duty freight transportation and fire-fighting. It has served with more than 100 air transport operators in the US, Australia, Canada, China, Mexico, and Central and South America, and its career runs through virtually the entire story of pre-war airline development in the United States. To list here all of the original and subsequent owners of the one hundred and ninety-eight production Tri-motors would be impossible, but even to record the principal original airline customers is more than adequate to make the point. These were, in alphabetical order: American Airways (one 5-AT-C); British Columbia Airways (one 4-AT-B); CLASSA (one 4-AT-E and one 4-AT-F); Colonial Air Transport (three 5-AT-B); Colonial Western Airways (one 4-AT-B and one 5-AT-C); Compania Mexicana de Aviacion (five 5-AT-B); Curtiss Flying Service (four 4-AT-B); Eastern Air Transport (two 4-AT-E); Jefferson Airways (one 4-AT-B); Maddux Air Lines (two 4-AT-A, six 4-AT-B, six 5-AT-B and two 5-AT-C); Mamer Flying Service (two 4-AT-E); Mohawk Airways (one 4-AT-E); National Air Transport (one 4-AT-A, eight 5-AT-C and three 5-AT-D); Northwest Airways (two 5-AT-A and two 5-AT-C); NYRBA (one 4-AT-A and three 5-AT-C); Pacific Air Transport (six 5-AT-D); Pan American Airways (six 5-AT-B, one 5-AT-C and two 5-AT-D); Pan American-Grace Airways (three 5-AT-C and one 5-AT-D); Pennsylvania Air Lines (one 4-AT-E); Pitcairn Aviation (one 4-AT-E); Queen City Air Lines (one 4-AT-B); Rapid Air Lines (one 4-AT-B); Robertson Aircraft Corporation (three 4-AT-B and one 5-AT-B); SCADTA (one 5-AT-D); Southwest Air Fast Express (six 5-AT-B and two 5-AT-C); Spokane Airways (one 4-AT-B); Stout Air Services (two 4-AT-A, three 4-AT-B, two 5-AT-B and two 5-AT-C); Transcontinental Air Transport (ten 5-AT-B and one 5-AT-C); and Universal Flyers (two 4-AT-D).

There has been an element of controversy concerning who truly designed the Ford Tri-motor, but credit for inspiring it is generally given to William B. Stout, owner of the Stout Metal Airplane Company, which produced in the early 1920s two single-engined cantilever high-wing monoplanes, the 4-seat Air Sedan and the Model 2-AT mailplane. Both were of all-metal construction, with a corrugated metal skin, and when, in August 1925, the Stout company was purchased by the Ford Motor Company, work was begun on developing the 2-AT into a three-engined design. The resulting 3-AT prototype was both ugly and ungainly, and was destroyed in a hangar fire early in its career. A drastic redesign was undertaken, led by Harold Hicks and Thomas Towle, which emerged in 1926 as the 4-AT. The prototype, which first flew on 11 June 1926, was powered by three 200 hp Wright J4 Whirlwind uncowled engines and had accommodation for a crew of 2, in an open cockpit, and 8 passengers. The initial production model, of which fourteen were built, was designated 4-AT-A. In 1927 there followed the 4-AT-B, an improved model with 220 hp J5 Whirlwinds, increased wing span and seating for up to 12 passengers. Thirty-five of this version were built. The 4-AT-C (one built) was a variant of the 4-AT-B with the nose engine replaced by a 400 hp Wasp radial, and three 4-AT-D's (all different) were built with various powerplants and other modifications. The last major 4-AT model was the 4-AT-E (twenty-four built), powered by three 300 hp J6 Whirlwinds. Production of the 4-AT series was brought to a total of seventy-eight with a single 4-AT-F, built in 1931 and differing only in detail from the E model.

Apart from the 4-AT-F, production of the 4-AT series had ended in 1929, but by that time a new basic Tri-motor had appeared in the form of the Model 5-AT. This had the wing span increased from 74 ft 0 in (22.56 m) to 77 ft 10 in (23.72 m), the cabin enlarged to seat 13 passengers, and the power increased to three 420 hp Pratt & Whitney Wasp radials. Three were built in 1928 as Model 5-AT-A, after which seating capacity was further increased in the 15-seat 5-AT-B (forty-two built) and 17-seat 5-AT-C (forty-eight built) and 5-AT-D (twenty-four built).

During its career the 'Tin Goose' inevitably underwent both official and unofficial modification to meet the needs of particular operators. It was flown with wheel, float and ski landing gear, and several aircraft were subjected to changes in equipment, interior layout, door sizes and so on. Development by no means ended with the 5-AT series. Later designations included the 6-AT-A (5-AT-C with 300 hp J6 engines; three built); 7-AT-A (conversion of one 6-AT-A with a 420 hp Wasp in the nose; later converted back to 5-AT-C); 9-AT (conversion of one 4-AT-B with three 300 hp Wasp Juniors); 11-AT (conversion of one 4-AT-E with three 225 hp Packard Diesel engines; originally designated 4-AT-G, later converted to 4-AT-B); and 13-A (conversion of one 5-AT-D with a 575 hp Cyclone in the nose and two 300 hp J6's; later restored to 5-AT-D). The Model 8-AT was a one-off single-engined freighter, later sold to Pacific Alaska Airways, and was a 5-AT-C with the outer engines removed; Models 10-AT and 12-A were unbuilt projects. The final development, built in February 1932, was the Model 14-A, a 40-passenger machine powered by Hispano-Suiza engines (1,100 hp in the nose and two 715 hp outer engines), but this was never flown.

35 Savoia-Marchetti S.71

The Società Idrovolanti Alta Italia originally specialised in the design and manufacture of flying-boats and seaplanes, several of which achieved prominence in the 1920s. During the second post-war decade it became better known for its multi-engined landplanes designed for commercial transport and bomber roles. The first such transport design was the S.71, designed by Ing Alessandro Marchetti. The first S.71, I-AAYP, was flown in late 1930 and on 29 January 1931 Sandro Passaleva set up a world load-to-height record at Cameri by reaching an altitude of 21,457 ft (6,540 m) in this aircraft while carrying a payload of 4,409 lb (2,000 kg). The first four S.71's (the others being I-SIAI, I-EOLO and I-PALO) were powered by three 240 hp Walter Castor seven-cylinder radial engines, and were followed by two more (I-ROMA and I-ALPI) with 370 hp Piaggio Stella VII radials. All six were delivered to Società Aerea Mediterranea (SAM), which inaugurated a service between Rome and Brindisi with the S.71 on 6 July 1931. When SAM became part of Ala Littoria in October 1934 its S.71 fleet continued to be employed, eventually operating a through service from Rome to Salonika. The Ala Littoria fleet still included four S.71's as late as 1937, though with the advent of the later S.73 and S.M.75 (which see) they may by then have been relegated to the company's services in Italian East Africa. A seventh S.71, the Stella-engined I-ABIV, was specially adapted as a mail transport.

The standard version was designed to seat a crew of 3 and up to 10 passengers, although it is likely that 8 was a more usual load.

36 Fokker F.VII and F.VII-3m series

From the modest initial batch of five F.VII's built for KLM in 1924–25, there grew up a family of single- and three-engined high-wing transport aircraft whose influence was world-wide, and which was eventually to realise a production total well in excess of two hundred and fifty aircraft. In mid-1921, to US requirements, Fokker built two examples of the F.IV, which was essentially an enlarged version of the F.III powered by a 400 hp Packard Liberty engine. They were evaluated by the US Army Air Service in the transport (T-2) and ambulance (A-2) roles, though no production order was placed. Fokker's next transport was the one-off F.V, first flown in December 1922, a parasol-wing monoplane that could be converted quickly into a biplane by adding a lower pair of wings. It seated a crew of 2 and 8 passengers, was powered by a 360 hp Rolls-Royce Eagle IX engine, and was eventually acquired by Olag, the Austrian airline.

The F.VII, which first flew (H-NACC) in 1924, had the same powerplant and seating capacity as the F.V, except for the final example, which was fitted with a 450 hp Napier Lion engine. Three of the five were later refitted with Bristol Jupiter engines. The F.VII was used primarily on KLM's European and domestic network; two were lost in accidents in 1926, one was resold via Fokker in 1927 to Standard Air Lines in the US, and one in 1931 to Pacific Aerial Transport in New Guinea.

A year after the appearance of the F.VII, Fokker produced a refined version known as the F.VIIa. Powered by a 400 hp Packard Liberty engine, the prototype (H-NACZ) flew for the first time on 12 March 1925 and was subsequently demonstrated in the United States. While in America Anthony Fokker heard about the Ford Reliability Tour to be staged later that year, and decided to compete. The obvious way to improve the reliability of the F.VIIa was to provide it with additional engines, and an example was quickly converted by fitting it with three 200 hp Wright J4 Whirlwind engines, one in the nose and two slung beneath the wings. This, the first trimotor Fokker, flew for the first time on 4 September 1925. It won the

Ford contest easily, and of some sixty-three or more F. VIIa's and F.VIIa-3m's eventually built, eighteen were exported to the United States. The original tri-motor was acquired by the Byrd Arctic Expedition and named *Josephine Ford*; on 9 May 1926 it became the first aeroplane ever to fly over the North Pole, and is to-day preserved as an exhibit in the Ford Museum at Dearborn, Michigan. Other preserved Fokkers include the F.VIIa *Alaskan*, now in the Liberty Museum, and another tri-motor, the famous *Southern Cross* flown by Charles Kingsford Smith on the first trans-Pacific flight (from Oakland to Brisbane) in May/June 1928, which is now on display in Brisbane. The latter aircraft had longer-span wings than previous tri-motors; it was originally built with three Whirlwind engines as *Detroiter* for the 1926 Arctic Expedition led by Hubert Wilkins, and was refitted with 220 hp Whirlwinds and a modified rudder to become the *Southern Cross*. Single-engined F.VIIa's were built for Balair, CIDNA (seven), DDL (two), KLM (eleven), Lot (six), Malert (two) and STAR (three); those for KLM and Balair were powered by 400 hp Gnome-Rhône Jupiter radial engines, while the aircraft for Lot and STAR had French Lorraines. Tri-motor F.VIIa-3m's were sold to Pan American (five), Reynolds Airways (two) and Western Air Express (one) in the United States, where this version was built by Fokker's American company, Atlantic Aircraft Corporation, for civil and military customers.

The production total of the F.VIIa and F.VIIa-3m was more than doubled by that of the slightly larger F.VIIb-3m, which was the most widely-built of any pre-war Fokker commercial transport. The F.VIIb-3m flew with at least a dozen alternative types of power-plant, ranging in output from the 215 hp Armstrong Siddeley Lynx to the 365 hp Gnome-Rhône Titan Major. Other engines, of intermediate ratings, included the 220 hp Wright J5, 240 hp Gnome-Rhône Titan, 250 hp Avia DR 14, 260 hp Walter Castor, 300 hp Wright J6, 300 hp Pratt & Whitney Wasp Junior, and 340 hp Armstong Siddeley Serval. The standard F.VIIb-3m airframe differed primarily from the F.VIIa-3m in having the longer-span wings first seen on the *Detroiter*, but with the taper interrupted inboard of the wing engines by a section with its trailing-edge at right-angles to the fuselage. It has been estimated that Fokker built about fifty-seven F.VIIb-3m's, including a few early examples with shorter-span wings. The overall total, excluding US production (see below), was about one hundred and forty-five, and included licence-built batches by Avia (fourteen), Avro (thirteen as Avro Ten, which see), Meridionali (two or more), Plage and Laskiewicz (eighteen) and SABCA (twenty-eight). Customers included Air Orient (two); Avio Linee Italiane (six or more); Balair (five); CIDNA (six); CLASSA (four); CLS (eight); CSA (five); Japan Air Transport (ten); KLM (eight); KNILM (seven); LAPE (three); Lot (eighteen); Sabena (thirty); Swissair (three); and Western Canada Airways (one). By resale and/or re-formation of airlines, the total number of operators was, of course, considerably greater, ranging throughout Europe, Africa and the Middle and Far East. The

F.VIIb-3m carried a crew of 2 (sometimes 3), and had standard accommodation for 8 passengers, although the latter figure varied according to circumstances.

Developed versions were also built in the United States in 1928–29 as the F-10 and F-10A. The F-10, developed to meet a requirement of Western Air Express, had Dutch-built F.VIIb-3m wings, a US-built fuselage seating 12 passengers, and 420 hp Wasp engines. Seven were built, of which five were delivered to WAE, entering service in May 1928; four of these were later inherited by TWA. The other two were converted to F-10A standard, which introduced extended-span, US-built wings (with unbroken trailing-edge taper) and had higher operating weights and an improved performance. The F-10A could be powered by 420 hp or 450 hp Wasp engines. Approximately sixty civil F-10A's were built (plus others to military contracts); the principal initial customers were Pan American (twelve); Standard Air Lines (six); Universal Airlines (fifteen); West Coast Air Transport (three); and Western Air Express (twenty-one). Six of the WAE F-10A's passed into TWA ownership; another major operator was American Airways, which purchased sixteen from other airlines.

37 Avro Ten, Five, Six and Eighteen

These four types, combined production of which totalled twenty-one aircraft, stemmed from a licence acquired by A.V. Roe and Co in 1928 to build the Fokker F.VIIb-3m in the UK. Their names reflected the number of people, in-cluding crew, which each could carry.

The first to enter production was the Avro Ten (Type 618, seating a crew of 2 and 8 passengers). This differed only slightly from the standard Dutch-built F.VIIb-3m, and twelve were built between 1929 and 1933 for Australian National Airways (seven); Imperial Airways (two, for charter operations); Midland and Scottish Air Ferries (one); and the Egyptian Air Force (two). One of the Egyptian pair was sold in 1935 to Indian National Airways.

In 1930 a smaller version, re-designed by Avro, appeared as the Avro Five (Type 619), seating a pilot and 4 passengers and powered by three 105 hp Armstrong Siddeley Genet Major 1 radial engines. Wilson Airways of Kenya ordered two, later adding a third to replace one that had been lost. Two other Fives were built.

The Avro Six (Type 624) carried one more passenger than the Five. It had the same powerplant, and the gross weight was increased from 4,420 lb (2,005 kg) to 5,000 lb (2,268 kg). Two Sixes were built, both sold eventually to the Chinese government.

The Avro Eighteen (Type 642/2m, seating 2 crew and 16 passengers), which appeared in 1934, represented a considerable re-design and bore little resemblance to the Fokker F.VIIb-3m. It utilised wings of the same span as the Avro Ten, though of slightly greater area, but the fuselage was com-pletely new and considerably more streamlined. Only one was built, built, powered by two 460 hp Armstrong Siddeley Jaguar VID radial engines; it was operated for a short period in 1934 by Midland and

Scottish Air Ferries, and later as a freighter, first in Europe and eventually in New Guinea. Avro also built one four-engined Type 642/4m for an operator in India.

38 Fokker F.VIII, F.IX, F.XII and F.XVIII

Except for the twin-engined F.VIII, these four airliners all represented variations on the Fokker tri-motor theme of the late 1920s and early 1930s. The F.VIII, which first flew (H-NADU) on 12 March 1927, was developed to meet a KLM requirement for a transport with greater capacity than the single-engined F.VII, and was powered by two uncowled underslung 480 hp Gnome-Rhône Jupiter VI radial engines. The cabin was designed to accommodate 15 persons, although actual loads varied between 10 and 24 passengers. The F.VIII carried a crew of 2, and there was a spacious hold for baggage, mail or freight in the nose section, which could be swung open for loading. The prototype served only briefly with KLM before being lost in a crash in August 1927, but during the following year six others (H-NAED/E/F/G/H/I) were delivered for service on the airline's European network. In addition, Fokker supplied one F.VIII (H-MFNA) to Malert, and two 13-passenger examples (H-MFNB and 'NC) were built under licence in Hungary in 1929–30 by Manfred Weiss. The KLM aircraft remained in service for several years, undergoing various refits with 500 hp Wasp or 690 hp Cyclone engines and receiving PH- registrations. One of the KLM aircraft went to the Netherlands West Indies, one to

AB Aerotransport in Sweden (1934) and two to British Airways in 1936; one of the British-registered F.VIII's was sold to a Swedish customer in 1939.

The F.IX, only two of which were built in Holland, was Fokker's largest tri-motor transport, and was intended to carry up to 6 passengers in sleeper accommodation over the route from Amsterdam to the Netherlands East Indies. In fact, although a proving flight was made in late 1930, it was used only on European services (mostly Amsterdam-London) with seating for up to 17 daytime passengers. The prototype (PH-AGA *Adelaar*) flew on 26 August 1929; it was delivered to KLM in May 1930 and remained in service until the autumn of 1936. The second Fokker-built F.IX (PH-AFK), also powered by three 480 hp Gnome-Rhône Jupiter VI engines, had a longer and more spacious fuselage which could accommodate up to 20 passengers. It served with KLM only from January to August 1931 before being lost in a crash. Avia in Czechoslovakia, which built a bomber development of the F.IX known as the Avia F.39, developed from the latter a transport version designated F.IXD. This also seated 20 passengers, and apart from having three 580 hp Walter-built Bristol Pegasus IIM2 engines was generally similar to the Dutch-built version. Two Avia F.IXD's (OK-AFF and 'AFG) were built for CSA in 1935.

The F.XII, though smaller than the F.IX, was also of larger capacity than the F.VII-3m series and was basically a three-engined development of the F.VIII. The prototype (PH-AFL) flew in early 1931, and during 1931–32 eleven

F.XII's were built by Fokker: two for KNILM (PK-AFH and 'AFI), one for AB Aerotransport (SE-ACZ *Värmland*), and eight for KLM (PH-AFL *Leeuwerik*, PH-AFU *Uil*, PH-AFV *Valk*, PH-AID *Duif*, PH-AIE *Ekster*, PH-AIH *Havik*, PH-AII *Ibis* and PH-AIJ *Ijsvogel*). The KLM aircraft, used for the Amsterdam-Batavia service, seated 16 passengers and were powered by three 425 hp Wasp C engines; the Swedish example had 500 hp Wasp T_1D_1's and seated 14 passengers. The F.XII entered service with KLM in March 1931 and continued until 1936, when six were sold to Crilly Airways and British Airways in the UK and one to Air Tropic in France. Two additional F.XII's, OY-DIG *Merkur* (1933) and OY-DAJ *Kronprinsesse Ingrid* (1935), were manufactured under licence by Orlogsvaerftet in Denmark and operated by DDL, initially on services from Copenhagen to Berlin, Hamburg and Hanover.

The last tri-motor to follow the traditional Fokker pattern of the period was the F.XVIII, built in 1932 to replace the twin-engined F.VIII on the KLM Amsterdam-Batavia route, with sleeper-type accommodation for 4 passengers. Five were built, and were delivered as PH-AIO *Oehoe*, PH-AIP *Pelikaan*, PH-AIQ *Kwartel*, PH-AIR *Rijstvogel* and PH-AIS *Snip*. They were powered originally by three 420 hp Wasp engines. After 2 or 3 years on this route, *Oehoe* and *Snip* were allocated to the West Indies network, the other three serving on for a while as 13-passenger day transports on KLM's European routes. In 1935–36 PH-AIQ and 'AIR were sold to CLS in Czechoslovakia, and 'AIP to Air Tropic.

36 Junkers G 38

On 12 December 1915 the first flight took place of the Junkers J 1, an all-metal cantilever monoplane which represented the first practical application of a patent taken out five years previously by Prof Hugo Junkers for a thick-section aerofoil with a load-bearing metal skin. For many years thereafter Prof Junkers pursued studies for large transport aircraft which would be virtually flying wings, with the main power-plant, fuel and passenger loads housed almost entirely within the wings. This ambition was approached very closely by the G 38, designed in 1928 by a team under Dipl Ing Ernst Zindel and flown for the first time at Dessau on 6 November 1929.

Everything about the G 38 was huge. Its wings were 6 ft $7\frac{1}{2}$ in (2.02 m) deep at their thickest point and had a root chord of 35 ft $5\frac{1}{4}$ in (10.80 m), decreasing to 9 ft $5\frac{3}{4}$ in (2.89 m) at the tip. The maximum depth of the fuselage was 11 ft $9\frac{3}{4}$ in (3.60 m), and the biplane tail unit spanned 30 ft $9\frac{1}{4}$ in (9.38 m). Within the multi-spar wings were the engines, fuel load, part of the passenger accommodation and a large freight storage area. It has been said that the first G 38 (D-2000) was powered originally by two L 88 and two L 8 Junkers petrol engines, but an account of a visit to Dessau during construction of the prototype, published in *l'Aéronautique* in March 1930, describes the inboard pair as Junkers L 55 twelve-cylinder Vee-type engines of 650 hp, each driving a four-blade propeller, and the outboard pair as 400 hp Junkers L 8 six-cylinder in-lines, each driving a two-blade propeller. A change to 800 hp L 88's in the inboard positions was perhaps made during the early months of 1930. All propellers were of 14 ft 9¼ in (4.50 m) diameter, coupled to the engines through a gearbox and shafting. A small diesel APU in the port wing provided compressed air for the main-wheel brakes, engine starting and fire extinguishing . system. There was complete accessibility to all engines during flight. Between the two engines in each wing was a machine-room, into whose space the underwing radiators could be retracted, and aft of the engine bays was a continuous tunnel running from port to starboard through the wing between the two outer engines. Aft of this tunnel, and astern of the two machine-rooms, fuel for up to 20 hours' flying was contained in 28 interconnected tanks. Inboard of the fuel area (i.e. in the wing roots) and underneath the fuselage cabin floor were compartments capable of housing a total of 6,614 lb (3,000 kg) of freight. Passenger accommodation was for 30 persons, 26 seated in successive cabins within the single-level fuselage and 2 each in the wing leading-edges inboard of the inner engines. The forward fuselage cabin, virtually buried within the wing centre-section, had four circular skylights in the roof, and for long flights there was provision to convert part of the fuselage accommodation to sleeper configuration. A further engine change in 1932 replaced the two L 8 engines by 800 hp L 88a's, the aircraft then having four-blade propellers on all engines and being redesignated G 38a.

Junkers built a second G 38, which received the registration D-2500. This was apparently powered at the outset by the L 8/L 88 engine combination, but was redesignated G 38ce in 1932 after being refitted with four L 88a's. It introduced some major structural alterations, primarily in connection with the flying control surfaces and passenger accommodation. The wings of the first G 38 had no flaps, but were fitted with long-span ailerons which terminated just outboard of the outer engines. The second G 38 had the full Junkers 'double wing' system, with three-section movable surfaces over virtually the whole of each trailing-edge. These improved airfield performance to the extent that D-2500, despite its higher gross weight, could take off and land over a 66 ft (20 m) obstacle in 1,890 ft (575 m) and 1,495 ft (455 m), compared with 2,510 ft (765 m) and 2,020 ft (615 m) for D-2000. The vertical tail surfaces comprised three fins and three rudders, as compared ·with three rudders and a single centre fin on the first G 38. The forward section of the fuselage was built up above the wing centre-section, permitting a substantial increase in the number of side windows; the fuselage was laid out to seat 11 passengers in the elevated forward cabin, 11 in the lower centre cabin and 4 in a third compartment for smokers only. Aft of this was a toilet; a second toilet was located in the starboard wing root, and there was a pantry on the port side of the fuselage ahead of the forward passenger cabin. Passenger accommodation was brought up to a total of 34 by seating 3 persons in each of the wing leading-edge cabins and 2 in the extreme nose. Provision was made for a 7-man crew, consisting of a captain, two pilots, two flight engineers, a wireless operator and a steward. In due course, D-2000 was brought up to a similar standard.

Both G 38's were acquired by Deutsche Lufthansa, D-2000 in 1930 and D-2500 in the following year. The former entered service on 1 July 1931, followed by the latter on 1 September 1931. The two aircraft were named *Deutschland* (D-2000) and *Hindenburg* (D-2500, re-christened *Generalfeldmarschall von Hindenburg* in April 1933), and when all-letter civil registrations were introduced in Germany their identities became D-AZUR and D-APIS respectively. In 1934 each was re-engined with four 750 hp Junkers Jumo 204 engines. D-2000/D-AZUR appears to have been used on an ad hoc basis rather than on regular scheduled services, but between them the two aircraft took part in DLH operations on routes from Berlin to Frankfurt, Königsberg, Munich, Rome, Stockholm and London. The original aircraft was lost in a take-off crash at Dessau in 1936, but D-APIS survived to be taken over by the Luftwaffe in September 1939.

10 Potez 62

Perhaps the most noticeable external feature of the Potez 62 was its fuselage, which in profile had been carefully contoured to reproduce that of an aerofoil cross-section. This resulted in an aeroplane of considerably more attractive appearance than the Potez 540 bomber (see *Bombers 1919–39*), from which the commercial transport was developed. Design of the Potez 62 was undertaken in 1934, and the prototype (F-ANPG) was flown for the first time on 28 January 1935, powered by two 870 hp Gnome-Rhône 14 Kirs Mistral Major fourteen-cylinder radial engines. The wing/powerplant/landing gear arrangement was generally similar to that of the Potez 540, with the main wheels retracting backward into the rear of the engine nacelles. A roomy flight deck, with generous window area, was provided for the 2-man flight crew, while the fuselage was divided into two cabins accommodating 6 persons forward and 8 aft in individual seats. Up to 16 passengers could be carried. Toilet and pantry were located between the flight deck and forward cabin, and there were compartments for baggage, mail or small freight in the nose and aft of the rear cabin.

The prototype, and eleven generally similar Potez 62-0's, were delivered to Air France, one (F-AOTZ) being an executive aircraft for the French Air Minister. The remainder, which began to enter service in June 1935, included F-ANPG, named *Albatros*, and F-ANPH *Cormoran*, F-ANPI *Cigogne*, F-ANPJ *Courlis*, F-ANQK *Gypaété*, F-ANQL *Ramier*, F-ANQM *Martinet*, F-ANQO *La Berceuse*, F-AOTU *La Séduisante*, F-AOUA *Flamant* and F-AOUE *Ibis*. Initially they were employed on services from Paris to Madrid, Marseilles and Rome. Nine were refitted in 1937 with 900 hp Gnome-Rhône 14N 16/17 engines.

Prior to this, there had appeared in 1935 the Potez 62-1 (first example F-ANQN *Aguila*), which had 720 hp Hispano-Suiza 12Xrs engines and very slight sweepback to the wings. Air France took delivery of F-ANQN (later renamed *Flamant*) and ten other Potez 62-1's comprising F-ANQP *L'Etourdie*, F-ANQQ *Falcon* (later *La Capricieuse*), F-ANQR *La Tapageuse* F-ANQS *La Fidèle*, F-AOTT

L'Entreprenante, F-AOTV *Alcyon,*
F-AOTX, F-AOTY *Magoary,*
F-APOC *Héron* and F-APOD
Pluvier. In addition, three of its
Potez 62-0's were modified to 62-1
standard.

With the build-up of its Potez
62 fleet, Air France gradually increased the number of routes on
which these aircraft were employed.
They began to operate to Scandinavia and other European centres,
on the Far Eastern routes which
Air France had inherited from the
former Air Orient, and (in 1936)
on South American routes across
the Andes between Buenos Aires
and Santiago. On the latter routes
it is believed that the three 62-0/
62-1 converted aircraft were
operated in a mixed-payload
capacity, carrying a cargo of mail
and up to 7 passengers. Most Potez
62's had been retired by the outbreak of World War 2, but at least
one is known to have been operated
by the Free French forces.

41 Armstrong Whitworth A.W.15 Atalanta

The Atalanta did not attract the
same publicity as some of its more
illustrious companions in the
Imperial Airways fleet of the 1930s,
yet its adaptability and safe operating record were no less deserving of
attention. It has been said that its
career was one of 'unobtrusive
efficiency'. It is a measure of that
efficiency that, of the small batch of
eight Atalantas built, only one was
lost in a flying accident in the first
6½ years of service; three continued
to operate until 1942, and two
others until 1944.

Designed in 1931 under the
leadership of J. Lloyd, the Atalanta
was evolved to meet the specific
needs of Imperial Airways' African

and Far Eastern routes. Particular
attention was paid to the provision
of adequate reserve power for flight
in 'hot and high' conditions, the
comfort of passengers during long
flights in tropical temperatures, and
a healthy cruising speed. The
Atalanta carried a crew of three
and could accommodate various
combinations of passengers and mail
or other freight, or 17 persons in
all-passenger configuration. The
prototype (G-ABPI), named
Atalanta, made its first flight on 26
June 1932; the streamlined fairings
over the main wheels were later
removed. The prototype was
awarded its C of A in August 1932
and was then renamed *Arethusa.*
The name *Atalanta* was re-allocated
to a later aircraft, G-ABTI, which
on 31 December 1932, piloted by
H. G. Brackley, left on the first
proving flight to Cape Town, where
it arrived on 14 February 1933. All
eight Atalantas had been delivered
by the end of April 1933, and on
29 May the seventh aircraft
G-ABTL *Astraea,* left on the first
proving flight to Australia. Fitted
with auxiliary fuel tanks, it reached
Melbourne on 30 June 1933.

The Atalantas were intended
primarily for employment on the
Karachi-Singapore and Nairobi-
Cape Town sectors of Imperial Airways' Far Eastern and South
African routes, and the former
service was opened by G-ABPI on
7 July 1933. From Singapore
passengers were taken on to
Australia by QANTAS aircraft.
The Karachi-Singapore service continued until 1 March 1938, when
it terminated at Calcutta, and
was suspended in mid-1939. One of
the four Far Eastern Atalantas,
G-ABTK *Athena,* was burnt out in
a hangar fire at Delhi in September

1936, and G-ABTH *Andromeda* was withdrawn from service in June 1939. The other two, G-ABPI and G-ABTM *Aurora*, had operated since August 1933 as VT-AEF and VT-AEG in the colours of Indian Transcontinental Airways (ITCA), an associate airline formed on 21 June 1933 in which Imperial Airways had a 51 per cent holding. The two ITCA Atalantas, and G-ABTI, G-ABTJ *Artemis* and G-ABTL from the African service (G-ABTG *Amalthea* having been lost in a crash at Kisumu in July 1938), were impressed in April 1941 for service with the Indian Air Force.

42 Armstrong Whitworth A.W.27 Ensign

Following the decision in 1934 to inaugurate the Empire Air Mail Scheme, two major new aircraft types were ordered by Imperial Airways with particular emphasis on greater range and payload than the types then in its fleet. Of these two, unquestionably the more successful was the Short 'C' class flying-boat, described in the companion volume *Flying-Boats and Seaplanes since 1910*. The other was the Armstrong Whitworth Ensign, which, although representing less of a gamble on the part of the airline, was the largest British landplane of its time. As events turned out, it was something of a disappointment, and had performed little useful airline service before the outbreak of war.

The airline made its requirements known early in 1934, and a design team led by J. Lloyd of Armstrong Whitworth evolved a four-engined monoplane with a thick, shoulder-mounted cantilever wing, and accommodation for up to 40 passengers in an elegantly-contoured fuselage. In 1935 Imperial Airways ordered twelve aircraft, including the prototype, but it was nearly three more years before the first aircraft (G-ADSR) made its first flight at Hamble on 24 January 1938. The second A.W.27 flew for the first time on 26 May of that year. Preliminary test flights revealed shortcomings in the rudder control and fuel feed system, but the chief problem lay in the unreliability of the four 880 hp Armstrong Siddeley Tiger IX engines. Nevertheless, Imperial Airways initiated route-proving flights with the Ensign in October 1938, and with the approach of Christmas assigned three to fly the heavy seasonal mail to Australia. The results were, to say the least, unfortunate: two of the aircraft succumbed to engine trouble, and the third to a fault in the landing gear. The Ensigns were returned for modification, from which they emerged refitted with 920 hp Tiger VIII or IXc engines and de Havilland constant-speed propellers. From mid-June 1939 they began to be re-delivered to Imperial Airways, flying on European routes on a limited basis until the outbreak of war, and all twelve were back with the airline by October 1939. During 1940 four of the twelve were lost: two to enemy action, one in a forced landing, and one scrapped. However, in late 1936 the original order for twelve aircraft had been increased by two, which had not been delivered prior to the outbreak of war. Moreover, Imperial Airways had in 1939 suggested a refit with 1,100 hp Wright GR-1820-G102A Cyclone engines. These were fitted in the two final aircraft in 1941, the first flight being made by G-AFZU as the prototype Ensign II on 20 June 1941, and the surviving Ensign Is were also brought up to Mk II standard. Four of the original dozen were completed to 'European' configuration, seating up to 40 passengers in three main cabins and an optional rear cabin. The 'Empire' version, using only the three main cabins, had daytime seating for 27 passengers (9 per cabin), or could be converted as a sleeper transport with 20 bunks. There was a flight crew of 3, and 2 stewards. Between the first and second cabins, beneath the wing centre-section, was a promenade deck (on the port side), a galley and 2 toilets. It was planned at one time that the four 'Empire' aircraft should be operated by Indian Transcontinental Airways, but this plan was abandoned after the outbreak of World War 2.

43 Junkers F 13
A Junkers policy of encouraging airline growth by making it so freely available, combined with its own undoubted merits, made the Junkers F 13 one of the real pioneers of early commercial air transport. It was in production from 1919 to 1932, during which time three hundred and twenty-two were built, and these served in two dozen or more countries, including almost every major state in South America. The origins of the F 13 can be traced back to the Junkers J 10 all-metal attack monoplane, described under its military designation CL.I in the *Fighters 1914–19* volume. Immediately after the end of World War 1 Junkers' chief designer, Dipl Ing Otto Reuter, was instructed to develop a transport aircraft using the same constructional techniques and materials.

Two designs were produced – the J 12, which was little more than a modified J 10 (and was not built) and the J 13, subsequently re-designated F 13. The identity of the prototype is not absolutely certain, but it seems possible that this was the aircraft registered D183 and named *Herta*, after the eldest daughter of Prof Junkers. The first flight, with a 160 hp Mercedes D.IIIa engine, was made on 25 June 1919, and on 13 September 1919 a Junkers F 13 – possibly the prototype – carrying 8 people flew to an altitude of 22,145 ft (6,750 m). Germany was excluded at the time from membership of the FAI, which precluded the flight from being recognised as an official international class record. It is probable that, for this flight, the aircraft was to production standard with increased wing span and a 185 hp BMW IIIa engine.

Major airline operators of the Junkers F 13 included AB Aerotransport (Sweden); Ad Astra Aero (Switzerland); Aero-Express (Hungary); Aerolot (Poland); Aeronaut (Estonia); Aero O/Y (Finland); Aero Traffic (Switzerland); CSA (Czechoslovakia); Deruluft (Germany-USSR); Deutscher Aero Lloyd; Deutsche Luft Hansa; Dobrolet (USSR); Junkers Luftverkehr; LARES (Romania); Lloyd Aereo Boliviano; Ölag (Austria); Pacific Airways (Canada); Sabena (Belgium); SAM (Italy); SAP (Portugal); SCADTA (Colombia); Sindicato Condor (Brazil); Transadriatica (Italy); UAE (Spain); Union Airways/South African Airways; Varig (Brazil); and Western Canada Airways. Eight were also operated by the US Post Office Department. Between them these carriers operated about two hundred F 13's, of which easily the largest fleets were those of Junkers Luftverkehr (sixty) and DLH (fifty-five). The former organisation, which existed from 1921 to 1926, served both to operate and to market the F 13, often making these aircraft available at extremely low rates, and sometimes entirely free of charge, to embryo airlines whose growth it wished to encourage.

The F 13 lived fully up to the description 'all-metal', having a metal-framed fuselage, multi-spar metal wings, and a complete covering, including the movable surfaces, of corrugated duralumin sheet. Standard accommodation was for a crew of 2 and 4 passengers. The crew cabin had a semi-enclosed appearance, but was without windows. Proof of the ruggedness of its airframe can be illustrated by the example depicted in the colour section. Delivered to AB Aerotransport in 1924, it was used initially on a Stockholm-Helsinki passenger service. In 1928 it was put into service for night mail operations on the Stockholm-Malmö-Amsterdam-London route, with fuselage letter-box and carrying a postal sorter in addition to the pilot. It was withdrawn from service in 1935 and presented to the Tekniska Museet (Science Museum) in Stockholm, where, except for a period in underground storage during World War 2, it stood outside in Nordic winter conditions for more than 30 years. Restored and repainted by SAS engineers in 1971, it now hangs inside the museum.

The system of designating variants of the F 13 was complicated, though apparently systematic. The original production version, with 185 hp BMW IIIa engine, was designated F 13a; subsequent changes to structure, gross weight etc, produced variants with suffix letters b, c, d, f, g, h, and k. To these were added a second suffix letter denoting the major types of powerplant fitted to later production batches; these were the 200 hp Junkers L 2 (suffix a); 310 hp Junkers L 5 (suffix e); 300 hp BMW IV (suffix i); 380 hp BMW Va (suffix o); and 480 hp Bristol, Gnome-Rhône or Siemens Jupiter VI (suffix ä). Other powerplants fitted at different times are reported to have included the Armstrong Siddeley Jaguar and Puma and the Pratt & Whitney Wasp. It seems that virtually any permutation of airframe standard and engine was possible, resulting in some 60 to 70 different variants of the F 13 during its lifetime. In addition, it was often referred to in a more general form as the F 13L, S or W, according to whether it was fitted with a wheel, ski or twin-float landing gear.

44 Junkers G 23 and G 24

These two closely-similar tri-motor transports were essentially scaled-up developments of the single-engined Junkers F 13. The same basic system of designating variants, by small suffix letters denoting changes in structure, weight and powerplant, seems to have been followed, but since much of the early flight testing and subsequent production could not be done openly in Germany the records of such activities are far from complete. The G 23, first flown in 1924, suffered particularly from these restrictions, which doubtless explains why the principal type was the larger and more adequately powered G 24. Dimensions of the

G 23 included a wing span and area of 92 ft 6 in (28.50 m) and 958.0 sq ft (89.00 sq m) and an overall length of 49 ft 11½ in (15.23 m). The prototype, with a 195 hp Junkers L 2 nose engine and a 100 hp Mercedes D.IIIa on each wing, was notably underpowered; but with a more realistic production installation of two wing-mounted L 2's and a 110 hp L 5 in the nose the G 23 had a cruising speed of 93 mph (150 km/hr) at a gross weight of 12,015 lb (5,450 kg).

The G 23 was clearly regarded as an interim model, and production seems unlikely to have exceeded about ten or a dozen aircraft, of which at least six are known to have been built in Sweden by AB Flygindustri. The principal operators were AB Aerotransport of Sweden and Ad Astra Aero of Switzerland, each of which had four. Two of the Swedish-built G 23's later went to UAE of Spain, and in Poland Aero Lloyd operated one twin-float G 23W. The G 23 entered service with ABA in May 1925 on its Malmö-Hamburg-Amsterdam route, later being relegated to night mail services.

The G 24, first flown in the summer of 1925, had wings of greater span and area than the G 23, but was otherwise similar externally. It had accommodation for 2 pilots, a wireless operator, and 9 passengers in individual armchair seats on each side of a central aisle. Behind the cabin were a toilet and a small baggage compartment, and aft of these a further baggage/freight compartment the full width of the fuselage. There was additional storage space in each wing, the total volume of all four compartments being some 156.4 cu ft

(4.43 cu m). The G 24 was flown originally with three 230 hp Junkers L 2a engines; more common was the use of three 310 hp L 5's or one L 5 and two L 2a's. Other installations, offered or reported, included a 500 hp Isotta-Fraschini nose engine (with what wing engines is not known); three 380 hp Bristol- or licence-built Jupiter radials; three 500 hp BMW Va's; and three 425 hp Pratt & Whitney Wasp or 525 hp Hornet radials.

Known constructor's numbers account for seventeen G 24's built in Sweden (three being conversions of G 23's) and twenty-seven in Germany; it is probable that the total built was about sixty, though it may have been as high as seventy. The principal operator was Deutsche Luft Hansa, which received up to twenty-eight between 1926–27 and kept the type in full-scale operation on its European routes until the end of 1933. In smaller numbers, G 24's were operated by AB Aerotransport (one); Aero O/Y of Finland (one); in Afghanistan (one); Chile (three); by Helleniki Eteria Enaerion Synghinonion in Greece (four); Ölag in Austria (two); Sindicato Condor in Brazil (three); Transadriatica in Italy (three); Turkey (one); and Union Aerea Espanola (four or five). In 1927–28 nine G 24's of DLH and one of the Spanish aircraft were converted to single-engined F 24's with shortened wings and, initially, 750 hp BMW VIu engines. An eleventh F 24 was built and used to flight-test the Junkers Jumo engine.

45 Junkers W 33 and W 34
The W 33 and W 34 (W for Werkflugzeug, or general-purpose aero-

plane) were, respectively, inline- and radial-engined refinements of the passenger-carrying Junkers F 13 intended for a wide range of duties. Many of these duties were military, and both types were produced in substantial numbers. One hundred and ninety-nine W 33's were built during 1927–34, and production of the W 34 and its military counterpart, the K 43, reached one thousand seven hundred and ninety-one.

The W 33 prototype (D-921), which first flew in 1926, was a converted F 13, powered by a 310 hp Junkers L 5 engine, the standard powerplant for most production aircraft. The W 33 was used by the under-cover Luftwaffe for communications and as a patrol seaplane; commercially-operated examples flew in 6-passenger, 2,205 lb (1,000 kg) cargo or mixed-payload configurations and were also used for aerial work. Airline operators included AB Aerotransport (two); Deruluft (one); Deutsche Luft Hansa (fifteen); Junkers Luftverkehr Persien (four or five); Lot (two, converted from F 13); Pacific Aerial Transport (one); and SCADTA (one). In early 1927 two landplane W 33's, D-1167 *Bremen* and D-1197 *Europa*, were prepared for an attempt to make the first east-west aeroplane crossing of the North Atlantic. They were powered by specially-boosted L 5G engines and the fuel load was increased to 660 Imp gallons (3,000 litres) by installing four additional tanks in the cabin. Both aircraft took off from Dessau on 14 August 1927, but had to abandon their attempts because of bad weather. Eventually, *Bremen*, flown by Kohl and von Hühnefeld, made a successful 37-hour crossing on 12/13 April 1928

between Baldonnel, near Dublin, and Greenly Island, Newfoundland.

Although it was used much more widely by airlines, commercial exploitation represented a comparatively small proportion of the large number of W 34/K 43 aircraft built. Operators included AB Aerotransport (two); Canadian Airways (five); Canadian Pacific Air Lines (three); China (one); Deutsche Lufthansa (ten or more); DNL (one); Guinea Airways (four or five); Lloyd Aereo Boliviano (two or more); Pacific Western Airlines (four); SCADTA (one); SETA (one); Sindicato Condor (five); Transadriatica (one); Union Airways/South African Airways (one); and Western Canada Airways (one). The prototype (probably D-922) was powered by a 420 hp Gnome-Rhône Jupiter VI radial engine and flew for the first time in 1926. Production began in the following year, and powerplants for later versions included the 540 hp Siemens Sh 20, 600 hp BMW Hornet C, Armstrong Siddeley Panther and Bristol Mercury VI.

46 Northrop Alpha, Gamma and Delta

Except that it lacked a retractable landing gear, the Northrop Alpha was as advanced a design as the Boeing Model 200 Monomail, of which it was a close contemporary. An all-metal, cantilever low-wing monoplane, the Alpha was designed in 1929 by John K. Northrop, and the prototype (X-2W) flew for the first time in April or May 1930, about the same time as the original Monomail. It was powered by a 420 hp Pratt & Whitney R-1340-C Wasp C nine-cylinder radial engine, and the original model, designated Alpha 2, was designed to carry 6 passengers in a fully-enclosed cabin in the front half of the fuselage. The pilot occupied a single open cockpit aft of the wing trailing-edge. An alternative model, the Alpha 3, was a mixed-payload version capable of carrying 3 passengers and 465 lb (211 kg) of mail or other cargo. Dimensions included a wing span and area of 41 ft 10 in (12.75 m) and 295.0 sq ft (27.41 sq m), and an overall length of 28 ft 5 in (8.66 m). At a gross weight of 4,500 lb (2,041 kg), the Alpha had a cruising speed of 145 mph (233 km/hr) and a range of 600 miles (965 km). It had a good airfield performance, including the ability to take off and land in 600 ft (183 m) or less. Production began in late 1930, and a Type Approval certificate was issued in November of that year. One aircraft, probably the prototype, was delivered to National Air Transport, and another (registered NS-1) was built as a personal transport for the US Assistant Secretary of Commerce for Aeronautics. The major customer, however, was TWA (Transcontinental and Western Air), which purchased three Alpha 2's (NC127W, NC11Y and NC966Y) and six Alpha 3's (NC933Y, NC942Y, NC947Y, NC961Y, NC993Y and NC999Y); these entered service in 1931. To these TWA added four examples (NC985Y, NC986Y, NC992Y and NC994Y) of a mail-only version known as the Alpha 4. This carried a pilot only, with a 1,060 lb (480 kg) cargo; it differed in having only a single cabin window on each side, and cantilever main undercarriage units enclosed in 'trouser' fairings. Eventually TWA brought all of its Alpha 2's and 3's (except NC966Y, which was converted to an Alpha

3) up to the standard of the Alpha 4 or the generally similar 4A. By the time TWA flew its last Alpha service, on 19 February 1935, the fleet had amassed a total of 5,413,736 miles (8,712,545 km) in some four years of operation. Three other Alphas were delivered to the US Army Air Corps for evaluation as a YC-19 and two Y1C-19's, but no military orders ensued.

The next major development of the design was the Gamma (the Beta having been a scaled-down Alpha for the private-owner and sport-flying market). The Gamma was essentially an extension of the mail/freight-carrying Alpha 4, produced in 1933. Among the thirty-eight built were NC12269, used by the Ellsworth transAntarctic Flight, and one Britishregistered example, G-AFBT, used as a testbed for a 1,400 hp Bristol Hercules fourteen-cylinder radial engine. An early Gamma was X12265, powered by a 700 hp Wright Cyclone. Named *Sky Chief,* it was flown by racing pilot Frank Hawks from San Diego to New York on 3 June 1933 in a time of 13 hours 27 minutes, at an average speed of 183 mph (294 km/hr). Three Gamma 2-D's (NR13757, NR13758 and NC13759) were delivered to TWA, and in the first of these the airline's vice-president, Jack Frye, set a new US cargo transport record on 13/14 May 1934 by flying from Los Angeles to Newark in 11 hours 31 minutes with a payload of 440 lb (200 kg). Though its commercial service was less extensive than that of its predecessor, the Gamma did much useful work in exploring the conditions later to be met by new generations of higher-flying transport aircraft travelling 'over the weather'. TWA's NR13758 had an Army turbo-supercharger fitted to its engine, with which it was able to explore icing, turbulence and other high-altitude weather phenomena at heights of up to 35,000 ft (10,670 m).

The final member of this Northrop family was the Delta, originally intended as an 8-passenger development of the Gamma, with the pilot seated in a fully-enclosed cockpit at the forward end of the fuselage. Comparatively few Deltas were built for commercial use. TWA had one only, a Model 1-A (NC12292), which had been in service (as a trans-continental express mailplane) for only three months before it was lost following an engine fire in November 1933. At least one (Model 1-B?) was supplied to Aerovias Centrales SA of Mexico in 1933, as X-ABED; and the third production Delta, designated Model 1-C, was sold to AB Aerotransport of Sweden as SE-ADI. It was intended as an entrant in the 1934 'MacRobertson' race, but did not after all compete and went eventually to a customer in Iraq. Canadian Vickers of Montreal acquired a manufacturing licence for the Model 1-D, derived from the Gamma 1-D, and in 1936-37 built three Mk I and seventeen Mk II Deltas for the Royal Canadian Air Force.

47 Boeing Monomail

Although it did not achieve production status, the Boeing Monomail represented, for its time, an advance in state-of-the-art design and construction techniques which foreshadowed the appearance of the true modern airliners typified later by the Boeing 247, the Douglas DC types and the twin-engined Lockheeds. When the original Model 200 Monomail (NX725W) made its first flight on 6 May 1930, the production of a smooth-skinned, all-metal cantilever low-wing monoplane with a neatly-cowled engine and semi-retractable main landing gear would have been a bold enough step for any manufacturer in the world. For Boeing, to thus break away from the safe tradition of wood-and-fabric-covered biplanes in the midst of the economic depression which followed the 1929 stock market collapse, it was doubly so. In one sense, perhaps, the Monomail was too far ahead of its time for its own good, for it appeared before the development of the variable-pitch propeller, which would have enabled it to make the fullest use of its engine power. As it was, the only propellers then available had to have their pitch pre-set before a flight, which meant that an operator could select for either a take-off with full payload or a high cruising speed once airborne, but not both. By the time that variable-pitch propellers were available, the Monomail was about to be superseded by aircraft of later design.

In one respect, which strikes an odd note in the light of its many other advanced features, the Monomail did retain what was soon to become an outworn concept. The pilot still sat in an open cockpit well back along the fuselage, aft of the centrally-located 220 cu ft (6.23 cu m) mail/cargo compartment in the fuselage. This was exactly the same layout as in the Boeing Model 40 biplane of 5 years earlier, and one of two links with the older design, for the Model 200 also had the same powerplant as the Model 40B, a 575 hp Pratt & Whitney Hornet B radial.

Boeing built a second Monomail, the Model 221, shortly after the Model 200. Registered NC10225, it was flown for the first time on 18 August 1930 and was identical to the Model 200 except in one respect. By adding 8 in (20.3 cm) to the length of the fuselage, and reducing the size of the mail compartment, Boeing was able to insert between the engine bay and the mail compartment a cabin to seat 6 passengers. Although this was endowed with four large oval windows on each side, access via the small forward door cannot have been easy and the small cross-sectional area of the fuselage must have made conditions in the cabin somewhat claustrophobic. Nevertheless Boeing put the Model 221 into commercial service with its own operating company, Boeing Air Transport. Eventually both Monomails underwent further modification, in which an additional 2 ft 3 in (0.69 m) was added to the overall length, allowing the carriage of up to 8 passengers and a 750 lb (340 kg) load of mail or cargo. In this configuration the aircraft were designated Model 221A, both serving for a time with Boeing Air Transport and the original aircraft later with United Air Lines.

48 Airspeed Courier

The Courier, a small, single-engined feeder-line transport, was not built in great numbers, but made a number of contributions to the advancement of aircraft design and operating techniques during the 1930s. Among British aircraft, it was the first type with a retractable landing gear to go into series production – yet, paradoxically, this feature was eliminated from many Couriers later in their service. Designed by A. H. Tiltman, the prototype A.S.5 Courier (G-ABXN) was completed in 1932, and made its first flight on 11 April 1933, powered by a 240 hp Amstrong Siddeley Lynx IVc engine. It was designed for use by Sir Alan Cobham in an attempt to make a non-stop flight from England to India, using the technique of aerial refuelling, and the cabin space was occupied by additional fuel tanks. The attempt, in September 1924, had to be called off after the aircraft reached the Sudan, though a successful refuelling from a Handley Page W10 tanker aircraft had been made over the English Channel.

A production line of fifteen Couriers was laid down, and twelve of these were eventually completed as A.S.5A's, having the same powerplant as the prototype but increased normal fuel tankage and a tailwheel instead of the prototype's tailskid. Standard accommodation was for a pilot and 5 passengers, equivalent to a payload of 881 lb (400 kg). The first production Courier, G-ACJL, was entered for the 1934 'MacRobertson' race from England to Australia; it gained fourth place in the handicap section, and at the end of the year was sold to an Australian buyer to become VH-UUF. First airline customer was Portsmouth, Southsea and Isle of Wight Aviation, which initially flew two Couriers (G-ACLR and 'LT) on its ferry service across the Solent in 1934. Two other A.S.5A's (G-ACSY and 'SZ) were delivered at about the same time to London, Scottish and Provincial Airways, which opened a Leeds-London-Paris service on 6 August 1934 but lost G-ACSY in an accident at the end of the following month. Another Courier, G-ACLS of Air Taxis Ltd, suffered a crash in October 1934, LSPA lost its second Courier in May 1937, and another aircraft, G-ACVE, was crashed in August 1936 in an attempted hijacking by its ground crew, who intended to fly it to Spain to take part in the Civil War. All of the other ten British-based Couriers survived until the outbreak of World War 2, eight of them (G-ABXN, G-ACLF, G-ACLR, G-ACLT, G-ACVF, G-ACZL, G-ADAX and G-ADAY) having spent most of the intervening period in the service of North Eastern Airways and/or Portsmouth, Southsea and Isle of Wight Aviation. The latter operator, finding the retractable undercarriage an unnecessary refinement for the short distances involved in its Ryde ferry service, had its aircraft converted to a fixed landing gear.

Of the eight Couriers listed above, G-ACLF differed in being an A.S.5B, having a 275 hp Armstrong Siddeley Cheetah V engine. One other A.S.5B (VT-AFY) was built in 1934 for the Maharajah of Jaipur. There were two other 'special' Couriers, the first being K4047, an A.S.5A used by the Royal Aircraft Establishment at Farnborough for anti-icing experiments and for testing with various wing and under-fuselage flap systems. The other was G-ACNZ, the sole A.S.5C, which was purchased by Napier for tests with the 325 hp Rapier IV sixteen-cylinder H-type engine. This Courier achieved an average speed of 166 mph (267 km/hr), as compared with the 132 mph (212 km/hr) cruising speed of the standard A.S.5A. It, too, later joined the PSIOW fleet. In 1940 all nine civil-registered British Couriers were impressed into the RAF.

49 Lockheed Orion

Last in the family that stemmed from J. K. Northrop's original Vega design (which see), the Lockheed Model 9 Orion was one of four low-wing derivatives of this famous line. These began with the Model 4 and Model 7 Explorers of 1929 and 1930, single-seat racers with a 450 hp Wasp engine and a top speed of 165 mph (265.5 km/hr). From the Explorer Gerard Vultee developed a long-range 2-seater, the Model 8 Sirius. The first customer for this was Charles Lindbergh who, with his wife as passenger, set up a new US trans-continental west-to-east flight record of 14 hours 45 minutes between Glendale, California, and New York on 20 April 1930. In 1931 and 1933, after it had been converted to a twin-float seaplane, Lindbergh flew it on many survey flights over the North and South Atlantic and the North Pacific on behalf of Pan American Airways. This Sirius, named *Tingmissartoq*, is now in the National Air Museum in Washington. In all, Lockheed built fourteen Sirius (five Model 8, eight Model 8A and one metal-fuselage Model DL-2), of which Bowen Air Lines and Wedell-Williams Air Service each had one. Sirius development continued with the Altair, six of which were built including two DL-2A's with metal-skinned fuselages. Six other Altairs were produced by converting Sirius airframes.

The fourth and last low-wing version, the Orion, was also the most numerous, thirty-five original Orions being built and an additional five produced by conversion.

Major models were the Model 9 (eighteen, including three conversions and one 'Special'), with a 450 hp Wasp SC and seating for 6 passengers inside the front fuselage; and the Model 9D (thirteen built, including one 'Special'), with the same seating capacity but fitted with wing flaps and a 550 hp Wasp S1D1 engine. Other Orion designations signified chiefly a difference in powerplant and included the Models 9B (575 hp Cyclone R-1820-E), 9E (450 hp Wasp SC1), 9F (645 hp Cyclone R-1820-F2) and 9F-1 (650 hp Cyclone SR-1820-F2).

In US domestic service the Orion was in operation at various times with American Airways and Varney Air Service (six each); Northwest Airways, Transcontinental & Western Air, and Wyoming Air Service (three each); Air Express, Bowen, Continental Airways, Inland Air Lines, New York & Western Airlines, and Pan American (two each); and New York, Philadelphia & Washington Airway (one). Outside of the US the major operators were Swissair, which had two, and three Mexican airlines: Trasportes Aéreos de Chiapas (five), Aerovias Centrales (three) and Compania Mexicana de Aviación (two).

50 Clark (General Aviation) G.A.43

Relatively unknown among transport aircraft of the inter-war years, the G.A.43 was nevertheless among the first of the breed of cantilever low-wing, all-metal, retractable landing gear airliners to appear in the early 1930s. Its precise origin is obscure, but the concept of the G.A.43 appears to have begun in about 1929–30 with its designer, Col Virginius Clark, whose name is best known in connection with the Clark aerofoil. Development of the design was somewhat protracted; it was undertaken by the American Airplane and Engine Corporation at Farmingdale, New York, until late 1932, when responsibility for continuing its development was transferred to the General Aviation Manufacturing Corporation of Dundalk, Maryland. The prototype (X775N), then known as the Pilgrim 150, almost certainly made its first flight in 1933, and originally had fabric-covered wingtips and a non-retractable landing gear with streamlined fairings over the main legs and all three wheels. So clean was the design aerodynamically that it was decided to make the main gear capable of retracting backwards into streamlined underwing fairings, and on production aircraft the outer wings had the same aluminium skinning as the rest of the aircraft. Only the wing and tail movable surfaces were fabric-covered.

So far as is known only five G.A.43's, including the prototype, were built. One was fitted with a 575 hp Pratt & Whitney Hornet C radial engine, the others having one version or another of the Wright Cyclone ranging from 625 to 700 hp. The enclosed cockpit seated a crew of 2 side by side, usually with dual controls, and the main cabin could accommodate 10 passengers in individual seats on each side of the central aisle, with a toilet at the rear. After being modified to production standard and serving as a demonstrator, X775N was delivered in 1934 to the Mitsui Bussan in Japan, where it was handed over to the Nakajima company and re-registered J-BAEP. It is believed that the aircraft was dissected, to give the Japanese industry an insight into American techniques of all-metal aircraft construction, later being reassembled and sold to the para-military transport force of Manchukuo.

Airline service of the G.A.43 was limited to the four production aircraft, the first of which was Swissair's CH 169, delivered in March 1934 and operated on the Zurich-Frankfurt night mail service and on passenger services to Vienna and between Zurich, Basle and Geneva. The fourth ·production aircraft was also operated by Swissair, over the same routes, as HB-ITU. Ordered in March 1935, it was lost in April of the following year when it flew into a mountainside in central Switzerland; fortunately, no passengers were on board at the time. Later in 1936 Swissair sold its original G.A.43 to a French organisation which then made it available to the Republican forces during the Spanish Civil War.

The other two G.A.43's were both sold to US customers, Western Air Express operating the second (NC13903) between Cheyenne and Albuquerque. The third (NC13904) was purchased by Pan American Aviation Supply Corporation and operated by SCADTA on a route along the Magdalena River in Colombia. Given the fleet name *Bolivar,* this was the Hornet-powered machine; it was designated G.A.43-J and differed also from the other examples in having twin Edo floats and an enlarged main fin; a small underfin was fitted initially, but was later removed.

51 General Aircraft Monospars

The original Mono-Spar concept, developed by H. J. Steiger, was an ingenious attempt to produce a strong but light cantilever wing at a time when most other wings of this type were both thick and heavy. As its name implied, it was built around a single main spar, which was of the Warren girder type, made of duralumin and braced by a series of load-bearing tie-rods, the whole structure being fabric-covered. The designations ST-1 and ST-2 were given to two sets of experimental wings built to this formula at the request of the Air Ministry, which flight-tested the latter set on a Fokker F.VIIb-3m.

The first complete aircraft built to the Monospar principle was the ST-3, the sole example of which (G-AARP) made its maiden flight during the first half of 1931, powered by two 45 hp ABC Salmson 9Ad radial engines. It was a 3-seat low-wing monoplane, constructed on behalf of the Monospar Wing Company by Gloster Aircraft Ltd, and had a maximum speed of 110 mph (177 km/hr). Although scrapped in September 1932, its flight performance was successful enough to lead to the formation of General Aircraft Ltd to build further aircraft to the Monospar formula. These began with six ST-4's, the first of which (G-ABUZ) was flown in May 1932. The ST-4 was basically a scaled-up ST-3, with two 85 hp Pobjoy R radial engines and accommodation for 4 persons. Two went into airline service: one with Alpar Bern of Switzerland and one in the UK with Portsmouth, Southsea and Isle of Wight Aviation, which used it for a ferry service between Portsmouth, Ryde and Shanklin. From 1933 there followed twenty-four ST-4 Mk II's, with detail improvements including a nose-mounted landing light. Most of these went to private owners, but airline customers included Highland Airways, International Airlines and Lundy and Atlantic Coast Air Lines. The next Monospar was the 5-seat ST-6, which had an enlarged cabin, restyled forward fuselage, improved engine cowlings and a manually-retractable main landing gear. Two were built, the first (G-ACGI) flying for a time with Southern Airways and the other being fitted with 90 hp Pobjoy Niagara I seven-cylinder radial engines. A third ST-6 was produced by converting one of the ST-4 Mk II's. The Niagara I was also the powerplant for the Monospar ST-10. This reverted to a fixed undercarriage, but had a much-redesigned fuselage, taller cabin, more pointed nose and restyled fin and rudder. Despite its greater frontal area, improvements in body shape and flying attitude gave the ST-10 an extra 10 mph (16 km/hr) on its top speed, which enabled G-ACTS to achieve a convincing win in the King's Cup air race on 13/14 July 1934. Flown by H. M. Schofield, with Steiger as passenger, the ST-10 completed the course at an average speed of 134.16 mph (215.91 km/hr). In later years it served with PSIOW on the Ryde ferry service and on the route to Heston. One other ST-10 was built; this was for an Australian customer, as were the two retractable-undercarriage ST-11's delivered to Eastern Air Transport for its Sydney-Canberra service in 1935. The ST-12 was a developed version with 130 hp Gipsy Major in-line engines, which gave it improved speed, ceiling and climb performance despite a slightly higher gross weight. Total production of this version is not known, but none of the four British-registered examples was built for an airline customer.

Two new Monospar designs appeared in 1935, the first of which was the ST-18 Croydon. This was a 10-passenger transport, with two 450 hp Pratt & Whitney Wasp Junior SB-9 radial engines and a fully-retractable undercarriage. Its sweptback wings, strut-braced to the top of the fuselage, had a span of 59 ft 6 in (18.14 m), and at a gross weight of 9,000 lb (4,082 kg) it had a maximum cruising speed of 176 mph (283 km/hr) at 9,700 ft (2,956 m) and a maximum range of 880 miles (1,416 km). Only one (G-AECB) was built, which was lost in October 1936 on a return flight from Australia.

The final Monospar built in quantity was the ST-25, a developed version of the ST-10 with 90 hp Niagara II engines. The prototype (G-ADIV) first appeared in mid-1935, and the initial 5-seat version was known as the ST-25 Jubilee. British airline operators included Crilly Airways (three), PSIOW (two) and Air Commerce (one). The ST-25 De Luxe, which appeared in March 1936 (prototype G-AEDY), had 4 seats, 95 hp Niagara III engines and an enlarged fin. This aircraft was later rebuilt as the prototype ST-25 Universal, and the only other De Luxe, G-AEGX, was converted from a Jubilee to ambulance configuration for the British Red Cross. The ST-25 Universal differed from all previous Monospars in having a twin-fin-and-rudder tail assembly, to improve directional control with one engine shut down, and 1 ft 0 in (0.31 m) shorter overall length. The outer wing panels could be folded, reducing the overall span to only 14 ft 11 in (4.55 m). The Universal could maintain an altitude of 4,500 ft (1,372 m) on one engine for prolonged periods. The original De Luxe, G-AEDY, was rebuilt to serve as the Universal prototype, and this twin-finned version entered production in the autumn of 1936. It was offered as a standard passenger transport (pilot, 3 passengers and baggage), ambulance, or freighter. Twenty-six Universals were built (a little less than half the total ST-25 production between 1936 and 1939), and several of these – mostly freighters – found their way into airline service. Seven went to Eastern Canada Air Lines, and others were operated by Utility Airways in the UK and Airlines (WA) in Australia. Other ST-25's were used for various experimental purposes, including cabin pressurisation, one with a nosewheel landing gear and another fitted with Cirrus Minor 1 engines. In the spring of 1940, twenty Monospars (three ST-4's, one ST-6, one ST-10, two ST-12's, four ST-25 Jubilees and nine Universals) were impressed for wartime duties with the RAF.

52 Boeing Model 247

The design and structural innovations introduced by Boeing with the single-engined Monomail first found their full commercial expression in the twin-engined Model 247, the first example of which (X13301) made its first flight on 8 February 1933. Prior to this, in 1931-32, Boeing and the potential operating members of United Aircraft and Transport Corporation had discussed a number of other proposals for a replacement for the ageing Boeing Model 80's and Ford Tri-motors in their current fleets. These included a biplane (Model 239) and two high-wing monoplanes

(Models 238 and 243), but all were rejected and Boeing instead developed a new aeroplane, the Model 247, based on the B-9 (Model 215) twin-engined bomber. The 247 introduced some innovations of its own, among them wing and tail de-icing and an aileron and elevator trim-tab system; and it was 50 mph (80.5 km/hr) or more faster than the standard types of airliner then in service. It carried a crew of 2 pilots and a stewardess, and the 10 passengers sat in individual arm-chair seats, at a comfortable 40 in (103 cm) pitch, on each side of the central aisle. There were a galley and toilet at the rear of the cabin, and nose and rear-fuselage compartments of 60 and 65 cu ft (1.70 and 1.84 cu m) for up to 400 lb (181 kg) of baggage and mail. Powerplant was two 550 hp Pratt & Whitney Wasp S1D1 nine-cylinder radial engines, fitted with Townend ring cowlings.

There was no separate prototype of the Model 247. The first flight had been made by a production aircraft, of which the airline members of UATC (Boeing Air Transport, Pacific Air Transport, National Air Transport and Varney Air Lines) had ordered no fewer than fifty-nine in early 1932, while the project was still in the mock-up stage. A sixtieth aircraft was delivered in November 1933 to Pratt & Whitney, which used it both as an executive aircraft and for research. Designated Model 247A, it was powered by two 625 hp Twin Wasp Junior radial engines, with narrow-chord NACA cowlings. Two other airline 247's were ordered, by Deutsche Luft Hansa. These were delivered in 1934 and operated as D-AGAR and D-AKIN. The first 247 delivery to a member of UATC was made on 30 March 1933, and by 1 January 1934 fifty-four of the fifty-nine ordered had been delivered. The four separate airlines combined to form United Air Lines, which became effective under the new title on 1 May 1934.

The next (and only other major) version was the Model 247D, of which thirteen were built. Ten of these, all delivered by November 1934, were for United, which then began to dispose of some of its original 247's to other American operators. The Model 247D had Wasp S1H1-G geared engines, with deep-chord NACA cowlings and variable-pitch propellers, fabric (instead of metal) covering on the rudder and elevators, and a conventionally-sloped cockpit windscreen instead of the undercut one of the initial production version. These modifications resulted in a notable improvement in all-round performance, and were later applied (except, in some cases, that to the windscreen), to most of the American-owned Model 247's. The UAL aircraft were used between points on the west coast, ranging from Vancouver down to San Francisco, Los Angeles and Aguascalientes (Mexico); and to New York and Philadelphia in the eastern United States, by way of Salt Lake City, Cheyenne, Omaha, Chicago and Cleveland. By January 1938 the United fleet had dwindled to twenty-four 247/247D's, thirty-six others having been sold to other operators during 1935–37. Prior to the outbreak of World War 2 they were to be seen in the colours of National Parks Airlines, Pennsylvania-Central Airlines, Western Air lines, Wyoming Air Service and Zimmerley Airlines in the US, and SCADTA in Colombia. One of

the three non-United 247D's had been exported as a 6-seat executive transport for the Chinese warlord Marshal Chang Hsueh-liang, and in January 1937 Boeing acquired an ex-United 247D for delivery to the same customer. This aircraft had two 0.50 in Colt machine-guns in the nose and a third on a ring mounting in a dorsal 'greenhouse' aft of the cockpit; it was then re-designated 247Y.

United Air Lines continued to operate its Boeings until early 1942, when a total of twenty-seven 247D's, including all except one of the UAL fleet which existed at that time, were impressed into the USAAF under the designation C-73.

53   Douglas DC-1 and DC-2
The United States air transport scene in the early 1930s was dominated by large, not particularly cost - effective and generally obsolescent types such as the Fokker and Ford tri-motor monoplanes and the Curtiss Condor twin-engined biplane. The injection into this scene of the smooth-skinned, all-metal Boeing 247, as the exclusive property of United Air Lines, naturally aroused an instinct of survival among UAL's competitors, and in particular at Transcontinental and Western Air Inc. In 1932 TWA's vice-president in charge of operations, Jack Frye, invited five US manufacturers to tender a design to compete with the Boeing 247. Frye specified a three-engined aircraft, to preserve the 'one engine out' safety factor of his existing fleet, but the twin-engined DC-1 (Douglas Commercial No 1) design promised to maintain this safety margin to TWA's satisfaction, and the DC-1 proposal was accepted. The basic configuration,

worked out by James 'Dutch' Kindelberger and Arthur Raymond, was left to John K. Northrop to translate into structural terms, which Northrop did by utilising the same basic multi-cellular system of construction that had proved successful in his earlier Gamma and Delta monoplanes.

Construction of the DC-1 began early in the following year, and the prototype (X223Y) flew for the first time on 1 July 1933, powered by two 700 hp Pratt & Whitney Hornet radial engines. Between the nacelles and the fuselage, forward of the wing leading-edge, were two slim struts. These were fairings over the leads of certain test equipment, and were soon removed. The Hornet-engined DC-1 received CAA Type Approval in November 1933, which was extended in the following February to cover the new installation of two 710 hp Wright SGR-1820-F3 Cyclone radials. In this form the DC-1 not only carried 12 passengers – 2 more than the Boeing 247 – but had a 35 mph (56 km/hr) faster cruising speed and a considerably better range. It was delivered to TWA in September 1933, and on 19 February 1934 set a new US trans-continental speed record between Los Angeles and Newark – the first of 11 US and 8 world speed and distance records which it was to set up within the next few months.

With this kind of performance margin over its nearest rival, it was clear that the DC-1 design was capable of being stretched further without surrendering its overall advantage. Accordingly, TWA decided instead not to order the DC-1 at all, but to purchase a slightly enlarged version, the DC-2. This had more powerful (720 hp)

Cyclone engines and a longer fuselage with an enlarged cabin, enabling it to accommodate 14 passengers and 1,740 lb (789 kg) of baggage and freight. Despite a 500 lb (227 kg) increase in gross weight, the DC-2's cruising speed was 6 mph (9.7 km/hr) faster than the DC-1 and its range was increased by 60 miles (97 km). The only other major differences from the DC-1 were a redesigned rudder and the provision of wheel brakes. An initial order for twenty DC-2's was placed by TWA, which eventually operated thirty-two. The first example, NC13711 *City of Chicago,* was delivered in May 1934, and scheduled DC-2 services began in the following August, between New York and Los Angeles. They remained on this service until their replacement by DC-3's in 1936, when they were relegated to shorter routes. Other US customers to operate the DC-2 included American Airlines (eighteen); Eastern Air Lines (ten); General Airlines (four); Pan American (ten); and Panagra (three).

One other event in 1934 was to have a profound effect upon the DC-2's success in the export market. This resulted from the decision by KLM to enter a DC-2, carrying a standard transport payload, in the 'MacRobertson' air race from England to Australia. When PH-AJU *Uiver,* carrying a cargo of 3 passengers and 30,000 air mail letters, came first in the transport class and second only (to the D.H.88 Comet) in the overall speed class, there was no denying the Douglas transport's capabilities. Eventually, KLM operated a fleet of nineteen DC-2's on its Amsterdam-Batavia service, while its subsidiary KNILM used three more on the Netherlands East Indies domestic network. Other customers included Amtorg, the Russian purchasing organisation, which had one; Australian National Airways (two); the Austrian government (one); Avio Linee Italiane (one); China (six, used by CNAC and Canton Airlines); CLS in Czechoslovakia (five); Deutsche Lufthansa (one); the French government (one); Holyman's Airways in Australia (two); Iberia (one); Japan (six); LAPE in Spain (three); Lot in Poland (two); and Swissair (four). Authorities differ over the exact number of DC-2's built, but the best estimate appears to be two hundred, this total including one hundred and thirty for civil customers, fifty-seven for the USAAC, five for the US Navy and eight others assembled from spares. There were four basic powerplants – 710 or 770 hp Cyclones, and 700 or 720 hp Pratt & Whitney Hornets – though some aircraft were fitted with 690 hp Bristol Pegasus VI engines. In the US, the DC-2 design was also the basis for the Douglas B-18 bomber; in Europe, DC-2 manufacturing licences were acquired by Airspeed and Fokker. Neither licence was taken up, but Fokker acted as European marketing agent for both the DC-2 and its successor, the DC-3.

54 Douglas DC-3

The birth of the DC-3 arose from circumstances similar to those which resulted in the creation of the DC-1 and DC-2. This time the airline chief involved was C. R. Smith, president of American Airlines, who was operating a substantial number of night sleeper services with ageing Fokker tri-motors and Curtiss Condor biplanes. To remain competitive Smith sought an equivalent to the DC-2, which could carry as many passengers in sleeping berths as the DC-2 did in daytime seating. John Northrop of Douglas, working closely with William Littlewood, American's chief engineer, solved the problem by stretching his original DC-1/DC-2 design still further, this time extending the girth as well as the length of the fuselage by making it 3 in (7.6 cm) deeper and 2 ft 2 in (0.66 m) wider. The resulting aircraft, known as the DST (Douglas Sleeper Transport), was thus able to accommodate 7 upper and 7 lower sleeping berths, plus a 'honeymoon suite' at the forward end of the cabin. Wing span was extended compared with the DC-2, and the fin and rudder were restyled and enlarged. The prototype (X14988) was flown for the first time on 17 December 1935.

The career of the DC-3 during and after World War 2 is described in three other volumes in this series; this volume is concerned only with its career as a pre-war airliner, which it is convenient to regard as continuing to the end of 1941. Up to this time a total of four hundred and fifty-five had been built, of which only thirty-eight were DST's – half of them powered by 1,000 hp Wright SGR-1820-G102 Cyclone engines and the other half by Pratt & Whitney R-1830-SB3G Twin Wasps of comparable power. The remaining four hundred and seventeen DC-3's were built as conventional day-passenger transports, and the DST's were eventually converted to this standard as well. The reason is a simple one of basic economics. While the DST was evolved to meet a relatively specialised requirement, Douglas was quick to realise that, by removing the sleeping berths, the larger DC-3 fuselage would accommodate a third row of seats, so giving an increase of 50 per cent in capacity over the DC-2. Airline customers were already impressed with the DC-2's operating costs; when offered a larger aircraft with costs only two-thirds those of the DC-2, even with more powerful (1,200 hp) Cyclone or Twin Wasp engines, they soon produced a flood of orders. Such was the impact of the DC-3 that by 1938 it was carrying 95 per cent of all US airline traffic, and was in service with 30 foreign airlines; a year later, 90 per cent of the world's airline trade was being flown by DC-3's.

The DST/DC-3 entered service on American Airlines' New York-Chicago service in June 1936. American eventually operated the largest pre-war DC-3 fleet, receiving sixty-six. Second largest operator (forty-five aircraft) was United Air Lines, which had to admit the eclipse of its Boeing 247 fleet, now losing money to its Douglas-equipped rivals. UAL began its DC-3 services in June 1937. Other US customers for the DC-3 included Braniff (ten); Delta (six); Eastern (thirty-one); Hawaiian (three); Northeast (two); Northwest (eleven); Pan American (twenty); Panagra (twelve); Pennsylvania-Central (fifteen); TWA (thirty-one); and Western (five). The major foreign customers included AB Aerotransport of Sweden (five); Aeroflot (eighteen); Air France (one); Australian National Airways (four); Canadian Colonial Airways (four); CLS (four or more);

Compania Mexicana de Aviacion; KLM (the first European operator, twenty-four); LAV of Venezuela; Lot of Poland; Malert of Hungary; Panair do Brasil; Sabena of Belgium (two); and Swissair (five). Licence manufacture was undertaken by Nakajima in Japan from 1938, for Dai Nippon K.K.K. (Greater Japan Air Lines), and Soviet licence production as the PS-84 (later Lisunov Li-2) began in 1940. Huge numbers were ordered in September 1940 (and later) for the US Army Air Corps (as the C-47 and C-53) and US Navy (as the R4D-1), and large numbers of civil DC-3's were impressed for military service with designations from C-48 to C-52 inclusive. Many were supplied to the RAF and other Allied air forces during World War 2. About five or six were acquired by advancing German forces in Europe, and were handed over to Deutsche Lufthansa.

55 Mitsubishi G3M2

The G3M was evolved in 1934–35 as a land-based, long-range medium bomber for the Imperial Japanese Navy, making its maiden flight in the summer of 1935. By the end of 1937 it was in full production as the G3M1 and G3M2, and an account of its military career is given in the *Bombers 1919–39* volume. In 1938, Mitsubishi also began the conversion of about two dozen G3M2's as commercial transports, with armament deleted and the interior furnished as a cabin for 8 passengers. Most of these were delivered to Greater Japan Air Lines (Dai Nippon Koku K.K.), by whom they were operated on an internal network and on services to China, Formosa, Korea, Thailand and various Japanese-held Pacific islands. Known members of the Dai

Nippon fleet included J-BEOA *Soyokaze,* J-BEOC *Yamato,* J-BEOE and J-BEOG *Matukaze.*

One other well-known civil G3M2 was J-BACI *Nippon,* which was acquired from the JNAF in late 1938 by the Mainichi Shimbun newspaper group. Originally a G3M2 Model 21, it was brought up to Model 22 standard with improved fuselage contours; the interior was modified in similar fashion to the airline G3M2's, and internal fuel capacity was substantially increased. Between 26 August and 20 October 1939 *Nippon* made a much-publicised world tour via Alaska, Canada, the USA, Central and South America, Dakar, Casablanca, Rome, the Middle East, south-east Asia and Formosa, covering 32,845 miles (52,860 km) in a total of 194 hours' flying. Europe had to be avoided owing to the outbreak of war, cancelling original plans to fly by way of Madrid, Paris, London and Berlin. After Japan's own entry into World War 2 the civil G3M2's were operated by Dai Nippon on military duties, together with a number of similar, but armed, conversions of G3M1's and G3M2's as L3Y1 and L3Y2 military transports.

56 Junkers Ju 86

Although it achieved greater prominence in its military guise (see *Bombers 1919–39),* the Ju 86 also achieved some status as a commercial transport during the 1930s, nearly fifty seeing service with eight operators in as many countries. Like its contemporary, the Heinkel He 111, the Ju 86 was designed in 1934 to a joint Lufthansa/RLM specification for a multi-engined aircraft for use both as a bomber and as a commercial transport. The design team was led by Dipl Ing Ernst Zindel, and the two civil prototypes were the Ju 86 V2 (D-ABUK) and V4 (D-AREV), which made their first flights on 22 March and 24 August 1935 respectively.

From the outset, the Ju 86's development was affected by problems with the Jumo engines selected to power it, but production began in 1935 of the initial commercial version, the Ju 86B, equipped with two 600 hp Jumo 205C-4 engines. At least eight examples were built of the pre-production Ju 86B-0, of which HB-IXI, in April 1936, was the first to be delivered to a customer airline (Swissair); five others were delivered to Deutsche Lufthansa, which put them into service in mid-1936 from Berlin to Gleiwitz, Bremen and Cologne and from Cologne to Breslau. The Swissair example, used for a night mail service between Zurich and Frankfurt, was damaged in a crash-landing in August 1936, but six months later was replaced by the Ju 86Z-1 HB-IXE (redesignated Ju 86Z-2 and re-registered HB-IXA after being re-engined with BMW 132 engines). Standard accommodation was for a flight crew of 3, and 10 passengers in individual seats, with a baggage compartment aft of the main cabin.

DLH became one of the two major airline operators of the Ju 86. In addition to accepting the V2, V4 and five B-0's, it also received six Ju 86C-1's, two Ju 86Z-2's and the Ju 86 V24, to make a total of sixteen altogether. By 1937 they were serving on 18 Lufthansa routes, and the Ju 86 fleet remained in service until 1939. In 1940 it was disposed of, probably for use by the Luftwaffe. The C-1 version retained the Jumo 205C

166

powerplant, but featured an extended rear fuselage. The 'Z' designation suffix for civil variants, introduced in 1936, was allocated to three models: the Jumo-engined Z-1 (corresponding to the former B-0 or C-1), sold to Swissair (one, as described above), Airlines of Australia (one) and LAN-Chile (three); the BMW 132H-engined Z-2 for Lufthansa (two) and the para-military Manchuria Air Transport (five or more); and the Hornet-engined Z-7, delivered to AB Aerotransport of Sweden (one, for use on mail services), Lloyd Aereo Boliviano (three) and South African Airways (seventeen). The ABA aircraft was later transferred to the Swedish Air Force, with which it served, under the designation Tp 9, until 1958.

SAA's original intention had been to have its Ju 86's powered by 745 hp Rolls-Royce Kestrel Vee-type engines. Six aircraft for SAA, flown with these engines, were refitted with Hornets before being delivered, and the remainder also were Hornet-powered. The fleet was impressed for service with the South African Air Force in 1939, joining an eighteenth aircraft (a Ju 86K-1 bomber) already acquired by the SAAF for evaluation.

In addition to the forty-eight known airline examples described above, at least ten other Ju 86's bore German civil registrations. Some were military development aircraft, but they included three owned by Hansa Luftbild, an aerial photography company, and D-AXEQ, a Ju 86A Junkers demonstrator.

57 Lockheed Model 10 Electra and Model 12

Just as the Vega and its derivatives formed the foundation on which Lockheed fortunes were based in the late 1920s, so the Electra was the aircraft on which its hopes were built anew after those fortunes suffered a near-fatal blow in the post-depression years of 1929–32. As related in the Vega description, the Detroit Aircraft Corporation acquired a controlling interest in the Lockheed Aircraft Co in July 1929. In October 1931 Detroit and its Lockheed division at Burbank went into receivership, and for eight months Lockheed was kept barely alive with orders for a handful of aircraft, until in June 1932 a small group of businessmen, including Robert E. Gross, airline owner Walter Varney and aircraft manufacturer Lloyd C. Stearman, acquired the company's assets for $40,000. It was re-formed, with Stearman as president, under the new title Lockheed Aircraft Corporation, and by the end of the year had resolved to base its return to world markets on a new, all-metal transport aircraft. At Stearman's instigation, the original proposal was to continue the previous Lockheed pattern of single-engined aircraft, but – probably prompted by the appearance of the Boeing 247, which had made its first flight in February 1933 – it was subsequently decided to change to a twin-engined, retractable-undercarriage project. In its original form this was designed with a single fin and rudder, but when wind-tunnel tests revealed a lack of control for flight on one engine the eventual twin-tailed configuration was evolved instead. The new aircraft, continuing the earlier Lockheed type-numbering sequence, was designated Model 10 and named Electra. It was designed for fast, economical airline operation carrying a crew of 2 and 10 passengers and their baggage. The prototype (X-233-Y) flew for the first time on 23 February 1934, by which time seven Electras had already been ordered, by Northwest Airlines and Pan American; by the following summer orders had increased to twenty-two. The first recipient was Northwest, which carried out proving flights from June 1934 and put the Electra into regular service some two months later. Including small quantities for the USAAC and US Navy, a total of one hundred and forty-nine Electras was built, and up to the outbreak of World War 2 they served widely in the USA, Canada, South America, Europe and Australasia. There were three basic versions: the Model 10A which, like the prototype, had 400 hp Wasp Junior SB2 engines; the Model 10B, with 420 hp R-975-E3 Whirlwinds; and the Model 10E with 450 hp R-1340-S3H1 Wasps and additional fuel capacity. US domestic and international operators included, in addition to the two original customers, Boston - Maine / Northeast, Delta, Eastern, Mid-Continent, National and Pacific Alaska. Elsewhere in the Americas, Electras were operated by Trans Canada Air Lines, Compania Mexicana de Aviacion, Linea Aeropostal Venezolana and Panair do Brasil, and by KLM in the West Indies. On the other side of the Pacific they were to be found in the fleets of MacRobertson Miller Aviation (Australia), Guinea Airways and Union Airways of New Zealand. In Europe, they were operated by British Airways (seven), Lot in Poland (ten), the Romanian airline LARES (eleven) and Aeroput in Yugoslavia (four). Those of British Airways entered service in March 1937 on the Viking Mail Service (Croydon-Hamburg-Copenhagen-Malmö-Stockholm) and were also used between Croydon and Le Bourget.

Many Electras served during the war, after impressment by the USAAC and RAF or, in the case of some Polish escapees, after seizure in Romania by the Luftwaffe. One other military Electra, which flew before the war, deserves mention for its significance in the subsequent development of both civil and military aircraft design. This was the XC-35 (serial number 36-353), sponsored by the USAAC and first flown on 7 May 1937. This had 550 hp XR-1340-43 turbocharged Wasp engines and a modified, circular-section fuselage with a fully-pressurised cabin. It had a service ceiling of 32,000 ft (9,754 m), and won for the Army the 1937 Collier Trophy for its work in high-altitude flight research.

With Electra production in full swing, Lockheed turned in 1936 to the development of a scaled-down version for the feeder-line and business aviation market. This was the Model 12, sometimes known as the Electra Junior. It had the same powerplant as the Model 10A, but seated 6 passengers instead of 10. The Model 12 prototype flew for the first time on 27 June 1936, shortly afterwards winning both the first and second prizes in a design competition staged by the US Department of Commerce. It was built as the Model 12A, a total of one hundred and fourteen being completed, including small quantities for the US Army and Navy. Among just over a dozen which came on to the British Civil Register were two pre-war examples (G-AFKR and G-AFTL) owned by

Sidney Cotton, the latter being used for clandestine aerial photography of German naval installations in the early weeks of World War 2.

58 Lockheed Model 14 and Model 18 Lodestar

The Models 14 and 18 were, in essence, scaled-up developments of the Lockheed Model 10 Electra, the former seating 12 passengers and the latter 14. Each carried a 2-man flight crew and a stewardess. Noteworthy innovations in the Model 14, which earned designer Clarence L. Johnson the 1937 Lawrence Sperry Award, were the introduction of Fowler wing trailing-edge flaps and the use of 'letter-box' slots near the outer wing leading-edges. The first Model 14 was flown in July 1937, and one hundred and twelve were built by Lockheed in three main versions: the 14-H2 (750 hp Hornet S1E2G engines), 14-F62 (760 hp Cyclone GR-1820-F62's) and 14-G3B (820 hp Cyclone GR-1820-G3B's). In 1942, by which time US production of the Model 14 had ended, three were impressed into the USAAC and designated C-111, and one was built as the R4O, a staff transport for the US Navy. Commercial orders were received from a number of US domestic airlines, notably Continental Air Lines and Northwest Airlines, and foreign operators included Aer Lingus, British Airways/BOAC, DNL, Flugfelag, Greater Japan Air Lines, Guinea Airways, KLM (the first European operator), KNILM, Lot, Sabena, Trans Canada Air Lines, and Wideroe's. Most of these were already in service before the outbreak of war in Europe, and the British Airways fleet included G-AFGN, the aircraft used by Prime Minister Neville Chamberlain to fly to his meeting in Munich with Hitler in 1938. A flight of happier import took place in July 1938, when Howard Hughes and a crew of 4 flew NX18973 on a round-the-world flight of 14,791 miles (23,804 km) in 3 days 19 hours 8 minutes. Thirty Model 14-G3B's were exported in 1938 to Japan, where a further one hundred and nineteen, with 900 hp Mitsubishi Ha-26-I engines, were built as military transports for the JAAF by Kawasaki and Tachikawa. Kawasaki also built a similar quantity of a developed version as the Ki-56. BOAC inherited or acquired nine Model 14's: six from British Airways, two ex-Lot and one ex-KLM; they were used chiefly in north-eastern and central Africa during the war years.

The prototype Model 18 Lodestar, converted from a Model 14, made its first flight on 21 September 1939, and differed chiefly in having a lengthened fuselage, to seat up to 14 passengers, and a wing with compound taper. A small number of Model 14's later underwent similar conversion. Total Lodestar production was six hundred and twenty-five, of which four hundred and eighty were to US Army or US Navy wartime contracts (see *Bombers 1939–45*). The civil Lodestar was produced in six principal versions: Models 18-07 (750 hp Hornet S1E3G engines), 18-08 (900 hp Twin Wasp SC3G's), 18-14 (1,050 hp Twin Wasp S4C4G's), 18-40 (900 hp Cyclone GR-1820-G102A's), 18-50 (1,000 hp Cyclone GR-1820-G202A's) and 18-56 (1,000 hp Cyclone GR-1820-G205A's). United States operators included Continental, Mid-Continent (the first Lodestar operator),

National, United, and Western Air Express. In Latin America, Lodestars went into service with Panair do Brasil and LAV of Venezuela, and from October 1942 Sabena considerably extended its Congo network with a mixed fleet of Model 14's and 18's. Another substantial order was placed by South African Airways. Perhaps the largest single airline operator was BOAC, which had in all (though not all at the same time) thirty-eight Lodestars, comprising fifteen Model 18-07's and twenty-three Model 18-08's. This fleet eventually took over all BOAC wartime services in Africa and the Near East, and played a prominent part in running the enemy blockade of Malta.

From the Model 14 and Model 18 were developed, respectively, the Hudson and Ventura bomber and reconnaissance aircraft of World War 2, described in *Fighters and Bombers of World War II*, Book II.

59 Bloch 220

The company headed by Marcel Bloch (better known today as Marcel Dassault) produced two commercial transport designs in 1935 to meet the requirements of Air France. The larger of these, the Bloch 300 Pacifique, a 30-passenger airliner powered by three Gnome-Rhône 14K radial engines, underwent testing in 1935, but was not adopted. Bloch was more successful with the twin-engined Bloch 220, which flew for the first time in December 1935. The wings and horizontal tail surfaces were essentially those of the Bloch 210 bomber, flown a year or so earlier and in production for the Armée de l'Air. The Bloch 220 prototype (F-AOHA) apparently did not go into airline service, but six-

teen production Bloch 220's were built for Air France, to replace its existing Potez 62's and Wibault 282's.

The Bloch 220 carried a crew of 1 or 2 pilots, a wireless operator and a steward. Passenger accommodation was divided into 6-seat forward and 10-seat rear cabins, with a toilet and bar at the rear of the latter and a main baggage/freight compartment in the rear fuselage. The passengers were provided with individual seats, each beside a window, on either side of a central aisle. On 11 August 1936 came the decision to nationalise the major constituents of the French aircraft industry, and the Bloch factories were incorporated in the new Société Nationale de Constructions Aéronautiques du Sud-Ouest, formed on 16 November of that year. In the following month Bloch formed a new company, Société des Avions Marcel Bloch, of which he was the sole administrator and shareholder, and gained the right to receive royalties from the state for his previous designs and to continue to provide, via the SNCASO, certain military prototypes, engines and other equipment of which his company was the constructor.

These administrative rearrangements were no doubt one main reason why Air France did not receive its first five Bloch 220's (F-AOHB *Gascogne*, F-AOHC *Guyenne*, F-AOHD *Auvergne*, F-AOHE *Aunis* and F-AOHF *Saintonge*) until the latter part of 1937. By the following summer another five had been delivered, and when delivery was completed the fleet included F-AOHG *Flandre*, F-AOHH *Savoie*, F-AOHI *Berry*, F-AOHJ *Poitou*, F-AQNK *Anjou*, F-AQNL *Languedoc*, F-AQNM

Provence, F-AQNN *Champagne*, F-AQNO *Alsace*, F-AQNP *Lorraine* and F-ARIQ *Roussillon*. Their first airline operations were in late 1937/early 1938 on Air France's Paris-Marseilles service, followed by the Paris-London service from 27 March 1938 and others to Amsterdam, Bucharest, Prague, Stockholm and Zurich by the end of that year, completely replacing the Potez 62 and Wibault 282 on all Air France European primary routes. An 'every hour, on the hour' service between London and Paris began in the summer of 1939. During World War 2 at least three Bloch 220's were commandeered by the German authorities and allocated to Deutsche Lufthansa.

60 Tupolev ANT-35

Although outwardly of modern appearance for its day – it was designed in 1935 – the ANT-35 did not prove particularly outstanding, and remains a comparatively obscure type. It was designed by a Tupolev design team led by A. A. Archangelski, and the first flight was made in the spring or summer of 1936. On 15 September of that year the prototype (URSS No35) made a demonstration flight from Moscow to Leningrad and back, a round trip of 787 miles (1,266 km) covered in 3 hours 38 minutes at an average speed of 216 mph (348 km/hr). In December 1936 it was displayed statically at the Salon de l'Aéronautique in Paris. Reporters noted, among other things, a poor overall standard of workmanship in its all-metal construction. The wings appear to have been essentially similar to those of the Tupolev SB-2 twin-engined bomber. The main landing gear retracted rearward into the engine nacelles, the

tailwheel being non-retractable. Accommodation was for a crew of 2 or 3 and up to 10 passengers, the cabin being air-conditioned and insulated against external noise. There were baggage compartments under the floor and to the rear of the cabin. Observers were surprised to note the absence of any de-icing provision, and the only concessions to the wintry conditions in which the aircraft later operated were the fitting of spinners to the propellers and perforated baffle-plates in the cowlings in front of the engine cylinders.

Production of the ANT-35 was initiated in 1937, and introduction into regular Aeroflot service came on 1 July of that year from Moscow to Stockholm via Riga. Powerplant for production aircraft was two 850 hp M-85 (Gnome-Rhône 14N) radials which, although each nominally capable of developing some 50 hp more than the engines in the prototype, were not satisfactory in service. As a result the maximum speed of the ANT-35 (alternatively known as the PS-35) was well below the expected 268 mph (432 km/hr).

The total number of ANT-35's built is not known, but is unlikely to have been high; production ended in 1938. The only known operator was Aeroflot, whose fleet included aircraft registered URSS-M131 and -M134. The presence in the Aeroflot fleet at about this time of a Douglas DC-3 registered URSS-M132, and the acquisition in 1938 of a Soviet licence to manufacture the American transport (later designated Li-2), would appear to indicate a fairly short life for the ANT-35, although some may have been used for military transport duties during World War 2.

61 Junkers Ju 52/3m

In the field of commercial aviation between 1919 and 1939, three tri-motor types stand out for their particularly prominent contribution to the world-wide development of air transport: the Fokker F.VIIb-3m, the Ford Tri-motor and the Junkers Ju 52/3m. Of these the German design was eventually built in far greater numbers, though production was predominantly for military purposes. Nevertheless, the pre-war employment of close on two hundred Ju 52/3m's by nearly 30 airlines is a measure of the type's importance in the commercial transport scene.

The original Ju 52 was a single-engined aircraft, designed as a cargo transport and having a 590 cu ft (16.7 cu m) cabin capable of accommodating a 4,067 lb (1,845 kg) payload. The prototype (D-1974), which first flew on 13 October 1930, was powered initially by an 800 hp Junkers L 88 engine, but among the five Ju 52's known to have been built numerous alternative engines were fitted at different stages of their careers. One of these aircraft was operated by Deutsche Verkehrsfliegerschule (DVS) and another by Canadian Airways.

The seventh Ju 52 was fitted with three 575 hp BMW (Pratt & Whitney) Hornet radial engines, with which it flew for the first time in April 1931, and all subsequent aircraft were completed as tri-motor Ju 52/3m's. Accommodation was for a crew of 2 or 3 and up to 17 passengers, with a toilet and a baggage/freight compartment at the rear of the passenger cabin. Like the other Junkers transports described in this volume, it was produced in many variants, with distinguishing suffix letters signifying changes of powerplant, interior layout and so on. Production of the Ju 52/3m began in 1932, the first two examples being delivered to Lloyd Aereo Boliviano. Most pre-war Ju 52/3m's were powered by one version or another of the Hornet engine or its German counterpart, the BMW 132, but other powerplants included Pratt & Whitney Wasp or Bristol Pegasus radials and Hispano-Suiza Vee-type engines. Predictably, the largest single commercial operator was Deutsche Lufthansa. By the end of World War 2 no fewer than two hundred and thirty-one Ju 52/3m's had appeared in the DLH inventory, although the majority of these were operated in wartime on behalf of the Luftwaffe. The highest known DLH peacetime total is fifty-nine, the number taken on charge by the Luftwaffe prior to the outbreak of war in 1939. Other Ju 52/3m's were operated on an almost world-wide basis, by AB Aerotransport (seven); Aero O/Y (five); Aeroposta Argentina (four); AGO, Estonia (one); Ala Littoria (five); British Airways (three); CAUSA (two); the Colombian government (three); DDL (three); Deruluft (five or more); DETA (three); DNL (eight); Eurasia Aviation Corporation, China (five); Iberia; LARES (one); Lloyd Aereo Boliviano (seven); Lot (one); Malert (five); Ölag (three); Sabena (nine); Servicos Aereos Portugueses (one); SEDTA, Ecuador (two); SHCA, Greece (three); Sindicato Condor (seventeen); South African Airways (fifteen); Varig (one); and VASP (three).

62 Spartan Cruiser

Developed from the 1931 Saro-Percival (later Spartan) Mailplane, the Cruiser, which appeared in the following spring, was a small feeder-line transport which served on several British and foreign internal routes during the 1930s. The original Percival-designed aircraft, G-ABLI, was built by Saunders-Roe; its development was subsequently transferred to Spartan Aircraft Ltd. It was powered by three 120 hp de Havilland Gipsy III engines. The original single fin and rudder was replaced by a twin assembly in 1932, when the aircraft was named *Blackpool*, but there was no demand for an all-mail aircraft and G-ABLI was scrapped in early 1933.

Spartan, however, continued to develop the design as a passenger transport, and in May 1932 flew the prototype Cruiser I (G-ABTY), which retained the Gipsy III powerplant but was slightly smaller and had an all-metal fuselage. The accommodation provided for a total of 8 persons, including 1 or 2 pilots. After a number of demonstration flights in Britain and Europe, Spartan initiated a modest production line in 1933 which by May 1935 turned out twelve Cruiser II's and three Cruiser III's. The Cruiser II was generally similar to the Cruiser I, except in the type of engines installed. Standard powerplant, fitted in nine of the twelve aircraft built, was three 130 hp Gipsy Majors; two others, including G-ACBM, the first Cruiser II, had 130 hp Cirrus Hermes IV's, and one was equipped with Walter Major 4's, also of 130 hp. Six of the Cruiser II's were built for foreign customers, G-ACBM being operated by Iraq Airwork as YI-AAA between Baghdad and Mosul. Two were delivered (as YU-SAN and YU-SAO) to the Yugoslav airline Aeroput, two others to the Bata Shoe Company in Czechoslovakia, and one to the Maharajah of Patiala. The manufacturer set up its own operating company, Spartan Air Lines, which on 1 April 1933 opened a service between Heston and Cowes (later Ryde) using, initially, the sole Cruiser I and the Cruiser III's G-ACDW and G-ACDX. After control of Spartan Air Lines had been acquired by the Southern Railway, operation continued under the name Southern Air Services. By that time G-ACDW had been sold (in April 1934) to Misr Airwork of Egypt as SU-ABL, and when G-ACDX (which had briefly borne the fleet name *Hampshire*) was destroyed in a crash in October 1935 its place was filled by the repurchase of G-ACBM from Iraq. Three other Cruiser II's were built for Spartan Air Lines/ Southern Air Services: G-ACSM *Sussex*, G-ACVT and G-ACZM. These, together with the single Cruiser II G-ACYL built for United Airways, and two of the three Cruiser III's, passed into British Airways ownership in late 1935.

The Cruiser III was a development of the Cruiser II, with an aerodynamically-refined fuselage, modified windscreen and tail unit, and fully-faired 'trousered' main landing gear. The overall length was increased to 41 ft 0 in (12.50 m) and the cabin redesigned to seat up to 8 passengers. At the same gross weight as the Cruiser II, cruising speed was increased to 118 mph (190 km/hr) and range to 550 miles (885 km). Three of this version (G-ACYK, G-ADEL and G-ADEM) were built, of which the last-named was destroyed in a crash at Blackpool in November 1936. None of the Cruisers remained long in British Airways service, their performance being too modest for the 'image' required of Britain's second largest airline. Three Cruiser II's and one Cruiser III (G-ACSM, G-ACYL, G-ACZM and G-ADEL) were resold in 1936–37 to Northern and Scottish Airways, which, under its later title Scottish Airways, operated them until the beginning of World War 2. Three were then impressed into the RAF in April 1940, but little or no military use was made of them owing to structural deterioration.

63 Stinson Model A

A comparative anachronism in the era of the Boeing, Douglas and Lockheed all-metal twins, the Stinson Model A tri-motor was built only in modest numbers and remains a relatively little-known type of the latter 1930s. It first appeared in 1933, and was built essentially along similar lines, structurally, to an earlier Stinson tri-motor, the Model 6000 of 1931. A novel feature was its one-piece wing structure, built up on a single steel-tube truss spar, with steel ribs. A dural stressed-skin covering was applied inboard of the wing engines, and fabric covering on the outer panels. The low wing was a genuine cantilever type, the two thick struts on each side being provided solely to absorb part of the landing loads. Standard accommodation was for a crew of 2 and 8 passengers, with a toilet and the main baggage/freight hold at the rear of the cabin. Additional storage space was provided in the rear of each outboard nacelle, and an extra hold could be installed if only one pilot was carried. On some aircraft, an NACA cowling was fitted over the nose engine.

The Model A entered service in mid-1934 with Delta Air Corporation, on the Dallas-Atlanta-Charleston air mail route, and with Central Airlines (later a part of Pennsylvania-Central Airlines) on a five-a-day each-way service between Detroit and Washington, DC. In 1935 the Delta Stinsons were relegated to a night service between Atlanta and Fort Worth. Model A's also operated for a short period in the colours of American Airlines. So far as is known the only other customer was Airlines of Australia, which took delivery of three Model A's (VH-UKK and two others) in 1936 for service on its Sydney-Brisbane route. These passed in 1942 into the hands of Australian National Airways, which at the end of World War 2 modified them to twin-engined aircraft by deleting the nose engine and replacing the wing pair with Australian-built 600 hp Pratt & Whitney R-1340-S3H1 Wasp radial engines, fully cowled and driving larger-diameter propellers. An extra freight hold was installed in the nose. In this form, sometimes known as the Model A/2m, the aircraft's gross weight rose to 11,200 lb (5,081 kg), and performance included a take-off run of 690 ft (210 m) and a cruising speed of 166 mph (267 km/hr) at 7,000 ft (2,135 m).

64 Wibault-Penhoët 28

Produced by Michel Wibault in 1930, this compact French tri-motor in its original Wibault 280 form had accommodation for 2 crew and 8 passengers. The prototype first flew in November 1930, was powered by 300 hp Hispano-Suiza 9Qa uncowled radial engines, and originally bore the unofficial registration F-ADEK. This was changed to F-AKEK when it was acquired by the French government, which subjected it to official acceptance trials in early 1931. Prior to these it had been redesignated Wibault 281T after being refitted with 300 hp Gnome-Rhône 7Kb radials, and Wibault 282T when these were replaced by Gnome-Rhône 7Kd Titan Major radials of 350 hp each. With the increased power available, passenger capacity was increased to 10, in individual seats with a central aisle and toilet and baggage facilities at the rear of the cabin. A second 282T prototype (F-AKEL, also purchased by the French government) was completed, and these two prototypes were certificated in March and July 1932 respectively.

During 1931 Wibault joined forces with Chantiers de Saint-Nazaire Penhoët to form a new company, Chantiers Aéronautiques Wibault-Penhoët, and in 1933 this company built six production Wibault 282's. One of these, F-AMHK, together with F-AKEK, was delivered to CIDNA in 1933, which operated them from Paris to Warsaw via Prague. Apparently the dearth of passengers on the east-west run of this service led CIDNA to develop a cargo contract for carrying lobsters in the cabin – the aroma from which was not entirely appreciated by passengers travelling on the return journey! Two other Wibault-Penhoët 282's (F-AMHN and F-AMHO) were used by Air Union on its Golden Clipper (la Voile d'Or) service which replaced the LeO 213 on its Paris-London service. The CIDNA and Air Union 282's, and the second prototype, all passed to Air France (as F-AKEK Le Frondeur, F-AKEL Le Rapide, F-AMHN Le Vaillant, F-AMHK Le Diligent and F-AMHO Le

Téméraire) upon its formation in August 1933, and the remaining three 282's were delivered direct to Air France as F-AMHL Le Fougueux, F-AMHM L'Intrépide and F-AMHP La Voile d'Or.

Various improvements were made after the 282's entry into service, including the adoption of cowling rings for two (and later all three) engines. The next production version, the Wibault-Penhoët 283, had NACA-type cowlings and its main undercarriage units enclosed in deep 'trouser' fairings. The latter feature created airflow problems over the tail surfaces, resulting in the addition of auxiliary fins and an increase in rudder area.

In 1934 (during which time Wibault-Penhoët was taken over by the Breguet company) ten 283's were built, all for Air France. These were F-AMTS L'Infatigable (prototype, first flown January 1934), F-AMTT L'Imbattable, F-AMYD Le Glorieux, F-AMYE L'Intrigant, F-AMYF Le Vengeur, F-ANBK L'Ambitieux, F-ANBL L'Aventureux, F-ANBM Le Conquérant, F-ANBN L'Invulnérable and F-ANBO Le Merveilleux. In addition, the much-modified F-AKEK and also F-AMHO were also brought up to 283 standard. The Wibault-Penhoët tri-motors were used on the primary European routes of Air France until their replacement in 1938 by the Bloch 220 (which see).

65 Savoia-Marchetti S.73 and S.M.75

By the outbreak of World War 2 Savoia-Marchetti had established a tradition of large tri-motor designs, including the S.M.79 and S.M.84 bombers and S.M.81 and S.M.82 bomber-transports for the Regia

Aeronautica. The commercial tri-motor transport line had begun with the high-wing S.71 (which see), and was followed in the mid-1930s by two low-wing types, each built in quantity. The first was the S.73, which flew on 4 June 1934. The prototype bore no civil registration, and may have been built at the instigation of the Italian Air Ministry; it had the vertical red-white-green fin and rudder stripes then applicable to military aircraft, and the customary fasces symbol beneath the rearmost cabin window. It was powered by three 600 hp Gnome-Rhône Mistral Major 9Kfr engines, and had a tall fin and rudder similar to that of the earlier S.71. The cabin windows were continuous on each side, divided by vertical pillars. Production S.73's differed in having a broader, more squat fin and rudder, separate cabin windows, lengthened nose, and a wide variety of different power-plants. Dimensions included a wing span and area of 78 ft 9 in (24.00 m) and 1,001.0 sq ft (93.00 sq m) and an overall length of 57 ft 3 in (17.45 m). Gross weight of the Stella-engined version was 22,994 lb (10,430 kg), at which the S.73 had a cruising speed of 174 mph (280 km/hr) at 13,125 ft (4,000 m) and a normal range of 634 miles (1,020 km).

So far as can be ascertained, forty-seven S.73's were built in addition to the prototype. The major customer was Ala Littoria, which received twenty-one: ten with 760 hp Wright GR-1820 Cyclone engines, five with 700 hp Piaggio Stella X.RC's, two with 800 hp Alfa Romeo 126 RC 10's, and four others. Sabena had twelve, seven of them licence-built by SABCA and all with 600 hp Mistral Major

9Kfr engines; other recipients were Avio Linee Italiane (six, with Alfa Romeos); CSA (six, with 615 hp Walter-built Bristol Pegasus IIM2's); and the Regia Aeronautica (one, presumably for evaluation).

The S.73 went into service in mid-1935, and operated over a wide area of Europe, including routes to Scandinavia, across the Mediterranean to North and Central Africa, and in the Belgian Congo. Accommodation was for a flight crew of 4, a steward, and 18 passengers. The main cabin lay aft of the wing main spars, and seated 14 persons in individual armchairs on each side of a centre aisle. There was a toilet to the rear of the cabin and space for baggage and small freight beneath the cabin floor. The remaining 4 passengers were seated in a separate forward cabin, elevated above the wing centre-section (which housed the fuel tanks) and on the same level as the flight deck. Beneath the flight deck was a second, smaller freight compartment. The S.73 was still in widespread service at the outbreak of war in Europe, and after Italy's entry into the war in June 1940 thirteen of the Ala Littoria fleet were acquired by the Commando Servizi Aerei Speciale of the Regia Aeronautica.

The S.M.75 was a considerably larger aircraft, and was the first Savoia-Marchetti tri-motor to have a retractable main landing gear. There was apparently no separate prototype, the first flight on 6 November 1937 probably being made by the first production S.M.75 (I-TACO). This and at least twenty-nine more S.M.75's were delivered to Ala Littoria, with whom they entered service in 1938. Standard powerplant was three 750

176

hp Alfa Romeo 126 RC 34 radial engines, although one example (in 1942) is known to have been fitted with 860 hp Alfa Romeo 128's and the five S.M.75's delivered to the Hungarian airline Malert were powered by Gnome-Rhône K14 engines. One S.M.75 was delivered to the Regia Aeronautica, and at least nine others were built whose ownership is uncertain; some of these may also have gone to Ala Littoria.

The S.M.75 carried a flight crew of 3 and a steward, and had standard 3-abreast seating for 24 passengers in two 12-seat cabins separated by a refreshments bar. Passenger capacity could be increased to 30. Aft of the rear cabin were a toilet and a baggage/freight compartment, with additional baggage space under the floor of the rear cabin. A smaller compartment was located beneath the front of the forward cabin, ahead of the wing leading-edge. On 9 January 1939 an S.M.75, piloted by N. Prota and G. Bertocco, set up international speed records of 207 mph (333 km/hr) and 205 mph (330 km/hr) over 621 mile (1,000 km) and 1,243 mile (2,000 km) closed circuits while carrying a 22,046 lb (10,000 kg) payload. About a dozen of the Ala Littoria aircraft were impressed for military service when Italy entered World War 2, and a modified version known as the S.M.75*bis* was built specifically as a military transport. A twin-float derivative, the S.M.87, appeared in 1943.

66 Dewoitine 338

This elegant French tri-motor, which formed an important component of Air France's long-range fleet during the late 1930s, was a development of the record-breaking Dewoitine 332 (F-AMMY *Emeraude*), which flew for the first time on 11 July 1933 and subsequently made many much-publicised flights in Europe and to North and West Africa, the USSR and French Indo-China. The D 332, acquired by Air France in November 1933, was a smaller aircraft than the D 338, and accommodated a 3-man flight crew, 8 passengers and 882 lb (400 kg) of baggage or freight. It was powered by three 575 hp Hispano-Suiza 9V engines, and had a non-retractable landing gear with 'trouser' fairings over the main units. In January 1934, when almost home after a triumphant flight to Saigon, it crashed in appalling weather, with no survivors.

The sole D 332 was followed by three examples of the larger Dewoitine 333 (F-AKHA *Antares,* later F-ANQA, F-ANQB *Cassiopée* and F-ANQC *Altair*), delivered to Air France in 1935. The D 333 had accommodation for 2 more passengers than the D 332, and on 17 May 1935 inaugurated a Toulouse-Dakar service as part of the Air France route to South America. The type was later used in South America, on the sector between Buenos Aires and Natal, Brazil.

Air France placed an initial order for twenty-one examples of the D 338, which first flew in 1935, and eventually acquired twenty-nine D 338's of its own, as well as being responsible for operating one of the two others that were built for the French government. Seating capacity varied according to the routes flown, ranging from 22 passengers on short-haul routes in Europe and to North Africa, to 15 or 18 on middle-distance routes and 12 (including 6 in sleeper accommodation) on long-range sectors. The cabin was well soundproofed, which perhaps was just as well if one accepts a wartime attempt to aid identification of the Dewoitine 338 which declared: 'In the air this aeroplane emits a great noise, like a flight of Harvards'. First operations began in mid-1936, at first between Paris and Cannes; later it was flown on the Paris-Dakar route. An experimental Paris-Hanoi flight in January 1938 paved the way for a regular Damascus-Hanoi service, and on 10 August that year the route was extended to Hong Kong. During the early months of World War 2 the Dewoitine 338 was used on the Paris-Heston service; after the fall of France a number were operated by LAM (Lignes Aériennes Militaires) between Beirut and Brazzaville, and seven were seized by the German forces and allocated to Deutsche Lufthansa.

67 Focke-Wulf Fw 200 Condor

Several of the German warplanes of World War 2 originated before the outbreak of hostilities in designs intended to meet joint military and civil requirements. One which originated purely as a commercial transport design was the Focke-Wulf Condor, developed to meet a Lufthansa requirement for a 26-passenger long-range airliner. Design work, led by Prof Dipl Ing Kurt Tank, began in the spring of 1936 and was rewarded with a development contract in July of that year. In the following autumn Focke-Wulf began the construction of three prototypes, and made plans for a pre-series production batch of nine more. The Fw 200 V1 first

prototype, which flew on 27 July 1937, was powered by four 875 hp Pratt & Whitney Hornet S1EG radial engines. Shortly after this flight it received the identity D-AERE Saarland. The V2 second prototype (D-AETA Westfalen) was essentially similar, but was powered by 720 hp BMW 132G-1 engines. The similarly-powered V3, one of two Condors acquired by the Luftwaffe as VIP transports for the use of Adolf Hitler and his staff and advisers, became D-2600 and was named Immelmann III; later in its career its markings were varied as WL+2600 and later still as 26+00. The BMW 132 was retained for seven of the nine Fw 200A-0 pre-production batch, five of which were allocated to Deutsche Lufthansa and were also given Versuchs numbers. These were the V4 (D-ADHR Saarland), V5 (D-AMHC Nordmark), V6 (D-ACVH Grenzmark), V7 (D-ARHW Friesland) and V9 (D-AXFO Pommern). Of these, the V6 and V7 were powered by 750 hp BMW 132L engines, the remainder being powered by the BMW 132G-1. Two BMW-powered Fw 200A-0's were delivered, in July and November 1938, to the Danish airline DDL as OY-DAM Dania and OY-DEM Jutlandia respectively. The remaining two pre-series aircraft, which were Hornet-powered, were delivered to Sindicato Condor SA of Brazil in August 1939 as PP-CBI Abaitara and PP-CBJ Arumani. Standard accommodation in the Condor included a 9-passenger smoking compartment in the forward fuselage and a rear main cabin for 16 or 17 passengers.

The Condor first demonstrated its long-range capabilities outside Germany when the V4 made a flight from Berlin to Cairo via Salonika on 27 June 1938, and quite soon after this DLH and DDL put the Condor into operational airline service. Further publicity came on 10 August 1938, when the Fw 200 V1 left Berlin for a non-stop flight to New York, for which it was redesignated Fw 200 S1, re-registered D-ACON and renamed *Brandenburg*. It arrived at Floyd Bennett airfield 24 hours 55 minutes later, and completed the return flight in 19 hours 47 minutes. On 28 November 1938 it began an equally spectacular flight, this time reaching Tokyo in 42 hours 18 minutes flying time from Berlin, with refuelling stops at Basra, Karachi and Hanoi. Unfortunately the aircraft was lost shortly after-wards, when it ditched on its approach to land at Manila, but its visit to Japan had not been without success, for it brought an order for five Fw 200B's from Dai Nippon KKK, and a request from the Imperial Japanese Navy for a sixth equipped as a potential reconnais-sance-bomber. In the event, the fulfilment of this order – and of another from Aero O/Y of Finland for two Fw 200B's – was prevented by the outbreak of war in Europe, but four B-series Condors were completed and allocated to Deutsche Lufthansa. These comprised one B-1 (D-ASBR *Holstein*), with 850 hp BMW 132Dc engines; and three B-2's (D-ABOD *Kurmark*, D-ASHH *Hessen* and D-AMHL *Pommern*), with 850 hp BMW 132H-1 engines. The new *Pommern* was a replace-ment for D-AXFO, which was lost shortly after the outbreak of World War 2. One other Condor – D-ASVX *Thüringen*, the first Fw 200C-0 – was allocated to Luft-hansa, but before delivery it and

the rest of the DLH fleet were ac-quired by the Luftwaffe in the spring of 1940 and employed as troop transports during the Ger-man invasion of Norway.

The two Danish Condors con-tinued to operate a Copenhagen-Amsterdam-UK service for some months after the outbreak of war, until OY-DAM was impounded in Britain early in April 1940. It sub-sequently flew for a time in BOAC markings as G-AGAY *Wolf*.

68   Junkers Ju 90

The first design studies which led to the commercial transport version of the Ju 90 were made in the spring of 1936, using as a basis Junkers' existing design for the Ju 89 long-range bomber. At the end of that year, when it became apparent that the latter project would prove abortive, Dipl Ing Ernst Zindel and his design team obtained permission to utilise the wings, powerplant, landing gear and tail assembly of the Ju 89 V3 in the construction of a prototype for the proposed transport. This proto-type, the Ju 90 V1 (D-AALU *Der Grosse Dessauer*), made its first flight on 28 August 1937, powered by four 1,050 hp Daimler-Benz DB 600A engines, but broke up in flight on 6 February 1938 while under-going flutter tests. The life of the V2 (D-AIVI *Preussen*) was almost as short: it crashed at Bathurst in December 1938 while undergoing tropical trials for Deutsche Luft-hansa. The Ju 90 V2 was the first of a second batch of three proto-types powered by 800 hp BMW 132H radial engines. A crew of 4 was carried, and the passenger accommodation was offered in two basic alternative layouts. In one the fuselage was divided into 5 equal cabins, each having facing pairs of seats on each side of a centre aisle, i.e. 40 seats in all. The two forward cabins were designated as smoking compartments. The alternative layout provided for two larger cabins, a 16-seat smoker forward and a main rear cabin seating 22 or 24 passengers. Forward and aft of the passenger cabins were cloakrooms, toilets, a galley and mail or baggage compartments, and there was additional baggage space in the wing centre-section beneath the cabin floor.

In view of the early demise of the first two prototypes, much of the publicity and route-proving flying devolved upon the Ju 90 V3 (D-AURE *Bayern*), which was completed early in 1938 and was used for the first Lufthansa services with the type between Berlin and Vienna later that year. The V4 (D-ADLH *Sachsen*) was the prototype for the Ju 90B-1 production version, of which eight were ordered by DLH. These were the V5 (D-ABDG *Württemberg*), V6 (D-AEDS *Preussen*, replacement for the V2), V7 (D-ADFJ *Baden*), V10 (D-ASND *Mecklenburg*), V11 (D-AFHG *Oldenburg*), V12 (D-ATDC *Hessen*), V13 (D-AJHB *Thüringen*) and V14 (D-AVMF *Brandenburg*). Two other B-type aircraft, with Twin Wasp SC3G engines, were ordered by South African Airways and designated Ju 90Z-2; they were allocated registrations ZS-ANG and ZS-ANH, but were not delivered and instead received Versuchs numbers V8 and V9 respectively.

Not all of the aircraft listed were actually operated by Lufthansa, and the Ju 90's pre-war airline service was of a rather limited nature, although a daily Berlin-Belgrade service was operated in 1940. Earlier, a project had been launched in 1937 to develop a more powerful version, the Ju 90S. After the conquest of Poland the Ju 90S development team transferred its activities to the Letov works at Prague-Letnany, where development work led, not to a new commercial transport version, but to the Ju 290 military transport for which D-AFHG eventually became the prototype.

69 Boeing Stratoliner

The Stratoliner, the first four-engined pressurised airliner to be built in the United States, originated in December 1935 as a transport counterpart to the Boeing Model 299 Flying Fortress bomber. The original project, initiated in parallel with the Model 299, was known as the Model 300, but was soon developed into a later project with the Boeing Model number 307. This was designed to use, virtually unchanged, the complete wings, power installation and tail assembly of the B-17C Flying Fortress, the only notable change being the introduction of leading-edge 'letter-box' slots on the outer wings. An entirely new fuselage, some 3 ft 6 in (1.07 m) greater in diameter than that of the bomber, could accommodate a flight crew of 5 and 33 passengers. If required, the cabin could be converted to a 16-berth sleeper transport, with space for 9 other passengers in reclining sleeper chairs.

No separate prototype was built, Boeing preferring to await firm airline orders before beginning manufacture. These came in 1937, when Pan American Airways ordered four Stratoliners and TWA six (later reduced to five). A production line of ten aircraft was then laid down, and the first flight, on 31 December 1938, was made by NX19901, the first of the Pan American aircraft. This, unfortunately, was destroyed during a test flight in March 1939, but the programme was continued by subsequent aircraft off the line. The second and subsequent Stratoliners had a fully-pressurised passenger cabin, as envisaged in the original design. Only one major design change, an increase in the vertical tail area, was found to be necessary. The second PanAm aircraft, NX19902, flew experimentally in early 1939 with a long, straight dorsal fin fairing, but the configuration eventually adopted was a complete redesign incorporating a smaller-area rudder and an enlarged fin with curving dorsal fairing, resembling closely the surfaces introduced later on the B-17E Flying Fortress.

The three Pan American Stratoliners (NC19902, NC19903 and NC19910) were delivered in 1940. They were named *Clipper Rainbow, Clipper Flying Cloud* and *Clipper Comet*, and were designated Model S-307, although often referred to as PAA-307. They were powered by four Wright GR-1820-G102A Cyclone engines, each developing 1,100 hp for take-off, and were used on services from Brownsville and Los Angeles to Mexico City. The TWA aircraft, designated SA-307B, were generally similar, except for GR-1820-G105A Cyclones and triangular flap hinge fairings under the inboard wing trailing-edges. Identities were NC19905 *Comanche,* NC19906 *Cherokee,* NC19907 *Zuni,* NC19908 *Apache* and NC19909 *Navajo.* Prior to America's entry into World War 2 the utilisation of all eight Strato-

liners was high, and by the time of Pearl Harbor the TWA quintet alone had flown 4,522,500 miles (7,278,210 km) without an accident. From 1942 the PAA trio, flown by airline crews and retaining their civilian markings, were employed on military transport schedules between the USA and South America, being returned to airline ownership in late 1944. The five TWA aircraft, although also flown by airline crews, were given the military designation C-75 during their service with Air Transport Command.

One other Stratoliner was built. This was an SB-307B, delivered in July 1939 to millionaire Howard Hughes and equipped for an attempt – prevented by the outbreak of war – on his own record of July 1938 in a Lockheed Model 14 for a round-the-world flight.

70 de Havilland D.H.91 Albatross

More than 35 years after its first appearance the de Havilland Albatross would still qualify for any list of the world's most handsome aeroplane designs. It was conceived originally as a passenger transport, capable of cruising at 200 mph (322 km/hr), but was ordered in the first instance as a long-range mailplane, capable of carrying a 1,000 lb (454 kg) payload non-stop across the North Atlantic. This order, for two aircraft to Specification 36/35, was placed by the Air Ministry in January 1936, and the design team was led by A. E. Hagg, who had been responsible not only for the D.H.84, D.H.86 and D.H.89 biplane airliners (which see) but for the D.H.88 Comet racing aeroplane which had won the famous 'MacRobertson' race from England to Australia in 1934. For the Comet, Hagg had developed a form of all-wood stressed-skin construction which resulted in an extremely strong thin-section cantilever wing, and the same philosophy was employed in the construction of the new D.H.91. Other noteworthy features of the design were the Gipsy Twelve engines – evolved by Major Frank Halford by uniting two six-cylinder Gipsy Six in-line engines to form a twelve-cylinder Vee – and electrical actuation of the split flaps and main landing gear extension and retraction.

The first of the two trans-Atlantic Albatrosses flew for the first time on 20 May 1937. Originally the twin fins and rudders were strut-braced and inset on the upper surface of the tailplane. After preliminary flight testing, however, the standard form of unbraced endplate vertical surfaces was adopted. Fuel was contained in four fuselage tanks, over the wing centre-section, having a total capacity of 1,320 Imp gallons (6,000 litres), giving the mailplane version a maximum range of 3,230 miles (5,198 km) – considerably better than the 2,500 miles (4,023 km) demanded by the Air Ministry Specification. The mail payload was stowed in a compartment in the rear fuselage, aft of the wings, with access via a door in the starboard side. The aircraft was operated by a 4-man crew, consisting of captain, first officer, wireless operator and navigator. The two Albatross mailplanes, although allotted the military serial numbers K8618, and K8619, instead appeared on the British Civil Register as G-AEVV and 'VW.

Quick to appreciate the economic and visual appeal of the Albatross, Imperial Airways ordered a fleet of five with a 22-passenger interior, and these were delivered from October 1938 as G-AFDI *Frobisher* (flagship), G-AFDJ *Falcon*, G-AFDK *Fortuna*, G-AFDL *Finga* and G-AFDM *Fiona*. In 1939 the two original aircraft were added to the fleet for experimental mail services and were named *Faraday* and *Franklin* respectively. The Albatross passenger version interior was divided into three cabins for 8, 8 and 6 persons, in 4-abreast seating with a central aisle. There was a 4-man flight crew, as in the mailplane, and a cabin steward. Forward of the front passenger cabin, on the port side, was a 58 cu ft (1.64 cu m) baggage compartment, with a galley opposite on the starboard side. Aft of the rear cabin was a toilet and the main mail/freight hold, with a capacity of 158 cu ft (4.47 cu m). The passenger version had about one-third of the fuel capacity of the mailplane, this being disposed in under-floor tanks at the front and rear of the fuselage of 270 gallons (1,227 litres) and 170 gallons (773 litres) respectively. Over a 1,000 mile (1,610 km) range, the passenger version could carry a payload of 4,188 lb (1,900 kg); a maximum payload of 5,388 lb (2,444 kg) could be carried over ranges of up to 600 miles (965 km). Take-off and landing could be accomplished in less than 1,000 ft (305 m). Externally, it could be distinguished by its additional cabin windows (6 each side) and slotted underwing flaps.

After experimental Christmas mail flights (by *Frobisher* and *Falcon*) to Cairo in December 1938, the passenger fleet settled down in January 1939 to operate Imperial Airways' service from Croydon to Paris, Brussels and Zurich. After the outbreak of World War 2 *Faraday* and *Franklin*, after conversion to passenger/mail configuration and a brief period of service with BOAC, were impressed into the RAF. G-AFDI to 'DM, retaining their civilian identities, passed into BOAC ownership in 1940 and were employed on the airline's services to Lisbon (inaugurated on 6 June 1940 by *Fingal*) and Shannon.

BOOK II

AIRLINERS FROM 1946
TO THE PRESENT DAY

THE AIR transport scene after the end of World War 2 was a motley one indeed. Most of the available aircraft plant in Europe had been turning out warplanes at the direction of the Axis dictators; Britain and Russia, too, had concentrated their efforts on mass production of the more militant types. Thus, only the United States had been able to maintain a continuity of transport aircraft production since the pre-war era. With her massive resources she had been able to sustain, for four years, the output of enough aircraft to meet virtually the entire transportation needs of all the major Allied powers: a fact which gave her a marked advantage over the other aircraft-producing nations at the war's end. With the tremendous run-down of military forces that immediately followed, many thousands of war-surplus transports became readily available for sale to airline operators both inside and outside the United States. These aeroplanes had already proved their capabilities under operational conditions far more arduous than any they would meet in peacetime, and so could be put straight into service once their interiors had been 'civilianised'. Furthermore, although many of them had not been developed with operating economics uppermost in mind, their availability provided a valuable breathing space while types with better commercial attributes were designed and tested.

Not all of the aircraft used by airlines during the mid-1940s started their lives as pure transports, however. The mainstay of the French internal and international networks, for instance, was for several years the veteran Junkers Ju 52/3m, designed nearly a decade and a half earlier as a Luftwaffe bomber and only diverted to transport duties after its shortcomings as a bomber had been revealed during the Spanish civil war. Bombers of more recent design, too, were obvious targets for stop-gap conversion to passenger- and freight-carrying duties, because of their size and their ability to fly long distances. The US Flying Fortress and Liberator, and Britain's Halifax and Lancaster, all underwent conversion in this way. Their comparatively modest payloads made them costly to operate, and from an economic viewpoint it was as well that they were only short-term equipment for the larger airlines; but their contribution to the Berlin airlift a year or two later was beyond price. One bomber development that deserves separate mention is the Boeing Stratocruiser, for this descendant of the B-29 Superfortress can justly be regarded as a true airliner in its own right, and its interior appointments for the comfort and safety of its passengers in flight set new standards that were not matched by any other type for several years.

Meanwhile, the latter half of the 1940s saw the gradual emergence of new airliner designs, or developments of older ones, that had been growing on the drawing boards since the middle years of the war. In Britain these were geared chiefly to the recommendations of the Brabazon Committee, and the aeroplanes that eventually resulted from the requirements laid down by this committee met with widely differing degrees of success. The Dove and Viscount, for example, subsequently proved to be first-class money-spinners; rather less fortune attended the Ambassador and the Marathon, while the giant Brabazon suffered the penalty of being ahead of its time and the ignominy of being reduced to scrap after only a few hundred hours in the air.

For many years the four-engined airliner market was largely taken care of by the progressively developed Douglas DC-4/6/7 series and the Lockheed Constellation/Super Constellation range, both originated before and developed during the war. In the realm of the short/medium-range twin-engined airliner, however, despite the numerical preponderance of war-surplus C-46s and C-47s, several new designs began to emerge during the late 1940s and early 1950s. The principal British contender in this field was the Vickers Viking, a tubby but efficient and hardworking design that was a familiar sight on the European networks until the middle 1950s. The more elegant Ambassador also sustained the popularity which attended its introduction by BEA in 1952, and its built-in passenger appeal was surpassed only by the Viscount among post-war British propeller-driven airliners. In retrospect it may be considered a great pity that only about a score of them were built. The fact that fifteen were still in active airline service at the end of 1966 speaks highly for the aeroplane's safety record, as well as for its popularity; and the two factors are not without connection. A similar observation might be made in regard to the Swedish Scandia, another medium twin also built only in modest numbers yet with a service record extending into the late 1960s.

In the Soviet Union, the veteran designer Sergei Ilyushin made his contribution to the medium twin scene, first with the interim Il-12 design and later with the Il-14. The latter, in terms of length and breadth of service, of numbers built and of duties performed, well deserves to be called 'the Russian DC-3', and has been the staple equipment of many Communist bloc airlines, not to mention military squadrons, for much of the post-war period.

The US aviation industry produced two major types in this category, namely the Martin 2-0-2 and the Convair 240. The former, and its derivative the Martin 4-0-4, were built in comparatively modest numbers by US standards, and their employment was confined largely to the Americas. The Convair 240, on the other hand, was ordered extensively by both military and civil customers and its development continued into the second half of the 1960s, following the alliance of its well-proven airframe with the latest turboprop engines.

It was of course the Vickers Viscount which really brought home to the airlines the virtues of turboprop powerplants, and subsequently it became not only the first but – until overtaken in more recent times by the twin-Dart-powered Friendship – by far the most successful airliner since the war to be powered in this fashion. The Americans, curiously, did not pursue the application of the turboprop to passenger aircraft to the degree that might have been expected of a world leader in air transport design. While the Viscount was fast establishing new standards of speed, comfort and efficiency, the US aero-engine industry was still wringing the last ounce of energy out of the piston engine in the form of the Wright Turbo Compound that powered its DC-7s and Super Constellations. The only American airliner designed from the outset for propeller-turbine engines was the Electra, which entered service some years later than the Viscount and in less than half the numbers.

Apart from Britain, where the Viscount and Hawker Siddeley 748, and the larger Britannia and Vanguard, have fully demonstrated the efficacy of the turboprop engine, the only other nation really to pursue it in relation to large passenger-carrying aircraft has been the USSR. So much so, in fact, that the Soviet Union has the most powerful propeller-turbine engines in the world: those installed in the giant Tu-114 each develop nearly 15,000 shp, while those of the An-22 military freighter are more powerful still. Russian designers, and Oleg Antonov in particular, chose turboprop powerplants for a considerable range of new civil aircraft which began to appear in the mid-1950s. Most of these are used within the Soviet Union, where the turboprop's economy with heavy loads over long distances, and its less demanding runway requirements than the pure jet, are important factors in its favour.

France, despite its considerable success in other categories of aviation, has made comparatively little impact on the turboprop transport scene, the twin-Bastan N 262/Frégate having mustered only about fifty sales in seven years. Greater success has attended the Japanese designed and built YS-11, which relies on that most proven of all propeller-turbines, the Rolls-Royce Dart.

As with the turboprop, so with the turbojet, and the first jet airliner on the scene was also of British design. The wartime Brabazon Committee was inclined to be somewhat reticent about the potentialities of the jet engine in relation to mass passenger transport; or perhaps it felt that the development costs of a large intercontinental jet airliner would be too prohibitive for a nation still recovering from the unprecedented expense of the war. At any rate, its Type IV recommendations related only to a medium-range jet transport with modest payload capabilities, and it was left to de Havilland to prove that a larger machine could compete with propeller-driven transports on the Empire routes. In 1952 the Comet proudly entered service with BOAC; the tragic accidents and subsequent grounding of all Comets in 1954 are now a matter of history, and it was another four and a half years before the much-improved Comet 4 took the place of its forebear. True, it still beat the Boeing 707 into service across the North Atlantic, and the intervening years were far from being entirely wasted; but they still represented much lost time, one of the commodities least dispensable to any aviation industry.

Meanwhile, the distinction of being the second jetliner into service had gone, not to America, as might have been expected, but to the Soviet Union, whose twin-jet Tu-104 had taken the western nations by surprise early in 1956 and entered service inside Russia a year later. Some western observers, seeming almost to take the Tu-104's existence as a personal affront, dwelt heavily on the fact that it was 'only a converted bomber', and ridiculed the Victorian-style décor of the passenger accommodation; but the Tu-104 was no prestige lash-up, as its subsequent years of airline service have demonstrated beyond question.

At last, in October 1958, the first American jetliner, the now ubiquitous Boeing 707, entered service across the North Atlantic. Pan American was the pioneer airline, but a comparable fleet of Boeings had simultaneously been ordered by PanAm's great rival, Trans World Airlines, and this was to spark off the greatest and most expensive one-upmanship race in the history of aviation. Rightly or wrongly – we shall never know – airline after airline decided that it would have to have jets itself or go out of business, and the Boeing order book grew almost daily. For almost a year the Seattle manufacturer had things virtually all its own way, for its greatest rival, Douglas, was not to have the competing DC-8 in service until September 1959. Since then both American types have grown into 'families' of jet airliners with a variant for almost every conceivable route requirement.

One by-product of the great scramble for jet equipment was that the secondhand airliner market began to receive a glut of redundant but by no means retirement-worthy piston-engined aircraft. As a result, quite a few less affluent (or less hot-headed) airlines found themselves in a buyers' market where they could discard piston-engined aircraft that had worn out and replace them at an unexpectedly low cost with similar or better machines that still had plenty of service left in them. One such airline, Icelandair, was even able to make advertising capital of the fact that it was the only *non*-jet airline flying the North Atlantic.

The other major impact on the jet scene during the late 1950s was made by the Sud-Aviation Caravelle, which entered service in May 1959 and was the pioneer of the 'clean' wing and rear-mounted engine layout. Numerically the Caravelle has not attained the sales record of the Boeing or Douglas jets, but it was a pace-setter when it first appeared and in its later forms remains one of the world's leading jetliner types. For several years Sud-Aviation ran a highly successful sales campaign with the slogan 'Oh! Ils ont copié Caravelle!', and the proof of this statement can be seen in over a score of other designs, large and small and of many nationalities, now flying.

The aft-engine vogue has brought forth, in the second generation of jet transports, designs with two, three and four engines mounted in this fashion at or in the rear of the fuselage. The principal twin-engined types are the BAC One-Eleven and the McDonnell Douglas DC-9, both selling well according to their respective standards. The tri-jet formula is exemplified by the British Trident, Russia's Tu-154 and the American Boeing 727. The British story, unfortunately, is the all too familiar one of disappointing sales after being first in the field, while at the opposite extreme the Boeing 727 has proved to be the greatest-selling jet airliner in history. No American producer of a four-engined jet type has used the rear-engine formula, preferring the established underwing pod configuration instead; thus the only two exponents in this class are the VC10 and the Russian Il-62.

With the gradual improvement of the by-pass turbojet, or turbofan as it is more commonly called, there has been an increasing tendency to use this form of powerplant in preference to the turbojet, both in airliners and in smaller types of aircraft. Many of the established turbojet designs are available with, or have been converted to, fan engines, and an increasing number of newcomers are using this type of powerplant from the outset. First into service with a turbofan design was the Soviet Union with the Tu-124, a descendant of the Tu-104 already mentioned.

The most radical step in recent years in the field of subsonic jet transports was Boeing's decision to go ahead with what was quickly named the 'jumbo jet', the Boeing 747. More of a mammoth than a mere elephant, the 747 is designed to carry up to 500 people in an interior with 10-abreast seating whose proportions are more akin to a theatre auditorium than an airliner. Initial scepticism of whether there was really a need for an aeroplane of such a size seems to have been more than answered by the size of the order book and the traffic statistics during its first few years of operation. The 747 is, indeed, only the first of a new generation of wide-bodied airliners that began flying the world's air routes in the 1970s. It was followed in 1971 by the McDonnell Douglas DC-10, and by 1974 had been joined also by the Lockheed TriStar, the A300 European Airbus and the smaller, shorter-range Dassault Mercure. Russia's equivalent, the Ilyushin Il-86, flew in prototype form in December 1976.

Big though the 747 is, Boeing went out on an even longer limb financially when its design was chosen as the United States' entry in the supersonic airliner stakes. The other two world entrants, the Anglo/French Concorde and Russia's Tupolev Tu-144, are similar in basic concept and based on relatively straightforward airframes. The initial Boeing SST submission, by comparison, was more complex by virtue of its adoption of the variable-geometry or 'swing-wing' concept. The complexity of this design led to its eventual withdrawal and replacement by the more conventional fixed-wing Boeing 2707-300, which itself fell victim to the 'environmentalist' lobby of American politics and was cancelled by a one-vote majority of the US Senate in March 1971. It is impossible to believe that America will not, eventually, build a supersonic transport aircraft; but for the moment that remains in the future.

Perhaps it is not altogether irrelevant to conclude with a reference to an aeroplane at almost the opposite end of the speed spectrum to the SST: the perennial DC-3. With less than a quarter of the capacity and little more than a tenth of the speed of the Concorde this ageless, seemingly irreplaceable aeroplane has an unrivalled record in airline service stretching back over more than half the entire history of powered flight. How many Concordes, one wonders, will still be in service forty-five years from now?

THE COLOUR PLATES

As an aid to identification, the colour plates which follow have been arranged mainly on a visual basis, divided according to whether the aeroplane is propeller-driven or jet-driven and arranged in ascending order of the number of engines installed. The 'split' plan view technique is adopted to give, within a single plan outline, upper and lower surface markings of whichever aspect is represented by the side view.

The reference number of each aircraft corresponds to the appropriate text matter. An index to all types appears on pp. 351–352.

CURTISS C-46 (U.S.A.)

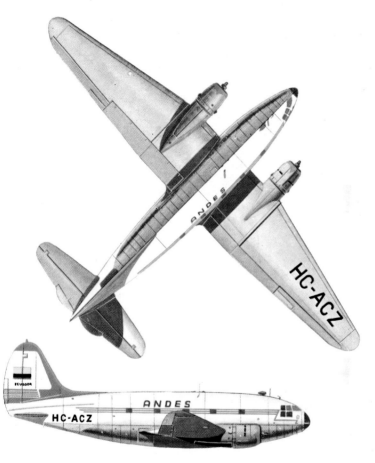

1

Curtiss C-46 of Lineas Aéreas Andes S.A., *ca* 1965. *Engines:* Two 2,000 h.p. Pratt & Whitney R-2800-51M1 Double Wasp eighteen-cylinder radial engines. *Span:* 108 ft. 0 in. (32·92 m.). *Length:* 76 ft. 4 in. (23·26 m.). *Wing area:* 1,358·0 sq. ft. (126·16 sq. m.). *Maximum take-off weight:* 48,000 lb. (21,772 kg.). *Typical cruising speed:* 195 m.p.h. (314 km/hr.) at 9,000 ft. (2,750 m.). *Service ceiling:* 24,500 ft. (7,470 m.). *Range with payload of 9,584 lb. (4,347 kg.):* 1,800 miles (2,897 km.).

II–14 (U.S.S.R.)

2

Avia 14 Salon (Czech-built Ilyushin II-14) of Air Guinée, *ca* 1963. *Engines:* Two 1,900 h.p. Shvetsov ASh–82T fourteen-cylinder radial engines. *Span:* 106 ft. 8 in. (32·41 m.). *Length:* 73 ft. 2 in. (22·30 m.). *Wing area:* 1,076·4 sq. ft. (100·00 sq. m.). *Maximum take-off weight:* 39,683 lb. (18,000 kg.). *Typical cruising speed:* 186 m.p.h. (299 km/hr.) at 6,500 ft. (1,980 m.). *Service ceiling:* 22,000 ft. (6,700 m.). *Range with maximum payload of 8,620 lb. (3,910 kg.):* 280 miles (450 km.).

DOUGLAS DC-3 (U.S.A.)

3

Douglas DC–3 of Compania de Aviacion Faucett S.A., *ca* 1965. *Engines:* Two 1,200 h.p. Pratt & Whitney R–1830–92 Twin Wasp fourteen-cylinder radial engines. *Span:* 95 ft. 0 in. (28·96 m.). *Length:* 64 ft. 0½ in. (19·52 m.). *Wing area:* 987·0 sq. ft. (91·70 sq. m.). *Maximum take-off weight:* 25,200 lb. (11,431 kg.). *Typical cruising speed:* 178 m.p.h. (286 km/hr.) at 10,000 ft. (3,050 m.). *Service ceiling:* 24,000 ft. (7,300 m.). *Range with maximum payload of 5,000 lb. (2,268 kg.):* 660 miles (1,062 km.).

VIKING (U.K.)

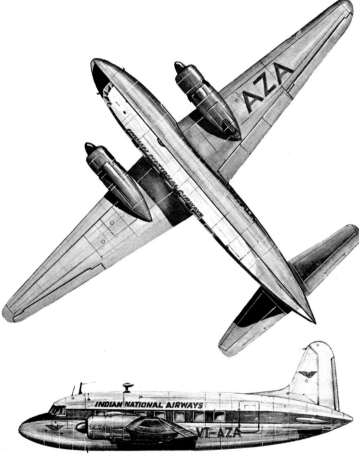

4

Vickers Type 604 Viking 1B *Jumna* of Indian National Airways, *ca* 1950. *Engines:* Two 1,690 h.p. Bristol Hercules 634 fourteen-cylinder radial engines. *Span:* 89 ft. 3 in. (27·20 m.). *Length:* 65 ft. 2 in. (19·86 m.). *Wing area:* 882·0 sq. ft. (81·94 sq. m.). *Maximum take-off weight:* 34,000 lb. (15,422 kg.). *Maximum cruising speed:* 210 m.p.h. (338 km/hr.) at 6,000 ft. (1,830 m.). *Service ceiling:* 23,750 ft. (7,240 m.). *Range with maximum payload of 7,240 lb. (3,284 kg.):* 520 miles (837 km.).

SCANDIA (Sweden)

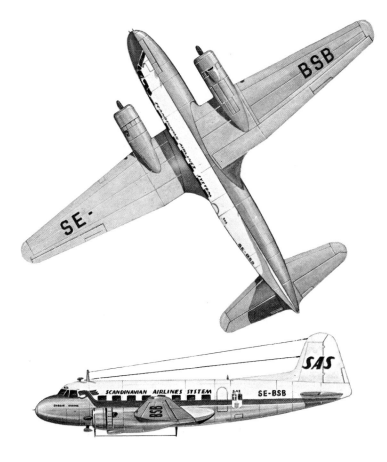

5

Saab 90A2 Scandia *Gardar Viking* of Scandinavian Airlines System, *ca* 1955. *Engines:* Two 1,800 h.p. Pratt & Whitney R–2180–E1 Twin Wasp eighteen-cylinder radial engines. *Span:* 91 ft. $10\frac{1}{4}$ in. (28·00 m.). *Length:* 69 ft. $10\frac{1}{2}$ in. (21·30 m.). *Wing area:* 922·5 sq. ft. (85·70 sq. m.). *Maximum take-off weight:* 35,274 lb. (16,000 kg.). *Maximum cruising speed:* 242 m.p.h. (391 km/hr.) at 10,000 ft. (3,050 m.). *Service ceiling:* 22,850 ft. (7,500 m.). *Range with 6,173 lb. (2,800 kg.) payload:* 920 miles (1,480 km.).

AMBASSADOR (U.K.)

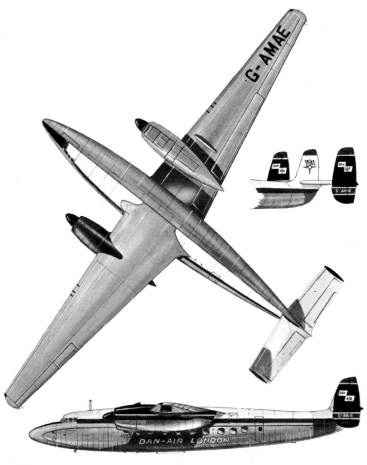

6

Airspeed A.S.57 Ambassador Srs. 2 of Dan-Air Services Ltd., *ca* 1967. *Engines:* Two 2,625 h.p. Bristol Centaurus 661 eighteen-cylinder radial engines. *Span:* 115 ft. 0 in. (35·05 m.). *Length:* 82 ft. 0 in. (24·99 m.). *Wing area:* 1,200·0 sq. ft. (111·48 sq. m.). *Maximum take-off weight:* 55,000 lb. (24,948 kg.). *Typical cruising speed:* 240 m.p.h. (386 km/hr.) at 15,000 ft. (4,570 m.). *Range with maximum payload of 10,800 lb. (4,900 kg.):* 445 miles (716 km.).

MARTIN 2-0-2 (U.S.A.)

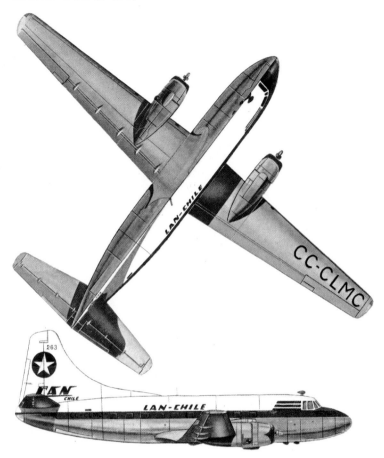

7

Martin 2–0–2 of Linea Aérea Nacional de Chile (LAN-Chile), *ca* 1948/49. *Engines:* Two 2,400 h.p. Pratt & Whitney R–2800–CA18 Double Wasp eighteen-cylinder radial engines. *Span:* 93 ft. 3 in. (28·42 m.). *Length:* 71 ft. 4 in. (21·74 m.). *Wing area:* 864·0 sq. ft. (80·27 sq. m.). *Maximum take-off weight:* 39,900 lb. (18,098 kg.). *Typical cruising speed:* 286 m.p.h. (460 km/hr.) at 12,000 ft. (3,660 m.). *Service ceiling:* 33,000 ft. (10,060 m.). *Range with maximum payload of 9,270 lb. (4,205 kg.) and reserves:* 635 miles (1,022 km.).

CONVAIR 240 (U.S.A.)

8

Convair 240 of Ethiopian Airlines S.C., *ca* 1959/60. *Engines:* Two 2,400 h.p. Pratt & Whitney R–2800–CA18 Double Wasp eighteen-cylinder radial engines. *Span:* 91 ft. 9 in. (27·96 m.). *Length:* 74 ft. 8 in. (22·76 m.). *Wing area:* 817·0 sq. ft. (75·90 sq. m.). *Maximum take-off weight:* 41,790 lb. (18,955 kg.). *Typical cruising speed:* 235 m.p.h. (378 km/hr.) at 8,000 ft. (2,440 m.). *Service ceiling:* 30,000 ft. (9,150 m.). *Range with maximum payload of 9,250 lb. (4,195 kg.):* 690 miles (1,110 km.).

CONVAIR 440 and 540 (U.S.A.)

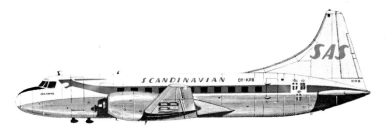

9

Convair 440 Metropolitan *Egil Viking* of Scandinavian Airlines System, *ca* 1964. *Engines:* Two 2,500 h.p. Pratt & Whitney R–2800–CB16/17 eighteen-cylinder radial engines. *Span:* 105 ft. 4 in. (32·10 m.). *Length:* 81 ft. 6 in. (24·84 m.). *Wing area:* 920·0 sq. ft. (85·47 sq. m.). *Maximum take-off weight:* 49,100 lb. (22,270 kg.). *Typical cruising speed:* 289 m.p.h. (465 km/hr.) at 20,000 ft. (6,100 m.). *Service ceiling:* 24,900 ft. (7,590 m.). *Range with maximum payload of 12,700 lb. (5,760 kg.):* 470 miles (756 km.).

10

Convair 540 (ex-340) leased to Allegheny Airlines Inc. in July 1959 for experimental services. *Engines:* Two 3,500 e.h.p. Napier Eland 504A turbo-props. *Span:* 105 ft. 4 in. (32·10 m.). *Length:* 79 ft. 2 in. (24·57 m.). *Wing area:* 920·0 sq. ft. (85·47 sq. m.). *Maximum take-off weight:* 53,200 lb. (24,131 kg.). *Maximum cruising speed:* 325 m.p.h. (523 km/hr.) at 20,000 ft. (6,100 m.). *Service ceiling:* 21,000 ft. (6,400 m.). *Range with maximum payload of 12,986 lb. (5,890 kg.):* 905 miles (1,456 km.).

NAMC YS-11 (Japan)

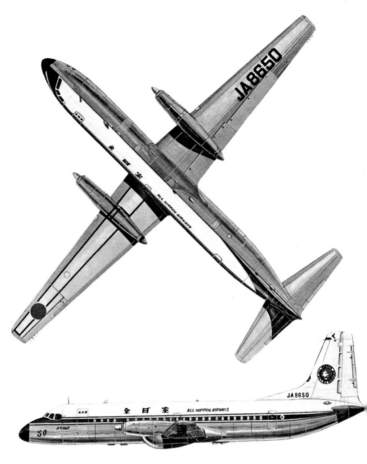

11

NAMC YS–11–102 of All Nippon Airways Co., *ca* 1966. *Engines:* Two 3,060 e.h.p. Rolls-Royce Dart Mk.542–10 turboprops. *Span:* 104 ft. 11¾ in. (32.00 m.). *Length:* 86 ft. 3½ in. (26·30 m.). *Wing area:* 1,020·4 sq. ft. (94·80 sq. m.). *Maximum take-off weight:* 51,808 lb. (23,500 kg.). *Maximum cruising speed:* 297 m.p.h. (478 km/hr.) at 15,000 ft. (4,575 m.). *Service ceiling:* 27,500 ft. (8,380 m.). *Range with maximum payload of 12,350 lb. (5,600 kg.):* 860 miles (1,390 km.).

HS 748 (U.K.)

12

Hawker Siddeley 748 Srs. 2 of Air Ceylon Ltd., *ca* 1965. *Engines:* Two 2,105 e.h.p. Rolls-Royce Dart Mk. 531 turboprops. *Span:* 98 ft. 6 in. (30·02 m.). *Length:* 67 ft. 0 in. (20·42 m.). *Wing area:* 810·75 sq. ft. (75·35 sq. m.). *Maximum take-off weight:* 44,495 lb. (20,182 kg.). *Maximum cruising speed:* 287 m.p.h. (462 km/hr.) at 15,000 ft. (4,570 m.). *Service ceiling:* 25,000 ft. (7,620 m.). *Range with maximum payload of 11,512 lb. (5,221 kg.):* 690 miles (1,110 km.).

FRIENDSHIP (Netherlands)

13

Fairchild Hiller F-27A of Bonanza Air Lines Inc., *ca* 1959. *Engines:* Two 2,050 e.h.p. Rolls-Royce Dart Mk. 528–7E turboprops. *Span:* 95 ft. 2 in. (29·00 m.). *Length:* 77 ft. 2 in. (23·50 m.). *Wing area:* 753·5 sq. ft. (70·00 sq. m.). *Maximum take-off weight:* 42,000 lb. (19,050 kg.). *Maximum cruising speed:* 300 m.p.h. (483 km/hr.) at 20,000 ft. (6,100 m.). *Service ceiling:* 32,600 ft. (9,935 m.). *Range with maximum payload of 12,500 lb. (5,670 kg.):* 912 miles (1,468 km.).

An-24 (U.S.S.R.)

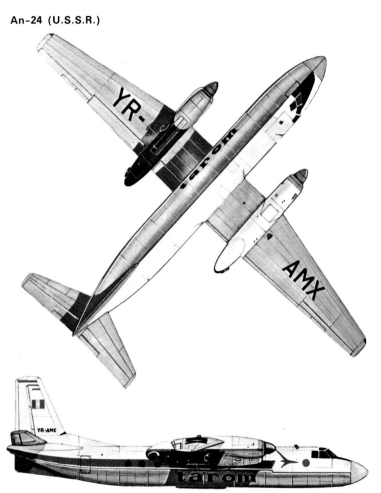

14

Antonov An–24V Series I of Transporturile Aeriene Romîne (Tarom), *ca* 1967.
Engines: Two 2,550 e.h.p. Ivchenko Al–24 turboprops. *Span:* 95 ft. $9\frac{1}{2}$ in.
(29·20 m.). *Length:* 77 ft. $2\frac{1}{2}$ in. (23·53 m.). *Wing area:* 780·0 sq. ft. (72·46
sq. m.). *Maximum take-off weight:* 46,300 lb. (21,000 kg.). *Maximum cruising
speed:* 310 m.p.h. (500 km/hr.) at 19,700 ft. (6,000 m.). *Service ceiling:*
29,500 ft. (9,000 m.). *Range with maximum payload of 12,565 lb. (5,700
kg.):* 404 miles (650 km.).

HERALD (U.K.)

15

Handley Page H.P.R.7 Herald 214 of Sadia S.A. Transportes Aéreos, *ca* 1966. *Engines:* Two 2,105 e.h.p. Rolls-Royce Dart Mk. 527 turboprops. *Span:* 94 ft. 9 in. (28·88 m.). *Length:* 75 ft. 6 in. (23·01 m.). *Wing area:* 886·0 sq. ft. (82·31 sq. m.). *Maximum take-off weight:* 43,000 lb. (19,500 kg.). *Maximum cruising speed:* 275 m.p.h. (443 km/hr.) at 15,000 ft. (4,575 m.). *Service ceiling:* 27,900 ft. (8,500 m.). *Range with maximum payload of 11,242 lb. (5,100 kg.):* 700 miles (1,125 km.).

AÉROSPATIALE N 262 (France)

16

Aérospatiale N 262 Series A of Japan Domestic Airlines (Nippon Kokunai Koku), *ca* 1966. *Engines:* Two 1,065 e.h.p. Turboméca Bastan VIC turboprops. *Span:* 71 ft. 10 in. (21·90 m.). *Length:* 63 ft. 3 in. (19·28 m.). *Wing area:* 592·0 sq. ft. (55·00 sq. m.). *Maximum take-off weight:* 22,930 lb. (10,400 kg.). *Maximum cruising speed:* 233 m.p.h. (375 km/hr.) at 15,000 ft. (4,570 m.). *Service ceiling:* 19,200 ft. (5,850 m.). *Range with maximum payload of 7,280 lb. (3,302 kg.):* 545 miles (875 km.).

SAUNDERS ST-27 (Canada)

17

Saunders ST–27 in manufacturer's demonstration livery, 1971. *Engines:* Two 715 e.h.p. United Aircraft of Canada PT6A–27 turboprops. *Span:* 71 ft. 6 in. (21·79 m.). *Length:* 59 ft. 0 in. (17·98 m.). *Wing area:* 499·0 sq. ft. (46·36 sq. m.). *Maximum take-off weight:* 13,500 lb. (6,124 kg.). *Maximum cruising speed:* 230 m.p.h. (370 km/hr.) at 7,000 ft. (2,135 m.). *Service ceiling:* 25,000 ft. (7,620 m.). *Maximum range:* 817 miles (1,315 km.).

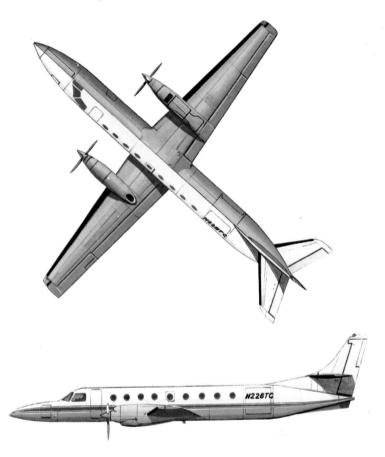

18,

Swearingen SA–226TC Metro prototype in manufacturer's demonstration livery, 1970. *Engines:* Two 940 s.h.p. AiResearch TPE 331–3UW–303G turboprops. *Span:* 46 ft. 3 in. (14·10 m.). *Length:* 59 ft. 4¼ in. (18·09 m.). *Wing area:* 277·5 sq. ft. (25·78 sq. m.). *Maximum take-off weight:* 12,500 lb. (5,670 kg.). *Maximum cruising speed:* 294 m.p.h. (473 km/hr.) at 10,000 ft. (3,050 m.). *Typical range with 3,080 lb. (1,397 kg.) payload:* 500 miles (805 km.).

TURBOLET (Czechoslovakia)

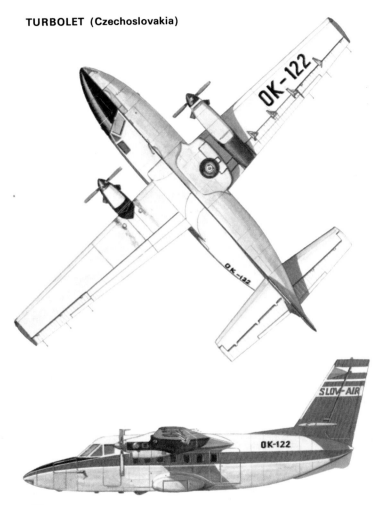

19

Let L–410A Turbolet of Slov-Air, Czechoslovakia, 1972. *Engines:* Two 715 e.h.p. United Aircraft of Canada PT6A–27 turboprops. *Span:* 56 ft. 1½ in. (17·10 m.). *Length:* 44 ft. 7¾ in. (13·61 m.). *Wing area:* 349·8 sq. ft. (32·50 sq. m.). *Maximum take-off weight:* 12,566 lb. (5,700 kg.). *Maximum cruising speed:* 233 m.p.h. (375 km/hr.) at 9,850 ft. (3,000 m.). *Service ceiling:* 22,966 ft. (7,000 m.). *Maximum range:* 808 miles (1,300 km.).

TWIN OTTER (Canada)

20

de Havilland Canada DHC–6 Twin Otter Series 100 of Trans-Australia Airlines, 1967. *Engines:* Two 579 e.h.p. United Aircraft of Canada PT6A–20 turboprops. *Span:* 65 ft. 0 in. (19·81 m.). *Length:* 49 ft. 6 in. (15·09 m.). *Wing area:* 420·0 sq. ft. (39·02 sq. m.). *Maximum take-off weight:* 11,579 lb. (5,252 kg.). *Maximum cruising speed:* 184 m.p.h. (297 km/hr.) at 10,000 ft. (3,050 m.). *Service ceiling:* 25,500 ft. (7,770 m.). *Maximum range:* 920 miles (1,480 km.).

Ju 52/3m (Germany)

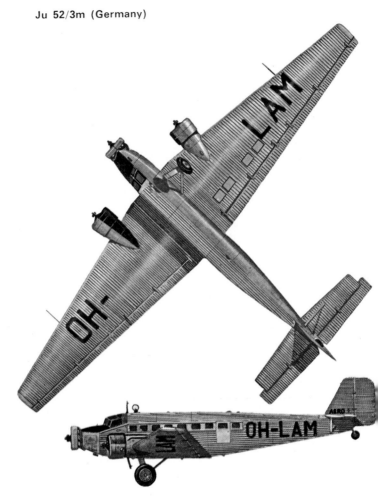

21

Junkers Ju 52/3m *Karjala* of Aero O/Y (Finnair), *ca* 1947. *Engines:* Three 770 h.p. BMW 132H nine-cylinder radial engines. *Span:* 95 ft. 11½ in. (29·25 m.). *Length:* 62 ft. 0 in. (18·90 m.). *Wing area:* 1,189·4 sq. ft. (110·50 sq. m.). *Maximum take-off weight:* 23,150 lb. (10,500 kg.). *Typical cruising speed:* 154 m.p.h. (248 km/hr.) at 8,200 ft. (2,500 m.). *Service ceiling:* 19,025 ft. (5,800 m.). *Typical range:* 545 miles (880 km.).

TRISLANDER (U.K.)

22

Britten-Norman BN–2A Mk III Trislander of Aurigny Air Services, 1971.
Engines: Three 260 h.p. Lycoming O–540–E4C5 six-cylinder horizontally-
opposed type. *Span:* 53 ft. 0 in. (16·15 m.). *Length:* 43 ft. 9 in. (13·335
m.). *Wing area:* 337·0 sq. ft. (31·31 sq. m.). *Maximum take-off weight:*
10,000 lb. (4,536 kg.). *Maximum cruising speed:* 166 m.p.h. (267 km/hr.)
at 6,500 ft. (1,980 m.). *Service ceiling:* 13,150 ft. (4,010 m.). *Maximum
range:* 1,000 miles (1,610 km.).

LANCASTRIAN (U.K.)

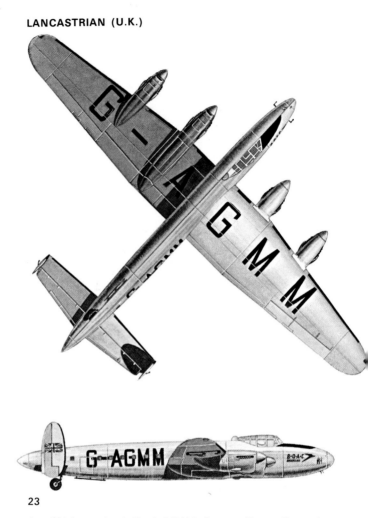

23

Avro 691 Lancastrian 1 *Nepal* of British Overseas Airways Corporation, *ca* 1948. *Engines:* Four 1,635 h.p. Rolls-Royce Merlin T.24/4 twelve-cylinder Vee-type engines. *Span:* 102 ft. 0 in. (31·09 m.). *Length:* 76 ft. 10 in. (23·42 m.). *Wing area:* 1,297·0 sq. ft. (119·49 sq. m.). *Maximum take-off weight:* 65,000 lb. (29,484 kg.). *Typical cruising speed:* 280 m.p.h. (451 km/hr.) at 11,000 ft. (3,350 m.). *Service ceiling:* 24,300 ft. (7,400 m.). *Range with maximum fuel:* 2,820 miles (4,540 km.).

HALTON (U.K.)

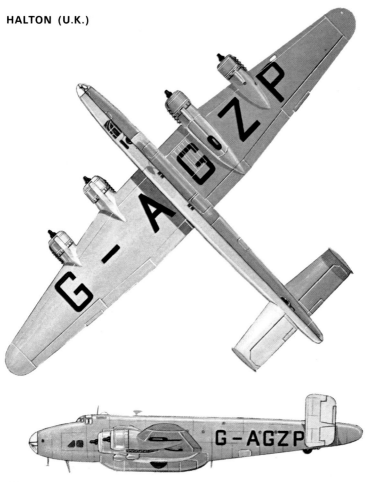

24

Handley Page H.P.70 Halton 2 operated by British American Air Services Ltd. in 1946 on behalf of The Maharajah Gaekwar of Baroda. *Engines:* Four 1,675 h.p. Bristol Hercules 100 fourteen-cylinder radial engines. *Span:* 103 ft. 8 in. (31·59 m.). *Length:* 73 ft. 7 in. (22·43 m.). *Wing area:* 1,278·0 sq. ft. (118·73 sq. m.). *Maximum take-off weight:* 68,000 lb. (30,844 kg.). *Maximum cruising speed:* 260 m.p.h. (418 km/hr.) at 15,000 ft. (4,570 m.). *Service ceiling:* 21,000 ft. (6,400 m.). *Range with maximum payload of 8,000 lb. (3,629 kg.):* 2,530 miles (4,072 km.).

BRABAZON (U.K.)

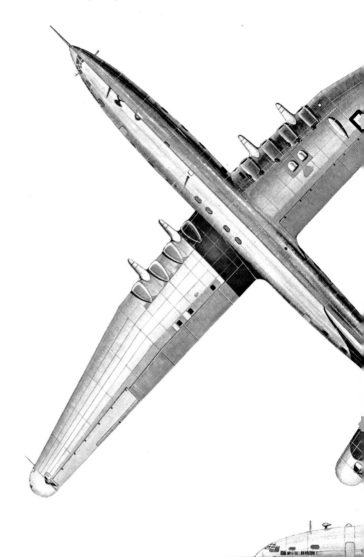

216

25

Bristol 167 Brabazon 1 prototype, *ca* 1950. *Engines:* Eight 2,500 h.p. Bristol Centaurus 20 eighteen-cylinder radial engines. *Span:* 230 ft. 0 in. (70·10 m.). *Length:* 177 ft. 0 in. (53·95 m.). *Wing area:* 5,317·0 sq. ft. (493·97 sq. m.). *Maximum take-off weight:* 290,000 lb. (131,540 kg.). *Maximum cruising speed:* 250 m.p.h. (402 km/hr.) at 25,000 ft. (7,620 m.). *Range with maximum fuel:* 5,500 miles (8,851 km.).

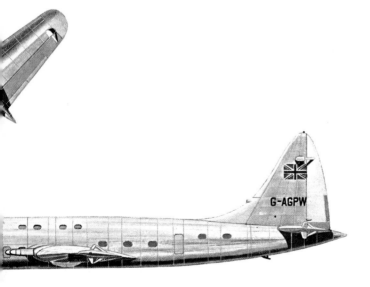

TUDOR (U.K.)

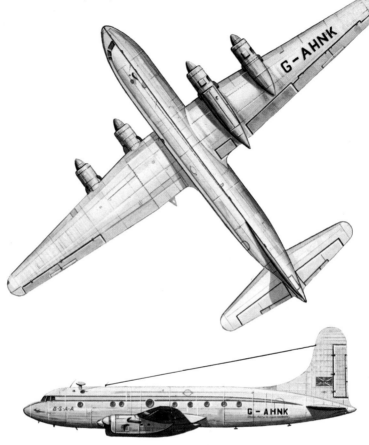

26

Avro 688 Tudor 4 *Star Lion* of British South American Airways, *ca* 1948. *Engines:* Four 1,770 h.p. Rolls-Royce Merlin 621 twelve-cylinder Vee-type engines. *Span:* 120 ft. 0 in. (36·58 m.). *Length:* 85 ft. 3 in. (25·98 m.). *Wing area:* 1,421·0 sq. ft. (132·01 sq. m.). *Maximum take-off weight:* 80,000 lb. (36,287 kg.). *Maximum cruising speed:* 210 m.p.h. (338 km/hr.) at 20,000 ft. (6,100 m.). *Service ceiling:* 27,400 ft. (8,350 m.). *Range with maximum fuel:* 4,000 miles (6,437 km.).

HERMES (U.K.)

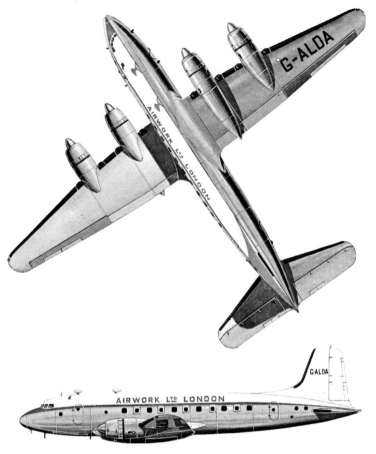

27

Handley Page H.P.81 Hermes 4A of Airwork Ltd, *ca* 1953. *Engines:* Four 2,125 h.p. Bristol Hercules 773 fourteen-cylinder radial engines. *Span:* 113 ft. 0 in. (34·44 m.). *Length:* 96 ft. 10 in. (29·51 m.). *Wing area:* 1,408·0 sq. ft. (130·80 sq. m.). *Maximum take-off weight:* 86,000 lb. (39,009 kg.). *Maximum cruising speed:* 270 m.p.h. (435 km/hr.) at 20,000 ft. (6,100 m.). *Service ceiling:* 23,800 ft. (7,250 m.). *Range with payload of 14,125 lb. (6,407 kg.):* 2,000 miles (3,219 km.).

STRATOCRUISER (U.S.A.)

28

Boeing 377–10–26 Stratocruiser *Clipper Washington* of Pan American World Airways Inc, *ca* 1951. *Engines:* Four 3,500 h.p. Pratt & Whitney R–4360–B6 Wasp Major twenty-eight-cylinder radial engines. *Span:* 141 ft. 3 in. (43·05 m.). *Length:* 110 ft. 4 in. (33·63 m.). *Wing area:* 1,769·0 sq. ft. (164·35 sq. m.). *Maximum take-off weight:* 142,500 lb. (64,634 kg.). *Maximum cruising speed:* 340 m.p.h. (547 km/hr.) at 25,000 ft. (7,620 m.). *Service ceiling:* 33,000 ft. (10,000 m.). *Range with maximum payload of 23,930 lb. (10,855 kg.):* 2,750 miles (4,426 km.).

DOUGLAS DC-4 (U.S.A.)

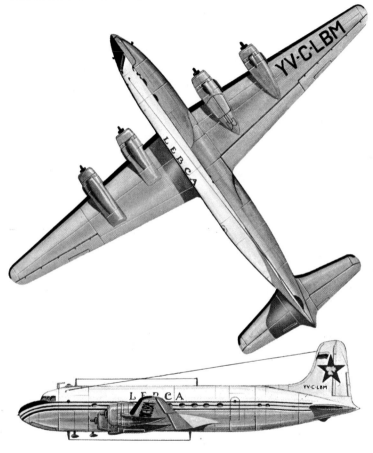

29

Douglas DC–4 of Linea Expresa Bolivar C.A. (LEBCA), *ca* 1963. *Engines:* Four 1,450 h.p. Pratt & Whitney R–2000–SD13G Twin Wasp fourteen-cylinder radial engines. *Span:* 117 ft. 6 in. (35·81 m.). *Length:* 93 ft. 11 in. (28·63 m.). *Wing area:* 1,463·0 sq. ft. (136·91 sq. m.). *Maximum take-off weight:* 73,000 lb. (33,112 kg.). *Typical cruising speed:* 227 m.p.h. (365 km/hr.) at 10,000 ft. (3,050 m.). *Service ceiling:* 22,300 ft. (6,800 m.). *Range with maximum payload of 12,700 lb. (5,760 kg.):* 2,140 miles (3,444 km.).

DOUGLAS DC-6 (U.S.A.)

30

Douglas DC–6B of Hawaiian Airlines Inc, *ca* 1965. *Engines:* Four 2,500 h.p. Pratt & Whitney R–2800–CB17 Double Wasp eighteen-cylinder radial engines. *Span:* 117 ft. 6 in. (35·81 m.). *Length:* 106 ft. 8 in. (32·51 m.). *Wing area:* 1,463·0 sq. ft. (136·91 sq. m.). *Maximum take-off weight:* 106,000 lb. (48,081 kg.). *Typical cruising speed:* 311 m.p.h. (500 km/hr.) at 22,500 ft. (6,860 m.). *Service ceiling:* 25,000 ft. (7,620 m.). *Range with maximum payload of 19,200 lb. (8,709 kg.):* 3,050 miles (4,908 km.).

DOUGLAS DC-7 (U.S.A.)

31

Douglas DC–7F *Irish Sea* of Koninklijke Luchtvaart Maatschappij N.V. (K.L.M. Royal Dutch Airlines), *ca* 1963. *Engines:* Four 3,400 h.p. Wright R–3350–988TC–18EA–4 eighteen-cylinder Turbo Compound radial engines. *Span:* 127 ft. 6 in. (38·86 m.). *Length:* 112 ft. 3 in. (34·21 m.). *Wing area:* 1,637·0 sq. ft. (152·08 sq. m.). *Maximum take-off weight:* 143,000 lb. (64,863 kg.). *Typical cruising speed:* 360 m.p.h. (579 km/hr.) at 23,500 ft. (7,165 m.). *Service ceiling:* 25,000 ft. (7,620 m.). *Range with maximum payload of 35,275 lb. (16,000 kg.):* 4,250 miles (6,840 km.).

S.M. 95 (Italy)

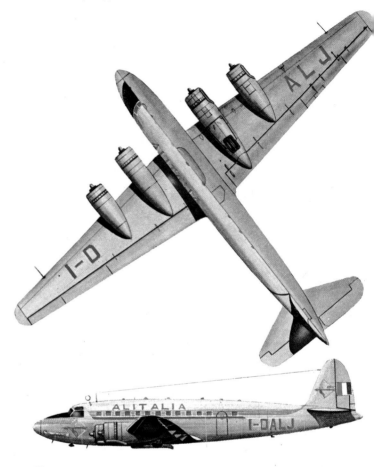

32

SIAI-Marchetti S.M.95 *Cristoforo Colombo* of Alitalia, *ca* 1948. *Engines:* Four 850 h.p. Alfa Romeo 128 RC 18 nine-cylinder radial engines. *Span:* 112 ft. $5\frac{1}{4}$ in. (34·28 m.). *Length:* 81 ft. $3\frac{1}{4}$ in. (24·77 m.). *Wing area:* 1,381·0 sq. ft. (128·30 sq. m.). *Maximum take-off weight:* 47,642 lb. (21,610 kg.). *Typical cruising speed:* 196 m.p.h. (315 km/hr.) at 11,480 ft. (3,500 m.). *Service ceiling:* 20,830 ft. (6,350 m.). *Range with payload of 8,977 lb. (4,072 kg.):* 1,242 miles(2,000 km.).

LANGUEDOC (France)

33

Sud-Est S.E.161 Languedoc of Polskie Linie Lotnicze (LOT), *ca* 1948. *Engines:* Four 1,200 h.p. Gnome-Rhône 14N 68/69 fourteen-cylinder radial engines. *Span:* 96 ft. 4¾ in. (29·38 m.). *Length:* 79 ft. 6¾ in. (24·25 m.). *Wing area:* 1,198·0 sq. ft. (111·30 sq. m.). *Maximum take-off weight:* 50,576 lb. (22,940 kg.). *Typical cruising speed:* 252 m.p.h. (405 km/hr.) at 10,825 ft. (3,300 m.). *Service ceiling:* 23,625 ft. (7,200 m.). *Range with maximum payload of 8,752 lb. (3,970 kg.):* 620 miles (1,000 km.).

MARATHON (U.K.)

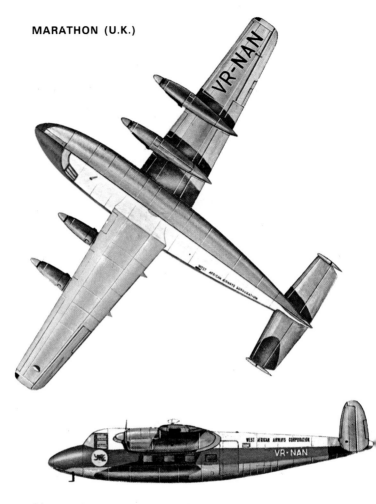

34

Handley Page H.P.R.1 Marathon 1A *Lagos* of West African Airways Corporation, *ca* 1952. *Engines:* Four 340 h.p. de Havilland Gipsy Queen 70 Mk. 4 six-cylinder inline engines. *Span:* 65 ft. 0 in. (19·81 m.). *Length:* 52 ft. 1½ in. (15·88 m.). *Wing area:* 498·0 sq. ft. (46·26 sq. m.). *Maximum take-off weight:* 18,250 lb. (8,278 kg.). *Maximum cruising speed:* 201 m.p.h. (324 km/hr.) at 10,000 ft. (3,050 m.). *Service ceiling:* 18,000 ft. (5,490 m.). *Range with payload of 4,172 lb. (1,892 kg.):* 720 miles (1,160 km.).

YORK (U.K.)

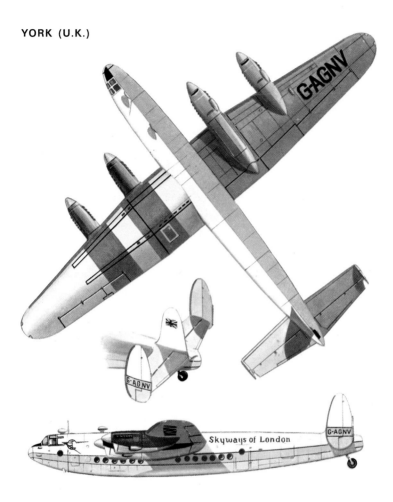

35

Avro 685 York 1 of Skyways Ltd, *ca* 1955. *Engines:* Four 1,610 h.p. Rolls-Royce Merlin 502 twelve-cylinder Vee-type engines. *Span:* 102 ft. 0 in. (31·09 m.). *Length:* 78 ft. 6 in. (23·92 m.). *Wing area:* 1,297·0 sq. ft. (119·49 sq. m.). *Maximum take-off weight:* 70,000 lb. (31,751 kg.). *Typical cruising speed:* 210 m.p.h. (338 km/hr.) at 10,000 ft. (3,050 m.). *Service ceiling:* 23,000 ft. (7,010 m.). *Range with maximum payload of 20,000 lb. (9,072 kg.):* 1,400 miles (2,253 km.).

CONSTELLATION (U.S.A.)

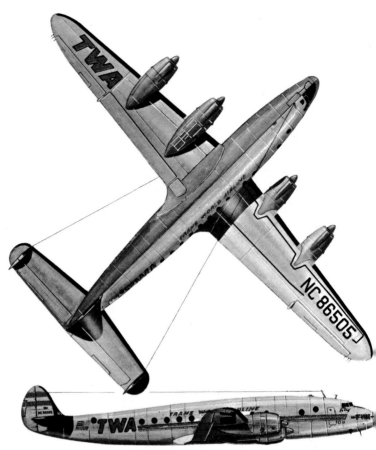

36

Lockheed Model 049 Constellation *Paris Sky Chief* of Trans World Airline, *ca* 1946. *Engines:* Four 2,200 h.p. Wright R–3350–C18–BA–1 Cyclone 18 eighteen-cylinder radial engines. *Span:* 123 ·ft. 0 in. (37·49 m.). *Length:* 95 ft. 2 in. (29·00 m.). *Wing area:* 1,650·0 sq. ft. (153·28 sq. m.). *Maximum take-off weight:* 86,250 lb. (39,112 kg.). *Typical cruising speed:* 313 m.p.h. (504 km/hr.) at 20,000 ft. (6,100 m.). *Service ceiling:* 25,000 ft. (7,620 m.). *Typical range:* 3,050 miles (4,908 km.).

SUPER CONSTELLATION (U.S.A.)

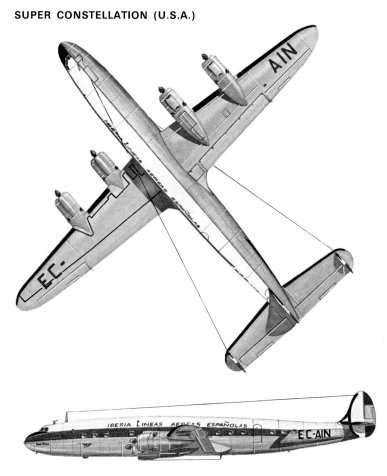

37

Lockheed Model L.1049E Super Constellation *Santa Maria* of Lineas Aéreas Españolas. S.A. (Iberia), *ca* 1955. *Engines:* Four 3,250 h.p. Wright R–3350– C18–DA–1 Turbo Compounds. *Span:* 123 ft. 0 in. (37·49 m.). *Length:* 113 ft. 7 in. (34·65 m.). *Wing area:* 1,650·0 sq. ft. (153·28 sq. m.). *Maximum take-off weight:* 150,000 lb. (68,100 kg.). *Maximum cruising speed:* 327 m.p.h. (523 km/hr.) at 20,000 ft. (6,100 m.). *Service ceiling:* 25,000 ft. (7,620 m.). *Range with maximum payload of 26,400 lb. (11,974 kg.):* 3,100 miles (4,990 km.).

VISCOUNT 700 (U.K.)

38

Vickers Viscount 779 of Fred. Olsen Air Transport Ltd, *ca* 1957. *Engines:* Four 1,740 e.h.p. Rolls-Royce Dart Mk.510 turboprops. *Span:* 93 ft. $8\frac{1}{2}$ in. (28·56 m.). *Length:* 81 ft. 10 in. (25·04 m.). *Wing area:* 963·0 sq. ft. (89·47 sq. m.). *Maximum take-off weight:* 64,500 lb. (29,257 kg.). *Maximum cruising speed:* 334 m.p.h. (537 km/hr.) at 20,000 ft. (6,100 m.). *Service ceiling:* 27,500 ft. (8,380 m.). *Range with maximum payload of 11,842 lb. (5,372 kg.):* 1,748 miles (2,813 km.).

VISCOUNT 800/810 (U.K.)

39

Vickers Viscount 807 *City of Wellington* of New Zealand National Airways Corporation, *ca* 1959. *Engines:* Four 1,740 e.h.p. Rolls-Royce Dart Mk. 510 turboprops. *Span:* 93 ft. 8½ in. (28·56 m.). *Length:* 85 ft. 8 in. (26·11 m.). *Wing area:* 963·0 sq. ft. (89·47 sq. m.). *Maximum take-off weight:* 64,500 lb. (29,257 kg.). *Typical cruising speed:* 305 m.p.h. (491 km/hr.) at 19,500 ft. (5,950 m.). *Service ceiling:* 27,000 ft. (8,230 m.). *Range with maximum payload of 12,900 lb. (5,851 kg.):* 1,290 miles (2,075 km.).

PROVENCE (France)

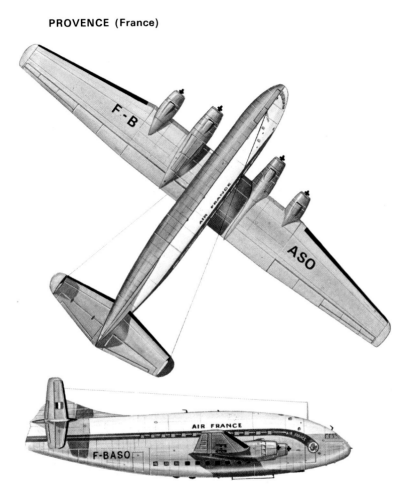

40

Breguet Br.763 Provence of Compagnie Nationale Air France, *ca* 1953. *Engines:*
Four 2,400 h.p. Pratt & Whitney R–2800–CA18 Double Wasp eighteen-cylinder
radial engines. *Span:* 141 ft. $0\frac{1}{2}$ in. (42·99 m.). *Length:* 94 ft. $11\frac{1}{2}$ in. (28·94
m.). *Wing area:* 1,995·6 sq. ft. (185·40 sq. m.). *Maximum take-off weight:*
113,759 lb. (51,600 kg.). *Typical cruising speed:* 218 m.p.h. (351 km/hr.)
at 10,000 ft. (3,050 m.). *Service ceiling:* 24,000 ft. (7,300 m.). *Typical range
with maximum payload of 26,960 lb. (12,228 kg.):* 1,345 miles (2,165 km.).

CARVAIR (U.K.)

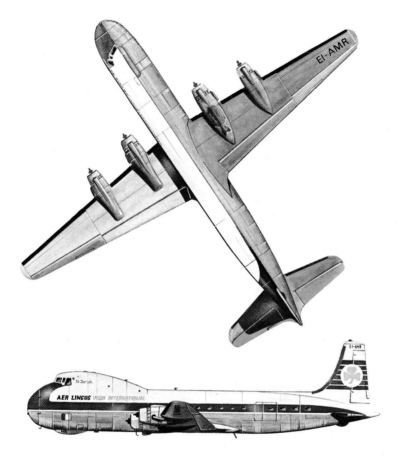

41

Aviation Traders ATL.98 Carvair *St Jarlaith* of Aer Lingus Teoranta, *ca* 1964. *Engines:* Four 1,450 h.p. Pratt & Whitney R–2000–7M2 Twin Wasp fourteen-cylinder radials. *Span:* 117 ft. 6 in. (35·81 m.). *Length:* 102 ft. 7 in. (31·27 m.). *Wing area:* 1,462·0 sq. ft. (135·82 sq. m.). *Maximum take-off weight:* 73,800 lb. (33,475 kg.). *Maximum cruising speed:* 213 m.p.h. (342 km/hr.) at 10,000 ft. (3,050 m.). *Service ceiling:* 18,700 ft. (5,700 m.). *Range with maximum payload of 17,635 lb. (8,000 kg.):* 2,300 miles (3,700 km.).

BRITANNIA (U.K.)

42

Bristol Britannia 312 *Justice* of British Eagle International Airlines Ltd, *ca* 1965. *Engines:* Four 4,445 e.h.p. Bristol Siddeley Proteus 765 turboprops. *Span:* 142 ft. 3 in. (43·36 m.). *Length:* 124 ft. 3 in. (37·87 m.). *Wing area:* 2,075·0 sq. ft. (192·78 sq. m.). *Maximum take-off weight:* 185,000 lb. (83,914 kg.). *Maximum cruising speed:* 402 m.p.h. (647 km/hr.) at 21,000 ft. (6,400 m.). *Service ceiling:* 24,000 ft. (7,300 m.). *Range with maximum payload of 34,900 lb. (15,830 kg.):* 4,268 miles (6,870 km.).

FORTY-FOUR (Canada)

43

Canadair CL–44D–4 of The Flying Tiger Line Inc, *ca* 1962. *Engines:* Four
5,730 e.h.p. Rolls-Royce Tyne Mk. 515/10 turboprops. *Span:* 142 ft. $3\frac{2}{3}$
in. (43·37 m.). *Length:* 136 ft. 8 in. (41·65 m.). *Wing area:* 2,075·0 sq.
ft. (192·78 sq. m.). *Maximum take-off weight:* 210,000 lb. (95,250 kg.).
Typical cruising speed: 316 m.p.h. (506 km/hr.) at 20,340 ft. (6,200 m.).
Service ceiling: 30,000 ft. (9,145 m.). *Range with maximum payload of 63,272
lb. (28,725 kg.):* 2,875 miles (4,600 km.).

ELECTRA (U.S.A.)

44

Lockheed L–188C Electra *Aotearoa* of Air New Zealand Ltd, *ca* 1967. *Engines:* Four 3,750 e.h.p. Allison 501–D13A turboprops. *Span:* 99 ft. 0 in. (30·18 m.). *Length:* 104 ft. 8 in. (31·90 m.). *Wing area:* 1,300·0 sq. ft. (120·77 sq. m.). *Maximum take-off weight:* 116,000 lb. (52,617 kg.). *Maximum cruising speed:* 405 m.p.h. (652 km/hr.) at 22,000 ft. (6,700 m.). *Service ceiling:* 27,000 ft. (8,230 m.). *Range with 22,000 lb. (9,979 kg.) payload:* 2,500 miles (4,023 km.).

VANGUARD (U.K.)

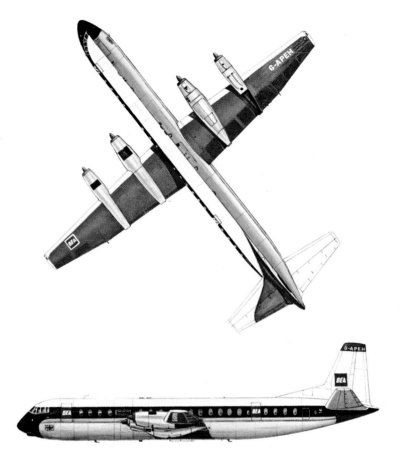

45

Vickers Vanguard 953 of British European Airways Corporation, *ca* 1966. *Engines:* Four 4,985 e.h.p. Rolls-Royce Tyne Mk. 506 turboprops. *Span:* 118 ft. 0 in. (35·96 m.). *Length:* 122 ft. 10½ in. (37·38 m.). *Wing area:* 1,529·0 sq. ft. (142·04 sq. m.). *Maximum take-off weight:* 146,500 lb. (66,451 kg.). *Maximum cruising speed:* 425 m.p.h. (680 km/hr.) at 20,000 ft. (6,100 m.). *Range with maximum payload of 37,000 lb. (16,783 kg.):* 1,590 miles (2,560 km.).

II-18 (U.S.S.R.)

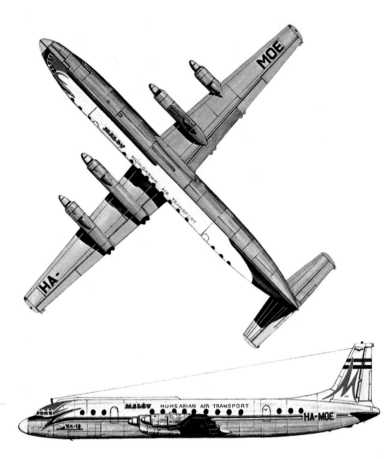

46

Ilyushin II–18V Moskva of Magyar Legiközlekedesi Vallalat (Malév), *ca* 1965.
Engines: Four 4,000 e.h.p. Ivchenko Al–20K turboprops. *Span:* 122 ft. $8\frac{1}{2}$
in. (37·40 m.). *Length:* 117 ft. 9 in. (35·90 m.). *Wing area:* 1,506·95 sq.
ft. (140·00 sq. m.). *Maximum take-off weight:* 134,925 lb. (61,200 kg.).
Maximum cruising speed: 404 m.p.h. (650 km/hr.) at 29,500 ft. (9,000 m.).
Service ceiling: 32,800 ft. (10,000 m.). *Range with maximum payload of
29,762 lb. (13,500 kg.):* 1,553 miles (2,500 km.).

An-10 (U.S.S.R.)

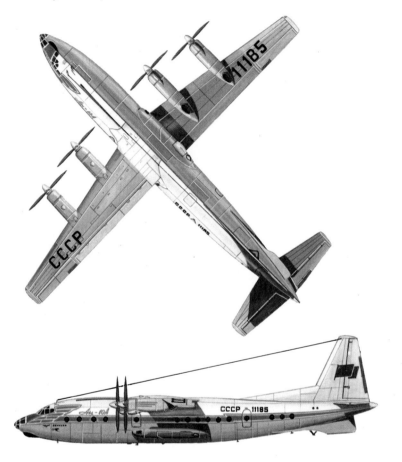

47

Antonov An–10A of Aeroflot, *ca* 1960. *Engines:* Four 4,000 e.h.p. Ivchenko AI–20K turboprops. *Span:* 124 ft. 8 in. (38·00 m.). *Length:* 111 ft. 6½ in. (34·00 m.). *Wing area:* 1,291·7 sq. ft. (120·00 sq. m.). *Maximum take-off weight:* 121,500 lb. (55,100 kg.). *Maximum cruising speed:* 422 m.p.h. (680 km./hr.) at 32,800 ft. (10,000 m.). *Service ceiling:* 33,465 ft. (10,200 m.). *Range with maximum payload of 32,000 lb. (14,500 kg.):* 745 miles (1,200 km.).

Tu-114 (U.S.S.R.)

48

Tupolev Tu-114 of Aeroflot, *ca* 1961. *Engines:* Four 14,795 e.h.p. Kuznetsov NK-12MV turboprops. *Span:* 167 ft. 8 in. (51·10 m.). *Length:* 177 ft. 6 in. (54·10 m.). *Wing area:* 3,348·6 sq. ft. (311·10 sq. m.). *Maximum take-off weight:* 376,990 lb. (171,000 kg.). *Maximum cruising speed:* 478 m.p.h. (770 km/hr.) at 29,500 ft. (9,000 m.). *Service ceiling:* 39,370 ft. (12,000 m.). *Range with maximum payload of 66,140 lb. (30,000 kg.):* 3,850 miles (6,200 km.).

COMET 1 and 2 (U.K.)

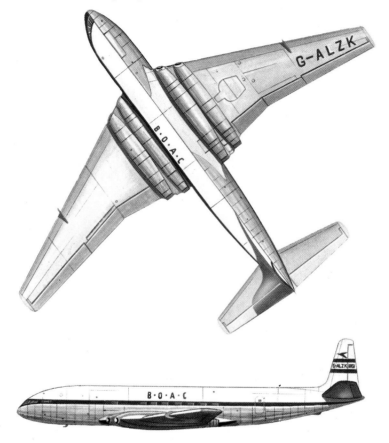

49

Second M.o.S. prototype for the de Havilland D.H.106 Comet 1 in the colours of British Overseas Airways Corporation, *ca* 1951. *Engines:* Four 4,450 lb. (2,018 kg.) s.t. de Havilland Ghost 50 Mk. 1 turbojets. *Span:* 115 ft. 0 in. (35·05 m.). *Length:* 93 ft. 1¼ in. (28·38 m.). *Wing area:* 2,015·0 sq. ft. (187·20 sq. m.). *Maximum take-off weight:* 105,000 lb. (47,627 kg.). *Maximum cruising speed:* 490 m.p.h. (788 km/hr.) at 35,000 ft. (10,700 m.). *Service ceiling:* 40,000 ft. (12,190 m.). *Range with maximum payload of 12,000 lb. (5,443 kg.):* 1,750 miles (2,816 km.).

Tu-104 (U.S.S.R.)

50

Tupolev Tu-104A *Brno* of Československé Aerolinie (CSA), *ca* 1958. *Engines:* Two 21,385 lb. (9,700 kg.) s.t. Mikulin AM–3M–500 turbojets. *Span:* 113 ft. 4 in. (34·54 m.). *Length:* 127 ft. $5\frac{1}{2}$ in. (38·85 m.). *Wing area:* 1,877·2 sq. ft. (174·40 sq. m.). *Maximum take-off weight:* 167,550 lb. (76,000 kg.). *Maximum cruising speed:* 560 m.p.h. (900 km/hr.) at 32,800 ft. (10,000 m.). *Service ceiling:* 37,750 ft. (11,500 m.). *Range with maximum payload of 19,840 lb. (9,000 kg.):* 1,645 miles (2,650 km.).

Tu-124 (U.S.S.R.)

51

Tupolev Tu-124V *Centrotex* of Československé Aerolinie (CSA), *ca* 1967.
Engines: Two 11,905 lb. (5,400 kg.) s.t. Soloviev D-20P turbofans. *Span:*
83 ft. 9½ in. (25·55 m.). *Length:* 100 ft. 4 in. (30·58 m.). *Wing area:* 1,280·9
sq. ft. (119·00 sq. m.). *Maximum take-off weight:* 83,775 lb. (38,000 kg.).
Maximum cruising speed: 540 m.p.h. (870 km/hr.) at 32,800 ft. (10,000
m.). *Range with maximum payload of 13,228 lb. (6,000 kg.):* 760 miles
(1,220 km.).

VFW 614 (Germany)

52

VFW–Fokker VFW 614G1 first prototype in manufacturer's livery, 1971. *Engines:* Two 7,280 lb. (3,302 kg.) s.t. Rolls-Royce/SNECMA M45H Mk. 501 turbofans. *Span:* 70 ft. 6½ in. (21·50 m.). *Length:* 67 ft. 7 in. (20·60 m.). *Wing area:* 688·9 sq. ft. (64·00 sq. m.). *Maximum take-off weight:* 43,980 lb. (19,950 kg.). *Maximum cruising speed:* 449 m.p.h. (722 km/hr.) at 25,000 ft. (7,620 m.). *Service ceiling:* 25,000 ft (7,620 m.). *Range with 40 passengers:* 748 miles (1,205 km.).

BOEING 737 (U.S.A.)

53

Boeing 737–293 operated by Air California, *ca* 1969. *Engines:* Two 14,500 lb. (6,575 kg.) s.t. Pratt & Whitney JT8D–9 turbofans. *Span:* 93 ft. 0 in. (28·35 m.). *Length:* 100 ft. 0 in. (30·48 m.). *Wing area:* 980·0 sq. ft. (91·05 sq. m.). *Maximum take-off weight:* 115,500 lb. (52,390 kg.). *Maximum cruising speed:* 576 m.p.h. (927 km/hr.) at 22,600 ft (6,890 m.). *Range with maximum payload of 35,700 lb. (16,193 kg.):* 2,370 miles (3,815 km.).

MERCURE (France)

54

Dassault Mercure second prototype in the livery of Air Inter, 1973. *Engines:* Two 15,500 lb. (7,030 kg.) s.t. Pratt & Whitney JT8D–15 turbofans. *Span:* 100 ft. 3 in. (30·55 m.). *Length:* 114 ft. 3½ in. (34·84 m.). *Wing area:* 1,248·6 sq. ft. (116·00 sq. m.). *Maximum take-off weight:* 119,050 lb. (54,000 kg.). *Maximum cruising speed:* 575 m.p.h. (926 km/hr.) at 20,000 ft. (6,100 m.). *Maximum range with 140 passengers and reserves:* 1,047 miles (1,680 km.).

AIRBUS A300 (International)

55

Airbus Industrie A300B2 development aircraft in Air France livery, 1973. *Engines:* Two 51,000 lb. (23,133 kg.) s.t. General Electric CF6-50C turbofans. *Span:* 147 ft. 1 in. (44·83 m.). *Length:* 175 ft. 11 in. (53·62 m.). *Wing area:* 2,798·6 sq. ft. (260·00 sq. m.). *Maximum take-off weight:* 302,000 lb. (137,000 kg.). *Maximum cruising speed:* 582 m.p.h. (937 km/hr.) at 25,000 ft. (7,620 m.). *Maximum operating altitude:* 35,000 ft. (10,675 m.). *Range with 281 passengers and baggage:* 1,615 miles (2,600 km.).

CARAVELLE (France)

56

Aérospatiale Caravelle VI–N *Canopo* of Alitalia, *ca* 1965. *Engines:* Two 12,200 lb (5,535 kg.) s.t. Rolls-Royce Avon Mk. 531 turbojets. *Span:* 112 ft. 6 in. (34·30 m.). *Length:* 105 ft. 0 in. (32·01 m.). *Wing area:* 1,579·1 sq. ft. (146·70 sq. m.). *Maximum take-off weight:* 105,820 lb. (48,000 kg.). *Maximum cruising speed:* 525 m.p.h. (845 km/hr.) at 25,000 ft. (7,620 m.). *Service ceiling:* 32,800 ft. (10,000 m.). *Range with 16,800 lb. (7,620 kg.) payload:* 1,553 miles (2,500 km.).

McDONNELL DOUGLAS DC-9 (U.S.A.)

58

McDonnell Douglas DC–9–10 Model 14 of Air Canada, *ca* 1967. *Engines:* Two 12,250 lb. (5,556 kg.) s.t. Pratt & Whitney JT8D–5 turbofans. *Span:* 89 ft. 5 in. (27·25 m.). *Length:* 104 ft. 4¾ in. (31·82 m.). *Wing area:* 934·3 sq. ft. (86·77 sq. m.). *Maximum take-off weight:* 77,700 lb. (35,245 kg.). *Maximum cruising speed:* 561 m.p.h. (903 km/hr.) at 25,000 ft. (7,620 m.). *Range with 50 passengers:* 1,310 miles (2,110 km.).

57

Aérospatiale Caravelle Super B *Turku* of Aero O/Y (Finnair), *ca* 1966. *Engines:* Two 14,000 lb. (6,350 kg.) s.t. Pratt & Whitney JT8D–1 turbofans. *Span and Wing area:* As for Caravelle VI–N. *Length:* 108 ft. 3½ in. (33·01 m.). *Maximum take-off weight:* 114,640 lb. (52,000 kg.). *Maximum cruising speed:* 512 m.p.h. (825 km/hr.) at 25,000 ft. (7,620 m.). *Service ceiling:* 32,800 ft. (10,000 m.). *Range with maximum payload of 20,060 lb. (9,100 kg.):* 1,650 miles (2,655 km.).

ONE-ELEVEN (U.K.)

59

BAC One-Eleven Model 203 of Braniff International Airways, *ca* 1965. *Engines:* Two 10,330 lb. (4,686 kg.) s.t. Rolls-Royce Spey–25 Mk. 506 turbofans. *Span:* 88 ft. 6 in. (26·97 m.). *Length:* 93 ft. 6 in. (28·50 m.). *Wing area:* 1,003·0 sq. ft. (93·18 sq. m.). *Maximum take-off weight:* 79,000 lb. (35,833 kg.). *Maximum cruising speed:* 541 m.p.h. (871 km/hr.) at 21,000 ft. (6,400 m.). *Maximum cruising height:* 35,000 ft. (10,670 m.). *Range with typical payload:* 875 miles (1,410 km.).

ONE-ELEVEN (U.K.)

60

BAC One-Eleven Model 518 of Court Line, 1970. *Engines:* Two 12,550 lb. (5,692 kg.) s.t. Rolls-Royce Spey Mk. 512 DW turbofans. *Span:* 93 ft. 6 in. (28·50 m.). *Length:* 107 ft. 0 in. (32·61 m.). *Wing area:* 1,031·0 sq. ft. (95·78 sq. m.). *Maximum take-off weight:* 104,500 lb. (47,400 kg.). *Maximum cruising speed:* 541 m.p.h. (871 km/hr.) at 21,000 ft. (6,400 m.). *Maximum cruising height:* 35,000 ft. (10,670 m.). *Range with typical payload:* 1,705 miles (2,744 km.).

FELLOWSHIP (Netherlands)

61

Fokker–VFW F.28 Fellowship Mk. 1000, Colombian Presidential transport, 1971. *Engines:* Two 9,850 lb. (4,468 kg.) s.t. Rolls-Royce Spey Mk. 555–15 turbofans. *Span:* 77 ft. $4\frac{1}{4}$ in. (23·58 m.). *Length:* 89 ft. $10\frac{3}{4}$ in. (27·40 m.). *Wing area:* 822·4 sq. ft. (76·40 sq. m.). *Maximum take-off weight:* 65,000 lb. (29,485 kg.). *Maximum cruising speed:* 523 m.p.h. (843 km/hr.) at 23,000 ft. (7,000 m.). *Range with 65 passengers:* 1,300 miles (2,093 km.).

Tu-134 (U.S.S.R.)

62

Tupolev Tu-134 of Polskie Linie Lotnicze (LOT), 1967. *Engines:* Two 14,990 lb. (6,800 kg.) s.t. Soloviev D-30 turbofans. *Span:* 95 ft. 1¾ in. (29·00 m.). *Length:* 112 ft. 8¼ in. (34·35 m.). *Wing area:* 1,370·3 sq. ft. (127·30 sq. m.). *Maximum take-off weight:* 98,105 lb. (44,500 kg.). *Maximum cruising speed:* 559 m.p.h. (900 km/hr.) at 27,900 ft. (8,500 m.). *Service ceiling:* 39,375 ft. (12,000 m.). *Range with payload of 15,430 lb. (7,000 kg.):* 1,490 miles (2,400 km.).

TRIDENT (U.K.)

63

Hawker Siddeley Trident 3B, first aircraft for British Airways (BEA), 1971. *Engines:* Three 11,960 lb. (5,425 kg.) s.t. Rolls-Royce Spey Mk. 512–5W turbofans and one 5,250 lb. (2,381 kg.) s.t. Rolls-Royce RB.162–86 turbojet. *Span:* 98 ft. 0 in. (29·87 m.). *Length:* 131 ft. 2 in. (39·98 m.). *Wing area:* 1,493·0 sq. ft. (138·70 sq. m.). *Maximum take-off weight:* 150,000 lb. (68,040 kg.). *Maximum cruising speed:* 601 m.p.h. (967 km/hr.) at 28,300 ft. (8,625 m.). *Range with maximum payload of 33,722 lb. (15,296 kg.):* 1,094 miles (1,760 km.).

BOEING 727 (U.S.A.)

64

Boeing 727–130 *Kiel* of Deutsche Lufthansa A.G., *ca* 1965. *Engines:* Three 14,000 lb. (6,350 kg.) s.t. Pratt & Whitney JT8D–7 turbofans. *Span:* 108 ft. 0 in. (32·92 m.). *Length:* 133 ft. 2 in. (40·59 m.). *Wing area:* 1,700·0 sq. ft. (157·90 sq. m.). *Maximum take-off weight:* 169,000 lb. (76,655 kg.). *Maximum cruising speed:* 607 m.p.h. (977 km/hr.) at 21,000 ft. (6,400 m.). *Service ceiling:* 36,500 ft. (11,125 m.). *Range with maximum payload of 34,500 lb. (15,649 kg.):* 2,025 miles (3,260 km.).

Yak-40 (U.S.S.R.)

65

Yakovlev Yak–40 of Aeroflot, *ca* 1972. *Engines:* Three 3,307 lb. (1,500 kg.) s.t. Ivchenko AI–25 turbofans. *Span:* 82 ft. 0¼ in. (25·00 m.). *Length:* 66 ft. 9½ in. (20·36 m.). *Wing area:* 753·5 sq. ft. (70·00 sq. m.). *Maximum take-off weight:* 35,275 lb. (16,000 kg.). *Maximum cruising speed:* 342 m.p.h. (550 km/hr.) at 23,000 ft. (7,000 m.). *Range with maximum payload of 6,000 lb. (2,720 kg.):* 900 miles (1,450 km.).

Tu-154 (U.S.S.R.)

66

Tupolev Tu-154 prototype in Aeroflot livery, 1971. Data apply to production version. *Engines:* Three 20,945 lb. (9,500 kg.) s.t. Kuznetsov NK–8–2 turbofans. *Span:* 123 ft. 2½ in. (37·55 m.). *Length:* 157 ft. 1¾ in. (47·90 m.). *Wing area:* 2,168·4 sq. ft. (201·45 sq. m.). *Maximum take-off weight:* 198,415 lb. (90,000 kg.). *Maximum cruising speed:* 605 m.p.h. (975 km/hr.) at 31,150 ft. (9,500 m.). *Normal operating altitude:* 36,000 ft. (11,000 m.). *Typical range with maximum payload of 44,090 lb. (20,000 kg.):* 1,565 miles (2,520 km.).

TRISTAR (U.S.A.)

67

Lockheed L–1011–1 TriStar, third aircraft in Eastern Air Lines livery, 1971. *Engines:* Three 42,000 lb. (19,050 kg.) s.t. Rolls-Royce RB.211–22B turbofans. *Span:* 155 ft. 4 in. (47·34 m.). *Length:* 178 ft. 8 in. (54·35 m.). *Wing area:* 3,456·0 sq. ft. (321·07 sq. m.). *Maximum take-off weight:* 430,000 lb. (195,050 kg.). *Maximum cruising speed:* 562 m.p.h. (904 km/hr.) at 35,000 ft. (10,670 m.). *Service ceiling:* 42,000 ft. (12,800 m.). *Range with maximum payload of 86,183 lb. (39,092 kg.):* 2,677 miles (4,308 km.).

McDONNELL DOUGLAS DC-10 (U.S.A.)

68

McDonnell Douglas DC-10 Series 10, second aircraft in American Airlines livery, 1971. *Engines:* Three 41,000 lb. (18,597 kg.) s.t. General Electric CF6–6D1 turbofans. *Span:* 155 ft. 4 in. (47·34 m.). *Length:* 182 ft. 2½ in. (55·54 m.). *Wing area:* 3,861·0 sq. ft. (358·70 sq. m.). *Maximum take-off weight:* 440,000 lb. (199,580 kg.). *Maximum cruising speed:* 584 m.p.h. (940 km/hr.) at 31,000 ft. (9,450 m.). *Service ceiling:* 35,000 ft. (10,670 m.). *Range with maximum payload of 101,700 lb. (46,130 kg.):* 2,705 miles (4,353 km.).

COMET 4 (U.K.)

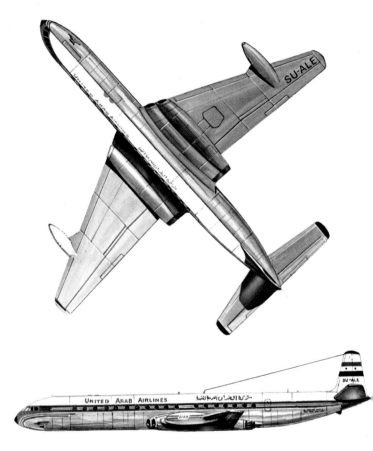

69

Hawker Siddeley Comet 4C of United Arab Airlines, *ca* 1964. *Engines:* Four 10,500 lb. (4,763 kg.) s.t. Rolls-Royce Avon Mk. 525B turbojets. *Span:* 114 ft. 10 in. (35·00 m.). *Length:* 118 ft. 0 in. (35·97 m.). *Wing area:* 2,121·0 sq. ft. (197·05 sq. m.). *Maximum take-off weight:* 162,000 lb. 73,500 kg.). *Typical cruising speed:* 542 m.p.h. (872 km/hr.) at 31,000 ft. (9,450 m.). *Service ceiling:* 39,000 ft. (11,890 m.). *Range with 19,630 lb. (8,900 kg.) payload:* 2,590 miles (4,168 km.).

BOEING 720 (U.S.A.)

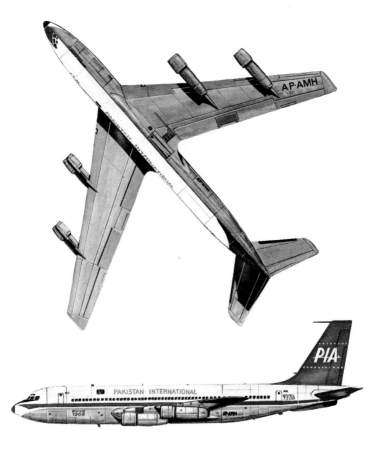

70

Boeing 720–040B of Pakistan International Airlines Corporation, *ca* 1963.
Engines: Four 17,000 lb. (7,710 kg.) s.t. Pratt & Whitney JT3D–1 turbofans.
Span: 130 ft. 10 in. (39·87 m.). *Length:* 136 ft. 9 in. (41·68 m.). *Wing
area:* 2,521·0 sq. ft. (234·21 sq. m.). *Maximum take-off weight:* 234,000
lb. (106,140 kg.). *Maximum cruising speed:* 611 m.p.h. (983 km/hr.) at 25,000
ft. (7,620 m.). *Service ceiling:* 42,000 ft. (12,800 m.). *Range with maximum
payload of 43,117 lb. (19,692 kg.):* 4,155 miles (6,690 km.).

McDONNELL DOUGLAS DC-8 (U.S.A.)

71

McDonnell Douglas DC–8–51 of Aeronaves de Mexico S.A., *ca* 1965. *Engines:* Four 18,000 lb. (8,172 kg.) s.t. Pratt & Whitney JT3D–3 turbofans. *Span:* 142 ft. 5 in. (43·41 m.). *Length:* 150 ft. 6 in. (45·87 m.). *Wing area:* 2,773·0 sq. ft. (257·62 sq. m.). *Maximum take-off weight:* 315,000 lb. (142,880 kg.). *Maximum cruising speed:* 579 m.p.h. (932 km/hr.) at 30,000 ft. (9,150 m.). *Range with maximum payload of 34,360 lb. (15,585 kg.):* 5,720 miles (9,205 km.).

CONVAIR 880 (U.S.A.)

72

Convair 880–M of Civil Air Transport (Taiwan), *ca* 1962. *Engines:* Four 11,650 lb. (5,285 kg.) s.t. General Electric CJ805–3B turbojets. *Span:* 120 ft. 0 in. (36·58 m.). *Length:* 129 ft. 4 in. (39·42 m.). *Wing area:* 2,000·0 sq. ft. (185·81 sq. m.). *Maximum take-off weight:* 193,000 lb. (87,540 kg.). *Maximum cruising speed:* 615 m.p.h. (990 km/hr.) at 22,500 ft. (6,860 m.). *Service ceiling:* 41,000 ft. (12,500 m.). *Range with 24,000 lb. (10,885 kg.) payload:* 2,880 miles (4,630 km.).

Tu-144 (U.S.S.R.)

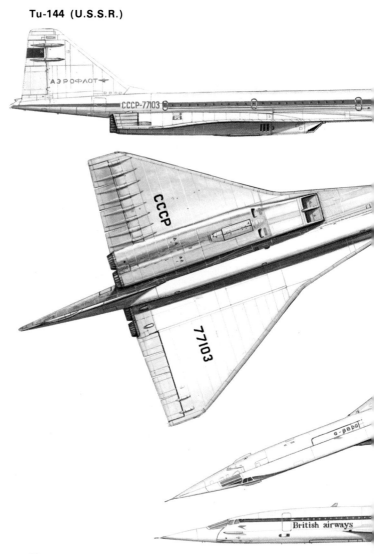

73

Tupolev Tu–144 (3rd production aircraft) in Aeroflot livery, 1973. *Engines:* Four 28,660/44,092 lb. (13,000/20,000 kg.) s.t. Kuznetsov NK–144 afterburning turbofans. *Span:* 94 ft. 5¾ in (28·80 m.). *Length:* 215 ft. 6½ in. (65·70 m.). *Wing area:* 4,714·6 sq. ft. (438·00 sq. m.). *Maximum take-off weight:* 396,830 lb. (180,000 kg.). *Maximum cruising speed:* 1,550 m.p.h. (2,500 km/hr.) at 59,050 ft. (18,000 m.). *Maximum range with 140 passengers:* 4,040 miles (6,500 km.).

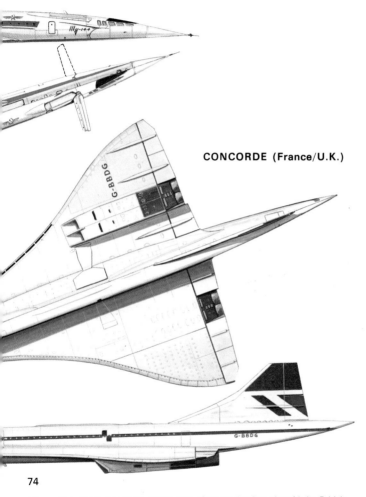

CONCORDE (France/U.K.)

74

Aérospatiale/BAC Concorde Series 200 (2nd production aircraft) in British Airways livery, 1974. *Engines:* Four 38,050 lb. (17,260 kg.) s.t. Rolls-Royce/ SNECMA Olympus 593 Mk. 602 afterburning turbojets. *Span:* 83 ft. 10 in. (25·56 m.). *Length:* 202 ft. 3·6 in. (51·66 m.). *Wing area:* 3,856·0 sq. ft. (358·25 sq. m.). *Maximum take-off weight:* 389,000 lb. (176,445 kg.). *Maximum cruising speed:* 1,354 m.p.h. (2,179 km/hr.) at 51,300 ft. (15,635 m.) (Mach 2·05). *Range at Mach 2·05 with maximum payload:* 3,970 miles (6,380 km.).

BOEING 707 INTERCONTINENTAL (U.S.A.)

75

Boeing 707–437 *Kanchenjunga* of Air-India, *ca* 1962. *Engines:* Four 17,500 lb. (7,945 kg.) s.t. Rolls-Royce Conway Mk. 508 turbofans. *Span:* 142 ft. 5 in. (43·41 m.). *Length:* 152 ft. 11 in. (46·61 m.). *Wing area:* 2,892·0 sq. ft. (268·68 sq. m.). *Maximum take-off weight:* 312,000 lb. (141,520 kg.). *Maximum cruising speed:* 593 m.p.h. (954 km/hr.) at 25,000 ft. (7,620 m.). *Service ceiling:* 42,000 ft. (12,800 m.). *Range with maximum payload of 57,000 lb. (25,855 kg.):* 4,865 miles (7,830 km.).

CONVAIR 990A (U.S.A.)

76

Convair 990A Coronado *Vaud* of Schweizerische Luftverkehr A.G. (Swissair),
ca 1966. *Engines:* Four 16,050 lb. (7,280 kg.) s.t. General Electric CJ805—23B
turbofans. *Span:* 120 ft. 0 in. (36·58 m.). *Length:* 139 ft. $2\frac{1}{2}$ in. (42·43
m.). *Wing area:* 2,250·0 sq. ft. (209·03 sq. m.). *Maximum take-off weight:*
253,000 lb. (114,760 kg.). *Maximum cruising speed:* 625 m.p.h. (1,006 km./hr.)
at 21,000 ft. (6,400 m.). *Service ceiling:* 41,000 ft. (12,500 m.). *Range with
25,770 lb. (11,690 kg.) payload:* 3,800 miles (6,115 km.).

SUPER VC10 (U.K.)

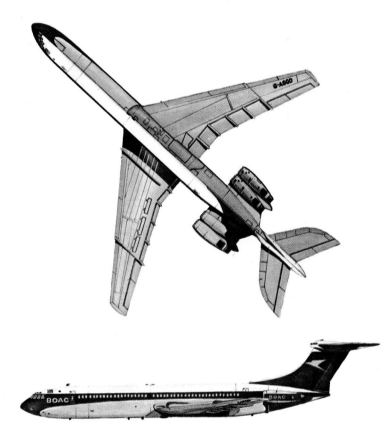

77

BAC Super VC10 Model 1151 of British Overseas Airways Corporation, *ca* 1965. *Engines:* Four 22,500 lb. (10,205 kg.) s.t. Rolls-Royce Conway 43 Mk. 550 turbofans. *Span:* 146 ft. 2 in. (44·55 m.). *Length:* 171 ft. 8 in. (52·32 m.). *Wing area:* 2,887·0 sq. ft. (268·21 sq. m.). *Maximum take-off weight:* 335,000 lb. (151,950 kg.). *Maximum cruising speed:* 568 m.p.h. (914 km/hr.) at 38,000 ft. (11,600 m.). *Service ceiling:* 42,000 ft. (12,800 m.). *Range with maximum payload of 50,406 lb. (22,860 kg.):* 4,630 miles (7,450 km.).

Il-62 (U.S.S.R.)

78

Ilyushin Il–62 of CSA, *ca* 1967. *Engines:* Four 23,150 lb. (10,500 kg.) s.t. Kuznetsov NK–8–4 turbofans. *Span:* 141 ft. 9 in. (43·20 m.). *Length:* 174 ft. 3½ in. (53·12 m.). *Wing area:* 3,009·05 sq. ft. (279·55 sq. m.). *Maximum take-off weight:* 357,150 lb. (162,000 kg.). *Maximum cruising speed:* 560 m.p.h. (900 km/hr.) at 39,370 ft. (12,000 m.). *Range with maximum payload of 50,700 lb. (23,000 kg.):* 4,160 miles (6,700 km.).

BOEING 747 (U.S.A.)

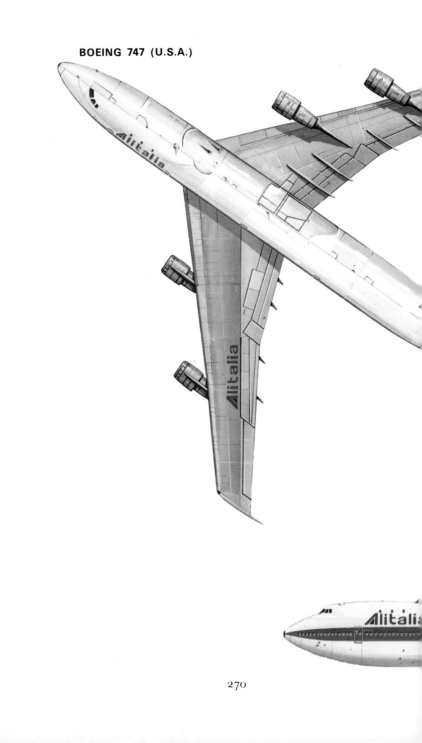

79

Boeing 747–143 *Neil Armstrong* of Alitalia, 1970. *Engines:* Four 43,500 lb. (19,730 kg.) s.t. Pratt & Whitney JT9D–3 turbofans. *Span:* 195 ft. 8 in. (59·64 m.). *Length:* 231 ft. 4 in. (70·51 m.). *Wing area:* 5,500·0 sq. ft. (510·97 sq. m.). *Maximum take-off weight:* 710,000 lb. (322,050 kg.). *Maximum level speed:* 595 m.p.h. (958 km/hr.) at 30,000 ft. (9,150 m.). *Maximum cruising height:* 45,000 ft. (13,715 m.). *Range with 374 passengers and baggage:* 5,790 miles (9,140 km.).

I-DEMA

McDONNELL DOUGLAS DC-8 SUPER SIXTY (U.S.A.)

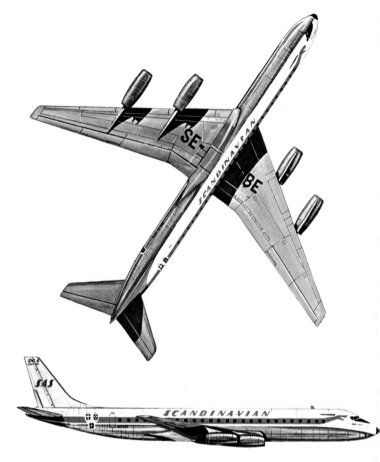

80

McDonnell Douglas DC–8–62 *Anund Viking* of Scandinavian Airlines System, *ca* 1967. *Engines:* Four 18,000 lb. (8,172 kg.) s.t. Pratt & Whitney JT3D–3B turbofans. *Span:* 148 ft. 5 in. (45·23 m.). *Length:* 157 ft. 5 in. (47·98 m.). *Wing area:* 2,927·0 sq. ft. (271·93 sq. m.). *Maximum take-off weight:* 335,000 lb. (151,950 kg.). *Maximum cruising speed:* 600 m.p.h. (965 km/hr.) at 30,000 ft. (9,150 m.). *Range with maximum payload of 47,335 lb. (21,470 kg.):* 6,000 miles (9,640 km.).

1 Curtiss C-46

Arising out of talks held in 1936 between the Curtiss-Wright Corporation and a number of US domestic airlines, the CW-20 (as the design was originally known) materialised three years later as the world's largest twin-engined transport and featured a generous 'double-bubble' fuselage. The twin-tailed CW-20 prototype, NX19436, powered by two 1,700 hp Wright R-586-C14-BA2 Double Row Cyclones, flew for the first time on 26 March 1940. After substitution of the now familiar single fin and rudder, the aircraft was evaluated briefly by the USAAF (as the C-55-CS), and then sold to BOAC in 1941 as G-AGDI *St Louis*, being used as a 24-seat war transport for the next two years. Commercial production of the CW-20 was precluded by America's entry into World War 2, but under the name Commando an unpressurised, Double Wasp-powered version was accepted for a military role. Over 3,180 C-46s were built for the USAAF and 160 R5C-1s for the US Marine Corps. Plans were made after the war to produce a CW-20E civil version for Eastern; but this failed to achieve production status. Instead, several hundred war-surplus Commandos were 'demilitarised' for the commercial market. Their adoption by civil operators was slow to reach appreciable proportions, largely due to some difficulty in meeting full CAA requirements regarding maximum operating weights. However, by 1960 over ninety carriers were operating C-46s, and there were still well over a hundred of these aircraft in airline service at the beginning of 1974, mostly in North and South America. The majority of those which saw service post-war were former C-46As (single loading door), C-46Ds (double cargo doors and modified nose), or generally similar C-46Fs; these had R-2800-51M1 engines, a 17,600 lb (7,983 kg) payload and 48,000 lb (21,772 kg) gross weight. Post-war modifications have included the 1956 CW-20T with various structural improvements, introduced by Air Carrier Engineering Services and the L.B. Smith Aircraft Corporation; the Super 46C, from the same source in 1958 with a 50,650 lb (22,975 kg) gross weight; and a similar version introduced by Riddle Airlines in 1957 as the C-46R.

2 Ilyushin Il-14 ('Crate')

For many years the piston-engined workhorse of the air forces and airlines in the Soviet Union and numerous satellite states, the Il-14 is still in commercial service, though in diminishing numbers: excluding those still operated by Aeroflot, more than a hundred were estimated to be still active early in 1974. The Il-14 is a derivative of Ilyushin's earlier Il-12, the design of which was begun in 1943 as a potential successor to the Li-2 (licence DC-3) built extensively in Russia during the war years. Construction of the prototype Il-12 (SSSR-L1380) began in 1945, and the aeroplane made its first flight early in 1946, its existence being made public in August of that year. The first transport to be built post-war in the Soviet Union, it was in production from 1946–53, during which time over three thousand are believed to have been built, most of them for military use. The original production Il-12, with 1,650 hp ASh-82FN engines, was supplanted by the Il-12B, which had a number of refinements including a small dorsal fin fairing and a strengthened nosewheel oleo. Both versions had unpressurised fuselages, accommodating a flight crew of four and 27 passengers; they served with Aeroflot and Il-12Bs were operated by the Czechoslovak and Polish state airlines, CSA and LOT. In 1953 the Il-12 was superseded in production by the Il-14, a development of the former and distinguishable by its more powerful engines, revised wings with squared-off tips and a larger and more angular vertical tail. In its original standard commercial version, the Il-14P, the new type seated only 18 passengers, although between 1956–59 about eighty examples of a 26-seat version were built under licence by the VEB Flugzeugbau of Dresden. The first VEB-built Il-14P was flown in April 1956, and aircraft from the Dresden production batch were supplied to airlines in Bulgaria, China, Hungary and Poland, as well as to the former East German Lufthansa. Licence production of the Il-14P was also undertaken by Avia in Czechoslovakia, which built fifty for the USSR, six for the national airline, CSA, and one for LOT. By far the most prolific model,

however, was the Il-14M, which first appeared in 1956 and entered service with Aeroflot in the summer of that year. Chief differences noticeable in the Il-14M are a 3 ft 3¼ in (1·00 m) longer fuselage, with seats for 24–32 passengers, and a slightly different wing planform. The Il-14M was subsequently built in many thousands in Russia (up to 1958), Czechoslovakia and East Germany for use both as a civil and a military transport. The Avia company refined the aircraft still further during its production period, which ended in 1962. The original Il-14M was produced as the Avia 14-32A in 1957, Avia 14T cargo transport, and finally as the Avia 14 Super, later known as the 14 Salon. Considerable structural re-design of this last-named version resulted in a much lower basic empty weight, a somewhat higher gross weight and additional range through the use of wingtip fuel tanks. Passenger cabin windows are circular in the 14 Salon, which can seat up to 42 passengers and has a pressurised fuselage.

3   Douglas DC-3

One of the most challenging activities for a high proportion of the world's aircraft designers and airline chiefs in post-war years has been the pursuit of an elusive and almost non-existent will-o'-the-wisp described as the 'DC-3 replacement'; for how does one begin to set about replacing a thirty-five-year-old aeroplane that in 1970 was still in the inventory of more than two hundred airlines, large and small, in every part of the globe, performing every kind of task imaginable? For a large percentage of the years since the end of World War 2, the DC-3s in commercial service outnumbered the total of all other types of transport aeroplane put together. A detailed *Flight International* survey published in December 1969 revealed nearly nine hundred DC-3s still in airline service. Five years later, that figure was still in excess of five hundred. The evolution of the DC-3, as a 'sleeper' development of the DC-2, began in 1935, with the first flight taking place later that year on 17 December. In the event, however, it was the day transport version which attracted most customer attention and became the principal production model prior to the outbreak of World War 2. The war brought about a tremendous output of these aircraft – nearly eleven thousand in the United States, together with some two thousand built under licence in the Soviet Union (as the Lisunov Li-2) and another four hundred and fifty in Japan as the L2D2. When the war ended, thousands of surplus C-47s and other military variants flooded the civil market and were snapped up eagerly by operators the world over for passenger, freight and general duties. A year or two later the DC-3 went through a rather bad patch, acquiring a reputation for being accident-prone – though the very number of them in service, by the law of averages, must have precluded an entirely trouble-free career. Some of these accidents were undoubtedly due to overloading:

nominally, the DC-3's capacity is 28–32 passengers, but there were plenty of hair-raising tales of more than twice this number being herded into some aircraft in Middle Eastern and African countries – perhaps due to the faith of simple people in the DC-3's ability to do almost anything asked of it – though most of these trips were accomplished without incident. Time, and the DC-3's sterling contribution to the Berlin airlift, erased the 'death-trap' image from the public mind, and it has enjoyed a virtually unblemished career ever since. Because of the widespread nature of the DC-3's employment, it would be impossible to list here the innumerable modifications, official and unofficial, that have been carried out during its past forty years of service. Generally speaking, these concern the employment of varying types of engine, including turboprops, differing shapes of passenger cabin windows and the arrangement of internal seating and furnishing. Most of those still in service are DC-3Cs, a structurally strengthened version of the wartime C-47 Skytrain or Dakota. In addition, many hundreds of military models continue in service with air arms throughout the world; the RAF retired its last in 1970.

4 Vickers Viking

The longevity of the Viking is typified by the machine chosen for the illustration on page 20; as the first production example of the long-nosed Viking 1B, it made its maiden flight on 6 August 1946, yet was disposed of for scrap by its original owner only in 1962. As Britain's first post-war civil transport to enter commercial service, the Viking was the result of a requirement issued in 1944 for a 'Wellington transport', and the three prototypes and first production model (the Viking 1A) utilised the geodetic-pattern outer wing panels, engine nacelles and landing gear assemblies of the celebrated wartime bomber. With two 1,675 hp Hercules 130 engines, the first prototype (G-AGOK) was flown at Wisley on 22 June 1945; G-AGOL and 'OM joined it before the end of the year, both of these featuring a curved dorsal fin extension which became standard on production aircraft. The Viking's C of A was issued on 24 April 1946. Nineteen Viking 1As, with 1,690 hp Hercules 630s, were built, eleven of them going to BEA. On 1 September 1946 the first Viking services (Northolt–Copenhagen) were inaugurated by BEA. Production continued with thirty-one Viking 1s, with more conventional stressed-skin exteriors replacing the fabric-covered geodetic structure, and these also were delivered chiefly to BEA and various associate airlines. Five 1As were brought up to Viking 1 standard and operated by British West Indian Airways. The major version was the Viking 1B, one hundred and thirteen of which were built before production ceased at the end of 1947. Like the Viking 1, the 1B was powered by 1,690 hp Hercules 634 radials, but differed in having a 2 ft 4 in (0·71

m) longer fuselage with seating capacity increased from 21 to 24 initially, and eventually to 27. Viking 1Bs were sold or leased to carriers in Africa, Argentina, Denmark, Eire, India, Iraq, Southern Rhodesia and the United Kingdom, operating both on scheduled services and with a large number of charter operators. As late as 1960 there were still about a hundred Vikings in service; by 1970 the number had dwindled to three, belonging to the French operator Europe Aero Service, and by 1974 these too had disappeared from service. Various internal modifications enabled some Vikings to carry heavier loads than those originally specified, for example the 'Mks 3/3A/3B' (unofficial designation of 1/1A/1Bs operated by Eagle), with an additional half-ton of payload, and BEA's 'Admiral' class of 1952, which seated a maximum of 36 passengers. Variants of the design included the RAF Viking C.2, Valetta and Varsity, small numbers of which appeared on the civil register in the 1950s. One distinction belonging to the Viking is that of G-AJPH, the Nene engine testbed, which on 6 April 1948 became the first purely jet-powered British transport aeroplane to fly.

5 Saab 90 Scandia

In broadly the same class as the Convair 240, Il-12 and Viking, the Scandia's design was begun by Saab in 1944 under the title Project CT. Later the designation Saab 90 was allocated, and the prototype (SE-

BCA) was flown for the first time on 16 November 1946. This aircraft, powered by two 1,350 hp Pratt & Whitney R-2000-2SD13-G engines, was widely demonstrated in the major European countries during 1947–48, but failed to collect more than one order, and that (for ten aircraft) from the home airline AB Aerotransport, which became a part of the SAS combine in February 1948. Six of the ABA order were delivered to SAS, the remaining four going to Aerovias Brasil. Two years later, Aerovias became part of VASP, which ordered a further five Scandias, and these were the only airlines to operate the type. In all, seventeen production Scandias were built, the last two being for SAS. The first eleven aircraft were completed entirely by Saab. The remaining six, because of Saab's heavy commitments to military production, were undertaken with assistance from the Aviolanda, de Schelde and Fokker factories in Holland. The production model, with more powerful engines of the R-2180 type, was known as the Saab 90A-2, and was introduced on SAS's Scandinavian domestic services in November 1950. It carried a flight crew of four (later reduced to three) and provided accommodation for 24–32 passengers in a non-pressurised fuselage. Seating capacity was later increased to 36. After their withdrawal from SAS service in 1957 the domestic Scandias were also bought by VASP, and with the purchase of the prototype by the same airline, all aircraft of this type gravitated to Brazil. In South America they continued a lengthy flying career, and in 1967 there were still nine Scandias in the VASP fleet. Two other variants of the Scandia were projected: the Saab 90A-3, enlarged to seat up to 38 passengers, and the Saab 90B-3, with similar capacity and a pressurised fuselage; but neither of these was built.

6 Airspeed Ambassador

The A.S.57 Ambassador resulted from the Brabazon Committee's requirement IIA for a European short-haul airliner (Specification 25/43), and work on building a prototype was started in 1945. Originally the aeroplane was scheduled to have Centaurus 130 engines and a capacity ranging from 28–50 seats, depending on stage length, though in BEA service the normal range was 40–47 seats. The first prototype (G-AGUA), powered by two 2,600 hp Centaurus 631 radials, flew at Christchurch on 10 July 1947, and from the outset it was evident that the design had great passenger appeal. The high wing permitted an extremely quiet and roomy passenger cabin, which offered an excellent view from the large panoramic windows. Cleanliness and elegance of line were apparent throughout the aeroplane, down to the interchangeable 'power eggs', each in a petal-type cowling specially designed by Airspeed to offer minimum drag. Furthermore, the Ambassador combined modest runway requirements with an outstanding single-engined performance. The second prototype

(G-AKRD) flew on 26 August 1948; two static-test airframes were built, followed by one pre-production Ambassador (G-ALFR) which was used to obtain the C of A and for route proving by BEA. This aircraft had the definitive Centaurus 661 powerplant, and flew for the first time in May 1950. Twenty production Ambassadors were built for BEA, the first of these flying on 12 January 1951. Airline acceptance trials were completed during the following August, and on 13 March 1952, under the BEA class name 'Elizabethan', the Ambassador entered service. It quickly proved to have better operating costs, especially over the shorter routes, than any other aircraft in the BEA fleet, and remained in service with the airline for five and a half years until the latter half of 1957. Three were then operated for a short time by Butler Air Transport, two others by Globe Air and another pair by the Royal Jordanian Air Force. These all returned eventually to the United Kingdom, where for several more years they flew with BKS, Dan-Air and other operators. One was still operating with Dan-Air in 1971. In the latter 1950s, G-AKRD and G-ALZR were extensively used as flying testbeds for Dart, Eland, Proteus and Tyne engines, and various turboprop developments (including one with four Darts) were projected under the designation A.S.59. Other projects included the A.S.60 Ayrshire, a military transport to Specification 13/45, and the A.S.67 freighter, but none of these came to fruition.

7 Martin 2-0-2 and 4-0-4

The Martin 2-0-2 made its first appearance slightly ahead of the Convair 240, and on 13 August 1947 became the first twin-engined airliner of US post-war design to receive a CAA type operating certificate. Two flying prototypes were built, the maiden flight taking place on 22 November 1946, and a third airframe was completed for static testing. Twenty-five 2-0-2s were produced to the order of Northwest Orient Airlines, plus four for LAN-Chile and two for LAV of Venezuela, LAN-Chile being first to put the type into service, in October 1947. Powered by two 2,400 hp R-2800-CA18 engines, the Martin 2-0-2 seated 36–40 passengers in an unpressurised fuselage. In 1948, investigation of an accident to an airline 2-0-2 revealed some structural weaknesses in the wing; all aircraft then in service were temporarily withdrawn for this to be rectified, and no further 2-0-2s were built. Two pressurised developments were proposed, the passenger 3-0-3 and the cargo 3-0-4, and a prototype of the former was flown on 20 June 1947, but in 1949 both designs were shelved in favour of the Martin 4-0-4. Initial orders for the 4-0-4 were placed by Eastern and TWA, for thirty-five and thirty respectively, and as an interim measure twelve Martin 2-0-2As (the first of which flew in July 1950) were built for use by the latter airline. These were unpressurised, but had -CB16 engines of 2,400 hp and a gross weight of 43,000 lb (19,504 kg); they entered

TWA service on 1 September 1950. The Martin 4-0-4 had the same powerplant and the same seating capacity as the 2-0-2A, but its pressurised fuselage was 3 ft 3 in (0·99 m) longer and the maximum payload and take-off weight were increased to 11,592 lb (5,259 kg) and 44,900 lb (20,366 kg) respectively. A converted 2-0-2 airframe, N40400, acted as the 4-0-4 prototype, flying for the first time at Baltimore on 21 October 1950. Between autumn 1951 and spring 1953 a total of one hundred and three Martin 4-0-4s were delivered: Eastern and TWA had increased their original orders to sixty and forty-one, and the remaining two aircraft were completed as RM-1s for the US Coast Guard. The Martin 4-0-4 entered service with TWA in October 1951, and with Eastern in January 1952. By the beginning of 1971 about forty Martins were still in airline service. Almost all of these were 4-0-4s, the largest fleets being those of Piedmont Airlines and Southern Airways. By the mid-1970s only about twenty 4-0-4s remained in service, Southern (fourteen) having the largest fleet.

8, 9 & 10 **Convair 240/340/440/ 540/580/600/640 series**

A requirement existed in many countries after World War 2 for a twin-engined, medium-range, medium-capacity passenger transport aircraft. Russia produced the Il-12, Britain the Viking, the United States the Martin 2-0-2 and Convair-liner; and of these the Convair proved to be the most adaptable and durable. Convair's first medium twin design was the Model 110, a prototype of which (NX90653) was flown for the first time on 8 July 1946. Powered by two 2,100 hp R-2800-S1C3-G engines, the Convair 110 was a 30-seater having a wing span of 91 ft 0 in (27·74 m) and a length of 71 ft 0 in (21·64 m). Though an attractive aeroplane, the 110 offered only limited payload/range capabilities and did not go into production. From it, however, Convair developed the slightly larger Model 240 with 2,400 hp R-2800-CA18 engines. Despite a slimmer-section fuselage the Convair 240 seated up to 40 passengers, and had appreciably better range than its predecessor. The prototype (N24501) was first flown at San Diego on 16 March 1947, and immediately met with favourable reaction. Series production started late in 1947, and by mid-1948 over a hundred and fifty 240s had been ordered. The largest initial order, for seventy-five aircraft, was from American Airlines; other US domestic carriers to order Convairs included Continental (five), Pan American (twenty) and Western (ten). Overseas customers included the Argentine operator FAMA, which ordered five, and KLM, Swissair and TAA, which ordered twelve, four and five respectively. The first certificated Convair 240 was delivered on 28 February 1948 to American, which put the type into scheduled service on 1 June. The first overseas delivery was made to TAA on 25

August the same year. The Model 240 remained in production until 1958, by which time five hundred and seventy-one examples had been built. The majority of these were completed as T-29 aircrew trainers and C-131A transports for the US services, but one hundred and seventy-six were civil 240s. These have served with nearly fifty airlines the world over; only about half a dozen were still in airline service in 1970, but a number continued to fly as business executive transports.

The basic soundness of the Convair 240 design led, inevitably, to consideration of a stretched version, and this duly appeared in the form of the Convair 340, the prototype of which (N3401) flew for the first time on 5 October 1951. More efficient R-2800-CB16 engines offered a somewhat better performance than that of the Model 240, but the major outward changes in the Model 340 were an increase of 13 ft 7 in (4·14 m) in the wing span and the insertion of additional fuselage sections of 1 ft 4 in (0·40 m) ahead of the wing and 3 ft 2 in (0·96 m) aft. These alterations enabled the Convair 340 to seat up to 44 passengers in a standard interior layout, and by the time the 340 received its FAA type certificate on 28 March 1952 more than a hundred and sixty had been ordered by nearly a score of domestic and overseas operators. The first delivery of a production 340 was made to United Air Lines on 28 March 1952. Two hundred and nine civil 340s were built, of which about two dozen were still in airline operation in the mid-1970s. Others were in service as company transports.

The Convair 440 Metropolitan retains the same overall configuration as the 340, but has more powerful R-2800-CB17 engines and a number of detail refinements. These include better cabin soundproofing and, on many aircraft, weather-warning radar. Maximum seating capacity is raised to 52. The first Metropolitan, a converted 340, was flown on 6 October 1955, but in addition to 340 conversions one hundred and eighty-six civil 440s were built from the outset to Metropolitan standard, and about eighty of these were still in service in 1974; the major operators at that time were Mackey in the United States, and SAS and Linjeflyg in Europe, and six have been acquired by the Bolivian Air Force. Convair-liners of one kind or another had thus been continuously in service for more than twenty-five years, some of them still with their original 1948 customers.

Conversion of Convair 240 and 340/440 airliners to turbine power began experimentally in the early 1950s, though it was only in the early and middle 1960s that the movement gained impetus. There are four basic series of turboprop Convairs, designated according to powerplant. These are the 540, with Napier Eland engines; the 580, with Allisons; and the 600 and 640, with Rolls-Royce Darts. The US Air Force tested a military YC-131C with Allison T56 turboprops in 1954, but it was Napier which started the civil conversion movement when, at the end of that year, it fitted 3,060 ehp Eland N. El. 1 engines to an ex-airline Convair 340. Re-registered G-ANVP, it flew for the first time with Elands on 9 February 1955. (Some years later, with the uprated Eland 504As which became the standard installation, this machine was leased to Allegheny Airlines, in whose colours it appears in the drawing on page 25.) Allegheny subsequently operated five more Convair 540s until 1962, when cessation of Eland development led to their withdrawal. One other was converted by the PacAero division of Pacific Airmotive for Butler Air Transport. Canadair undertook to produce Eland Convairs under the title Canadair 540, and converted three 440s, one as a demonstrator and the other two for Quebecair. No further civil orders materialised, but Canadair built ten, as complete aircraft, for the RCAF as CC-109 Cosmopolitans; preceded by the two former Quebecair machines as military prototypes, they were delivered from July 1960. PacAero followed up its original interest in the 540 by proposing the more powerful Convair 580, using 3,750 shp Allison 501 D-13 turboprops. With increased tail control surface area, the Convair 580 was certificated in April 1960, although the first to enter service (with Frontier Airlines) did not do so until June 1964. Seating was increased from 44 to 52. Main operators of the 580 in 1975 were Allegheny, Frontier and North Central. A more recent alliance has been that with the 3,025 ehp Rolls-Royce Dart RDa.10/1 to produce the Convair 600. This conversion, unlike the others, applied to the Convair 240 as well as the 340/440, although in the former case additional strengthening of the structure was necessary. The first 600 conversion was in fact carried out on a former Model 240D which, as N94294, made its first flight with Darts on 20 May 1965. The first Convair 600 to enter service was Central Airlines' N74858 on 30 November 1965; Martin's Air Charter became the first European operator of the type in April 1966. With Dart engines, seating can be increased to 48 in former 240s and to 56 in ex-340/440s, the latter being designated Model 640 in their converted form. Caribair, on 22 December 1965, became the first Convair 640 operator. Nearly fifty Convair 600/640s were in airline service in the 1970s, including some two dozen with Texas International.

11 NAMC YS-11

In May 1957 the Japanese Ministry of International Trade and Industry set up a Transport Aircraft Development Association consisting of six of the major aircraft constructors in the country. Its objective was the design and production of an indigenous medium-range commercial transport. After establishing a basic specification for the aeroplane, the TADA set up a committee under Dr Hidemara Kimura to study various design proposals, and by January 1959 a basic configuration had been agreed upon. Work started shortly afterwards on a full-size mock-up of the design. This was carried out at Sugita, Yokohama, and the aeroplane was allotted the designation YS-11. On 1 June 1959 the Nihon Aeroplane Manufacturing Company (NAMC) was created to assume responsibility for development, flight testing and marketing of the aircraft. At this time the YS-11 was cast as a 60/70 seater, but a revision of customer requirements during the next two or three years caused this to be scaled down to 52–60 seats. The first of the two flying prototypes (two others were built for static testing) made its maiden flight on 30 August 1962 and the second on 28 December 1962. The YS-11 entered production in 1964, the first series-built aircraft flying on 23 October of that year. Construction was allocated as follows: tail units to Fuji, main wings and engine nacelles to Kawasaki, main fuselage (and final assembly) to Mitsubishi, flaps and ailerons to Nippi, rear fuselage to Shin Meiwa and honeycomb structural components to Showa. The NAMC was responsible for design work, production and quality control and sales. A domestic C of A was issued for the YS-11 on 25 August 1964, and an FAA certificate for exported models on 18 October 1965. The first YS-11 delivery was made, in March 1965, to Toa Airways, domestic services commencing on 1 April, and before the end of the year the first foreign delivery, to Filipinas Orient Airways, had also been made. The YS-11, the first airliner in service to use the RDa.10

version of the Dart turboprop, has since acquired a highly satisfactory reputation among its operators. Of the 60-passenger initial production version, designated YS-11-100, forty-seven examples were built, including four for the JASDF and one cargo model for the JMSDF. Subsequent production aircraft have YS-11A designations, beginning with the YS-11A-200 (60-seat all-passenger version); the YS-11A-300 is a mixed-traffic version, seating 46 passengers and featuring a cargo-loading door at the front; the YS-11A-400 is an all-cargo counterpart. The YS-11A-500 and -600 versions correspond broadly to the -200 and -300 but have a 1,102 lb (500 kg) increase in maximum take-off weight. Production, which ended after completion of the 182nd aircraft, comprised ninety-five YS-11A-200s (including one for the ASDF and four for the MSDF), sixteen -300s (including one for the ASDF), nine -400s (seven for the ASDF and two for the MSDF), four -500s and nine -600s (including three for the MSDF). The largest civil fleets were those operated by Piedmont, Toa Domestic and All Nippon.

12 Hawker Siddeley 748

The Hawker Siddeley 748 was a somewhat slow starter in the world airliner stakes, but the sales total had exceeded six hundred (including military purchases) and there were some sixty operators throughout the world by late summer 1981. Design development, as the 20-seat Avro 748, began as early as

1957, but until an enlarged, Dart-powered development of the aeroplane was proposed, the project attracted very little interest from the airlines. Nevertheless, on 9 January 1959, Hawker Siddeley announced its intention to go ahead with the project and build an initial batch of twelve aircraft, and work started a month later on the construction of two flying prototypes and two other aircraft for static tests. Encouragement came in July 1959 when the Indian government announced its intention to assemble the HS 748 under licence at Kanpur as a military transport for the Indian Air Force. The first HS 748 prototype, G-APZV, was flown at Woodford on 24 June 1960, the second (G-ARAY) on 10 April 1961 and the first production 748 (G-ARMV, one of three for Skyways) on 30 August 1961. This initial production model, known as the Series 1, had a slightly greater wing span than the prototypes, and was powered by 1,880 ehp Dart Mk 514 (RDa.6) engines. During 1961, components for five Series 1s were despatched to Kanpur for assembly, and the first Indian-assembled machine was flown on 1 November. The HS 748 Series 1 entered airline service with Skyways Coach Air and with Aerolineas Argentinas in April 1962, following the issue of a C of A on 9 January. Meanwhile, on 6 November 1961, G-ARAY had flown for the first time with a new powerplant of 2,105 ehp Dart Mk 531s (RDa.7s) to act as the prototype for the HS 748 Series 2. This second model, apart from an enhanced performance and higher operating weight, is generally similar to the Series 1, which it supplanted in production; both versions have a seating range of 40–58 passengers. The first Series 2 production machine flew in August 1962, and certification of this version followed two months later. The Series 2 is the subject of Indian licence assembly: the first Kanpur HS 748 Srs 2 was flown on 28 January 1964, and orders up to mid-1978 totalled seventeen for Indian Airlines Corporation and sixty-two for the Indian Air Force. Military orders for British-built 748s have been placed by the Belgian Air Force, Brazilian Air Force, Colombian Air Force, Ecuadorean Air Force, Royal Australian Air Force and Navy, Nepal Royal Flight, Venezualan Ministry of Defence, and Zambian Air Force. Air Support Command operated thirty-one as the Andover CC Mks 1 and 2 tactical transport. Others serve the Queen's Flight. Superseding the Series 2 from mid-1967, the Series 2A has improved performance resulting from the installation of 2,280 ehp Dart RDa.7 Mk 532-2L or -2S engines. The first Series 2A entered service with Varig of Brazil in August 1978. The Coastguarder is a maritime patrol version. The Series 2B replaced the 2A in 1979. It has an advanced wing with extended tips from the Coastguarder, low-noise level and wide-body interior styling. By mid-1980 HS 748 sales totalled three hundred and forty-nine to seventy-five operators in forty-eight countries.

13   Fokker-VFW Friendship

Probably the nearest approach to the elusive 'DC-3 replacement' is the Fokker Friendship, whose steady sales for over twenty-three years have established it as the world's biggest-selling turboprop-powered commercial transport by a handsome margin. Design studies for the F.27, Fokker's first airliner since the 1930s, were initiated in 1950, and after study of a variety of configurations a decision was made in favour of a twin-Dart aeroplane with pressurised accommodation for 28 passengers and a minimum range of 300 miles (483 km) with a capacity payload. Like the pre-war Fokkers, the new design, named Friendship, favoured a high wing layout, and the first of the two flying prototypes, PH-NIV, flew for the first time on 24 November 1955, powered by Dart Mk 507 turbo-props. The second and subsequent Friendships were 3 ft 0 in (0·91 m) longer, permitting four more passengers to be carried, and the higher-powered Dart Mk 511 was selected for the initial production version. In April 1956 the Dutch manufacturer signed an agreement with Fairchild, which had been building Fokker trainers in the United States for several years, to build and market the Friendship on that side of the Atlantic. The first Fairchild machine (N1027) was flown on 12 April 1958. Production Friendships built in Holland are identified by Mark numbers, and those from Fairchild (now Fairchild Industries) by F-27 or FH-227 designations. The first and basic 44-seat production model was the Mk 100 (= F-27), which entered service with West Coast Airlines (F-27) in September and with Aer Lingus (Friendship Mk 100) in December 1958. Eighty-four Mk 100s were built. They were followed by the Mk 200 (= F-27A), generally similar but with 2,050 shp Dart RDa. 7 Mk 532-7 engines. The Mk 300 (= F-27B) was a Fairchild-developed passenger/cargo version of the Mk 100 with reinforced floor and a large port-side freight door, of which thirteen were built; and the Mk 400 Combiplane a similar counterpart, by Fokker only, of the Mk 200. Fokker is responsible for the Mk 400M Troopship, a military troop- and freight-carrier version of the 200, and also for the first stretched version, the Mk 500, which has a 4 ft 11 in (1·50 m) longer fuselage, freight-loading door, Dart 528s and space for 52 passengers. The Mk 600 is a cargo version of the Mk 200, with optional quick-change capability. Fairchild developments included the F-27F and F-27J business variants, with Dart Mk 529 and 532 engines respectively, and the high-altitude F-27M. After the amalgamation with Hiller Aircraft in 1964 the American manufacturer produced its own stretched versions in the FH-227, FH-227B, C, D and E, which were 52-seaters, 6 ft 6 in (1·98 m) longer than the F-27 and powered by Dart Mk 532s. The first FH-227 flew in March 1966 and was delivered to Mohawk Airlines during the following month. By August 1974, six hundred and twenty-one Friendships had been ordered, of which nearly five hundred were for airline customers. American production (total two hundred and five) has ended, but Dutch production of Mks 200, 400, 500 and 600 in civil, Maritime and Troopship versions continues with five hundred and ten sold to one hundred and fifty-eight operators in sixty-three countries by late 1980.

14 Antonov An-24 ('Coke'), An-26 ('Curl') and An-30 ('Clunk')

Even without the high wing layout which has become a regular feature of Antonov designs, the An-24 would obviously bear close comparison with such western counterparts as the Friendship and the Herald. It is particularly comparable to the Friendship, being nearly identical in terms of overall size, weight and general performance; the chief point of difference is the Russian aeroplane's shorter range. However, the An-24 was intended for short-stage local service routes between communities with only second-class or unprepared airfields – hence the rather high available power and the high wing position, which has the added advantage of minimising the risk of propeller damage while using such strips. Design of the An-24 was begun, after discussions with Aeroflot in the spring of 1958, to provide the Soviet state airline with a 32/40-seat short-hauler to replace its veteran piston-engined Il-14s and Li-2s. The first of two prototypes ('SSSR-1959') was flown for the first time at Kiev at the end of April 1960, by test pilot G. Lysenko. Several modifications were apparent in the second machine, 'SSSR-1960', when it appeared later that year. Among these were an extended fuselage nose, elongated engine nacelles, a dorsal fin and additional fin area under the tailcone. This external configuration has remained basically unaltered, though internal rearrangement has increased the seating capacity of the An-24V first to 44 and then, in the Series II which has been the standard passenger version since 1968, to 50. A flight crew of up to five can be carried. Two static-test aircraft and three pre-series machines were built before the An-24V entered regular production in 1962. The early aircraft were subjected to typically thorough flight test and route-proving programmes before, in September 1963, Aeroflot introduced the type on scheduled services from Moscow to Voronezh and Saratov. In 1964 the An-24V became available for export, and the list of civil customers include Air Guinée, Air Mali, Balkan Bulgarian Airlines, CAAC (China), Cubana, Egyptair, Interflug, Iraqi Airways, Lina Congo, LOT, Mongolian Airlines and Tarom.

The standard version in production in 1974 was the An-24V Series II, which has AI-24A water-injection engines and is available in mixed-traffic, convertible, all-cargo or executive versions in addition to the standard 50-seater. The An-24T is a specialised freighter version, distinguishable by its twin ventral fins and hemispherical window above the flight deck. Variants of the An-24V and T, known as the

An-24RV and RT, have a 1,985 lb (900 kg) st Type RU 19-300 auxiliary turbojet engine in the rear of the starboard nacelle, to improve engine starting, take-off and in-flight performance. An aerial fire-fighting version, appearing in 1971, was the An-24P, and in 1973 first details were revealed of the An-30, an aerial survey version with an extensively-glazed nose and a specially-equipped main cabin.

The An-26, first revealed in 1969, is a version generally similar to the An-24RT but having more power-ful (2,820 ehp) AI-24T engines and redesigned rear fuselage incorporat-ing a large 'beaver-tail' rear-loading ramp/door. The An-32 ('Cline') flew in 1976. A much improved An-26, it has 4,190 ehp engines mounted overwing.

15 **Handley Page Herald**

The Herald suffered somewhat from the decision to persevere, in the early stages, with a piston-engined version of the design. Handley Page's decision to proceed with a 44-seat feederliner was taken in the early 1950s. As the H.P.R.3, work began in 1954 to complete two prototypes, each powered by four Alvis Leonides piston engines. By the time that the first of these (G-AODE) made its maiden flight on 25 August 1955, Handley Page had received orders for nearly thirty Heralds from Queensland Airlines, Australian National Airlines and Lloyd Aero Columbiano, together with a provi-sional order from Air Kruise, and plans were well advanced to lay down a production line. By this time, however, the advent of the Friendship and Viscount had caused many operators to revise their attitude to turbine transports, and some Herald customers declined to accept it in piston-engined form. As a result, Handley Page offered the twin-Dart H.P.R.7 as an alterna-tive, this being basically the same design except for a slightly longer fuselage seating up to 44 people and modifications made necessary by the change of powerplant. In its new form, G-AODE made its second 'maiden' flight on 11 March 1958 followed on 17 December by the second Dart Herald, G-AODF. In June 1959 the first order for the new Herald was placed by the British government, which bought three Series 100 for use on the 'Highlands and Islands' services of BEA; and subsequent sales continued steadily if not spectacularly. Major produc-tion version was the Series 200, which is 3 ft 6 in (1·07 m) longer and seats up to 56 passengers. The Series 400 was a military freighter equivalent with reinforced flooring and side-loading doors. It had accommodation for up to 50 troops or equivalent freight, or 24 stret-chers. Eight only were built in 1964–65 for the Royal Malaysian Air Force which sold them in 1977. The three BEA Series 100s were sold to Autair in 1966; operators of the thirty-six Series 200s built included Air Manila, Alia (Jordan), Arkia (Israel), Bavaria Flug, BUIA, East-ern Provincial (Canada), Europe Aero Service, Far Eastern Air Transport (Taiwan), Itavia and

Sadia. British Island Airways was the main operator by 1980.

16 Aérospatiale N 262 and Frégate

The N 262 has been labelled as a 'DC-3 replacement', though in view of the number of earlier attempts to replace the apparently irreplaceable, such a tag might have been thought more of a hindrance than a help. Its origins date back to 1957 and the M.H. 250 Super Broussard 22-seat feederliner, a square-bodied, twin-engined aeroplane developed by Avions Max Holste after experience in operating the smaller single-engined Broussard general purpose aircraft. With two 600 hp Pratt & Whitney R-1340 piston engines, the M.H. 250 prototype flew on 20 May 1959, but further development was shelved in favour of the alternative M.H. 260, which was 4 ft 7 in (1·39 m) longer and powered by Turboméca Bastan turboprops. The first M.H. 260 (F-WJDV) flew on 29 July 1960 with two 805 ehp Bastan IIIAs, these giving way three months later to 986 ehp Bastan IVs. The French government provided financial assistance towards a first batch of ten M.H. 260s to be completed by Nord-Aviation, the first of which (F-WJSN) flew on 29 January 1962. However, no more than these ten were completed, for Nord had continued separately to develop the M.H. 262, which had more powerful Bastan VI engines and seated up to 29 passengers in a circular-section pressurised fuselage. It was this, as the Nord 262, which became the definitive design. The prototype flew on 24 December 1962, and the first of three pre-series machines in the following May. Air Inter became, in the summer of 1963, the first Nord 262 customer; pending delivery of these a number of M.H. 260s were acquired on lease and put into service immediately the 262 had received French type certification on 16 July 1964. The remaining M.H. 260s were lease-operated by Widerøe's Flyveselskap for a similar period. The first four production aircraft, for Air Inter, were designated Series B; production then continued with the Series A for other customers. The Nord 262 broke into the American market when, in June 1964, Lake Central Airlines confirmed an initial order for eight aircraft, but hopes of further American sales did not materialise. It entered service with Lake Central in mid-1965, following FAA type approval in March, but by mid-1974 total sales had reached only ninety-seven aircraft, of which thirty-nine were for the French Air Force and Navy. In parallel production with the N 262 is the Frégate, which is being built for civil or government operators and the French Air Force. The Frégate has more powerful (1,145 ehp) Bastan VII engines and raked tips to the wings and tailplane, the former for better performance at 'hot and high' airfields and the latter improving low-speed handling. The French Air Force operates the N 262 Frégate on transport and communications duties, the Navy as a multi-engined trainer and transport.

17 Saunders ST-27

One of the growing areas of air travel in recent years has been that of the third-level operators – those flying commuter and other local services – and the aircraft needs of these operators are thus a worthy subject of current study for aircraft designers and manufacturers. Low-budget operators flying short-stage routes at low-level fares are clearly not in the market for expensive or highly-sophisticated aeroplanes, and one way to meet their needs at minimum cost is to adapt an existing aircraft design to a more economical means of operation. One of the more attractive results of such an exercise is that evolved by David Saunders, of Saunders Aircraft Corporation, Canada, whose ST-27 is basically a modernised adaptation of the de Havilland Heron. The major outward changes are the replacement of the original four de Havilland Gipsy Queen piston engines by a pair of PT6A turboprops, and the insertion of additional sections totalling 8 ft 6 in (2·59 m) in the fuselage, which permits the passenger accommodation to be increased from 17 to 23. Other changes include a 1 ft 6 in (0·46 m) longer nose-cone, re-shaped rudder and a redesigned wing structure; otherwise the wings, landing gear and tail assembly are essentially those of the retractable-undercarriage Heron Series 2. The prototype ST-27 (CF-YBM-X) was completed in England by Aviation Traders (Engineering) Ltd at Southend from a Heron 2 formerly belonging to The Queen's Flight. It made its first flight on 28 May 1969 and received a British C of A on 16 September 1970. A pre-production ST-27 was flown in April 1970, and by mid-1974 six ST-27s had been ordered: three by Aerolineas Centrales de Colombia, and one each by three Canadian operators – St Andrews Airways, Bayview Air Services and Voyageur Airways. Certification by the Canadian Ministry of Transport was received on 14 May 1971. Saunders also developed the ST-27B, a new-build aircraft with improved interior layout, partially-pressurised cabin, and increased gross weight. This made its first flight on 17 July 1974.

18 Swearingen Metro

Of generally similar overall appearance to the Saunders ST-27 (see above), the 20-passenger Metro third-level/commuter transport is, however, an entirely new design. Swearingen Aircraft of San Antonio, Texas, is well known for its range of Merlin twin-engined business executive aircraft, and the SA-226TC Metro is in fact an outgrowth of the Merlin IIB/III. The Metro I prototype (N226TC) made its first flight on 26 August 1969, having been developed originally at the instigation of Fairchild Hiller. It carries a crew of 2 and can, if required, be converted easily to a cargo transport, carrying a 5,000 lb (2,268 kg) payload. Weather radar is mounted in the aircraft's nose. FAA certification was granted in June 1970. The Metro II differs in detail but the III has a 10 ft (3 m) greater span and 950 shp engines.

The first scheduled services by Metro were begun in 1973 by Commuter Airlines. By late 1980 almost 200 had been ordered. It is in widespread service in the USA as a commuter airliner; Sabena and Cross Air operate several in Europe.

19 Let L-410 Turbolet

The Let National Corporation of Kunovice, Czechoslovakia, established in 1950, has in the past been responsible for manufacture of the Soviet Yak-11 trainer and the twin-engined Aero 45 air taxi, and is currently building the Z-37 Cmelák single-engined agricultural aeroplane. The twin-turboprop L-410 short-haul airliner programme, which was started in 1966, thus represents its biggest and most ambitious venture to date. Design was under the leadership of Ing Ladislav Smrcek, and details of the Turbolet were first announced in 1968, coinciding with the 50th anniversary of the Czechoslovak aircraft industry. The first of four prototypes (OK-YKE) made its maiden flight on 16 April 1969 on the power of two Canadian PT6A-27 turboprops, and these engines were also fitted to the three subsequent prototypes. The original intention was that production aircraft should be powered by Czech-designed M 601 turboprop engines of 736 ehp, with the Canadian engines available optionally – primarily for the benefit of potential western customers, since the L-410 was intended to be sold to a wide international market. Development of the M 601 was, however, much slower

than expected, as a result of which the L-410A initial production version has PT6A-27s as standard but was able to introduce the M 601 version on to the production line in 1975. The first L-410A operator was Slov-Air, a newly-formed Czechoslovak internal airline, which began operating regular services with four Turbolets in late 1971. The L-410A has also been evaluated by Aeroflot, which is operating this type in lieu of the now-abandoned Beriev Be-30. The high-wing configuration and the style of the landing gear speak of the rough-field capabilities of the Turbolet, which in its passenger transport form seats from 15 to 19 people, with a one- or two-man crew, in the non-pressurised fuselage. As an all-cargo aircraft, the L-410 can carry a 4,078 lb (1,850 kg) freight load; mixed-traffic, executive, survey, ambulance or training layouts are possible, and a ski landing gear is available optionally.

20 De Havilland Canada DHC-6 Twin Otter

Design of the DHC-6 Twin Otter originated as a private venture, in the early months of 1964, following research flying carried out by a specially-modified DHC-3 Otter aircraft. The objective was to combine a carrying capacity somewhat greater than that of the single-engined Otter with the additional safety factor inherent in a twin-engined design, while at the same time retaining the first-class STOL performance and economy of operation that had characterised the company's earlier products. Production costs were kept down by using as many components as possible from the wings and fuselage of the DHC-3, and no small contribution to the Twin Otter's success has been made by the PT6A engine, the first turboprop to be manufactured in Canada. An initial pre-production batch of five Twin Otters was started at Downsview, and the first of these (CF-DHC-X) made its first flight on 20 May 1965. This and the next three aircraft were each powered by two 579 ehp PT6A-6 engines, but subsequent aircraft adopted as standard the PT6A-20 engine of the same power. To begin with, the Twin Otter was envisaged as a 15-passenger aircraft, but standard accommodation in the Series 100, as the initial production model became known, was increased to 18. The first one hundred and fifteen aircraft were completed as Series 100s. FAA type certification, granted in mid-1966, was quickly followed by the first customer delivery, to the Ontario Department of Lands and Forests. First exports, to the Fuerza Aérea de Chile, were made before the end of the year.

In April 1968, DHC introduced the Series 200 on to the production line. This was essentially similar to the original model, except for a much-increased baggage capacity achieved by extending the aft baggage compartment further into the rear of the fuselage and by lengthening the nose by 2 ft 3 in (0·68 m). An identical number of Series 200 Twin Otters were built

before, in 1969, this model was in turn superseded by the Series 300, offering improved operating characteristics by combining the Series 200 airframe with more powerful 652 ehp PT6A-27 engines. In late 1980, just over fourteen years after the first delivery, the seven hundredth was delivered, over 80 countries having purchased the type. These are in service in every part of the world as passenger and/or cargo aircraft with several third-level operators or on a variety of other duties which include police, forestry or fishery patrol, Antarctic and other geophysical surveys, troop or paratroop transport, casualty evacuation, and search and rescue. They included six Series 300S aircraft specially modified for an experimental two-year service (1974–76) between STOLports in Ottawa and Montreal. The largest single operator of Twin Otters is Golden West Airlines of Los Angeles, which had a fleet of more than thirty of these aircraft. Others are included in the fleets of such major airline operators as Aeronaves de Mexico, Ansett/ MAL, East African, Guyana, Pakistan International, Sudan and Trans-Australia. Military operators include all three services in the Argentine which bought nine and the air forces of Canada (eight), Chile (six), Jamaica (one), Norway (four), Paraguay (one), Panama (one) and Peru (eleven). The Canadian Armed Forces' aircraft are designated CC-138. Another valuable service performed by Twin Otters is that of water-bombing in forest fire areas, the water load being carried either in specially-designed twin floats or, in the landplane, in an expendable membrane tank fitted under the fuselage. When fitted with floats the Twin Otter must also have the short nose (irrespective of Series number) and be fitted with wing fences and auxiliary tail fins.

21 Junkers Ju 52/3m

Nearly five thousand Ju 52/3m were built in Germany during a production life spanning eleven years, and more than half of this number was made up of those completed during World War 2 for use by the Luftwaffe on a variety of transport duties. There were many variants of this 'European DC-3', but all were basically similar airframes, the principal variation being the type of powerplant installed. These were nearly all radial-type engines, including the Pratt & Whitney Hornet, Wright Cyclone, BMW 132, Bristol Jupiter and Pegasus, Armstrong Siddeley Panther and Gnome-Rhône 9-Kbr; the Junkers Jumo 5 inline engine was also fitted successfully to some aircraft. The characteristic corrugated-metal skinning was a typical trade mark of Junkers aircraft of the 1920s and 1930s, and was designed to give great structural strength and resistance to torsional loads. Other unmistakable recognition features of the Ju 52/3m included the Junkers double flaps and elevators, and the toeing-out of the two wing-mounted engines. A substantial number of ex-Luftwaffe Ju 52/3m became spoils of war after VE-day, and were employed in Europe as stop-gap airline equipment for the next two or three years. There were also a hundred and seventy CASA-built aircraft, and more than four hundred were completed in France by the Ateliers Aéronautiques de Colombes as the AAC. 1. In the immediate post-war years, the Ju 52/3m was in service with commercial operators in Norway, Sweden and Denmark; ten, converted by Short & Harland Ltd, were employed by BEA from November 1946 to August 1947. The Ju 52/3m was most numerous, however, in France, being supplied to several domestic operators and to the national carrier, Air France, which at one time had a fleet of eighty-five of these veteran aircraft. Some of the Scandinavian machines were later sold to customers in Spain and elsewhere. The Ju 52/3m is now entirely extinct in both a military and a civil capacity, but one was still believed to be in service with Transportes Aéreos Orientales of Ecuador as recently as 1971.

22 Britten-Norman Islander and Trislander

The partnership formed in 1952 between John Britten and Desmond Norman made its first major impact in aviation circles with an aerial crop-spraying service, but in more recent years this has been overshadowed by the remarkable success of its second fixed-wing aircraft design, the BN-2 Islander. In November 1963, having seen a gap in the market for an extremely cheap feeder/charter aircraft – a latter-day Dragon Rapide, in effect

– Britten-Norman began work on such a design. The first prototype (G-ATCT), completed with a little assistance from F. G. Miles and Westland Aircraft, was flown for the first time on 13 June 1965 with two Rolls-Royce Continental IO-360 engines and a 45 ft 0 in (13·72 m) wing span. The original engines failed to realise their promised 210 hp each, and were replaced by 260 hp Lycoming O-540 engines. These, and a 49 ft 0 in (14·94 m) wing span, became standard features, and when the Islander appeared at the 1966 Biggin Hill Air Fair its STOL capabilities were dramatically demonstrated by a take-off accomplished within the length of the runway threshold markings. This followed a public début at the 1965 Paris Air Show and the collection, by the end of that year, of orders for more than thirty Islanders. By the autumn of 1974 that total was nearly six hundred and fifty, representing operators in nearly 70 countries – a tribute not only to the Islander's performance but to an equally attractive price. A British C of A was granted on 10 August 1967, followed on 19 December 1967 by FAA type approval. To cope with the fast-rising order list, Britten-Norman sub-contracted the manufacture of two hundred and thirty-six Islanders to the British Hovercraft Corporation, and in 1968 a licence agreement was concluded with IRMA (Intreprinderea de Reparat Material Aeronautic) in Romania, for the production of two hundred and fifteen. The first Romanian Islander flew on 4 August 1969. A new production line at Gosselies in Belgium was opened after Britten-Norman became a member of the Fairey group in 1972, and PADC in the Philippines was to build one hundred. The first Islander operator was Loganair of Scotland, to whose inter-island services the aircraft was ideally suited – a fact echoed in later years by Aurigny Air Services which, with a fleet of eight on Channel Island operations, became one of the major Islander customers. Initial production aircraft were designated BN-2; they were superseded from mid-1969 by the BN-2A with a side-loading baggage facility and detail equipment and aerodynamic improvements. Islander options offered to customers have included 300 hp IO-540-K fuel-injection engines (for 'hot and high' operations with somewhat reduced payload); a 'bolt-on' engine turbocharging installation developed by Rajay in the United States; wing-tip extensions, with raked-back tips, which contain an extra 49 Imp gallons (223 litres) of fuel and increase the overall span to 53 ft 0 in (16·15 m); and an extended nose providing an extra 28 cu ft (0·79 cu m) of baggage space. A militarised version known as the Defender, with provision for underwing stores, operators including Abu Dhabi, Ghana, Guyana, Hong Kong, Jamaica, Malagasy, Mexico, Oman and the British Army.

The BN-2B superseded the BN-2A in 1978. It has a higher all-up landing weight and smaller diameter propellers to reduce noise. By early 1979 some nine hundred Islanders had been ordered.

On 11 September 1970 the first flight was made of the BN-2A Mk III, subsequently named Trislander. This has 'Speedpak' wings, a 7 ft 6 in (2·29 m) longer fuselage than the standard BN-2A, enabling the maximum passenger seating to be increased from 9 to 18, and three 260 hp O-540-E engines, the third one being mounted as an integral part of the modified vertical tail. British certification of the Trislander was granted on 14 May 1971, and by late 1980 orders had been received for over eighty examples of what one contemporary report has described as 'the twopenny Trident'. The first customer for the Trislander was Aurigny Air Services, whose first aircraft (of an initial order for three) was delivered on 29 June 1971.

23 Avro Lancastrian

The first transport conversion of the celebrated Lancaster bomber was carried out in 1943 on behalf of Trans-Canada Air Lines. This aircraft was converted by A. V. Roe from a British-built bomber and, as CF-CMS, inaugurated a trans-Atlantic mail and VIP transport service on behalf of the Canadian government on 22 July 1943. During the following year a rather less elegant Lancaster conversion, with the nose and tail turrets crudely faired over, was flown as G-AGJI in BOAC colours as a testbed for new equipment intended for the Avro Tudor 1. Altogether, nineteen Lancaster transports of a similar kind appeared on the British register, although five of them served only to provide spares for the other fourteen. British South American Airways operated four long-nosed Lancasters for a time from 1946, and Skyways and Alitalia each acquired one as a crew trainer, but little other use was made of this rough Lancaster conversion. More widely employed as an interim airliner in the immediate post-war years was the Avro 691 Lancastrian; this, like the earlier CF-CMS, was characterised by streamlined nose and tail cones, the nose cone in this case being rather longer than that of the original machine. Again it was TCA who set the ball rolling, by ordering twelve Lancastrian conversions (with 1,250 hp Packard-built Merlin 38 engines and seating for 10 passengers) from Victory Aircraft of Toronto. The first of these (CF-CMV) was delivered in 1945, and a similar adaptation (with 1,640 hp Merlin 24s) was embarked upon by the parent company. British-built Lancastrians were produced to both civil and military orders, the RAF receiving sixty-five Mks II and IV from October 1945 to meet the requirements of Air Ministry Specification C. 16/44. These were respectively 9- and 13-passenger aircraft, whose commercial counterparts were BOAC's Mk I and the Mk III for British South American Airways. The first Avro-built Lancastrian was G-AGLF (formerly Lancaster VB873) for BOAC, which obtained the type's Certificate of Airworthiness early in 1945; G-AGLS was the second of BOAC's initial twenty-one, with which scheduled services were initiated on 31 May 1945. In addition to the North Atlantic route, BOAC flew its Lancastrians on the 'Kangaroo' service to Australasia in collaboration with Qantas. In 1946 the larger-capacity Lancastrian IIIs of BSAA opened services to Buenos Aires and other points in South America; other Lancastrians saw service in the fleets of Alitalia, Silver City and Skyways. The Lancastrian was the first British commercial type physically capable of crossing the South Atlantic, and both in this and in the reduction of England–Australia travelling time (to three days) it had no small prestige value at the time, despite its modest carrying capacity. But it was far from making economic sense on any route, and by 1947–48 had been relegated to hack transport work and the carriage of liquids in bulk, milk and petroleum in particular. It accepted its share of the work of the Berlin airlift in 1949 – as did some Lancaster transports too – but by the end of the decade had disappeared from service, and the last Lancastrians were reduced to scrap in 1951–52.

24 Handley Page Halifax and Halton

After the end of World War 2, as an interim step until genuine transport designs became established, each of Britain's two principal wartime bombers underwent somewhat rough-and-ready adaptation to provide cargo- and passenger-carrying facilities over ranges beyond the capacity of the smaller American C-46s and C-47s. The Lancaster-turned-Lancastrian was the more successful of the two, but some years of useful service were also given by adaptations of the Halifax. During what remained of the 1940s, one hundred and forty-seven Halifaxes appeared on the British civil register as passenger and/or cargo carriers, these comprising two B. IIIs, thirty-four B. VIs, seventy-nine C. VIIIs and thirty-two A. IXs. The first of these 'civilianisations' was G-AGXA *Waltzing Matilda*, converted from a B. III bomber early in 1946 and demonstrated (and ultimately sold) in Australia. Further bomber conversions followed, being joined later by civil counterparts of the military Halifax transports. The large ventral freight pannier of these aircraft, capable of holding an 8,000 lb (3,630 kg) payload, made it particularly useful as a cargo aeroplane, although the fuselage provided seating accommodation for 10 passengers as well. Two of the largest fleets of Halifax transports and Haltons were operated by the Lancashire Aircraft Company and LAMS (London Aero and Motor Services). The LAMS Halifaxes operated chiefly to Australia and New Zealand, and many others were flown by small charter operators in Britain and Europe. Whereas the Halifax transport involved the minimum of adaptation necessary for civilian operation, a more serious attempt was made with its stablemate, the Halton, to restyle the aeroplane for commercial service. The Halton 1, twelve of which were produced, was adapted from the Halifax C. VIII to provide BOAC with a fleet of long-range transports to bridge the gap created by the development delays affecting the Avro Tudor. Externally, the principal differences noticeable were the larger passenger entrance door and the rectangular passenger cabin windows. The first Halton 1, G-AHDU *Falkirk*, was delivered to BOAC in July 1946, and Halton services began soon afterwards to West Africa, Cairo and Karachi. The Halton illustrated was the one and only Halton 2 which, after a short period of operation in the United Kingdom on behalf of the Maharajah of Baroda, ended its days in South Africa. By the end of 1947, BOAC had begun to replace its Haltons with Canadair DC-4Ms, and by mid-1948 the decline in freight traffic appeared to have marked the end of the Halifax/Halton's usefulness. A temporary respite was afforded by the Berlin airlift, during which forty-one of these aircraft flew over eight thousand sorties with diesel fuel and dry cargo; but when the emergency ended in August 1949 the days of the surviving machines were indeed numbered, and by the end of the decade nearly all of them had been reduced to scrap.

25 Bristol Brabazon

One of the biggest and most ambitious projects ever attempted by the British aircraft industry, the Bristol Type 167 Brabazon was, technologically, far ahead of its time. Its development costs were therefore naturally high; as a consequence, it was a political embarrassment for virtually the whole of its eight-year career before the one and only completed aircraft went to the breakers after amassing less than four hundred hours flying in four years. The design originally submitted by Bristol was to meet the requirement – for a high-speed, high-capacity airliner capable of crossing the Atlantic non-stop – that later crystallised as the Brabazon Committee's Type I. It was based on the company's proposals, formulated in 1942, for a butterfly-tailed one-hundred-ton bomber. In May 1943 Bristol received a letter of intent covering two prototypes and up to ten production aircraft, so long as this did not affect war production. Various body configurations were studied during the ensuing year and a half, and by November 1944 the basic design had been established sufficiently for construction of a mock-up to begin. A conventional tail assembly was then proposed, and the powerplant was to consist of eight Centaurus radial piston engines, completely enclosed in the wings and geared in pairs to drive contra-rotating propellers. In October 1945 construction of the first prototype began. The sheer size of the venture posed many problems – intrinsic ones, such as pressurising a fuselage of some 25,000 cu ft (708 m³) capacity, and associated ones like the erection of an 8-acre (3·24 hectare) final assembly shed. The necessity to extend and strengthen the Filton runway involved demolishing part of a nearby village and closing a new by-pass road; and, combined with a thorough programme of stress tests at Filton and the Royal Aircraft Establishment, served to defer the first flight by G-AGPW until 4 September 1949. This machine was intended to serve only as a flight test aircraft, but during 1950 thirty seats were installed in the rear passenger cabin for demonstration flight purposes. It was the intention to develop the Brabazon Mk I as a 72/80-seater for BOAC's North Atlantic services. The Brabazon Mk II was to have been a 100-seater with four 7,000 ehp Coupled-Proteus 710 turboprops, but this version was shelved in 1952 before the second prototype (which would have served as the development aircraft) was fully completed. The Brabazon's unhappy career was then nearly at an end. True, much was learned while building and flying it that benefited the Britannia and other Bristol designs; but the belief remains that, when G-AGPW was reduced to scrap in October 1953, a potentially great aeroplane had been sacrificed for political reasons rather than technological failings.

26 Avro Tudor

When the Avro Tudor 1 prototype G-AGPF took off from Ringway Airport for its maiden flight on 14 June 1945, it seemed to embody every ingredient for success. Its handsome lines would undoubtedly appeal to passengers; its pressurised fuselage was the first on any British transport; and its wings, based on those of the Lincoln

bomber, carried four Rolls-Royce Merlins, among the most reliable engines in the world. Yet the Tudor's unfortunate career was one of modification, changing customer requirements and support, failure to achieve its design performance and several serious accidents. There were two basic Tudors, the design of which was started in mid-1944. The Avro 688 was represented by the short-fuselage Tudors 1, 3 and 4; while the Avro 689 (Tudors 2, 5 and 7) featured a fuselage 1 ft (0·30 m) greater in diameter and ultimately lengthened by 26 ft 1 in (7·95 m). The most noticeable outward revisions of the Tudor 1 design were the longer inboard nacelles of the Merlin 621 engines (the prototype had Merlin 102As) and the much-enlarged tail assembly. The Tudor 2 prototype, G-AGSU, also underwent similar modification after its first flight on 10 March 1946. In April 1947, two years after ordering twenty-two of the 24-seat Tudor 1s, BOAC decided that the aircraft was not suited to the North Atlantic and cancelled its order. It had also ordered seventy-nine 60-seat Tudor 2s, with a view to operating them in pool with Qantas and South African Airways on the Empire routes; but when the latter version proved overweight and underpowered, this order too was reduced until BOAC abandoned interest in the Tudor altogether. The experiment of fitting 1,715 hp Hercules 120 radial engines to G-AGRX, the first production Tudor 2 (making it the sole Tudor 7) proved unsuccessful; and the crash of G-AGSU on 23 August 1947 in which the Tudor's designer, Roy Chadwick, was among those killed, dealt a further blow to the aeroplane's prospects. Of the production Tudor 1s laid down, two were completed for the Ministry of Supply as 9-seat Tudor 3 official transports, and it was planned to complete the remainder for British South American Airways as 32-seat Tudor 4s or 4Bs with a 6 ft (1·83 m) longer fuselage. Six were delivered to BSAA, but the early loss of two in crashes led to the remainder being relegated to a freight-only role. Five Tudor 5s (44-seat conversions of the Tudor 2) for BSAA were also withheld from passenger service. The Berlin airlift saw several Tudor 4, 4B or 5 aircraft in service as freighters or tankers. These were withdrawn after the emergency, but in 1952 about a dozen Tudors, mostly 4Bs, were given a new lease of life by Aviation Traders Ltd, who re-engined them with Merlin 623s, fitting out some with 42-seat interiors and others (as Super Trader 4Bs) for cargo duties. A new C of A was granted early in 1954, and for several years the modified Tudors were employed by Air Charter on passenger flights to West Africa and on long range trooping or commercial charters. Air Charter maintained its small fleet for some years, but by the end of 1960 there were no longer any Tudors in regular service.

27 Handley Page Hermes

The Hermes was the first new British aircraft built after the war to go into service with British Overseas Airways Corporation, although the design had its origins in a specification for a 34/50-passenger airliner issued in 1944. An early project, based largely on Halifax components and known as the H.P. 64, was dropped in favour of the single-finned H.P. 68 Hermes 1. The latter was powered by 1,650 hp Bristol Hercules 101 engines and featured a pressurised passenger cabin. Development of the Hermes received a serious setback when the first prototype (G-AGSS) crashed on taking off for its maiden flight on 3 December 1945, and attention was for a time diverted to its military counterpart, the RAF Hastings, whose prototype (TE580) was flown successfully on 7 May 1946. However, following an order in April 1947 for twenty-five production Hermes airliners for BOAC, a second development aircraft was flown for the first time on 2 September 1947. This was G-AGUB, the sole H.P. 74 Hermes 2, which had a 15 ft 4 in (4·67 m) longer fuselage, 1,675 hp Hercules 121 engines and, like the Hermes 1, circular passenger windows and a tailwheel undercarriage. The definitive production model was the H.P. 81 Hermes 4, the first of which (G-AKFP) made its maiden flight on 5 September 1948. Among the changes noted in the production version were a nosewheel landing gear, rectangular windows and a significant increase in available power, the employment of 2,100 hp Hercules 763s permitting a maximum payload of 17,000 lb (7,711 kg) to be carried. The first Hermes 4 was delivered to BOAC on 2 February 1950, and the type entered service later that year on the Corporation's routes to West and South Africa. Normal complement was 40 passengers in addition to the five-man crew, although the Hermes was capable of seating as many as 63 people. The Hermes was meant only as an interim BOAC type, and its replacement by Canadair Argonauts began after only some two years of service. Among the first customers for the ex-BOAC aircraft was Airwork Ltd, who modified their machines to Hermes 4As by fitting 2,125 hp Hercules 773s before putting them to use as 68-seaters on military trooping charters. These were restored in 1957 to Mk 4 standard and, with other surviving Hermes 4s, served for the remainder of the 1950s and early 1960s with such British independents as Air Safaris, Falcon Airways, Skyways and Silver City. Two others were operated as 78-seaters by Bahamas Airways. Fifteen Hermes 4s were still active in 1960, but by the mid-1960s the type was no longer operational. Two other aircraft, H.P. 82 Hermes 5s, were completed in 1949–50 as turbine development aircraft with 2,490 ehp Bristol Theseus 502 turboprops, but no production of this version was undertaken.

28 Boeing Stratocruiser

The requirement for a transport development of the B-29 Superfortress bomber was first drawn up, in the middle years of World War 2,
as a military one for Air Transport Command of the USAAF. To meet this need, Boeing produced the Model 367, or YC-97, which utilised the same wing, engines, landing gear and tail assembly as the B-29 in conjunction with a two-deck 'double-bubble' fuselage of great strength and capacity, and fully pressurised. The first YC-97 was flown on 9 October 1945, and nearly nine hundred military Stratofreighters (C-97s) and Stratotankers (KC-97s) were subsequently completed. One of these was adapted as prototype for a postwar civil development, the Boeing 377, planned to carry 100 passengers or a 35,000 lb (15,876 kg) payload over long ranges. This prototype was flown for the first time on 8 July 1947. The first customer for the Stratocruiser, as the civil version was named, was Pan American, which placed an order for twenty in June 1946; other orders followed from American Overseas Airlines (eight), Northwest (ten) and United Air Lines (seven) in the United States, and BOAC (six) and SAS (four) in Europe. In the event, the Stratocruiser did not serve with SAS, whose order was added to the original BOAC requirement. Production of the fifty-five came to an end in March 1950. The first Stratocruiser services were operated by Pan American, which put the type into service on 7 September 1948; BOAC began its Stratocruiser services on 6 December 1949. Pan American later increased its fleet to twenty-seven by purchase of the prototype and six of the AOA air-

craft. Both its crews (normally comprising five men) and its passengers appreciated the spaciousness of the Stratocruiser's flight deck and passenger cabin, the latter including a lounge or cocktail bar on the lower deck at the rear of the generous luggage hold. The Stratocruiser could accommodate up to 89 passengers in a typical five-abreast tourist configuration, or up to 112 in a high-density layout, and its standards of comfort were scarcely bettered until the large-scale introduction of jets began in 1958. On 16 July 1958, one of the BOAC aircraft (which had been augmented by a further six aircraft purchased from United and one from Pan American) inaugurated services between London and Accra on behalf of the newly formed Ghana Airways Corporation; but by mid-1959 the British operator had withdrawn all its Stratocruisers from service. In 1960 about a score of Stratocruisers were still extant (mostly with Transocean), but by 1963 the type had disappeared completely from the commercial passenger scene. Some Stratocruiser and some C-97 airframes were utilised in the construction of the 'Guppy' series of outsize freighters produced by Aero Spacelines.

29 Douglas DC-4

A contemporary of the DC-3, the original Douglas DC-4 began its evolution in mid-1935 to the requirement of a number of US domestic operators for a 52-passenger airliner for medium-stage lengths of up to 2,500 miles (4,023 km). Two prototypes to this specification were completed, the first (NX18100) flying for the first time on 7 June 1938 powered by four 1,150 hp Pratt & Whitney R-2180 Twin Hornet engines. This early DC-4, although certificated in May 1939, was rejected by the airlines, who felt that a smaller-capacity machine would be more viable economically; accordingly Douglas began work on a smaller single-finned design (the first DC-4 had a triple tail unit) seating up to 42 passengers. American, Eastern and United placed orders for the smaller version totalling sixty-one aircraft, but by the time that the prototype flew on 14 February 1942 the United States was committed in World War 2, and all transport aircraft in production, the DC-4 included, were diverted to the US armed services. Large numbers of DC-4s were built during the war as C-54 and R5D Skymasters, and by the time production finally ceased in August 1947 a total of one thousand and eighty-four Skymasters and seventy-nine civil DC-4s had been completed. A substantial number of surplus Skymasters joined the post-war DC-4s on the civil market, and became one of the standard types used to re-equip leading international airlines in the early years until the appearance of post-war designs. There were still more than a hundred DC-4s in commercial service in 1974; they had a seating capacity ranging from 44 to 86 passengers according to layout, but most of them were soon converted to freighters with appropriate modifications which included strengthened floors and large cargo doors in the side. Twenty-three were converted by Aviation Traders as ATL. 98 Carvair freighters; this conversion is described separately on page 134. Another DC-4 variant was the 40/55-seat Canadian conversion known as the North Star. This was first produced by Canadair for the RCAF, and comprised twenty-three C-54Gs, fitted with 1,740 hp Rolls-Royce Merlin 620 engines and embodying appropriate structural changes. Six of these were loaned to Trans-Canada Airlines, these being unpressurised aircraft bearing the civil designation DC-4M-1. They were put into service in April 1947, but returned to the RCAF in the following year. Their place was taken by twenty DC-4M-2s, incorporating a number of features of the DC-6 including pressurisation and square passenger cabin windows. These aircraft commenced trans-Atlantic operation with TCA in April 1948. Following its disenchantment with the Avro Tudor, BOAC ordered a fleet of twenty-two DC-4M-2s in 1948 which it put into service (to the Far East) from August 1949 under the class name Argonaut. In the late 1950s this fleet was sold off to BOAC associates or independent airlines, with whom they continued in operation until the late 1960s.

30 Douglas DC-6 series

Design of the DC-6 actually began to military requirements during World War 2 for a 'heavy' develop-ment of the C-54 Skymaster (DC-4), and the first aircraft of this type to fly, on 15 February 1946, was an XC-112A ordered by the USAAF. Aircraft of the DC-6 type did indeed serve with the US forces, but it is as a civil transport that the aeroplane is generally known. Unlike its predecessor, the DC-6 had a pressurised cabin accommodating up to 68 passengers in addition to the crew of three and was 6 ft 8 in (2·03 m) longer than the DC-4. Other improvements included more powerful engines, large square passenger windows and revision of the wing and tail areas. Among the first domestic carriers to be interested in the DC-6 were United Air Lines, which placed an order for thirty-five aircraft, and American Airlines, which ordered forty-seven. Production deliveries began early in 1947 to United, which put the type into operation across the United States in April of that year. First European delivery was OO-AWA, made to the Belgian airline Sabena three months later, and other European recipients included KLM and SAS. Altogether, one hundred and seventy-five DC-6s were built, these being succeeded by seventy-seven DC-6As, a freight development which first flew on 29 September 1949 and entered service in 1951. Five feet (1·52 m) longer than the DC-6, the DC-6A incorporated cargo-loading doors, a strengthened fuselage floor and -CB17 engines. Payload was considerably better than that of the DC-6, and some DC-6As were converted to DC-6C passenger or cargo aircraft with a maximum seating, in the former role, for 107 people. Major production of DC-6As, however, concerned one hundred and sixty-seven C-118 or R6D Liftmasters for the US Air Force and Navy. The variant produced in greatest numbers for the civil market was the DC-6B, which flew for the first time on 10 February 1951 and began to be delivered (starting with Western Airlines) in April. With a further 1 ft 1 in (0·33 m) extension to the fuselage, the DC-6B was otherwise a passenger-carrying equivalent of the DC-6A and -6C, having maximum accommodation for 107 passengers or a payload nearly half as great again as the original DC-6. Two hundred and eighty-six DC-6Bs were built for commercial customers before its production, and that of the entire DC-6 series, came to an end late in 1958. The DC-6B has proved that it has excellent operating economics, and more than one hundred and fifty DC-6 variants of one kind or another were still in airline service during the 1970s.

31 Douglas DC-7 series

The DC-7 was the outcome of an approach to Douglas by American Airlines in 1951 to produce a stretched version of the DC-6B, with which American hoped to counter the introduction by TWA of the Super Constellation on domestic trunk routes. Douglas met this requirement by extending the DC-6B fuselage by 2 ft 3 in (0·69 m) to make it a 69/95-seater, and making use for the first time in the

DC-4/DC-6 line of development of the Wright Turbo Compound engine. Four R-3350-988-TC18-DA4 engines, each of 3,250 hp, were installed in the prototype DC-7, which flew for the first time on 18 May 1953. In terms of capacity, the DC-7 compared well with the DC-6B, gross weight being increased to 122,200 lb (55,429 kg) and maximum payload to 20,000 lb (9,072 kg); but in operation it proved to be less economical, and engine vibration and noise levels were excessive by comparison. Nevertheless, one hundred and twenty DC-7s were built. In addition, Douglas completed ninety-six DC-7Bs, an essentially similar version for overseas routes which flew on 25 April 1955 and entered service (with Pan American) in the following month. The DC-7B retained the powerplant and seating capacity of the DC-7, differing principally in the additional fuel tankage necessary for long-range flying. Maximum take-off weight was increased to 126,000 lb (57,152 kg) and payload to 21,516 lb (9,759 kg). However, the DC-7B still did not have the truly intercontinental range demanded by such operators as PanAm, and to try and provide this capability Douglas embarked upon a further programme of modifying and stretching which resulted in the DC-7C. This model made its maiden flight on 20 December 1955 and was the first to make effective use of the Turbo Compound engine. The problems of finding additional fuel storage and reducing the cabin noise level were met by the single step of inserting an additional 5 ft 0 in (1·52 m) of wing between the fuselage and each inboard nacelle. Flap and aileron area was increased, and the more powerful -EA4 version of the Wright engine adopted as powerplant. The fuselage was extended a further 3 ft 4 in (1·03 m), seating up to 105 passengers, and fin and rudder areas were increased. Other aerodynamic improvements were made, and up-to-date weather radar, de-icing and other equipment fitted. Thus improved, the DC-7C had a better airfield performance than any of its forebears, despite an all-up weight now as high as 143,000 lb (64,863 kg) which included a 25,350 lb (10,592 kg) payload. Moreover, it could achieve ranges in excess of 4,000 miles (6,437 km) with such loads. Production of the DC-7 series ended late in 1958 after the completion of three hundred and thirty-six aircraft, one hundred and twenty of these being DC-7Cs. Since 1959 a number of operators have had their DC-7s or -7Cs converted to DC-7F all-freight aircraft. By the beginning of 1974 only about twenty DC-7 series aircraft remained in regular airline operation.

32 SIAI-Marchetti S.M. 95

The S.M. 95 actually began life as a war transport, the first prototype making its maiden flight on 8 May 1943, before the Italian surrender, on the power of four 850 hp Alfa Romeo 131 RC 14/50 radial engines. This powerplant was later replaced by Alfa Romeo 128 RC 18 radials,

which also powered the two other S.M. 95s completed, by SAI Ambrosini at Perugia, before the end of the war in Europe. These were medium-range 18-seaters, with a 73 ft 0 in (22·25 m) fuselage, gross weight of 46,297 lb (21,000 kg) and a range of 1,243 miles (2,000 km), carrying a flight crew of four or five. After the war the design was enlarged to enable the S.M. 95 to operate over shorter stage lengths carrying up to 26 passengers in a fuselage lengthened to 81 ft 3¼ in (24·77 m). Despite the S.M. 95's good handling qualities, production of the civil version was extremely limited, and probably totalled little more than a dozen aircraft. The post-war production S.M. 95s were delivered either with Alfa Romeo 128 engines, with 740 hp Bristol Pegasus 48s or with 1,065 hp Pratt & Whitney R-1830-S1C3Gs. Six S.M. 95s were delivered to the Italian national carrier, Alitalia, with whom they entered service in April 1948. Alitalia later acquired three ex-LATI Twin-Wasp-engined S.M. 95s (its own having been Pegasus-powered), and continued to operate the type until 1951. Three S.M. 95s, reportedly seating 38 passengers, were also operated by SAIDE of Egypt. One of the wartime trio operated for a while in 1945–46 between Great Britain and the Continent bearing post-war Italian Air Force insignia.

33 Sud-Est Languedoc

The origins of this post-war French airliner are to be found in the 12-passenger MB 160 evolved for Air

Afrique in 1937 by Marcel Bloch (now Marcel Dassault). Powered by four 720 hp Hispano-Suiza 12 Xirs engines, the MB 160 set up two speed-with-payload records late in 1937, but it did not enter production. In its place Bloch developed the MB 161, a parallel design to the MB 162 heavy bomber, as a 33-seat passenger airliner tailored to the needs of Air France for operation over medium stage lengths. The 'MB' was retained in the designation despite the Bloch organisation's absorption in the nationalised SNCA du Sud-Ouest in January 1937, and a prototype of the Bloch 161 (F-ARTV) was flown for the first time in September 1939. After the fall of France, continued development of the aeroplane was authorised by the Vichy government, and preparations were made to begin production in 1941 at the SNCA du Sud-Est factory at Toulouse, to meet a German order for the completion of twenty aircraft. The prototype resumed test flying in 1942, and was later used as a VIP transport, but no production aircraft were completed until after the liberation. The first Toulouse-built SE 161 Languedoc (as the type then became known) was flown on 17 September 1945, with the registration F-BATA and a powerplant of four 1,150 hp Gnome-Rhône 14N 44/45 engines. Forty Languedocs were ordered by Air France for its European and North African services, and other operators included Air Atlas, Air Liban, Iberia, Misrair, LOT and Tunis Air. Initially it was planned to

power the production Languedoc with Gnome-Rhône engines, but these did not prove entirely satisfactory and the standard engine on most of the one hundred machines completed became the 1,200 hp Pratt & Whitney R-1830-S1C3-G. The Languedoc's fuselage, although long, had a narrower internal cabin width than the DC-3, and the 33 passengers were accommodated in three-abreast seating; the payload capacity was 8,650 lb (3,924 kg). Several Languedocs were supplied to the Armée de l'Air and Aéronavale, the latter force still retaining a few for aircrew training as late as 1960. By that time Aviaco of Spain, with a fleet of five, was the sole remaining civil operator of the Languedoc, and the type is no longer in commercial use. A number of Languedocs were used during the late 1940s as flying testbeds for aero-engines and other devices; among these were four aircraft employed as carriers for the Leduc series of ramjet research vehicles which were mounted, pick-a-back fashion, above the Languedoc fuselage.

34 Handley Page Marathon

As the M. 60, the Marathon was designed by Miles Aircraft Ltd to Specification 18/44 to meet the Type VA requirement of the Brabazon Committee for a feederliner for the British internal route network. Originally registered U-10, and later G-AGPD, the first of three 14/18-seat prototypes ordered was completed in fourteen months and made a successful maiden flight on 19 May 1946, powered by four

330 hp Gipsy Queen 71 engines. This, like the production aircraft, featured a triple-tail assembly, though the second prototype (G-AILH, first flown on 27 February 1947) was given only twin fins and rudders for comparative purposes. In 1948, Miles Aircraft went into liquidation, the company's remaining assets being taken over by Handley Page in June. Renamed as Handley Page (Reading) Ltd, the former Miles factory continued development of the Marathon under the new designation H.P.R. 1. Forty production Marathon 1s were at this time on order for British European Airways, and the first production Marathon (G-ALUB) was used on proving flights in 1951. But the airline decided that the Marathon did not fully meet its requirements; and finally, in 1952, it secured government approval to withdraw the order. The Royal Air Force, after evaluating two Marathon 1s from 1951, took a further twenty-eight converted as T. 11 advanced navigation trainers. Of the remainder of the final total of forty-three Marathons built, including prototypes, six (of a total of eight completed originally for BEA) were supplied to West African Airways Corporation in 1952, three to Union of Burma Airways, two to Far East Airlines (Japan) and one in 1954 to King Hussein of Jordan as a VIP transport. Powerplant of the standard Marathon 1 was four 340 hp Gipsy Queen 70-3 engines, but those in WAAC service were re-engined with Gipsy Queen 70-4s of similar power and designated Mara-

thon 1A. Seating capacity of the Marathon was for up to 22 passengers, and maximum payload was 5,036 lb (2,284 kg). In 1954 the West African aircraft were returned to Britain, where, in subsequent times, the principal operator was Derby Aviation; but none now remain in service. The Marathon's high-wing layout and roomy fuselage made it popular with its passengers, and Miles-designed high-lift flaps gave it a creditable short-field performance for its time. The third prototype Marathon to be completed, G-AHXU, was a development aircraft for the proposed M. 69 Marathon 2, and was powered by two 1,010 ehp Armstrong Siddeley Mamba 502 turbo-props. This aircraft flew for the first time on 23 July 1949, but no production of a turbine-engined version was undertaken. This prototype became, in 1955, an engine and nacelle testbed for the Leonides Major-powered H.P.R. 3 Herald.

35 Avro York

The Avro 685 York came into being as a military transport for the RAF, evolved as a private venture to meet the requirements of Air Ministry Specification C.1/42 and flown for the first time (LV626) at Ringway on 5 July 1942. The York's design relied heavily on that of the Lancaster, utilising the bomber's wing, power units and dual tail assembly allied to a square-section fuselage of about twice the Lancaster's volume. Mounting the wing high while retaining Lancaster-length main-wheel legs ensured that the fuselage was suitably close to ground level to facilitate the loading of cargo, but the additional side area of the transport body necessitated the introduction of a central fin on the third and all subsequent aircraft. Although designed quickly, the York's production priority was low, and comparatively few were built until 1945, when a full-scale programme got under way. Up to April 1948, when production ended, two hundred and fifty-six Yorks were built, most of them for RAF Transport Command. The first civil Yorks were five RAF aircraft allocated to BOAC in 1944 as 12-seat passenger/cargo aircraft, with which the airline inaugurated a service to Cairo in April. BOAC operated (though not all at one time) a total of forty-three Yorks, including four reserved for crew training. This total included nineteen acquired from its sister airline BSAA after the dissolution of that airline in 1949. Most of these had a standard 18-seat daytime interior, although a few 12-berth sleeper models were also in use. Overseas operators included South African Airways and FAMA of Argentina. Another pioneer operator of Yorks was the British independent Skyways, which had had three of the early Yorks in 1945–46; and when BOAC began to sell off its Yorks in 1951, Skyways built up a substantial fleet of these aircraft. When Hastings transports began to replace the RAF Yorks from 1951 (although the last York was not retired from service until five years later), about thirty more Yorks came on to the British civil register during the early 1950s. At the end of 1957, BOAC disposed of its last two Yorks to Skyways, and for the next few years Skyways, Dan-Air and Hunting Clan were the principal operators. About a score of Yorks remained in service in the United Kingdom in 1960, but within the next two or three years these had all been withdrawn. Two Yorks preserved in Britain are the RAF Museum's G-AGNV at Cosford and Dan-Air Preservation Group's G-ANTK at Lasham. The first aircraft, LV626, was re-engined with Bristol Hercules radials as the prototype for a York II, but no production of this model was undertaken.

36 Lockheed Constellation

One of the veterans of trans-Atlantic and other long-haul air routes since 1945, the Constellation and its descendants performed yeoman service for more than two decades, but had entirely disappeared from airline service by 1978. The Constellation's design originated in 1939 as a 40-passenger aircraft to the requirements of TWA (which ordered forty) and, later, Pan American Airways, but the United States had entered World War 2 by the time the first prototype (NX25600) was flown on 9 January 1943, and the Constellation's first career was as a military transport under the designation C-69. A large C-69 order was later cut drastically, and by VJ-day fifteen of these had been accepted by the USAAF. The remainder were immediately converted to civilian interiors and allocated to commercial customers. As the L-049 Constellation, this early version received CAA operating approval on 11 December 1945. The L-049 was basically a 43/48-seat aircraft, with a high-density capacity for up to 60 passengers. The first two customers, as before, were Pan American and TWA. The former became the first airline to operate Constellations when it introduced the type on its New York–Bermuda route in February 1946; TWA, which received its first Constellation in November 1945, opened the first US–Europe service (to Paris) on 6 February 1946. On 1 July 1946 the first of five L-049s for BOAC (G-AHEJ *Bristol II*) opened a trans-Atlantic service between London and New York. The first wholly civil Constellation was the so-called 'gold plate' Model L-649. This was flown for the first time (NX101A) on 19 October 1946 and entered service (with Eastern Air Lines) in May 1947. With 2,500 hp R-3350-C18-BD1 engines, the L-649 was able to accommodate 48–64 passengers (maximum 81) or a maximum payload of 20,276 lb (10,197 kg). This version was itself replaced in production in 1947 by the L-749, to which standard a number of L-649s were later converted. The L-749 Constellation was basically similar to the L-649, with the same seating capacity, but having additional fuel storage within the wings, enabling non-stop flights to be made between New York and Paris (3,660 miles = 5,890 km). PanAm's NC86530 *Clipper America* started the first round-the-world air service in June 1947. The L-749A was a variant with sturdier landing gear, permitting the gross take-off weight to be increased by 5,000 lb (2,268 kg) to 107,000 lb (48,534 kg). Excluding twelve military L-749As, total Constellation production of all variants reached two hundred and twenty-one (twenty-two C-69/L-049 conversions, sixty-six L-049s, twenty L-649/649As and one hundred and thirteen L-749/749As) before giving way to the Super Constellation in 1951.

37 Lockheed Super Constellation

Representing the greatest single stretch carried out on any propeller-driven airliner, the transformation of the already-long Constellation into the serpentine form of the Super Constellation took place in 1950. The insertion of additional sections fore and aft of the wing to lengthen the fuselage by 18 ft 4 in (5·59 m) was only one of several major design changes; others included a general reinforcing of the entire airframe, the provision of larger, rectangular passenger windows and a substantial increase in fuel capacity; and the utilisation of Wright R-3350 piston engines of greater power. To test all these modifications in the air the original Constellation (NX25600, re-registered NX6700) was turned into the prototype L-1049 Super Constellation, making its maiden flight in this form on 13 October 1950. The New 'Connie' proved to have excellent operating characteristics, but with 2,700 hp R-3350-CB1 engines was somewhat underpowered. Consequently only twenty-four L-1049s were built, for Eastern and TWA, the former airline leading in putting the type into service on 17 December 1951. The L-1049A and L-1049B were, respectively, the military RC-121D/WV-2 and -3 and the RC-121C/R7V-1, and from the latter was derived the next civil model, the L-1049C. Both the B and C models overcame the power shortage by using the Turbo Compound version of the R-3350 engine, which offered 3,250 hp for take-off, and successively later marks of the engine were selected for all subsequent Super Constellations. The first L-1049C (PH-TFP) was flown on 17 February 1953, and this type was first delivered to KLM and TWA, which commenced operating it in August and September 1953 respectively. Sixty of this version were completed, four of them as L-1049D cargo counterparts of the C model; the first D conversion flew in September 1954. Further detail refinements appeared in the L-1049E, but only eighteen of these were completed; the remainder of the fifty-six originally ordered were completed during assembly, at their purchaser's request, as L-1049Gs. (The L-1049F was a military model.) The L-1049G, known colloquially as the Super G, represented an even greater improvement than its predecessors, having 3,400 hp Turbo Compounds available optionally, more fuel (in wingtip tanks) and even better payload/range capabilities. The first Super G was flown on 12 December

1954, and entered service with Northwest Airlines in the spring of 1955; in addition to the thirty-eight former L-1049Es, sixty-six Super Constellations were completed as Super Gs, and fifty-three more as cargo/passenger L-1049Hs, bringing total civil production of the Super Constellation variants to two hundred and fifty-four aircraft. Maximum capacity of the two last-named versions was 95 passengers (L-1049G) or 24,293 lb (11,021 kg) of cargo (L-1049H). One further and final stretch of this highly elastic design produced the L-1649A Starliner, which flew for the first time on 11 October 1956. The Starliner was 2 ft 7 in (0·79 m) longer than the Super Constellation, seating 58–75 passengers normally, and was evolved to TWA's request as a counter to Douglas's long range DC-7C. An entirely new thin-section, straight-tapered wing, spanning 150 ft 0 in (45·72 m) and carrying much more fuel, did indeed give the Starliner more range than the DC-7C, but it was behind its rival in entering service (June 1957) and its career was overtaken by the big jets a year or two later. Forty-three Starliners were built, these going initially to TWA, Air France and Lufthansa. The major Constellation family operators ceased regular passenger services in 1967–68 and the last service anywhere was flown in 1978.

38 & 39 Vickers Viscount

The Brabazon Committee's Type IIB requirement, later covered by Ministry of Supply Specification

8/46, was for a 24-seat short/medium-range airliner for European routes, powered by four turboprop engines. Vickers, who had already made several design studies along similar lines, liaised with BEA in developing the proposed VC2 to meet this requirement, and were eventually rewarded by an order for two Type 609 prototypes. Construction of these began in December 1946, modified to a 32-seat capacity at the request of BEA, powered by Dart RDa.1 engines, renumbered Type 630 and named Viceroy. The name was changed to Viscount in 1947 for diplomatic reasons after the partition of India. The first 630, G-AHRF, was flown at Wisley on 16 July 1948, but before the year was out BEA had been instructed to cancel its order, and the second prototype became a testbed for the Tay turbojet. However, with the higher-powered RDa.3 available, Vickers embarked upon an enlarged, 53-seat development which reawakened BEA interest, and work on this continued under Specification 21/49 as the Viscount 700. The prototype, G-AMAV, flew for the first time on 28 August 1950. A few days before this, BEA had completed nearly four weeks' intensive use of the 630 prototype, which it had borrowed to augment summer peak services. The passengers' reaction to the Viscount's speed, comfort and quietness, together with the airline's appreciation of its operating economy and ability, affirmed BEA's interest in the larger model, and an order for twenty-six Viscount 701s was placed before the end of the year. By the time the first of these entered service in April 1953, substantial orders for Viscount 700 variants had been placed by Air France, Aer Lingus, TAA and TCA. The last named order, received in November 1952, was the Viscount's first breakthrough into the lucrative North American market, and was soon followed by others from a number of US operators for the only propeller-turbine-powered airliner then in production anywhere in the world. The largest US orders, totalling more than sixty, came from Capital Airlines, but when this operator went bankrupt its Viscount fleet was taken over by United Air Lines; and United, together with TCA (now Air Canada), became the largest operators of Series 700 Viscounts. Although there are many Viscount Type numbers, signifying interior layouts to individual customer requirements, there are basically only three models in the 700 Series: the original 700, with Dart 505 or 506 engines; the 700D with Dart 510s and extra fuel tankage; and the 770D, the North American equivalent of the 700D. Some Viscount 700Ds were fitted with slipper fuel tanks on the wing leading edges. Excluding prototypes, two hundred and eighty-seven Series 700 Viscounts were built; about seventy were still in regular service early in 1974, a small number as military or business executive transports.

The promise of progressively more powerful versions of the Dart turboprop led Vickers in the early 1950s to propose a stretched version of the Viscount 700 with high-density seating for up to 86 passengers over shorter stage lengths. To do this it was proposed to extend the fuselage by as much as 13 ft 3 in (4.04 m) but, after ordering twelve Type 801s to this specification in February 1953, BEA asked instead for a 65-seat aircraft. This emerged as the Type 802, being only 3 ft 10 in (1.17 m) longer than the 700 and having Dart 510 engines. The Viscount 802 was first flown on 27 July 1956, and was put into BEA service in February 1957. Generally similar Series 800 Viscounts were completed for Aer Lingus, KLM, New Zealand National Airways and other customers, together with a batch of Dart 520-powered Type 806s for BEA, but the next major stage of development was the Series 810 with 1,990 ehp Dart 525s, flown for the first time (G-AOYU) on 23 December 1957. The Series 810, evolved initially to the requirement of Continental Airlines, was subsequently built in considerable numbers for Cubana, Lufthansa, Pakistan International, South African Airways, TAP and VASP. The 810's gross weight of 67,500 lb (30,618 kg) and 402 mph (647 km/hr) speed, compared to the 43,000 lb (19,504 kg) and 300 mph (483 km/hr) of the little Viscount 630 prototype, give some idea of the Viscount's development over the years. Seating increased in proportion from the original 32 to a maximum of 75 which could be carried by some Viscount 810s.

Viscount production on any scale ceased in 1959, though a few additional orders were executed between 1959 and 1964. Sixty-eight Series 800 and eighty-six Series 810 aircraft were completed, and the grand total of all Viscounts built, including prototypes, amounted to four hundred and forty-four. They can be distinguished from the 700 Series by the longer fuselage and additional passenger windows forward of the wing, and by rectangular instead of oval doors. Some one hundred Viscounts remained in military and commercial service with about fifty operators in 1981.

40 Breguet Provence
An aeroplane whose shape and bulk made it easily recognisable, the Provence design originated in 1944, although the prototype (F-WFAM), known as the Br 761 Deux Ponts and powered by four 1,580 hp SNECMA-built Gnome-Rhône 14R radial engines, did not fly until 15 February 1949. It was followed by a pre-production batch of three Br 761Ss in which these were replaced by 2,020 hp Pratt & Whitney R-2800-B31 engines. All four aircraft were intended for a four-man flight crew and, apart from the powerplant, modified wingtips and the addition of a third, central fin, the Br 761Ss were similar to the prototype.

One of the pre-series machines was leased for a time to Air Algérie, and one later operated in Silver City colours before, in the middle 1950s, all three were handed over to the Armée de l'Air for service trials.

Meanwhile, in 1951 Air France had ordered twelve examples of a developed version, the Br 763. Equipped with more powerful R-2800 engines, the Br 763 also had strengthened wings of greater span and a cabin redesigned for a three-man crew; it made its maiden flight on 20 July 1951. The first Br 763 was delivered to Air France in August 1952, and under the class name Provence the type was first put into regular service, Lyons–Algiers, on 16 March 1953. Six of these aircraft were handed over to the Armée de l'Air in 1964 for military duties in the Far East, but Air France continued to operate the type, with the name Universel, in a freighter role until 1971. The Br 763, which has been described as 'a glutton for work', has a double-deck interior layout which in the passenger configuration originally seated 59 on the upper deck and 48 on the lower; 135 people could be carried in a high-density layout. As an all-cargo aeroplane it could accommodate some 11 tons of freight; it could also be operated as a mixed passenger/cargo aircraft or vehicle ferry. In the mid-1960s the Br 763 was flown on trans-Mediterranean routes to Corsica and North Africa, where it provided valuable supply support to companies developing the petroleum and mineral resources of the Sahara desert. The six former Air France Provences, under the military name Sahara, were allocated initially to the 64e Escadre de Transport along with four Br 765s with removable cargo doors and the original trio of Br 761Ss. The last

of them was retired from service (with Groupe Aérien Mixte 82 in the Pacific) in late 1972.

41 Aviation Traders Carvair

The need for an aeroplane such as the Carvair arose in the late 1950s when Air Charter Ltd of Southend, an associate of Aviation Traders (Engineering) Ltd, began to seek a replacement for its ageing Bristol Freighters. What they wanted was a four-engined aeroplane, capable of flying five cars and 25 passengers over fairly long ranges, which would be comparatively cheap both to buy and to operate. No existing design filled the bill, and the cost of an entirely new design would have been prohibitive. Aviation Traders met the challenge by producing an adaptation of the Douglas DC-4, thus combining the advantages of using an already proven airframe with low initial cost. With technical assistance from Douglas, Aviation Traders began to convert their first machine, the alterations consisting basically of substituting an entirely new and longer front fuselage, with a sideways-hinged nose door through which the vehicles could be loaded, and an enlarged DC-7C pattern vertical tail. The flight deck was situated high above the front cargo hold. The aeroplane was named Carvair – a contraction of 'car-via-air' – and the first converted machine, G-ANYB, made its maiden flight at Southend on 21 June 1961. It had already flown 37,000 hours as a DC-4. In March 1962 the Carvair went into service with the

Channel Air Bridge division of Air Charter (by then incorporated in British United Air Ferries), on vehicle ferry routes to the Continent. The Carvair's main freight hold is 68 ft (20·73 m) long, holding four large or five standard size cars; the rear passenger cabin, 12 ft 2 in (3·71 m) long, seats 23 passengers, and, with the 151 cu ft (4·27 cu m) under-floor baggage hold, gives a total internal volume of 4,630 cu ft (131·1 cu m). Alternative passenger and/or freight accommodation can be installed, a maximum passenger load of 65 being possible. British United Air Ferries operated a fleet of ten Carvairs on both long- and short-haul routes; the three flown by Aer Lingus were equipped to carry racehorses as well as vehicles and other cargo; Aviaco used three Carvairs on mixed-traffic runs from Spain to France and the Balearic Islands; Compagnie Air Transport operated the two freighters formerly belonging to Interocean Airways of Luxembourg, and converted to a 55-passenger layout; and Ansett/ANA operated three Carvairs, two of them as pure freighters with slightly enlarged nose doors. Thirteen Carvairs were still in service in early 1974: nine with British Air Ferries, two with Ansett and one each with Air Cambodge and Dominicana. Few remained by 1980.

42 Bristol Britannia

The Britannia, or Bristol Type 175, was one of several designs submitted in response to a 1947 specification to fulfil the future requirements of BOAC. From these the airline selected a relatively small (48-seat) aircraft with Centaurus piston engines, and in July 1948 three prototypes were ordered on its behalf by the Ministry of Supply. Four months later BOAC indicated that it would have twenty-five of these aircraft. The first six only would have Centaurus engines, the remainder the Bristol Proteus turboprop, which all along had been nominated as an alternative powerplant; and the aircraft would be increased in size to seat up to 74 people. In the event only two prototypes (Britannia 101) were completed; the first of these (G-ALBO) flew on 16 August 1952 with Proteus 625s, the second, G-ALRX, with Proteus 705s. Production ensued of fifteen Britannia 102s for BOAC which, after some development delays, entered service on the Corporation's South African routes on 1 February 1957 and to Australia a month later. BOAC had reserved the final ten of its order for an enlarged version capable of working the North Atlantic route non-stop with a more worthwhile payload. The first appeared in the form of the Britannia 300, in which 4,120 ehp Proteus 755 engines were combined with a 10 ft 3 in (3·12 m) longer fuselage, seating up to 133 tourist-class passengers. The prototype for this series was the Britannia 301 (G-ANCA) which made its first flight on 31 July 1956. It was succeeded by seven production aircraft with increased tankage, laid down as Britannia 302s for BOAC, whose order had meanwhile been reduced to that figure. In the event, however,

BOAC relinquished its claim to these aircraft, which were completed and delivered as Britannia 302s (two for Aeronaves de Mexico), 305s (two for Transcontinental SA), 307s (two for Air Charter) and one 309 (for Ghana Airways). The last five were to have gone to Northeast Airlines, but the American company found itself unable to finance them. The principal long-range model was the Series 310. Its prototype, the Britannia 311 (G-AOVA), flew on 31 December 1956, later being converted to a 312 for BOAC but then diverted to replace the crashed G-ANCA as a development aircraft. BOAC ordered ten Britannia 312s in August 1955, later increasing this to eighteen. Delivery began in September 1957; trans-Atlantic services started on 19 December. Britannias (100 and 310 Series) were operated by many of BOAC's overseas associate airlines. Trans-Atlantic services were also flown by the Israeli airline El Al (four Britannia 313s) and Canadian Pacific (six 314s); other customers included Hunting Clan (two 317s) and Cubana (four 318s). Three Britannia 252s and twenty 253s, basically similar to the Series 310 except for a large forward freight door, were completed by Short Bros for RAF Transport Command as Britannia C. Mk 1s. The final stage in the Britannia's development was the Series 320: this differed chiefly in having 4,445 ehp Proteus 765 engines. The only Britannias actually designated in this series were two 324s for Canadian Pacific, but one Britannia 312, one 313 and

two 318s were also completed to similar standard, and other Series 310 aircraft were re-engined with Proteus 765s. BOAC retired its long-range fleet in 1965, many of these going to British Eagle. Some forty Britannias remained in scheduled airline service in 1970, mostly of the 310 series and nearly all of them in the fleets of European operators; but by 1981 this figure had dwindled considerably.

43 Canadair CL-44 Forty-Four

In spite of a strong superficial resemblance to the Bristol Britannia, from which it was derived, the Canadair Forty-Four is an almost complete redesign of the British airliner. The first step leading to the ultimate production of the commercial CL-44 was taken in 1956, when Canadair began studies to evolve a trooper/freighter transport for the Royal Canadian Air Force. The Argus maritime patrol aircraft, then in production, had been based on the Britannia, and to take the same aircraft as a basis for developing the transport requirement was a logical extension of the company's licence arrangement with Bristol. The RCAF's need was fulfilled in the form of the CL-44-6, twelve of which were delivered from 1960 as the CC-106 Yukon. These aircraft had conventional side-loading facilities via front and rear fuselage doors, but in aiming for the civil market Canadair had decided, in November 1958, to pursue the novel idea of swinging the entire tail section of the aeroplane to one side to enable straight-in loading of bulky cargoes.

The first machine with this feature, designated CL-44D4 and registered CF-MKP-X, was flown for the first time on 16 November 1960. First customer was The Flying Tiger Line, which received the first of an order for twelve CL-44D4s in May 1961. The first of seven for Seaboard World Airlines was delivered in June – in which month the aircraft also received its FAA certification – and both airlines commenced operations with the freighter in July. Seaboard leased one of its Forty-Fours to BOAC from 1963–65 for trans-Atlantic cargo services. Slick Airways received the first of four CL-44D4s in January 1962; the fourth customer was Loftleidir of Iceland, whose three brought total production of the D4 model to twenty-seven. One of these was later converted by Conroy to a wide-bodied fuselage configuration and designated CL-44-O. Loftleidir operated its Forty-Fours as 160-seat low-fare passenger aircraft across the North Atlantic, adding to its fleet in 1966 a fourth aircraft completed as a CL-44J. This is a stretched version, also known as the Canadair 400, with a 15 ft 1¾ in (4·62 m) longer fuselage, seating up to 214 passengers, though still retaining the swing-tail arrangement of the D4. It flew for the first time (as CF-SEE-X) on 8 November 1965. Loftleidir's three original CL-44D4s were later converted to 44J standard. Several Forty-Fours changed hands during the early 'seventies, the major operators in early 1974 including Transmeridian (nine), TAR (five) and Tradewinds (five). Loft-

leidir transferred its fleet to its cargo subsidiary Cargolux, and few Forty-Fours now remain in service.

44 Lockheed L-188 Electra

Lockheed's first appraisals of the short/medium-range airliner market were made in the early 1950s, experience with building the C-130 Hercules military transport leading it to choose a turboprop rather than a pure-jet design. In 1954 it offered to American Airlines a high-wing project, the CL-303, with four Dart or Eland engines, but this proved too small for American's needs, as did the low-wing, Allison-powered CL-310 which was Lockheed's next proposal. However, in January 1955 American issued its detailed requirements to the US industry at large, to which Lockheed announced in June a scaled-up development of the CL-310 known as the L-188 Electra. American's order for thirty-five Electras 'off the drawing board' was quickly followed by one from Eastern Air Lines for forty. A year after its announcement the Electra had attracted orders for a hundred and twenty-eight aircraft, and this total had risen to a hundred and forty-four by the time the first prototype (N1881) was flown on 6 December 1957. A second prototype was flown on 13 February 1958 and a third (N1883) on 19 August 1958, the latter being used as the US Navy's aerodynamic prototype for the P-3 (then P3V-1) Orion anti-submarine aircraft. On 22 August FAA type certification was granted (at a gross weight of 113,000 lb (51,257 kg)) to the L-188A, the initial production version. The first L-188A (N5501) was delivered to Eastern and put into scheduled operation on 12 January 1959; American Airlines' first Electra entered service eleven days later. The L-188A was supplanted as the standard model by the L-188C, which had increased fuel capacity and gross weight and seats for up to 99 passengers. The first recipient of the L-188C was Northwest Airlines. The only European operator to order the Electra was KLM Royal Dutch Airlines, whose first L-188C was delivered (as PH-LLA *Mercurius*) in the autumn of 1959, entering service in December. A setback to the Electra's career occurred after serious accidents to a Braniff aircraft in September 1959 and one of Northwest's aircraft in the following March. Speed restrictions were imposed (until January 1961) while all Electras on the production line and in service underwent a strengthening of the nacelle and surrounding wing structure. A total of one hundred and sixty-eight production Electras – the first US designed and built propeller-turbine airliner – were built, comprising one hundred and thirteen L-188As and fifty-five L-188Cs. About a hundred Electras remained in service in early 1974, when the two largest fleets were those of Eastern (sixteen) and Overseas National (ten). Since then, numbers have dwindled.

45 Vickers Vanguard and Merchantman

Although, in 1951, British European Airways still had nearly two years to wait before receiving its first Viscounts, the airline was already looking ahead to the time when it would need to replace them, and over the next few years a considerable number of design studies were considered in conjunction with Vickers. Some, naturally enough, were based on Viscount components, but in 1953 the Type 900 was begun as an entirely new and independent design. The BEA specification called for Rolls-Royce Tyne engines, a capacity of 93 passengers or a 21,000 lb (9,525 kg) payload and a gross weight of 115,000 lb (52,163 kg), but further examination revealed that the payload/range performance of such an aeroplane would not be acceptable economically. Vickers therefore scaled up the design to 135,000 lb (61,235 kg) as the Type 950. Work on building the 950 prototype, G-AOYW, began and in July 1956 BEA placed an order for twenty production Type 951s. Six months later came a second order for twenty, later increased to twenty-three, from Trans Canada Air Lines. The Canadian machines, designated Type 952, were to have Tyne RTy.11 Mk 512 engines of 5,545 ehp and a 146,500 lb (66,450 kg) gross weight, and in the summer of 1958 BEA also decided to take advantage of the heavier version. Accordingly it reduced its Vanguard 951 order to six, making up the total with fourteen 953s having the same gross weight as the Canadian model but retaining the Tyne 506 powerplant of the 951. The maiden flight of G-AOYW took place on 20 January 1959, to be followed on 22 April by G-APEA, the first of the 951s for BEA. Some non-scheduled BEA Vanguard flights began in December 1960, and on 1 March 1961 the airline began scheduled services. TCA Vanguard services began a month earlier, and in May 1961 the Vanguard 953 entered BEA service. Up to 139 passengers can be carried, according to layout, on the upper deck of the 'double-bubble' fuselage. By the spring of 1974 TCA (now Air Canada) had disposed of the Vanguards in its fleet; fourteen of the BEA aircraft remained in British Airways service, nine having by then been converted into Merchantman freighters. Other Vanguard operators in 1974 were Europe Aero Service (seven, including three freighters), Invicta (six) and Merpati Nusantara (two).

46 Ilyushin Il-18 Moskva ('Coot')

It is not coincidence that one of the most elegant Soviet transport designs of recent years has also been one of that country's most exportable products. The Ilyushin bureau began work on the Il-18 design in 1955, following discussions with Aeroflot for a 75-seat turboprop aircraft for trunk and principal feeder services. The prototype (SSSR-L5811) was flown for the first time by veteran test pilot Vladimir Kokkinaki on 4 July 1957, making its public début at Moscow's Vnukovo airport later that month. Three further trials aircraft were followed by an initial batch of twenty Il-18s. Ten of these were powered, like the prototype, with 4,000 ehp Kuznetsov NK-4 engines, while the remaining ten, for comparative purposes, were fitted with Ivchenko AI-20s of similar output. The latter engine was subsequently standardised for all further production Il-18s. An exhaustive two-year proving programme, during which the aircraft established a number of records, was conducted before the first Aeroflot passenger services with Il-18s were inaugurated on 20 April 1959. Further records and worldwide demonstration flights were made later that year, and from 1960 onwards several non-Soviet airlines began to operate the type. In 1974 these included Air Guinée (two), Air Mali (one), Balkan Bulgarian (nine), CAAC (nine), CSA (seven), Cubana (four), Interflug (fifteen), LOT (eight), Malév (six), Tarom (eleven) and Yemen Airways (one). The Aeroflot fleet then numbered about four hundred and fifty. The standard Il-18V has normal seating for 90 passengers, or 110 in a high-density layout. Other variants include the 122-seat Il-18E, which has 4,250 ehp AI-20M engines replacing the AI-20Ks of other models; and the basically similar Il-18D (prototype SSSR-75888), with substantially greater fuel capacity. All versions carry a normal flight crew of five, and the internal standards of accommodation are comparable to contemporary western types. A prototype was tested in about 1961 of the Il-18I, with up to 125 seats and increased fuel capacity, but this version did not go into production.

47 Antonov An-10A Ukraina ('Cat') and An-12 ('Cub')

The An-10 design was evolved to meet domestic civil and military requirements for a large passenger and freight-carrying aircraft for use from second-class airfields and those with unprepared landing strips. The design was begun in November 1955, following the general pattern of the smaller, twin-engined An-8. The high wing position conferred a double advantage, facilitating cargo loading arrangements and keeping the propellers well above ground level, thus reducing the risk of damage on rough airstrips. The first An-10 made its maiden flight at Kiev in March 1957 under the command of Y. I. Vernikov, and bore the contrived registration SSSR-L1957. An initial batch of twenty aircraft was built, ten powered by Kuznetsov NK-4 turboprops and the remaining ten by Ivchenko AI-20 engines; the latter was subsequently adopted as standard powerplant. Initial stability problems were overcome by applying marked anhedral to the outer wing sections, and adding lozenge-shaped endplate auxiliary fins to the tailplane and an elongated fin beneath the tail cone. In this form the An-10 entered Aeroflot passenger service from Simferopol to Moscow and Kiev on 22 July 1959. Passenger accommodation was increased to 84 from the original 75 planned, and a prolonged route-proving programme of freight-carrying to Siberia was begun. However, a comparatively small number of An-10s (possibly no more than the original twenty) was completed before they were replaced on the production line by an improved model, the An-10A. This, which became the major production model, was a 100-seater with twin under-tail strakes but minus the auxiliary finlets of the An-10; and it had a 6 ft 7 in (2·00 m) longer fuselage. The An-10A entered Aeroflot passenger service in February 1960, and in the following year was also employed (with a ski landing gear) to carry supplies to Soviet polar bases. Other events in 1961 included a closed-circuit speed record for propeller-driven aircraft of 454 mph (731 km/hr). The An-10A, which carried a flight crew of five, could seat up to 130 people in a high-density layout.

The An-12 is basically a freighter counterpart to the An-10A Ukraina. The principal differences between the two can be seen in the rear fuselage shape, which in the An-12 is swept upwards to a much modified vertical tail and incorporates a rear-loading door which can be lowered to act as a ramp for the loading of vehicles and other large cargo. The military troop- or freight-carrier serves in some numbers with several Middle Eastern, African and Asian states as well as the Soviet Air Force. Others are in service with Aeroflot for general cargo-carrying duties, including the transportation of agricultural and industrial machinery; one (SSSR-11359) was used to transport scenery and other equipment to various European centres for the Bolshoi Ballet Company, and the aircraft has been extensively tested and used by the Russians in Arctic and Antarctic areas. Aeroflot also introduced on its Moscow–Paris service in February 1966 a mixed passenger/cargo version in which 14 passengers are accommodated in a pressurised compartment ahead of a cargo hold. In the civil version a smooth fairing replaces the tail gun position of the military model. The An-10A is no longer in commercial service, but civil An-12s were being operated in early 1974 by Aeroflot, Balkan Bulgarian (two), CAAC of China (one) and Iraqi Airways (four).

48 **Tupolev Tu-114 ('Cleat')**
The Tu-114 *Rossiya* (Russia) prototype attracted as much attention at the 1959 Salon de l'Aéronautique as did the Antonov An-22 six years later, for it was at that time the world's largest commercial passenger aircraft. It is also the only swept-wing airliner with turboprop engines. As its general layout reveals, it is a sister design to the Tu-95 bomber developed for the Soviet Air Force, and employs basically the same wing, engine and landing-gear units and a similar tail assembly. Whereas the Tu-95 is a mid-wing aeroplane, however, the Tu-114 employs a low wing position combined with an entirely new and much larger fuselage seating a maximum (over short ranges) of 220 passengers and incorporating a 48-seat restaurant cabin amidships. Development and construction of this turboprop airliner took place at a time when the world's airlines were engaged on a spending spree for pure-jet types,

and it is a mark of the capabilities of its Kuznetsov engines that the Tu-114's top cruising speed is little less than that of such contemporaries as the Caravelle and Comet 4 – not to mention the prodigious payloads and ranges of which the Russian aeroplane is capable. These latter attributes are borne out by over thirty speed and height records, with various payloads, set up by the Tu-114 in 1960–61. First flight of the Tu-114 prototype was made by A. Yakimov at Vnukovo in October 1957, neatly timed to coincide with the 40th anniversary of the October Revolution. Following the various record attempts and the normal flight development programme, the Tu-114 finally entered service with Aeroflot on 24 April 1961 on the 4,350-mile (7,000-km) route from Moscow to Khabarovsk in eastern Siberia. Some two and a half years later the Tu-114 opened a non-stop service to Cuba, bringing Havana within 20 hours flying time of the Russian capital. Normal Aeroflot seating is for 170, mostly tourist class. Its fleet of Tu-114s was believed to number between twenty and thirty: this included a small number of the Tu-114D, a variant using a much slimmer fuselage – probably a direct adaptation of that of the Tu-95 – which is employed for very long-range transport of urgent mail or freight or small numbers of passengers. The prototype Tu-114D made news in the spring of 1958 by flying a non-stop round trip from Moscow to Irkutsk and back, a total of 5,280 miles (8,500 km), at an average speed of

497 mph (800 km/hr). Conversely, the standard Tu-114 fuselage has been employed for a military development, which has the NATO code name 'Moss' and is in service as an airborne command post aircraft, with modified tail surfaces, and mounted a huge saucer-shaped radome on a pylon above the rear fuselage. It is likely that the 'Moss' aircraft in service were produced by conversion of Aeroflot Tu-114s.

49 De Havilland Comet 1 and 2

The Brabazon Committee, formed during World War 2 to formulate post-war requirements for British civil aircraft, supported the notion of a pure-jet transport only as a modest-capacity aeroplane for medium distances. De Havilland, on the other hand, felt that the jet could hold its own, financially, with higher loads over longer stage lengths; and by 1945 had evolved a tail-less design powered by four DH Ghost turbojets. After consultation with BOAC, however, a more orthodox design was adopted, and two prototypes were ordered by the Ministry of Supply to Specification 22/46. The first of these (G-5-1, later G-ALVG) was flown on 27 July 1949, by which time the aeroplane had been developed into a 36-seater; and the second, G-ALZK, on 27 July 1950. The latter made extensive route-proving flights in the colours of BOAC, which had nine Comet 1s on order, and on 9 January 1951 the first production model for the airline (G-ALYP) made its maiden flight powered by

four 4,450 lb (2,018 kg) st Ghost 50 Mk 1s. In May and August 1952, Comet services were inaugurated to Johannesburg and Colombo – the first by jet airliner anywhere in the world; services to Singapore and Tokyo opened in October 1952 and April 1953. No further Comet 1s were built, the next model being the 44-seat Comet 1A with 5,000 lb (2,268 kg) st Ghost 50 Mk 2s and increased range at higher all-up weights. During 1952–53 ten Comet 1As were delivered to Air France (three), Canadian Pacific (two), UAT (three) and No 412 Transport Squadron of the RCAF (two). Meanwhile, on 16 February 1952, a Comet 1 (G-ALYT), which had been set aside for flight development of the Rolls-Royce Avon, was flown with four 6,600 lb (2,994 kg) st Avon 502s; and, re-styled Comet 2X, became the prototype for the Comet 2. Although still basically a 44-seater, the Comet 2 had a 3 ft (0·91 m) longer fuselage, additional fuel and a higher gross weight. Its four 7,300 lb (3,311 kg) st Avon 503 engines were installed with the outward-curving jet pipes which are a feature of subsequent marks. The first production Comet 2 (G-AMXA) was flown on 27 August 1953, and twenty-two more were in varying stages of completion when, in April 1954, further work was halted and all Comets in service grounded. This followed an accident on 8 April, the fifth since October 1952 involving Comets and the fourth to involve loss of lives. There followed the now-celebrated salvage act and exhaustive structural investigation which identified fatigue as the cause of these accidents; and fifteen of the Comet 2s were later completed in accordance with its recommendations. Ten went to No 216 Squadron and three to No 90 Group of the RAF; the other pair became Comet 2Es retained for further Avon engine development. The RCAF 1As and two of those belonging to Air France were rebuilt as 1XBs to the revised standard with 5,500 lb (2,495 kg) st Ghost 50 Mk 4s; the former pair were restored to service in September 1957, the others being repurchased by the Ministry of Supply. During almost two years' service the Comet 1s and 1As flew over thirty thousand revenue hours; what was lost through those tragic accidents – even though the aeroplane itself was completely vindicated – can never be calculated.

50 Tupolev Tu-104 ('Camel')

The existence of the Soviet Union's first jet airliner became known outside Russia when the prototype (SSSR-L5400) brought General Serov to London Airport on 22 March 1956. This aircraft had then been flying for about a year, being joined on 17 June 1955 by the first of a pre-production batch of Tu-104s built for evaluation. Appearing as it did during the temporary eclipse of the Comet, and more than two years before the entry of the Boeing 707 into service, the Tu-104 would have attracted plenty of attention even if it had not been of Russian origin; but it attracted even more because it was clearly an adaptation of the Tu-16 'Badger' medium bomber, about which little was known in the west at that time. Its qualities as an airliner were denigrated by many simply because of its military origins, and uncomplimentary remarks were passed on its 'Victorian' cabin décor; but the choice of the Tu-104 to make that particular visit to Britain was clearly made on grounds of prestige, for the aeroplane had not at that time entered airline service in its homeland. Deliveries of production Tu-104s to Aeroflot began in May, and the first domestic jet service (Moscow–Irkutsk) was opened on 15 September 1956. The 50-seat Tu-104 was purely an interim model, for in 1956 work was already in hand to produce the 70-seat Tu-104A, which in autumn 1957 set many international speed-with-payload and height-with-payload records. By the end of 1957 the Tu-104A was in service with CSA, which eventually operated six; Aeroflot deliveries did not begin until 1958, but eventually increased until the Tu-104A was the most widely used model. Aeroflot was the only operator of the Tu-104B, a 100-seat development with a 3 ft 11½ in (1·21 m) longer fuselage, which appeared on Russian internal routes from 15 April 1959. In 1962 many Tu-104As were modified internally to seat 100 passengers in the standard-length fuselage, these converted aircraft being designated Tu-104V. Generally speaking, the Tu-104 and Tu-104B are used on domestic services, production being of the order of fifty and one hundred respectively; while the hundred or more Tu-104As are reserved for international routes. During their first ten years of service, Tu-104s of all versions carried some nine million passengers. About a hundred and eighty of those built were still in service in 1974, and their success is no doubt one reason why two other projected developments were not pursued. The first of these, appearing in 1957, was the Tu-110 with four Lyulka turbojet engines, the second being the Tu-104E, which appeared in 1960 and was powered by two RD-3M turbojets with increased-diameter intakes.

51 Tupolev Tu-124 ('Cookpot')

Despite an external resemblance to the Tu-104, from which it was developed, the Tu-124 is a much smaller aeroplane and was intended primarily to replace the piston-engined Il-14 on short and medium stage routes in the Soviet Union and other Communist bloc countries. It also claims the distinction of being the Soviet Union's first turbofan-powered commercial type to go into regular operation, having flown its first scheduled service for Aeroflot (on the Moscow–Tallin route) on 2 October 1962 – some two years ahead of such western fanjets as the BAC One-Eleven. The prototype Tu-124 (SSSR-L45000), evolved under the designership of A. A. Archangelski, was flown in June 1960, and preliminary details of the aircraft were released by the USSR shortly afterwards. It is approximately three-quarters the size of the Tu-104, and

can also be distinguished on the ground by its much shorter-stroke landing gear. A flight crew of three is normally carried, and the Tu-124 is in service with four basic interior layouts. The original Tu-124 had seating for 44 passengers, but the standard (and most widely used) model has been the 56-seat Tu-124V. De luxe interiors are available in the Tu-124K for 36 people, and for 22 in the Tu-124K2, which are otherwise identical. The Tu-124 is complementary to the larger rear-engined Tu-134, providing high-speed inter-city travel in areas where the traffic growth is as yet insufficient to justify the use of the larger machine. The Czechoslovak airline CSA received three Tu-124s, one of which was the first example of this type to visit Britain, in 1965; and East Germany's Interflug also operates the type. About ninety were estimated to be in service with Aeroflot in 1974. Tu-124s have also been delivered to the East German, Iraqi and Indian Air Forces. Production ended in 1966.

52 VFW-Fokker VFW 614

Billed as the first of a new generation of 'door-to-door' transport aeroplanes, the VFW 614 is attractive, unorthodox and may be classed in a similar bracket operationally to the Soviet Union's Yak-40 as a small-capacity, very-short-range feeder-liner capable of operating from semi-prepared airfields. Its development progressed slowly – it was started in 1962 and did not reach the flight test stage until 1971 – but this was due very largely to successive attempts by VFW to find an ideal set of partners to join in the venture. Another factor contributing to the lengthy gestation period is that VFW, having established first the basic role and design of the aircraft, only then approached Rolls-Royce and SNECMA to develop a turbofan engine that would enable it to meet the performance required and to exploit a market which had previously been uneconomical for pure jet aircraft operations. The resulting M45H medium by-pass ratio, twin-speed turbofan was designed to establish new low-noise standards for small transport aircraft, with 'advanced technology' features from larger turbofans. The combination of a new airframe and new engine is rare today but the VFW 614 has proved excellent on shorthauls. The first order (by Cimber Air, for two) was placed in April 1974. The unique feature of the VFW 614 is the mounting of the engines on pylons above the wings, an arrangement dictated to a large extent by the need to have a short and sturdy landing gear for rough-field operations. The over-wing position is claimed to have several other advantages, such as inhibiting the ingestion of stones or other debris into the air intakes, minimising distortion of the engine air inlet pressure, permitting an undivided flap system, and greater safety in the event of an emergency landing or an engine fire. Other features which help to make the aircraft less dependent upon airfield support equipment include a passenger door with built-in stairs, and an APU

for ground conditioning and engine starting. The VFW 614 can take off and land in 3,610 ft (1,100 m) or less, and can be operated either as a passenger-carrier or as a freighter. In the latter form it will accept vehicles or standard pallets. The passenger version seats up to 44 (40 is standard), but break-even operating costs are claimed with only half of the available seats filled. Under normal operating conditions it is claimed to be cost-effective over stage lengths of 100 miles (160 km) upwards.

The development programme involved three prototypes (G1 to G3) and two structural test airframes, construction of which began in August 1968; the VFW 614G1 (D-BABA) flew for the first time on 14 July 1971, followed by 'BB on 14 January and 'BC on 10 October 1972. Manufacture is shared with MBB, Fokker-VFW and SABCA. Certification was received on 23 August 1974. The first production aircraft entered service on 2 August 1975, with Cimber Air.

53 Boeing 737

It was something of a novelty for Boeing to be in the position of a late starter in the field of commercial jet transport, but the career of the Boeing 737 does not appear to have suffered unduly from coming late on the scene. Boeing's announcement of the 737 as its candidate in the short-haul jet market came on 22 February 1965, only three days before the maiden flight of one rival (the DC-9) and some six weeks before the other major contender (the

BAC One-Eleven) entered airline service. It had already progressed from the original conception of a 60-seater to that of an aeroplane with accommodation for up to 103 passengers, and simultaneously with its disclosure Boeing was able to announce details of the first order, from Lufthansa, for twenty-one aircraft. The 737's external similarity to other Boeing airliners should not obscure the fact that it is essentially a new design; on the other hand, it has some 60 per cent commonality of structure and internal systems with its immediate predecessor, the Boeing 727. Furthermore, the retention of the same 12 ft 4 in (3·76 m) diameter fuselage as the earlier Boeings has contributed much to its roominess and appeal. Leading-edge Krueger flaps and triple-slotted trailing-edge flaps are combined with other wing high-lift devices to give the 737 a first-class small-airfield performance for a twin-jet aircraft. The first flight was made on 9 April 1967, and by mid-1981 the total sales of all 737 series had reached nine hundred and thirty-four. Lufthansa's order was for the basic 737 Series 100, which entered service on 10 February 1968, but the majority of subsequent orders have been for the 6 ft 4 in (1·93 m) longer Series 200. This seats up to 130, has larger doors and slightly modified tail surfaces, and flew for the first time on 18 August 1967. The second 737 customer, and first to order the Series 200, was United Air Lines, which had ordered seventy-five by 1970. The 737-200 is the 'local

service' commuter airliner member of the family, whereas the smaller 737-100 is for stage lengths of up to 1,400 miles (2,253 km). Standard powerplant for the 737-100 was the JT8D-7 of 14,000 lb (6,350 kg) st. The 14,500 lb (6,575 kg) st JT8D-9, which was optional on this model, was standard on the initial production 737-200 models; optional engines for the 737-200 were the JT8D-7 or the 15,500 lb (7,030 kg) st JT8D-15. Nineteen 737-200s, with JT8D-9 engines and modified interiors, were produced as T-43A navigation trainers for the USAF. Alternative versions of the Model 737-200 include the passenger/cargo -200C and the 'quick-change' 737-200QC, and the 737-200 Business Jet luxury transport. In 1971 Boeing introduced 'Advanced' versions of each 737-200 model, with improved short-field take-off and landing characteristics and the option of JT8D-15 engines, which superseded the earlier 737 models on the production line.

54 Dassault Mercure

Development of this high-capacity twin-turbofan transport was started in 1967, as an aircraft tailored directly to the needs of short-haul operations – routes of up to 1,150 miles (1,850 km) in length. The shorter the stage length, the greater percentage of block time spent in climbing out of airports and descending into them; therefore, the less time spent at optimum cruising conditions, the higher the relative operating costs compared with longer-range travel. Yet the majority of aircraft recently employed on these short routes – notably the Caravelle, One-Eleven, DC-9, Boeing 727 and Boeing 737 – are basically medium-range types, in versions stretched to carry extra passengers in an attempt to mitigate this economic imbalance. For service during the 1970s a new generation of 'airbus' types, such as the DC-10, TriStar and A300, were then under development, but there seemed to be a gap in the market for a short-range 'mini-airbus' seating about 130–150 passengers. It was to fill this gap that the Mercure was evolved. Although designed by Dassault, the Mercure's production is a collaborative international venture, with Aeritalia, Canadair, CASA, SABCA and Switzerland's Federal Aircraft Factory all contributing major assemblies. Since the selected powerplant, the Pratt & Whitney JT8D, is not notably one of the world's quietest engines, Dassault has developed a noise absorber for production aircraft. The six-abreast seating provides for up to 162 passengers in high-density configuration, though more standard layouts are for 132 or 140 passengers. The Mercure carries a normal flight crew of two.

Two prototypes and a structural test airframe were built for the development programme. The first prototype was flown on 28 May 1971 and was registered F-WTCC, a 'contrived' identity in which the last three letters signify Transport Court-Courrier (short-range transport). This aircraft was powered by 15,000 lb (6,804 kg) st JT8D-11 engines, but the more powerful JT8D-15 powered the second prototype (F-WTMD), which flew for the first time on 7 September 1972. The first production Mercure was flown on 19 July 1973, and French certification was awarded on 12 February 1974. At this time the first and only customer (for ten) was the Air France subsidiary Air Inter. This airline, which received its first Mercure on 8 April 1974, operated the aircraft under a government subsidiary made necessary by the lack of other orders. Two developments gained no orders.

55 Airbus A300

The term 'airbus', like 'jumbo jet', has come into widespread general use to describe a particular class of transport aircraft rather than one individual type; in this case the wide-bodied, high-capacity transport designed particularly for short to medium stage lengths. The only one entitled to the name officially, so to speak, is the A300 produced by the international company Airbus Industrie. The first industry discussions which led to the A300 took place in mid-1965, and the first design proposals were put up to the British, French and German governments in October 1966. A go-ahead was received in the following December, but the present Airbus stems from a modified A300B design which was proposed in December 1968. Four flight development aircraft were built, the first two being designated A300B1 and flying for the first time on 28 October 1972

(F-WUAB) and 5 February 1973 (F-WUAC). The original airframe partners were Aérospatiale (design leaders), Hawker Siddeley and Deutsche Airbus for the airframe, and Rolls-Royce, SNECMA and MAN-Turbo for the powerplant; Fokker-VFW and CASA joined the programme later. The two B1 aircraft had shorter-than-standard fuselages: the next two A300s were designated B2, and are representative of the initial production version, making their first flights on 28 June (F-WUAD) and 20 November 1973 (F-WUAA) respectively. The first production A300B2 (F-BGVA) flew for the first time on 15 April 1974, and this version entered service with Air France between Paris and London on 23 May 1974. The A300B4 flew on 26 December 1974. While externally similar, A300 variants differ in payload and range. The A300B2-100 is the basic variant. The B2-200 has a re-inforced wing centre section and optional Krueger flaps to improve short runway performance. The B2K for South African Airways was a 'hot and high' variant, while the B2-300 for SAS has a modified wing and Pratt & Whitney JT9D-59A engines for short-haul routes. The A300B4-100 and -200 have Krueger flaps as standard, and greatly increased range. The A300C4 is a convertible passenger/freight version. The Airbus is Europe's most successful commercial aircraft programme. By mid-1981 firm orders totalled two hundred and thirty-two A300s, with eighty-two options, by some forty operators. The A310, a shorter, 212/

255 seat, re-winged, long-range development attracted seventy-eight firm orders and seventy options by mid-1981. A projected 130/160 seat short-to-medium haul A320 was announced in 1980.

56 & 57 Aérospatiale Caravelle
The Caravelle was the outcome of a specification issued in November 1951 to which six major French aircraft constructors submitted design proposals. The SNCA du Sud-Est put forward two projects in June 1952, one a triple-Atar design and the other based on the use of two then-undeveloped by-pass engines; the former, known as the X-210, was finally chosen – but as a twin-jet, using the more powerful Rolls-Royce Avon in place of the Atar. In January 1953 the Secrétariat-Générale à l'Aviation Civile et Commerciale ordered two flying prototypes and two static-test airframes to be built, and the first prototype (F-WHHH) made its maiden flight on 27 May 1955. The second followed on 16 May 1956, both aircraft being powered by 10,000 lb (4,536 kg) thrust Avon RA.26 engines. The Caravelle -01 continued the flight-testing and certification programme, while the -02 flew extensive demonstration tours of Europe and the Americas. French certification was granted on 2 April and FAA type approval on 8 April 1958. The first production aircraft was flown on 18 May 1958. The first Caravelle Is, with 10,500 lb (4,763 kg) st Avon RA. 29 Mk 522s, were delivered in April 1959 to Air France and SAS, the latter being

the first to enter service, on 26 April. The Caravelle IA was similar except for Avon 526 engines, but in 1959 there appeared the Caravelle III, powered by 11,700 lb (5,307 kg) st Avon Mk 527 engines which offered a much improved performance with higher loads. Nineteen Caravelle Is and thirteen Caravelle IAs were built; all except one Caravelle I (which had been lost in service) were converted in 1960–61 to Caravelle III standard, and a further seventy-eight of the latter model were built. Two non-airline Caravelle IIIs were completed: one became the Caravelle VII prototype when fitted with General Electric CJ805-23C turbofans, and the other was the Series III prototype (F-WJAK), converted to serve as prototype for the Caravelle VI. Flown for the first time on 10 September 1960, this had 12,200 lb (5,535 kg) Avon 531 engines. A variant is the VI-R, which has Avon 533s with thrust reversers, enlarged flight deck windows and was first flown (F-WJAP) on 6 February 1961. The model without thrust reversers is known as the VI-N. Production of these two models totalled fifty-three VI-Ns and fifty-six VI-Rs. The first operator of the Caravelle VI-N was Sabena, which received its first aircraft in January 1961; United, six months later, was first into service with the VI-R. The fan-engined Caravelle 10 R has JT8D-7 turbofans of 14,000 lb (6,350 kg) thrust, but is otherwise similar to the VI-R. It flew for the first time on 18 January 1965 and twenty

were eventually built. A development is the 11 R, first flown on 21 April 1967, which is a mixed-traffic version also having JT8D-7 engines but with a 3 ft 0⅔ in (0·93 m) extension of the fuselage forward of the wing, incorporating a large freight door. Six examples of this version were built.

A further-stretched version is the Caravelle Super B, a considerably more redesigned, second-generation model, incorporating many aerodynamic and technical improvements. Among the modifications are a 3 ft 3⅓ in (1·00 m) longer fuselage than the standard Caravelle, with the maximum seating increased to 104; a 4 ft 7 in (1·40 m) wider tailplane, with a 'bullet' fairing at its intersection with the fin and rudder; double-slotted flaps with greater travel; and a leading-edge root extension to the wings. Additional internal tankage is an optional extra. The first production Super B was flown on 3 March 1964, and the first delivery made on 25 July 1964, to Finnair. Total production of the Caravelle Super B was twenty-two aircraft. The final stretch of the original design appeared in the Caravelle 12, which was flown for the first time on 29 October 1970. This incorporates the airframe improvements of the Super B with more powerful JT8D-9 turbofan engines of 14,500 lb (6,577 kg) st and fore and aft extensions of the fuselage which increase the overall length to 118 ft 10½ in (36·24 m). A total of two hundred and eighty Caravelles of all versions were built, including sixteen Caravelle 12s. All but about forty of these were still in regular airline service in 1974.

58 McDonnell Douglas DC-9

The first US twin-jet to employ tail-mounted engines, the DC-9 was conceived at a time when the BAC One-Eleven – its closest rival – was already under development; when airlines were still digesting the financial effects of buying big jets; and when the DC-8 modification programme was costing Douglas a considerable sum of money. The main hope of success for a short/medium-haul jetliner lay in the US domestic market, which showed little interest in Douglas's original Model 2000 project of 1959. In 1962 Douglas brought out the Model 2086, also using JTF10 turbofans. More interest was shown in this, but by April 1963, when Douglas decided to go ahead with what had then become the DC-9, there were still no firm orders. The size of the aeroplane had been progressively increased, and the JT8D chosen as the definitive powerplant; and Douglas had enlisted de Havilland Canada and a score of US equipment and component manufacturers to share the costs. In May 1963 came the first order, from Delta Air Lines, for fifteen aircraft with options on fifteen more. Bonanza, whose intended purchase of One-Elevens had been vetoed by the US government, ordered three DC-9s, and Douglas started building two prototypes in July. They were rolled out together in January 1965, the first making its maiden flight on 25 February. Delta opened its DC-9 services on 29

November 1965. One hundred and thirty-seven Series 10s were built in two basic versions, the Model 11 with JT8D-5 turbofans and the Model 15 with more powerful JT8D-1s. Both have seating for up to 90 passengers. A stretched version, with wing span increased to 93 ft 5 in (28·47 m) and an overall length of 119 ft 3½ in (36·37 m), seats up to 115 passengers and is designated Series 30. It has full-span leading-edge slats and double-slotted flaps, 14,000 lb (6,350 kg) st JT8D-7 turbofans, 98,000 lb (44,452 kg) gross weight and a 26,156 lb (11,864 kg) payload. By 1 August 1966 – when the first DC-9-30 was flown – total DC-9 sales had reached three hundred and seventy-five, of which two hundred and seventy-five were of Series 30 aircraft. Ten examples were built for SAS of the Series 20, which has the short body of the Series 10, the long-span wings of the Series 30 and 14,500 lb (6,577 kg) JT8D-9 engines. The JT8D-9 or 15,500 lb (7,031 kg) st JT8D-15 powers the Series 40, which has a further fuselage stretch giving an overall length of 125 ft 7¼ in (38·28 m) and a maximum seating capacity of 125 passengers, and flew for the first time on 28 November 1967. This version also was built to an order from SAS, with whom it entered service on 12 March 1968. The stretched Series 50 is 12 ft 7¼ in (1·87 m) longer still, seating up to 139 passengers, and has JT8D-15 or 16,000 lb (7,257 kg) st JT8D-17 engines. It flew in 1974. The Series 80, 14 ft 3 in (4·34 m) longer with extended wing and 19,250 lb (8,730 kg) st -209s began services in 1980.

Freight (DC-9F), convertible (DC-9CF) and passenger/freight (DC-9RC) versions are available of all Series. By mid-1981 total sales of the DC-9 were one thousand and sixty-one, and of this total well over half were of the Series 30. Military variants of the DC-9 include twenty-one C-9A Nightingales, built for service as ambulance aircraft with the 375th Aeromedical Wing of Military Airlift Command of the USAF; seventeen C-9B Skytrain II logistic support transports for the USN/MC; and three VC-9C for the USAF.

59 & 60 BAC One-Eleven

Praised by pilots and passengers alike, the BAC One-Eleven has gone a long way towards fulfilling its role of jet successor to the Viscount. Admittedly, it has not approached the Viscount's record in numbers built or length of service, but by mid-1981 it already had more than sixteen years service behind it and orders had passed two hundred and forty. Its origins go back to the P-107 (later H-107) design evolved in 1956 by Hunting Percival Ltd. This was first framed to use Bristol Orpheus turbojets, but in September 1958 was re-tailored to Bristol Siddeley BS 75 turbofans instead. The project then languished until Hunting's absorption into the newly formed British Aircraft Corporation in 1960, when the design was re-appraised in conjunction with Vickers' own VC11. As the BAC-107, the design was fattened up and given a 'T' tail; and an enlarged development of this was announced in May 1961 as the BAC One-Eleven. Advantages offered included Rolls-Royce Spey engines (then under development for the Trident) and maximum seating for 69 passengers. Simultaneously with the publication of preliminary details, BAC announced the first order for the type, from British United Airways, for ten aircraft with options on another five. With its second order, the One-Eleven broke into the US domestic market, Braniff International ordering six. Before the first One-Eleven had flown, seven operators – three of them in the United States – had ordered forty-five aircraft – all of the initial model, the Series 200. The prototype (G-ASHG) flew for the first time on 20 August 1963. The first One-Eleven services by BUA began on 9 April 1965, only three days after its British C of A was issued; and Braniff began services on 25 April 1965, nine days after the issue of FAA type approval. Also produced since 1966 are the Series 300, 400, 475 and 500, which carry more fuel and have more powerful Spey engines. Apart from a fractionally longer engine pod, the Series 300 and 400 are physically similar to the Series 200, and are powered by 11,400 lb (5,171 kg) st Spey Mk 511 turbofans. The development aircraft for these Series, G-ASYD, flew for the first time on 13 July 1965. The biggest single operator of the One-Eleven was then American Airlines, which put the first of thirty Series 400s into service on 6 March 1966. In 1967, G-ASYD was further modified, making another 'first' flight on 30 June of that year as development aircraft for the Series 500, a stretched version with 12,550 lb (5,692 kg) st Spey Mk 512 DW engines, extended wingtips giving a 5 ft 0 in (1·52 m) increase in span, and a 13 ft 10 in (4·22 m) increase in overall length permitting maximum seating capacity to be increased from 89 to 119 passengers. The normal flight crew is two on all models. On 27 August 1970 G-ASYD made yet another 'first' flight, this time as development aircraft for the Series 475, which combines the standard-length fuselage of the Series 400 with the wings and powerplant of the Series 500 and a modified landing gear for use at airports with low-strength runways. In June 1978 BAe signed a co-production agreement with Romania for eighty-two One-Elevens, twenty-two from BAe components in 1980–85, then full production of six a year until 1995. The Series 670, based on the Srs 475 has improved airfield performance, range and noise levels. Srs 670 modifications applied to the Srs 500 produce the Srs 600.

61 Fokker-VFW Fellowship

Fokker's proposed successor to the highly-successful Friendship took some time in coming to fruition, a result of deliberate policy following Fokker's declared objective that it should achieve steady sales over a long-term period, rather than collect a greater number of orders during a shorter production life. If the F.28 accomplishes this it will emulate its turboprop predecessor, from which many structural and production features have been inherited. The first details of the Fellowship were announced in April 1962, although detail design studies for a short/medium-haul fanjet had been under way at Fokker for more than two years before this. In February 1964 the project received a promise of financial support from the Netherlands government, and that summer agreements were signed whereby three other European manufacturers would collaborate in the production of the aeroplane. Short Bros and Harland is thus responsible for the outer wings and landing gear doors, while Germany's MBB and Fokker's German partner VFW-Fokker between them produce centre and rear fuselage sections, tail units and engine nacelles. Fokker-VFW builds front and centre fuselages and wing root fairings. The Fellowship Mk 1000, the initial production version, seats up to 65; it was first flown in prototype form (PH-JHG) on 9 May 1967, and three aircraft had flown by the end of the year. Certification of the Fellowship Mk 1000 by the Dutch authorities was granted on 24 February 1969, and was followed by FAA type approval on 24 March and German certification on 30 March. The first order for the F.28 was placed in November 1965 by LTU of Dusseldorf, which ordered five, though the first commercial services were inaugurated, on 28 March 1969, by the Norwegian operator Braathens, which also ordered five. Total orders, up to 1980, were for one hundred and sixty-five Fellowships. A short-fuse-lage version of the Fellowship, seating 50 passengers and powered by 9,730 lb (4,414 kg) st Rolls-Royce Trent engines, was proposed in 1967 by the Fairchild Hiller Corporation under the designation F-228. This was later abandoned, but on 28 April 1971 Fokker-VFW flew PH-JHG as the prototype for its stretched F.28 Mk 2000, which is 97 ft 1¾ in (29·61 m) long overall and seats up to 79 passengers. On 27 September 1973, PH-JHG made another 'first' flight this time with new, extended unslatted wings of 82 ft 3 in (25·07 m) span. With these wings, and improved Spey engines, the Mks 1000 and 2000 are known as the Mks 3000 and 4000 respectively, which superseded the earlier marks in production. The Mk 6000 has the Mk 2000/4000 fuselage but has extended span wings fitted with slats and has improved field and payload/range performance.

62 Tupolev Tu-134 ('Crusty')

The basic design layout of the Tu-104, developed via the fan-engined Tu-124, was taken a stage further in the Tu-134 which, in its early stages, was provisionally known as the Tu-124A. Several major design changes, however – notably the placing of the Soloviev fan engines at the rear of the aeroplane – justified the allocation of an entirely new bureau number. Work on the Tu-134 project began under Leonid Selyakov in June 1962, the first flight taking place in December 1963 with what the Russians described as 'existing' engines – presumably

D-20 turbofans of the type that power the Tu-124. Production Tu-134s are powered by the improved D-30. Five pre-production aircraft were built; production Tu-134s have minor external refinements including a smaller dorsal fin fairing and tailplane 'bullet'. The Tu-134 is Russia's second rear-engined civil aircraft, and operationally may be regarded as the Soviet counterpart to the BAC One-Eleven and the McDonnell Douglas DC-9. It entered service with Aeroflot on internal routes during 1966, and began international operation in September 1967 on the Moscow–Stockholm service. The configuration offers greater wing area and efficiency than that of the Tu-124, and greater seating capacity, the normal passenger complement being 64 (16 first-class and 48 tourist), maximum 72, with a flight crew of three. The Tu-134 has a maximum range with minimal payload of 2,175 miles (3,500 km), but is intended mainly for stage lengths of 310–1,240 miles (500–2,000 km). A soft-field landing gear (i.e. the front wheels of the main bogies touch down first) gives a good small-field performance in and out of second-class airports and those with grass runways, when the occasion arises.

The original 64-seat Tu-134 was followed in 1968 by a stretched version, the Tu-134A, which has a 6 ft 10¾ in (2·10 m) increase in overall length enabling up to 80 passengers to be accommodated in a lengthened cabin. It has more sophisticated avionics, an APU, and engine thrust reversers, but is otherwise generally similar to the earlier Tu-134. It underwent Aeroflot route-proving in the autumn of 1970, and began regular international services in early 1971. The Aeroflot fleet in 1974 was estimated to be about one hundred and thirty strong; foreign customers include Aviogenex of Yugoslavia, Balkan Bulgarian, CSA, Interflug, LOT and Malév. The Tu-134B has increased seating. Production exceeded three hundred and fifty by 1979.

63 Hawker Siddeley Trident

De Havilland's absorption into the Hawker Siddeley Group cannot disguise the ancestry of the Comet's successor in the BEA fleet, the (originally D.H. 121) Trident. The Trident was the outcome of a BEA requirement, outlined in July 1956, for a medium-range 'second generation' jet. It was the third de Havilland design considered for the role, the four-Avon D.H. 119 and the joint BEA/BOAC D.H. 120 both being discarded in the project stage. The D.H. 121, in company with the Avro 740 and Bristol 200, was intended at the outset as an 80/100-passenger aircraft for stage lengths of up to 1,000 miles (1,610 km), having 'more than two' engines and a minimum cruising speed of 600 mph (966 km/hr). In February 1958, BEA announced that it had chosen the de Havilland design. Six months later, the airline was given Ministry approval to proceed with its order, but another twelve months elapsed before it signed a firm contract for twenty-four aircraft. In January 1958 de Havilland formed

a consortium with Hunting Aircraft and Fairey Aviation, for which the name of The Aircraft Manufacturing Company (Airco) was revived. The BEA requirement had undergone some revision by 1959, resolving into a smaller 75/80-seater powered by Spey turbofans in place of the more powerful RB.141s previously selected. In 1960 de Havilland became a part of the Hawker Siddeley Group and work started on the first batch of aircraft, to which the name Trident had by then been given. The first Trident 1 for BEA (there was no separate prototype), registered G-ARPA, made its maiden flight on 9 January 1962. With a wing span of 89 ft 10 in (27·38 m) and three 9,850 lb (4,468 kg) st Spey 505-5 engines, the Trident 1 had a gross weight of 115,000 lb (52,163 kg) and seats for up to 103 passengers. Following the receipt of its C of A on 18 February 1964, the Trident 1 commenced scheduled services on BEA's European routes on 1 April. In June 1965 a BEA Trident 1 made the first automatic landing during a passenger service. Fifteen examples were built of the Trident 1E, a developed version with 11,400 lb (5,170 kg) st Spey 511-5s, a 5 ft 2 in (1·57 m) longer wing with full-span slats replacing the former drooped leading edge, up to 115 seats (139 in the four aircraft built for Channel Airways and BKS) and an enhanced payload/range performance. The first Trident 1E was flown on 2 November 1964 and the first delivery (to Pakistan International Airways) was made on 1 March

1966. In August 1965 BEA transformed its original option for twelve more Tridents into a firm ·order for fifteen of the 2E version, which has a further 3 ft (0·91 m) increase in span and 11,930 lb (5,412 kg) st Spey Mk 512-5Ws. At a gross weight of 143,500 lb (65,090 kg), it can carry 97 passengers (or up to 149 in high-density seating) over longer ranges than the Trident 1 and 1E. Delivery to BEA began on 15 February 1968, following the first flight of a 2E (G-AVFA) on 27 July 1967. BEA, which refers to this version simply as the Trident Two, began services with the 2E on 18 April 1968. In addition to the fifteen for BEA, two other examples of the 2E were built for Cyprus Airways, these being delivered in September 1969 and May 1970, and the Chinese airline CAAC ordered fifteen.

The last major version is the Trident 3B, of which twenty-six were initially ordered by British Airways (ex-BEA) as the Trident Three. This represents a further stretch of the basic design, having increased flap and total wing area compared with the 2E (though the span is the same) and an increase of 16 ft 5 in (5·00 m) in overall length. This permits the maximum seating capacity to be increased to 179. Basic powerplant is similar to the 2E, but the Trident 3B has in addition a 5,250 lb (2,381 kg) st Rolls-Royce RB. 162 installed at the base of the vertical tail, to improve performance during take-off and climb-out. First flights by the Trident 3B were made on 11 December 1969 (without the boost engine) and 22 March 1970 (with the RB. 162 installed), and this version of the aircraft entered service with BEA in April 1971. CAAC has ordered two Super 3Bs, which are generally similar except for an additional wing centre-section fuel tank.

64 Boeing 727

No other turbine-engined transport aircraft in history has achieved such a remarkable commercial success as Boeing's short/medium-haul triple-turbofan 727. Since 5 December 1960, when Boeing announced its decision to go ahead with the 727, one thousand eight hundred and four of these aircraft had been ordered by May 1981, and nearly all of these had been delivered. They serve with over sixty airlines in every part of the world. From mid-1956, a hundred and fifty different design studies were undertaken, and sixty-eight of them tunnel-tested, before Boeing settled on the final layout in September 1960, which involved three rear-mounted engines. The 727 design is noteworthy in two particular aspects. The first is the system of wing high-lift devices, which were thoroughly tested on the 'Dash Eighty' 707 prototype and which give the 727 outstanding take-off and landing characteristics; the second lies in the fact that, from the cabin floor upwards, its fuselage cross-section is identical with the 707 series, making possible a considerable degree of commonality in construction and interior systems and seating arrangements to speed production. The Boeing 727 was originally designed as an 88/119-seater, but the standard production 727-100 can seat a maximum of 131 passengers; a typical mixed-class layout seats 94 people. In June 1961 Boeing started cutting metal for the first aircraft, and this made its maiden flight at Renton on 9 February 1963. The 727 had been launched with the news of orders from United and Eastern, each for forty of the Series 100, and the first to be delivered was handed over to the former operator on 29 October 1963; Eastern was the first to put the 727 into scheduled service, on 1 February 1964. Lufthansa was the first non-American customer, with an order (since increased) for twelve. Later versions of the 727-100 are the -100C and -100QC (= Quick Change) convertible passenger/cargo models, both of which are in service, and the 727-100 Business Jet luxury transport. In September 1966 construction began of the first 727-200, a 20 ft 0 in (6·10 m) longer model with a standard powerplant of 14,500 lb (6,577 kg) st JT8D-9 turbofans and seating up to 189 passengers. The first 727-200 was flown on 27 July 1967 and received FAA Type Approval in the following November. This version is available optionally with 15,000 lb (6,804 kg) st JT8D-11 or 15,500 lb (7,030 kg) st JT8D-15 turbofans. In 1971 Boeing announced the Advanced 727-200, initially to meet orders from Ansett/ANA and Trans-Australia Airlines. This is basically a 727-200 with improved interior layout, additional

fuel capacity, engine noise suppressors and a maximum ramp weight of 191,000 lb (86,635 kg).

By the end of 1970 the Boeing 727 had become both the biggest-selling and fastest-selling jet transport in the world, having surpassed the Boeing 707/720 series in a shorter period of time and having also become the first-ever turbine-powered transport aircraft to exceed a sales figure of one thousand.

65 Yakovlev Yak-40 ('Codling') and Yak-42

In years gone by the design bureau headed by the veteran Soviet designer Alexander Yakovlev has produced piston- and jet-engined fighters, strike and training aircraft, piston-engined transports, fixed-wing VTOL aircraft and helicopters. The Yak-40 further extended this wide range and was not only Yakovlev's first entry into the realm of turbine-engined commercial transports but was also the first fan-engined feederliner to go into service anywhere in the world. It was evolved as a modern replacement for the piston-engined Lisunov Li-2 (licence DC-3), Il-14 and similar types on Aeroflot internal routes, and has been especially tailored for use from semi-prepared or grass airfields. As such it makes an interesting comparison with the German VFW 614, which is of similar size and purpose. The Yak-40 carries a flight crew of 2 and, in its normal production form, has standard seating for 27 or 32 passengers in a pressurised cabin. There is a ventral airstair door at the rear of the cabin, similar to that fitted to the Aérospatiale Caravelle and BAC One-Eleven.

The first of five development aircraft (SSSR-1966) flew on 21 October 1966, and production was started in the following year. By the end of 1967 twenty-four had been built. The Yak-40 flew its first scheduled passenger service for Aeroflot on 30 September 1968; within the next five years nearly five hundred had been delivered, with production continuing at a rate of eight aircraft per month. By the spring of 1973 the aircraft in service had carried more than eight million passengers and collectively had flown some 124¼ million miles (200 million km). Aeroflot's short-haul local services cover several thousand routes, and in addition to passenger-carrying the Yak-40 is employed or ambulance and cargo transportation. An executive version is also available. Weather radar and other equipment permit the aircraft to make automatic approaches in Category 2 weather conditions. A centre engine thrust reverser improves short landing performance.

By mid-1980 over one thousand Yak-40s had been built. A sales drive was launched to reach world markets. Foreign users include Aeritirrena, Air Calypso, Air Settante, Bakhtar, Afghan Airways, Egyptair, General Air and Templewood Aviation. However, some Italian, German and Greek users returned theirs, dissatisfied with their performance.

The larger Yak-42 ('Clobber') resembles the Yak-40. The first prototype flew on 7 March 1975 with eleven degrees sweep, the second in April 1976 with twenty-five, adopted on production aircraft, the first of which flew in February 1977. Aeroflot deliveries began in 1979. Powered by three 14,320 lb (6,500 kg) st Lotarev D-36 turbofans, designed to minimise noise and fuel consumption, it has a range of 620 miles (1,000 km) with maximum payload of 31,938 lb (14,500 kg). A short-to-medium haul, 76, 100 or 120 seat airliner, it is designed to operate from rough airfields with limited facilities. Span is 112 ft 2½ in (34·2 m) and length 119 ft 4 in (36·38 m).

66 Tupolev Tu-154 ('Careless')

Seldom, if ever, has a new Soviet aircraft design been announced with such a wealth of structural and performance data as that which accompanied the début of the Tu-154. In its original form the Tu-154 was the largest tri-jet airliner planned for production anywhere in the world, and is intended to be developed to carry even greater loads. Primarily intended as a medium/long-range replacement for Aeroflot's An-10, Il-18 and Tu-104B fleet in the 1970s, the Tu-154 was first announced outside Russia in the spring of 1966, at which time a prototype and five pre-production aircraft were already under construction; the first of these (SSSR-85000) flew for the first time on 4 October 1968. The initial production model seats up to 158 passengers, with a three- or four-man flight crew and a cabin staff of six. Airfield performance is good, normal take-off distance being

3,740 ft (1,140 m) and landing runs being shortened by the use of thrust reversers on the two outer engines. Aeroflot route-proving began in August 1971, and regular passenger services started in early 1972. However, there were operational problems – indeed, Egyptair returned all their eight to the manufacturers. The Tu-154A introduced 23,150 lb (10,500 kg) st Kuznetsov NK-8-ZU turbofans and several improvements. The similarly powered Tu-154B can accommodate 169 passengers and incorporates major changes in systems and controls; its maximum take-off weight is 211,644 lb (96,000 kg). By 1979 over three hundred Tu-154s of all versions were in Aeroflot service. Other users include Balkan Airways and Malév.

67 Lockheed L-1011 TriStar

Second of the new-generation wide-body airbuses to be conceived in the United States, the Lockheed TriStar had its origins in a 1966 study for a twin-turbofan 300-seat short/medium-range airliner for domestic routes, to meet a requirement of American Airlines; but by March 1968, when the development go-ahead was given, discussion with this and other American operators had resulted in Lockheed pursuing a tri-jet layout instead, using as powerplant the highly-promising Rolls-Royce RB.211 turbofan engine. The development programme for the aircraft, named TriStar, originally involved six aircraft – later reduced to five – and construction of the first of these began in March 1969. Designated L-1011,

and registered N1011, this aircraft flew for the first time on 16 November 1970; it was followed by N1012 on 15 February and N301EA on 17 May 1971.

These aircraft were representative of the basic L-1011-1 short/medium-haul version (as illustrated), which carries a crew (including cabin staff) of 13, has seating for up to 400 passengers in an all-economy class layout and an initial in-service gross weight of 430,000 lb (195,040 kg). Certification was granted in April 1972, and first deliveries (to Eastern) were made in the same month. This airline began passenger services with the TriStar on 15 April 1972. By 1981 Lockheed had received orders for two hundred and fifty TriStars. These orders include the extended-range L-1011-100 and -200, which have an extra centre-section fuel tank, higher operating weights and a choice of more powerful versions of the RB.211 engine, and the -500, a shorter-fuselage, longer-range, more powerful -1 derivative with extended wings, and the similar -400 which has -1 wings and engines.

68 McDonnell Douglas DC-10

A design contemporary of the Lockheed TriStar, the McDonnell Douglas DC-10 responded, as did the TriStar, to an American Airlines requirement of early 1966 calling originally for a twin-turbofan short/medium-haul aircraft for domestic routes, but eventually matured into a three-engined design. McDonnell Douglas's choice of the General Electric CF6 turbofan avoided the problems posed to Lockheed by the Rolls-

Royce collapse, and construction of the first of five development aircraft was started in January 1969. This aircraft (N10DC) made its first flight on 10 August 1970 and was allocated to stability and control testing. The third aircraft (N102AA) was the next to fly, on 24 October 1970, and was followed on 23 December 1970 by the second DC-10; by mid-1971 all five aircraft were flying. FAA type approval was received, and the first two deliveries were made, on 29 July 1971; these were to American Airlines and United Air Lines, which both began services in mid-August, their aircraft having seating capacities of 206 and 222 respectively.

These were of the basic US domestic model, which is known as the Series 10 and has also been ordered by THY and Laker Airways as well as by other US internal airlines. The Series 30 is a long-range intercontinental version, with a 10 ft 0 in (3·05 m) greater wing span and powered by 49,000 lb (22,226 kg) st CF6-50A or 51,000 lb (23,133 kg) st CF6-50C engines; the Series 40 (originally known as the Series 20) is generally similar except in having 48,500 lb (22,000 kg) st Pratt & Whitney JT9D-20 turbofans. Accommodation in all versions is for a flight crew of five and up to 380 passengers.

Orders and options, for some 30 airlines totalled two hundred and fifty-one by mid-1974, increasing to three hundred and fourteen by early 1979. As with the DC-9 a CF (convertible freighter) version of all Series is available; the first of these, a Series 30CF, flew for the first time on 28 February 1973. The CF versions can accommodate up to 380 passengers or 155,700 lb (70,626 kg) of cargo.

69 Hawker Siddeley Comet 4

Even before the first of the Comet 1 accidents, de Havilland had made studies for a 'stretched' Comet 3, and work continued on this prototype notwithstanding the subsequent grounding and investigation of the earlier models. Registered G-ANLO, it flew for the first time on 19 July 1954, differing from earlier Comets in having a 111 ft 6 in (33·98 m) fuselage and 10,000 lb (4,536 kg) st Avon 502 engines. Additional fuel was carried in leading-edge pinion tanks, and the gross weight was increased by some 25,000 lb (11,340 kg) over the Comet 2. By the end of 1954, however, with the full accident findings available, de Havilland decided to combine all the latest knowledge into a Mk 4 version; and a modified G-ANLO, now with Avon 523s, began the flight test programme for this model in February 1957. The two Comet 2Es, G-AMXD and 'XK, had meanwhile continued the Avon development flying programme with a 7,330 lb (3,325 kg) st Avon 504 in each inner position, and a 10,500 lb (4,763 kg) st Avon 524 in each outer one; and these two aircraft assisted further by flying an extensive route-proving programme during 1957–58. The first production Comet 4 (G-APDA), flown on 27 April 1958, was the first of nineteen ordered by BOAC: Aerolineas Argentinas ordered six others, and East African Airways three. Although originally meant for Commonwealth and Far Eastern services, New York was within the range of the Comet 4, and BOAC became involved in a race to beat Pan American (with the Boeing 707) in being the first with fare-paying jet services across the North Atlantic. The British airline, which opened its London–New York route on 4 October 1958, was the winner by some three weeks. Later, the Comet 4s were widely used in their intended territories, both by BOAC and by such associates as Air-India, Nigerian Airways and Qantas. By comparison with the Comet 1/1As, the Comet 4s, during their first two years of operation, flew some sixty-eight thousand revenue hours. The projected 70/92-seat Comet 4A for Capital Airlines, with 3 ft 4 in (1·03 m) longer fuselage and the wing cropped by 7 ft 0 in (2·13 m), was not built, but the same wing, minus the pinion tanks and mounting 10,500 lb (4,763 kg) st Avon 525B engines, was used for the Comet 4B ordered by BEA for short- and medium-haul routes. A further stretch of the fuselage to 118 ft 0 in (35·97 m) enabled the Comet 4B to seat up to 101 passengers. Fourteen 4Bs were ultimately ordered by BEA, the first of these (G-APMA) flying on 27 June 1959; four others, with an 86-seat layout, entered service with Olympic Airways in 1960. Marriage of the 4B fuselage and seating capacity with the original full-span wing of the Comet 4

produced the final Comet version, the 4C, which flew for the first time (G-AOVU) on 31 October 1959. This version was purchased by Aerolineas Argentinas (one), Kuwait Airways (two), Mexicana (three), Middle East Airlines (four), Sudan Airways (two) and United Arab Airlines (nine). When Comet production came to an end, a total of seventy-four Series 4s had been built, including five C.Mk 4 VIP transports for the RAF, one Mk 4 for the A & AEE and two which became Nimrod prototypes. Less than thirty remained in regular airline service at the end of 1973, most with Dan-Air, but the last had been retired by 1980.

70 & 75 **Boeing 707/720 series**

Boeing began to think seriously about a future jet airliner immediately after the end of World War 2, and made tentative approaches to selected potential customers in 1950. Before another two years had elapsed the company had decided in principle to start work on a private venture design capable of developing into both a passenger successor to the Stratocruiser and a jet tanker successor to its military counterpart, the KC-97. Developed initially under the designation Model 367-80, the prototype (9,500 lb (4,309 kg) st JT3P engines) was rolled out on 14 May 1954 and made its first flight on 15 July, its true identity being revealed by its civil registration N70700. Only three months later the USAF ordered a substantial number of KC-135 tankers, and the first order for the airliner version came on 13 October 1955 when Pan American ordered six 707-121s. (The 707 family are identified by basic 'dash' numbers, those in the -120 and -220 blocks being domestic models and those in the -320 and -420 blocks being intercontinental versions. Customer configurations in each series begin at '21; a B suffix indicates turbofan engines instead of turbojets, and a C suffix denotes a B model with cargo-carrying capability.)

The production 707-120, the basic domestic version, was somewhat larger than the original prototype. Qantas 707-138s were unique in this series in having a 134 ft 6 in (41·00 m) overall length; all other 707-120s were 144 ft 6 in (44·04 m) overall. The first production -120 flew on 20 December 1957 and was delivered to Pan American in the following August. On 26 October 1958 PanAm put its Boeings into operation on the New York–London route. The 707-120 was powered by 13,500 lb (6,124 kg) st JT3C-6 turbojets but the majority of those produced (except those for Continental Airlines and TWA) are of 707-120B standard with 17,000 lb (7,711 kg) st JT3D-1 or 18,000 lb (8,165 kg) st JT3D-3 turbofans. The first aircraft converted in this way, for American Airlines, was flown for the first time with turbofans on 22 June 1960. Three VC-137A transports with Military Airlift Command were similarly converted to fan-engined VC-137Bs. Domestic 707 variants – other than the 720, which is described later – were completed by the 707-220, a reduced-weight

version of the -120 powered by 15,800 lb (7,167 kg) st JT4A-3 turbojets and having a better 'hot and high' airfield performance. Five 707-220s were built, all for Braniff, bringing total production of the above-mentioned versions to one hundred and forty-six. Seventeen years after its first appearance, the original 'Dash Eighty' prototype was still flying as a testbed for various members of the Boeing jet airliner family, being retired in 1972.

Although the original -120s of Pan American opened the airline career of the Boeing 707 by flying on the North Atlantic route, the decision to use it across the Atlantic was taken more for prestige than for practical operating reasons; and, having made its point, the 707-120 reverted to the US internal network for which it was tailored. The genuine international model is the 707-320 Intercontinental, which flew for the first time on 11 January 1959. This was a much larger aeroplane, with wing span increased by 11 ft 7 in (3·43 m) and overall length by 8 ft 5 in (2·56 m) compared with the domestic -120 model, and more powerful JT4A turbojet engines. Pan American was also the first to buy the Intercontinental version, beginning services across the United States on 26 August 1959 and across the North Atlantic on 10 October. Another early customer for the long-range model was BOAC, which created a new 707 series, the -420, by specifying 17,500 lb (7,938 kg) st Rolls-Royce Conway 508 turbofans for its Boeings. The first Conway-powered 707 flew on 20 May 1959, and after evaluating the first four aircraft, BOAC requested modifications to enhance the stability and control, including an increase of 2 ft 11 in (0·89 m) in fin height, combined with additional fin area beneath the fuselage tail cone. These features were subsequently incorporated in most of the -320s and many of the earlier series aircraft built. The first -420 services by BOAC commenced in May 1960, and four other airlines also operated this version. Sixty-nine 707-320s and thirty-seven -420s were built. Inevitably, with the additional performance and carrying capacity made possible by the use of turbofan powerplants, a fan-engined variant of the -320 was not long in making its appearance in the United States. This was the -320B, first flown on 31 January 1962 and employing the JT3D-3 engine of 18,000 lb (8,165 kg) thrust. An additional feature of the -320B was the introduction of new minimum-drag wingtips, which increased the overall span by a further 3 ft 4 in (1·03 m). The 707-320B remained in production, as did the 707-320C, which appeared a year later until 1979. A passenger and/or cargo version of the B, distinguished by a large freight-loading door ahead of the wing on the port side, the -320C has proved the most popular of all the Intercontinental versions. By 1979 707 orders totalled nine hundred and forty. Military production continues.

The trio of basic Boeing 707 models was completed in July 1957,

when Boeing announced an intermediate-range version. The new arrival was, in terms of structure and weight, virtually a fresh design; and this fact was acknowledged in November 1957, when, concurrently with the news of its first order (from United Air Lines for eleven aircraft), the designation Boeing 720 was allocated. Dimensionally, the 720 is close to the 707-120, having a fuselage shorter by 7 ft 9 in (2·36 m) and an identical wing span. The wings, however, have slightly more sweep inboard than the other Boeings and full-span leading-edge flaps which enhance the 720's airfield performance. Powerplant is four JT3C series turbojets. The first Boeing 720 was flown on 23 November 1959, received operating approval from the FAA in June 1960 and entered service with United on 5 July 1960. A total of fifty-five were built for six customers, United being the major operator with an eventual fleet of twenty-nine. A fan-engined counterpart, the Boeing 720B, appeared in 1960. With JT3D series engines, the first aircraft of this type was flown on 6 October 1960 and received FAA type approval in March 1961. The first customer for the 720B was American Airlines, who put it into service on 12 March 1961. Combined production of the 720 and 720B, which ended in 1969, totalled one hundred and fifty-four.

71 McDonnell Douglas DC-8

The DC-8, which began life as the Douglas Model 1881, was announced in June 1955 and became available to the airlines about a year later than the first Boeing 707s. The decision to proceed with what was then envisaged as a domestic airliner was followed in October 1955 by the first order (from Pan American) for twenty-five. By the end of 1955 an intercontinental model had also been proposed, and Douglas had received DC-8 orders from three more US airlines, two in Europe and one in Japan. By 30 May 1958, when the JT3C-powered prototype (N8008D) made its first flight, the order book stood at more than a hundred and thirty aircraft. Standard DC-8s were built in five basic versions, two for domestic routes and three for intercontinental operation. The domestic models are the Series 10 with 13,500 lb (6,124 kg) st JT3C-6 turbojets, and the Series 20 powered by 15,800 lb (7,167 kg) st JT4A-3s. The intercontinental Series 30 is powered by JT4A-9 or -11 engines; the Series 40 by Rolls-Royce Conway 509s of 17,500 lb (7,945 kg) st; and the Series 50 by JT3D-1 or -3 turbofans. Later-production Series 50s, designated Model 55, have detail airframe improvements and JT3D-3B turbofans. The first DC-8-20 was flown on 29 November 1958, the DC-8-30 and -40 on 21 February and 23 July 1959, and the first DC-8-50 on 20 December 1960. The DC-8-10 was the first model to go into operation, entering service simultaneously with United and Delta on 18 September 1959. Meanwhile, Douglas had introduced drag-reducing modifications to the wing which involved a new leading-edge and wingtip profile with leading edge slots. A DC-8-40 thus modified made, on 21 August 1961, the first flight at over Mach 1 by a jet airliner when it reached 667 mph (1,073 km/hr) in a shallow dive, equivalent to Mach 1·012. Numerically, the most successful variant was the DC-8 Series 50, and some domestic-model DC-8s were later converted to this standard. In April 1961, Douglas announced a further variant, the DC-8F Jet Trader, an all-cargo or mixed- traffic version of the Series 50 with JT3D-3 fan engines, reinforced floor and increased gross weight. The first DC-8F was flown on 29 October 1962, and this version became available in basic form as the DC-8-54 and, in improved form, with JT3D-3B engines, as the DC-8-55. Maximum capacity of the Jet Trader is 95,282 lb (43,219 kg) or 189 passengers. Excluding the 'Super Sixty' variants, described separately, two hundred and ninety-four DC-8s (twenty-eight -10s, thirty-four -20s, fifty-seven -30s, thirty-two -40s, eighty-nine -50s and fifty-four -54/55s) were built before production ended in November 1968.

72 Convair 880

Although seating fewer passengers than the Boeing 707 or Douglas DC-8, the Convair 880 on its first appearance offered a better speed performance than its rivals. Its existence was announced in the spring of 1956, at which time it was known as the Convair 600 Skylark, with the news that TWA and Delta had ordered thirty and ten respectively. Soon afterwards the name was changed to Golden Arrow, reflecting a colourful if somewhat bizarre proposal to use gold-tinted skin panels in the aeroplane's construction. This proposal was short-lived, however, and the aeroplane was again redesignated, this time as the Convair 880 Model 22, the title Convair 600 being retained temporarily for a stretched version. The Model 22 became the standard US domestic version, and flew for the first time on 27 January 1959 with four 11,200 lb (5,081 kg) st CJ805-3 turbojet engines. First delivery of a production 880 was made on 31 January 1960 to Delta Air Lines, which introduced the aeroplane into service on 15 May, exactly two weeks after the granting of its FAA type certificate. A few of the TWA aircraft were leased to Northeast Airlines, which started services a month earlier than TWA, in December 1960. Two months before this, on 3 October 1960, the first flight had taken place of the original 880 prototype modified for service on intercontinental routes. This version, originating as the Convair 880 Model 31, carried substantially more fuel but offered the same accommodation as the domestic version. With a certain amount of its extra range sacrificed in favour of improvements designed to give better airfield performance and quicker turn-round times, the Model 31 was redesignated 880-M in October 1959. New features included leading-edge wing slats, increased fin area and CJ805-3B turbojets. Gross weight was increased from 184,500 lb (83,691 kg) in the domestic 880 to 203,400 lb (92,262 kg) in the 880-M, and maximum payload from 27,600 lb (12,519 kg) to 33,600 lb (15,241 kg). Standard seating in both models ranged from 88 to 110 passengers, with a maximum possible of 124. The first delivery of a Convair 880-M was made to CAT, the Chinese Nationalist airline, in June 1961, airline operations beginning shortly after the issue of an FAA type certificate on 24 July. Convair 880-Ms were ordered in small numbers by a few foreign operators, but neither this version nor its domestic counterpart competed very successfully against the Boeing or Douglas jets and only sixty-five examples of the two models were completed. Cathay Pacific acquired most of the survivors in the 1970s from their original operators.

73 Tupolev Tu-144 ('Charger')

It was obvious, even without positive confirmation, that the Soviet Union would not be left out of the race to develop and put into service a supersonic passenger aircraft. The confirmation came at the 1965 Salon de l'Aéronautique in Paris, where the Russians displayed a model of their proposed design, the Tu-144; and subsequently Andrei Tupolev himself publicly expressed his desire to have a prototype in the air ahead of the Anglo-French Concorde. There is much superficial similarity of outline between the production versions of the Concorde and Tu-144, each employing an ogival (dual-curve) delta wing and a 'droop-snoot' nose section which hinges down for landing and incorporates a retractable flight deck visor. The Tu-144 wings have undergone considerable redesign from those of the prototypes, which were less complex aerodynamically and more angular in shape. The vertical tail area is proportionally greater, and the fuselage underside is flatter, than on the Concorde. The Tu-144's four afterburning Kuznetsov turbofans were originally grouped together in pairs beneath the fuselage, each pair having a bifurcated, area-ruled exhaust duct and variable-geometry intakes. On the production version they are further outboard, in non-area-ruled nacelles, very similar to those of the Concorde. Design of the Tu-144 was led by Andrei Tupolev's son, Professor Alexei Andreievich Tupolev, and the USSR, like the manufacturers of the Concorde, flight-tested a scaled-down wing on a special research aircraft. A reduction in the capacity of the Tu-144 was noted in 1966: the original model shown at Le Bourget in the previous year had revealed a 36-seat forward cabin, galley amidships and a 90-seat rear cabin. In June 1966 Andrei Tupolev referred to the aircraft as a 121-seater, but the production aircraft have seating arrangements accommodating 11 persons in the forward cabin, 30 in the centre cabin and 99 in the rear cabin, making a total of 140. In service, the aircraft carries a flight crew of three.

Tupolev's ambition to beat the Concorde into the air was realised on 31 December 1968, when the first Tu-144 prototype (SSSR-68001) became the first supersonic transport aircraft to fly. This occasion was also, incidentally, the first time that the NK-144 engines had been tested in the air. Mach 1 was exceeded for the first time on 5 June 1969. On 21 May 1970 the aircraft made its public début at Moscow's Sheremetievo Airport, and five days later it became the world's first SST to fly at a speed in excess of Mach 2, actually achieving a speed of 1,336 mph (2,150 km/hr). By the time another twelve months had elapsed – when it made its first appearance to a western public at the 1971 Paris Salon – the Tu-144 had reached speeds of up to 1,518 mph (2,443 km/hr) during trials. At this time it was declared that only one aircraft had flown, but it is now known that two more Tu-144 development aircraft were completed for flight testing and one for structure tests.

Production aircraft, of which the second example (SSSR-77102) was exhibited – and lost – at Paris in 1973, embody retractable foreplanes aft of the flight deck windows to enhance the take-off and landing characteristics and transonic acceleration. The aircraft illustrated is similar to that shown at Paris. On 1 November 1977 the Tu-144 became the first SST to enter regular passenger service, on Aeroflot's 2,025 mile (3,260 km) Moscow–Alma Ata route over which it had flown mail and cargo since 26 November 1976, but it was withdrawn on 1 June 1978 after one crashed during test flying. Problems with efficiency, engines, systems and vibration were unsolved. Twenty had been built by 1978.

74 **Aérospatiale/BAC Concorde**
As an example of international collaboration the Concorde provides evidence in the most convincing form that associations of this kind can compete on equal terms with the giant aircraft-producing systems of Russia and the United States. Development and production of the west's first supersonic airliner is a fifty-fifty joint undertaking by England and France, for which formal agreements were signed at the end of November 1962. It incorporates background research conducted by the RAE in Britain in the mid-1950s into the properties of slim-delta wings, and inherits some of the design features of the 'Super Caravelle' displayed in model form by Sud-Aviation at the 1961 Paris Air Show. Intended to cruise at up to Mach 2·05, the Concorde employs an ogival (dual-curve) wing planform of which the characteristics were tested extensively on the BAC-221, rebuilt from the record-breaking Fairey Delta 2 of 1956. Low-speed handling characteristics were similarly determined from evaluation of the Handley Page H.P. 115 slim-delta research aircraft. Power is provided by a Rolls-Royce/SNECMA development of the Bristol Siddeley Olympus turbojet which powered the Vulcan bomber. This engine, in 593 Mk 602 form, gives a thrust of 38,050 lb (17,260 kg) with 17 per cent afterburning. All four engines are fitted with thrust reversers. Six aircraft, including two for structural testing, were involved in the development programme. Aérospatiale had responsibility for the first (prototype), third (static test) and fifth (pre-production) machines, and BAC for the second (prototype), fourth (pre-production) and sixth (static test) aircraft. The prototypes both had 'contrived' registrations, the French-built 001 being F-WTSS (Transport SuperSonique) and the British-built 002 G-BSST (British SuperSonic Transport). First flights were made on 2 March 1969 (001 at Toulouse) and 9 April 1969 (002 at Bristol) respectively. In 1964 the development potential of the Olympus 593 series engines permitted a slight scaling-up of the overall design, making possible an increase of 19 ft $3\frac{1}{2}$ in (5·90 m) in passenger cabin length and standard seating for 128 people (maximum 144). Mach 1 was first exceeded on 1 October 1969, and Mach 2 on 4 November 1970, in each case by the 001 prototype. This aircraft was retired from the test programme in October 1973. The Concorde 01 first pre-production aircraft (G-AXDN) made its maiden flight on 17 December 1971, followed by the French-assembled 02 (F-WTSA) on 10 January 1973. The latter was virtually representative of the initial Series 200 production version, with elongated tail-cone, thrust reversers, increased fuel capacity and modified intakes and wing leading edges. The intense flight, certification, route proving and endurance test programme was completed by the four development aircraft in late 1975.

After an initial reservation of delivery positions for seventy-four aircraft by sixteen airlines, this option system was abolished in March 1973. Initial firm orders were placed, in May 1972, by British Airways for five and Air France for four; 'preliminary purchasing agreements' with China (three) and Iran Air (two, with a third on option) were not taken up. These covered the initial batch of sixteen Series 200s, the first examples flying on 6 December 1973 (F-WTSB) and 13 February 1974 (G-BBDG). BA (London–Bahrain) and Air France (Paris–Rio de Janeiro) began passenger services on 21 January 1976. Services to Caracas, Washington and New York followed.

76 Convair 990A

The first proposals for an elongated and faster version of the Convair 600 (as it then was) were put forward in the early months of 1958. The desired increase in performance was to be obtained by aerodynamic improvements and the employment of a turbofan powerplant; while the increase in passenger capacity would be achieved by a 10 ft 0 in (3·05 m) overall lengthening of the fuselage. Convair remained faithful to General Electric in its choice of engine, selecting the CJ805-23B to power the new model; and, apart from the stretching of the fuselage, most of the aerodynamic changes involved the engine and mainplane layout. A thinner aerofoil section was achieved by retaining the same actual thickness while increasing the wing's chord and thereby its gross area. Area-ruled anti-shock fairings were added to the trailing edge primarily to enhance the aeroplane's high-speed cruising capabilities, though they provided additional fuel storage as well; and full-span leading-edge flaps were fitted. Originally known as the Convair 600 Model 30, development was somewhat protracted, and the designation was amended to Convair 990 to avoid the implication that it was an earlier design than the 880. There was no separate 990 prototype, the first flight being made, on 24 January 1961, by the first of twenty aircraft ordered by American Airlines. The first delivery to the airline, some three weeks after the 990 was certificated by the FAA, was made on 7 January 1962. Swissair, which named the aircraft Coronado, received its first delivery at about the same time and was actually the first airline to begin operating the type, towards the end of February; American began its 990 services, between New York and Chicago, on 18 March. Flight testing of the 990 during 1961 had revealed a number of aerodynamic shortcomings, one solution to which was to shorten the outboard engine pylons to reduce drag; other refinements deemed necessary after subsequent testing and operating experience included further streamlining of the pylons and the installation of full-span Krueger flaps on the underside of the wing leading edge. With these modifications, duly carried out on all thirty-seven 990s built, the aircraft became known as the Convair 990A. Fresh FAA certificates for the 990A were granted in October 1962 for those serving abroad and in January 1963 for the domestically operated aircraft. Some two dozen remained in service until the late 1970s, most of them with Modern Air Transport and Spantax.

77   BAC VC10 and Super VC10

Probably no airliner since the Viscount has evoked such enthusiasm from its passengers as the VC10 when it entered BOAC service in 1964. Few, since the Comet and the Caravelle, have had the VC10's aesthetic appeal; and when airline pilots – rarely given to effusive praise of the machines they have to fly – utter such phrases as 'thoroughly delightful to handle in every respect' it is safe to assume that the aeroplane in question is a cut above the average. Yet, despite this widespread appeal, the VC10's sales record was disappointing, for only fifty-five were sold, and only seven to foreign customers. To some extent this was because the VC10 was tailored closely – some would say too closely – to the requirements of BOAC and the Royal Air Force. It was in the mid-1950s that BOAC first outlined its requirements for a Comet successor on its African and Far Eastern routes. Vickers had already studied a number of jet airliner possibilities, including the Type 100 and the so-called 'Vanjet', a Conway-powered development of the Vanguard with swept wings. In May 1957, after further discussions between manufacturer and custo-

mer, BOAC confirmed its intention to order the VC10. Detailed design began in the spring of 1958, and construction of a Model 1100 prototype (G-ARTA) in January 1959. This made its maiden flight on 29 June 1962, powered by four 21,000 lb (9,525 kg) st Conway RCo. 42 turbofan engines. Twelve similarly-powered Model 1101s were completed for BOAC, and began operations, on the service to Lagos, on 29 April 1964, six days after the award of an ARB certificate. Other VC10s included the Model 1102 (two for Ghana Airways), the 1103 (three for British United) and the 1109 (one for Laker Airways); these were fitted with a large cargo door in the port side of the forward fuselage, and have increased chord at the wing roots. Save for their engines (RCo. 43s) and added fuel tankage, the fourteen 1106s for Air Support Command are generally similar, though interior equipment and operating weights naturally differ. The original BOAC order had been for thirty-five VC10s, which was later cut to twelve to enable the airline to order thirty of a stretched version, the Super VC10, but under government pressure this order for Supers was later limited to seventeen aircraft. Compared with the standard VC10, the Super is 13 ft 0 in (3·96 m) longer; seats a maximum of 174 passengers; and has RCo. 43 engines, with thrust reversers on all four (instead of the outer two). The first Super VC10 (G-ASGA) was flown on 7 May 1964. The Super VC10s of BOAC had the Model number 1151 and were all-passenger aircraft. East African Airways' five 1154s had a mixed cargo/passenger layout and forward freight door. Standard VC10s entered service with Caledonian/ BUA from November 1964, serving South America, Africa and the Middle East, and with Ghana Airways from February 1965. The first BOAC service with Super VC10s commenced on 1 April 1965. British Airways' services ended in 1981.

78 Ilyushin Il-62 ('Classic')

In the post-Stalin atmosphere of economic, as well as military, competition between Soviet Russia and the western nations, there have been several examples of the 'date' of an airliner being worked into the designation or prototype registration. One may guess, therefore, that the leap from 18 to 62 in the design bureau number sequence of Sergei Ilyushin's last commercial airliners is explained by the fact that the prototype of this elegant aircraft (SSSR-06156) emerged for the first time in 1962 – actually on 24 September, when it was inspected by Premier Khrushchev. The neat lines and general configuration of this long-haul Soviet airliner obviously invite comparison with the British Super VC10, and the power of its NK-8 turbofans compares closely with the Conways of the British aeroplane. Early flight trials of the Il-62, pending availability of the definitive NK-8 engines, were conducted with two prototype and three pre-series aircraft powered initially by 16,535 lb (7,500 kg) st Lyulka AL-7 turbojets; the maiden

flight, in the hands of veteran test pilot Vladimir Kokkinaki, took place in January 1963. Public début came at Vnukovo in the spring of 1965, and the aircraft displayed at Le Bourget in June (SSSR-06176, believed to be the third machine) had by then been re-engined with Kuznetsov turbofans. Other minor changes noted at this time included an extension of the drooped wing leading edge and a shorter nosewheel leg. Production of the Il-62 was initiated in 1965, the type entering Aeroflot national (cargo) service on 1 March 1967 and international service, on the Moscow–Montreal route, on 15 September 1967. Four alternative interior layouts are available, ranging from an 85-passenger international sleeper version to an all-economy class with 186 seats. Seating is from four to six abreast according to variant. The Aeroflot fleet was estimated to number about fifty of these aircraft at the end of 1973; foreign customers have included CAAC, CSA, Cubana, Interflug, LOT, Malév and Tarom.

In 1970 there appeared a higher-capacity, longer-range version known as the Il-62M-200. This seats up to 198 passengers in a fuselage unchanged dimensionally from the standard Il-62, and has an additional fuel tank installed in the fin. Major outward changes are the installation of 25,350 lb (11,500 kg) st Soloviev D-30KU turbofan engines, with thrust reversers on the two outer engines. This version has an increased range, with a maximum 50,700 lb (23,000 kg) payload, of 4,970 miles (8,000 km).

79   Boeing 747

The Boeing 747 is the outcome of several years' effort to produce a counter to the Super Sixty series of stretched Douglas DC-8s. Until 1965 Boeing was still canvassing potential customers in an endeavour to meet this threat by variously enlarged versions of the 720-320B, but by the beginning of 1966 it was evident that this idea had been abandoned in favour of what has since become popularly known as the 'jumbo jet', the Boeing 747. Although in terms of general configuration the 747 clearly followed the highly successful layout of the 707 series, it is nearly 80 ft (24·38 m) longer and has treble the capacity of the 707-320B. Into the 747 went much of the design thought and work originally given to Boeing's unsuccessful contender for the giant C-5A military contract. From the beginning the Boeing 747 was designed to be equally viable whether carrying passengers or cargo, and Boeing expected about half the ultimate 747 sales to be of freighter versions. Originally proposed with a two-deck 'double-bubble' fuselage, the 747-100 eventually became essentially a single-decker, seating 385 people in the basic passenger model (including 16 in an upper-deck lounge); the maximum possible load is 500 passengers. The first order was received from Pan American, which in April 1966 booked twenty-three all-passenger 747s and two 747F freighters. For the first half of the year this was Boeing's only order for the jumbo transport, but interest subsequently quickened and

by the end of the year over eighty had been ordered. These included the first contract – from Continental Airlines – for the third variant, the convertible passenger/cargo 747C. There was no 747 prototype as such, the first flight being made by a production aircraft on 9 February 1969. Type approval was granted by the FAA on 30 December 1969, and the 'jumbo' entered passenger service on 22 January 1970 on Pan American's route between New York and London. With eight-abreast seating in a 20 ft 0 in (6·10 m) wide, 185 ft 0 in (56·39 m) long cabin with up to 8 ft 4 in (2·54 m) headroom, the Boeing 747 has, quite literally, brought a new dimension to air travel – though the very spaciousness, coupled with the much greater number of passengers requiring attention, has created some new internal logistics problems for the cabin staffs. Total 747 orders, up to mid-1981, were for five hundred and seventy-one, of which some 60 per cent had been delivered. The initial model is designated 747-100; the later 747-200 (first flight 11 October 1970) has increased operating weights, more powerful JT9D-7 engines, and is available in B (passenger), C (convertible) and F (cargo) configurations. The C and F models have an upward-hinged nose cone to allow straight-in loading of bulky freight items. The first 747-200 operator was KLM, which introduced this version into service in 1971. Subsequent versions include the short-range 747SR, first ordered in 1972 by Japan Air Lines, and the

747SP ('special performance') version, first announced in 1973. The latter version seats up to 360 passengers in a 47 ft (14·33 m) shorter fuselage, has a taller vertical tail, and lighter-weight wing and landing gear structures. First customers for the 747SP were Pan American and Iran Air. Six 747-200Bs have been adapted for the USAF as E-4 advanced airborne command post aircraft.

80 McDonnell Douglas DC-8 Super Sixty series

Three stretched and improved variants of the DC-8 made a substantial contribution to the total order book for this four-jet transport after the first details were announced in April 1965. Under the generic title 'Super Sixty', these comprised the DC-8-61, -62 and -63, all with the same powerplant and completed with passenger, cargo or mixed-traffic layouts. First in service (with United Air Lines, from November 1966) was the DC-8-61, with a fuselage 36 ft 8 in (11·17 m) longer than the standard DC-8-50, seating up to 259 passengers and providing additional baggage/cargo space. Primarily a high-density domestic model, the DC-8-61 was flown for the first time on 14 March 1966 and received its type certification from the FAA on 2 September. The maiden flight of the DC-8-62 took place on 29 August 1966, and this was a much more drastically re-designed version. Although its 189-passenger fuselage was only 6 ft 8 in (2·03 m) longer than the DC-8-50, it had longer, repositioned engine pods and new drag-reducing wingtip extensions which increased the overall span by 6 ft 0 in (1·83 m). The internal wing structure was also modified to increase fuel tankage for ultra-long ranges. Certification of the DC-8-62 was granted in April 1967, with first deliveries (to SAS) taking place on 3 May 1967 and entry into service on 22 May. By then the first flight had taken place (on 10 April 1967) of the DC-8-63, which combined the long fuselage of the -61 with the new wings and other aerodynamic refinements of the -62 and was the heaviest of all the many DC-8 variants, with a maximum take-off weight of 350,000 lb (158,760 kg). Certification of the DC-8-63 was granted on 30 June 1967; the first deliveries were PH-DEA *Amerigo Vespucci* and -DEB *Christopher Columbus* for KLM, with whom the Super 63 entered service on 27 July 1967. The DC-8-63 prototype flew with JT3D-3B turbofan engines, but most of those built subsequently were fitted with JT3D-7s of 19,000 lb (8,618 kg) st each. 'Jet Trader' (all-freight or passenger/freight) versions of each Super Sixty model are identified by CF or F designation suffix letters. Largest single operator of Super Sixties was United, which ordered thirty 61s and ten 62s; other operators to order ten or more included Air Canada, Alitalia, Delta, Eastern, Flying Tiger, KLM, SAS and Seaboard World. Total Super Sixty production amounted to two hundred and sixty-two, comprising seventy-eight -61, ten -61F/CF, fifty-one -62, sixteen -62F/CF, forty-seven -63 and sixty -63F/CF.

INDEX TO BOOK I

The reference numbers refer to the illustrations and corresponding text.

INDEX TO BOOK II

The reference numbers refer to the illustrations and corresponding text.